**Poetic Modernism
in the Culture
of Mass Print**

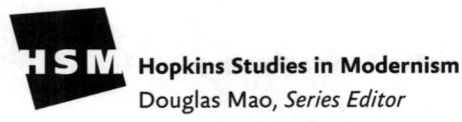
Hopkins Studies in Modernism
Douglas Mao, *Series Editor*

Poetic Modernism in the Culture of Mass Print

Bartholomew Brinkman

Johns Hopkins University Press
Baltimore

© 2017 Johns Hopkins University Press
All rights reserved. Published 2017
Printed in the United States of America on acid-free paper
9 8 7 6 5 4 3 2 1

Johns Hopkins University Press
2715 North Charles Street
Baltimore, Maryland 21218-4363
www.press.jhu.edu

Library of Congress Cataloging-in-Publication Data

Names: Brinkman, Bartholomew, 1979- author.
Title: Poetic modernism in the culture of mass print / Bartholomew Brinkman.
Description: Baltimore : Johns Hopkins University Press, 2017. | Series: Hopkins Studies in Modernism | Includes bibliographical references and index.
Identifiers: LCCN 2016010141 | ISBN 9781421421346 (hardback : acid-free paper) | ISBN 1421421348 (hardcover : acid-free paper) | ISBN 9781421421353 (electronic)
Subjects: LCSH: Modernism (Literature)—United States. | Modernism (Literature)—Great Britain. | American poetry—20th century—History and criticism. | English poetry—20th century—History and criticism. | Mass media and literature—United States. | Mass media and literature—Great Britain. | Poetics. | Publishers and publishing—United States. | Publishers and publishing—Great Britain. | Book collecting—United States. | Book collecting—Great Britain. | BISAC: LITERARY CRITICISM / Semiotics & Theory. | ANTIQUES & COLLECTIBLES / Books.
Classification: LCC PS228.M63 B75 2016 | DDC 810.9/112—dc23
LC record available at https://lccn.loc.gov/2016010141

A catalog record for this book is available from the British Library.

Special discounts are available for bulk purchases of this book. For more information, please contact Special Sales at 410-516-6936 or specialsales@press.jhu.edu.

Johns Hopkins University Press uses environmentally friendly book materials, including recycled text paper that is composed of at least 30 percent post-consumer waste, whenever possible.

Contents

Acknowledgments vii

Introduction: Modern Poetry, Cultures of Collecting, and the Mediation of Mass Print 1

1 As Good as Gold: Palgrave's *Golden Treasury*, Poetic Value, and the Objective Anthology 45

2 Making Modern *Poetry*: Format, Form, and Modern Poetic Genre 71

3 Scrapping Modernism: Marianne Moore and the Making of the Modern Collage Poem 105

4 Selecting Modernism: Eliot, Faber, and Poetic Reproduction 141

5 Instituting Modernism: The Rise of the Modern American Poetry Archive 168

Coda: Remaking Poetic Modernism after a Culture of Mass Print 200

Notes 207
Bibliography 245
Index 263

Acknowledgments

One thing I have learned studying modern poetry and mass print is that texts do not come into being through one individual. They are the products of vast networks of writers, readers, and publishers who entertain initial thoughts, offer suggestions for revision, and help words take material form. That is no less true here, and I would like to express my gratitude to the many people and institutions that helped this book come into being.

Much of the early research and writing for this book began at the University of Illinois at Urbana-Champaign, and many people helped in its initial shaping. Cary Nelson, a lion of the profession, has set an example with both his words and actions for how to be an intrepid researcher, a conscientious writer, and a generous mentor. He continues to show me the many ways poetry can make a difference in the world and why it is so necessary to teach the history of that poetry today. Likewise, Tim Newcomb helped me to expand and deepen my sense of modern poetry—often through long conversations over some fine bottles of wine. Bill Maxwell, Trish Loughran, and Jim Hansen all challenged and encouraged my ideas during the project's early stages, and the manuscript was further enriched over time through conversations with Mike Chasar, Melissa Girard, Natalia Cecire, and many others. My friends and colleagues at Framingham State University have warmly supported my work as a teacher and scholar of modern poetry, and have cheered me on through the book's completion.

This book was made possible through generous institutional and public support at several stages of its development. The English Department and Graduate College at the University of Illinois provided me with financial support that served as an early vote of confidence as much as it did a chance to focus my attention on research and writing. Many of my early ideas about modern periodicals and print culture were formed during my time as a participant in the National Endowment for the Humanities Summer Seminar, "Magazine Modernism," led by Sean Latham and Robert Scholes. I am happy to count as friends so many among that group. I owe much to my year as the National Endowment for the Humanities Post-Doctoral Fellow in Poetry at the Bill and Carol Fox Center for Humanistic Inquiry at Emory University, where I was able to devote my full attention to expanding my manuscript in the company of a supportive group of scholars from across the humanities. My manuscript was also immensely improved by my participation in the First Book Institute, held at the Center for American Literary Studies at Pennsylvania State University, and led by Sean Goudie and Priscilla Wald. Funding from Framingham State University, including a course release through the Center for Excellence in Learning, Teaching, Scholarship and Service gave me the necessary time to complete final revisions.

An early version of chapter 2 first appeared as "Making Modern *Poetry*: Format, Genre and the Invention of Imagism(e)" in *Journal of Modern Literature*; an early version of chapter 3 first appeared as "Scrapping Modernism: Marianne Moore and the Making of the Modern Collage Poem" in *Modernism/modernity* 18, no. 1. I am grateful for permission to reproduce work from those articles here. I am also grateful to poets' estates for granting permission to include text and images from key archival sources. This book could not have been written without the tireless efforts and generous assistance of librarians throughout the United States and the United Kingdom. There are far too many to name here, but I hope they will see their work in the pages that follow. I owe them special thanks.

I would like to thank Matt McAdam, Catherine Goldstead, Kim Johnson, and all the staff at Johns Hopkins University Press for believing in this book and for helping it come into being. Douglas Mao has been generously attentive to the details of the manuscript and has offered many kind and helpful suggestions for strengthening its bigger claims while expressing his unwavering support. Carrie Watterson and Becky Hornyak brought a careful eye to editing copy and generating the index. Additionally, I would like to thank the anonymous readers of the manuscript, who contributed valuable insights on multiple fronts. This book is certainly the better for it.

My parents have always impressed upon me the importance of learning and have kept so many wonderful books in the house. I am glad to be able to add one more to the shelves. My siblings, Britney, Bret, and Bryan, and my in-laws Julia, Sam, Kathi, and John have been a continuing source of conversation and inspiration. Oscar has been a constant writing companion and remains one of my toughest critics. Thessaly and Emmeline have helped put everything into perspective.

Finally, I dedicate this book to Colleen—my sounding board, my second guesser, my rah-raher, my travel partner in life's amazing adventure.

**Poetic Modernism
in the Culture
of Mass Print**

Introduction
Modern Poetry, Cultures of Collecting, and the Mediation of Mass Print

As if to mark the arrival of the new century, Lucy A. (Mixer) Britton of Brattleboro, Vermont, began in 1900 a scrapbook that she would actively keep for the next fifty years. The 130-page compilation, pasted into an old ten-by-thirteen-inch, leather-bound music book, records significant events in Lucy's life and in the lives of her loved ones (births, marriages, anniversaries, deaths), ornately celebrates Thanksgiving and Christmas, and touches on topics of domesticity, national politics, and war. Although there is the occasional handwritten item and photograph, Lucy's scrapbook for the most part conveys the various dimensions of her life through its incorporation of a variety of printed texts, including full-page book plates; freshly cut-out roses in pink, gold, ivory, and ruby (still vibrant today) that were likely printed just for such pasting; job-printed invitations and "Reward of Merit" cards; postcards from the far corners of the country; a few editorial cartoons and advertisements; and, overwhelmingly, clippings from a variety of newspapers and magazines.

These diverse textual media—portraying the widespread impact of an emerging mass print culture on a developing modern consciousness in a manner not unlike what a personal blog or a Facebook page might reveal about a compiler today—were deliberately assembled, often over decades (although Lucy's scrapbook begins in 1900, some materials date as far back as the middle of the nineteenth century), in an example of what Ellen Gruber Garvey has called "performing archivalness."[1] Far from being a scattershot pasting at will, such clippings frequently form complex collages on the page, centered on a particular subject or theme. A postcard of what appears to be California redwoods beside a lake; an 1840 newspaper advertisement for a stagecoach company; and a poem by Henry Van Dyke, "What America Means to Me," that acknowledges the attractions of Old Europe but unequivocally chooses America, "where the air is full of sunlight and the flag is full of stars," combine to celebrate the country's innocence and a just-closed frontier. Similarly, a two-page spread takes as its topic one of the best-known poems of all time: "Mary Had a Little Lamb" (fig. I.1). The pastiche includes a postcard and news story about Mary Sawyer's birthplace in Sterling, Massachusetts, reminding (or perhaps informing) us that the subject of this lullaby was an actual, recent historical figure. At the bottom of the page, an illustrated manger scene from George Vicat Cole's painting, *Pride and Humility*—Americanized through the inclusion of Benjamin Franklin's nominee for the national bird, the turkey—emphasizes the purity of the Christian Lamb and patriotic virtue. This connection is reinforced through a small sketch, *The Flight into Egypt*, depicting Jesus, Joseph, and Mary. The formal features of the lullaby are underscored by clippings of "An Indian Lullaby," "Old Mother Hubbard," and other short poems, and by the choice to leave exposed some of the notes from the underlying music book to emphasize the poem's melodic dimension. The scrapbook's constructed pages reveal the complex historical, aesthetic, and religious contexts of the poem while at the same time demonstrating Lucy's acts of interpretation in the literal bringing together of these multimedia elements.

One of the more notable (though not at all unusual) features of Lucy's scrapbook is the inclusion of hundreds of poems that, in addition to participating in intricate webs of association with other texts and genres, were placed into a personal anthology highlighting such topics as motherhood and soldiers returning from World War I—exemplifying a "poetics of scrapbooking," as Mike Chasar terms it, in which everyday readers would become both critical readers and producers of meaning through the deliberate collection and juxtaposition of poetic texts.[2] Although Lucy's scrapbook roughly corresponds to the period that literary critics generally refer to as "modernism," typified by such figures as Ezra Pound and Gertrude Stein, the works of these writers do not grace its pages. A few of the names might be familiar: James Russell Lowell, Ella Wheeler Wilcox, Edgar A. Guest, and Rudyard Kipling. Most of the poems Lucy includes, however, are sentimentally rhymed and anonymous—or might as well be. Lucy's scrapbook (like that of many other compilers) privileges an all but critically ignored and forgotten canon of poems, even as it makes the fierce case for poetry as a special means of understanding private life.

By contrast, at about the same time that Lucy was completing her scrapbook, on a stuffy July afternoon in 1952, an aging T. S. Eliot took the London

Introduction

Figure I.1. Scrapbook page from Lucy A. (Mixer) Britton on "Mary Had a Little Lamb." Author's collection.

Library's stately podium, amid the rattle of a book lift transporting volumes from the closed stacks to its main desk, to deliver a speech on the fine points of book collecting:

> There are three kinds of private collections of books. There is the collection of the collector: the man who collects valuable and rare editions, usually of some one author or of some type or period, and who, when he really knows what he is about, is a bibliographer. Such collections have great value: but, so far as they are

not dispersed on the death of the collector, but preserved intact in some public institution where they will be accessible to those worthy to examine them, we need not repine at their passage from private hands. There is what I call the "gentleman's library," a library of the best editions of such books as a person of general education and culture would wish to have at hand. And finally, there is the private library which is merely a haphazard accumulation. The last is the most frequently found to-day, and it is the kind that I own myself.[3]

Eliot's remarks suggest a very different relationship to print culture from that evident in Lucy's scrapbook—one interested less in incorporating the everyday ephemeral into a personal textual miscellany than in preserving those prized books that might stand in for a lasting culture in the face of such rapidly accumulating print. It is perhaps unsurprising that a poet-critic who made a career out of purifying our tribal traditions would take an active interest in the book collection as a site for literary and cultural preservation. Certainly *The Waste Land*, one of the most important and influential modernist poems, required wide reading to supply its quotations and allusions, and the process of selection would be enhanced by quoting from books not only read but also owned. But Eliot's meditations on book collecting suggest a deeper affective connection to the bibliographical basis of that tradition that goes beyond the instrumental. The high cultural identifications reinforced by acquiring limited editions or fine bindings and assembling literary references into poems such as *The Waste Land* speak to long-standing anxieties to shore up literary and cultural monuments against the same deluge of mass print that made Lucy's scrapbook possible. The context of the speech is also key: while Eliot addresses both private and public collecting in his speech, he does so in one of Britain's leading literary institutions, highlighting the importance of the book collection not only for the individual poet but also as an institutionalized cultural object in its own right.

T. S. Eliot and Lucy Britton present what I argue for throughout *Poetic Modernism in the Culture of Mass Print* as two contrasting collecting practices—one rooted in the book collector's conservation, the other in the scrapbooker's accumulation—that suggest radically different ways of responding to an emerging mass print culture. By studying a wide continuum of collecting practices framed by these extremes and by tracing a variety of print-media objects and institutions that relied on such collecting, we can begin to achieve a comprehensive accounting of poetic modernism that was largely conditioned by a culture of mass print. To invoke Eliot in a book about modern poetry hardly seems out of place, although one might be accused of foregrounding a kind of elite high modernism that is likely to provoke mixed reactions. But why should we care about Lucy Britton? She was not a figure of much historical or literary importance (a point confirmed by the fact that I purchased her scrapbook at an antique store in Maine, rather than consulting it in institutional archives, as I have with other better-known documents of modernism). Unlike some other women—including Amy Lowell, H.D., Edna St. Vincent Millay, and (the focus of chapter 3) Marianne Moore—Lucy would not become a famous modern poet, exploring in her writing subjects and themes she may have first tackled in scrapbooks, and rooting her poetics within the act of scrapbooking itself. The New Critics who dominated the literary landscape by the time Lucy was completing her scrapbook wouldn't have paid her any mind, even if they did know of her, and many critics today are likely to feel the same. But then Lucy's obscurity is part of the point. Although a mostly critically ignored dimension of modernism, scrapbooking was (to use the easy pun) a "commonplace" reaction to the rise of mass print in the latter half of the nineteenth century that involved not only many individual private compilers but also a pervasive public snippet culture that challenges high/low literary and cultural distinctions. These scrapbooks would in various ways come to inform the making of poetic modernism and as such prompt us to reconsider the role of popular production and reception in our understanding of that modernism.

Although I make frequent reference to figures like Lucy Britton, and to popular poems and poetic formations that have largely been neglected in studies of modernism, this book is not exclusively devoted to the popular. Rather, it charts a poetic modernism that is attentive both to the mostly forgotten quotidian and to the more familiar (if often more restrictive) "higher" modern poetry in an effort to make meaning through their points of contact, juxtapositions, contradictions, and jockeyings for position in fields of production and reception. As I argue throughout, these different dimensions of poetic modernism can best be understood through a continuum of collecting practices, typified by book collecting at one end and scrapbooking at the other, which highlighted both individual and more widespread cultural reactions to an emerging culture of mass print. These practices helped condition poetic modernism at several homologous formal, print-media, and institutional sites—including the anthology, the periodical, the collage poem, volumes of selected and collected poems, and the modern poetry archive—and a close study of these sites addresses in a new light long-standing issues of literary value, genre, form, reproduction, and institutionalization.

Beyond a particular engagement with modern poetry, I also suggest how mass print culture and the collecting of print-media objects as an expression of that culture serve to structure a variety of literary forms and institutions that became prominent in the first part of the twentieth century but that were themselves manifestations of decades-long cultural transformations. As such, this book also aims to speak more generally to literary, cultural, and print-media scholars of the nineteenth and twentieth centuries, which compels me to provide an overview of the rise of mass print culture and its attendant collecting practices before addressing their specific impact on poetic modernism.

Book Collecting in the Age of Mass Print

A good book is fruitful of other books; it perpetuates its fame from age to age, and makes eras in the lives of its readers.

—A. Bronson Alcott, "Influence of a Library"

The order of disorder reigns supreme
All round the room: here book on book lies piled. . . .

—Thomas Hutchinson, "Sonnets in the Library"

If asked to locate the watershed moment of our current information age, we might be tempted to offer a variety of dates. We might cite the rise of ARPANET in the 1960s, Tim Berners-Lee's proposal for the World Wide Web and its attendant standards (HTML, URI, HTTP) in 1989-1990, or the fuller realization of the Internet's potential in such applications as Google (incorporated in 1998), *Wikipedia* (launched in 2001), and Facebook (launched in 2004). If we choose instead to focus on the material substructure that makes such information sharing (and oversharing) possible, we might trace the rise of the microcomputer in the 1970s or look back to the vacuum-tubed mainframes of the 1940s and 1950s or even to these behemoths' own precursors in such mechanical wonders as the punch card-driven Jacquard loom, first demonstrated in 1801. Should we find a focus on the technology itself to be too deterministic, we might locate key political, social, and economic shifts—marked by such phenomena as creeping copyright law and the rise of the multinational corporation—which frequently frame our complex relationships to information media.

Similarly (and the similarities far from end here), the moment of mass print culture's emergence, and the emergence of its attendant print-collecting practices, proves to be a slippery fish. For example, Deidre Shauna Lynch has turned her attention to the earlier decades of the nineteenth century to argue for the ways in which collectors and scholars were "wedded to books" in an often pathologized bibliomania that located the love of the scarce book-object in a world of increasingly cheap print. This book love simultaneously promoted a consolidation of the literary canon through principles of ordering that looked to the collection of the material bibliographical object as well as the potential for a more intimate relationship with the text itself. Lynch also notes the gendered nature of book collecting, practiced overwhelmingly by men, and offers the female-dominated practice of paper-album collage construction (a forerunner to modern scrapbooking) as a counterpart to the bibliomaniac's library.[4]

For a host of reasons, however, these earlier impulses intensify by the latter decades of the nineteenth century in what can more fully be called a culture of mass print. These decades are typified by the rise of penny papers, weekly magazines, and inexpensive book reprints hawked at tobacco stores and on street corners outside train stations, which were made possible by a number of technological innovations and social transformations from throughout the century. Stereotyping (the process of casting pages onto metal plates to facilitate large print runs of books and periodicals, developed in the early eighteenth century and improved in the early nineteenth century) and lithography (the process of printing images using smooth stone or metal, developed at the end of the eighteenth century), improvements in typecasting throughout the nineteenth century (including the invention of monotype and linotype machines for quickly casting individual characters and entire lines of type), and the development of machine-made wood paper in the middle decades of the nineteenth century all made it possible to produce many more pages much more cheaply and rapidly than had been the case in the past.

Various social transformations, such as the repeal of the British advertising, newspaper, and paper taxes (the so-called taxes on knowledge) and the organization of factory-shop labor, were also integral to mass print's success. Rising literacy rates, resulting from such education legislation as the British Education Act of 1870 and a series of compulsory education laws in the United States, provided a reading public for this new material, ushering in the age of popular periodicals and cheap reprints of classics in the latter part of the century. These transformations were themselves conditioned by more basic economic transformations, including the increased mass production and consumption of a variety of goods that allowed newspapers and magazines to receive much of their money from advertising (often in verse) everything from books to bicycles to cure-all elixirs. Selling issues at or below the cost of production, periodical publishers were able to garner much larger readerships than they had previously been able to secure.

While precursors—such as penny papers and early paperbacks—can be traced to earlier decades, the prevalence of these material and social innovations brought about a saturation of mass print in the latter part of the nineteenth century, by which time books and periodicals had become a significant part of life for many (though by no means all) people across the socioeconomic spectrum in both Britain and the United States. By this point, print's liberating power was increasingly celebrated in what might be said to constitute a new genre of bibliographically based poems, typified by "Song of the Printing-Press":

> "*Vive la* PRESS!" a prophetic cry,
> For it tells that the glorious By and By
> Shall be nearer each other by the rule it owns;
> And that all of mankind, on the earth's broad zones,
> Shall the Gospel of Liberty plainly hear;
> And that darkness and error shall disappear
> That the poor and the lowly, the weak, oppressed,
> Uplifted shall be, and supremely blest![5]

The poem portrays the modern printing press as a democratic instrument, capable of disseminating information to the earth's far reaches and bringing about social and economic equality.

As liberating a force as the press could be, there was a flip side to its cultural potential. As newspapers and magazines syndicated their columns and participated in nationwide advertising campaigns, and as book publishers consolidated their power, pushing aside smaller competitors to serve the needs of a growing professional-managerial class, the modern press also inaugurated a hegemony of national mass culture that disrupted earlier social and regional formations.[6] One way that people sought to escape what they saw as the homogenization and dumbing-down of culture through the use of mass print was to give attention to the handcrafted book, imprinted with an individual style and the mark of personal production that defies standardized efficiency. This attention to craft helps to account for the socialist underpinnings of such titans of the Arts and Crafts movement as William Morris's Kelmscott Press in Britain and Elbert Hubbard's Roycroft Press in the United States, both of which emphasized direct, unalienated labor.

It was also often the case, however, that such attention to the finely made book indicated a literally (and frequently aesthetically and politically) conservative reaction to emerging mass print—an often anxious grasping at a residual cultural form that was losing ground to cheap, mass-produced books and magazines, which fueled a fetishization of old and rare books and a turn-of-the-century culture of collecting. The purview of such collecting is outlined in the first issue of the London-based bibliographical magazine *Book Lore* (1884-1887), which begins with the declaration that

> nothing that concerns books will be outside our range of sympathy. We shall deal with the methods of their production in ancient and modern times, the substances on which man has written, the instruments by which he has recorded his thoughts, and the manner in which art has added its beauty to literature. The blunders of scribes and printers, the fortunes and misfortunes of books and authors; the heroism, the folly, the fanaticism and the eccentricity embalmed in books will also have a place. Libraries, public and private, ancient and modern, will be noted. Episodes in the history of bookselling will be chronicled. Biographical particulars will be given of those less known worthies who have hitherto almost escaped attention.[7]

Book Lore's varied attention to the material, historical, and social aspects of the book stems from a proliferation of private book collecting—largely by middle-class men who trolled back-alley bookstalls and found camaraderie in bookstores, auctions, and book-collecting clubs. While for many bibliophiles collecting was a leisurely pastime, the most committed of collectors were said to suffer from the disease of bibliomania, being reduced to theft, poverty, and even to marrying inheritors of collections to get their hands on a prized book.[8] As one book lover put it, there is "as much difference between the inclinations and taste of a bibliophile and a bibliomaniac as between a slight cold and the advanced stages of consumption."[9]

Betraying the pervasiveness of the very mass print that was being challenged, this private book collecting entered public discourse through several bibliographical magazines springing up on both sides of the Atlantic at the turn of the twentieth century.[10] These magazines, along with a host of manuals, pamphlets, and other books on the subject, ushered in what has been called the "golden age of book collecting," roughly spanning the years from 1890 to 1930.[11] The rise of book collecting is in one respect a particular manifestation of a larger nineteenth-century phenomenon, where those with the means to do so were collecting everything from tapestries to teapots. The mass production of various "unlimited" goods led to a surge in private collecting that collapsed the boundaries between the useful and artistic object, deferring its meaning and serving as a marker of distinction for the collector.[12] This culture of collecting was put on public display in the Crystal Palace exhibitions in London (1851) and New York (1853)—which showcased exotica and colonial spoils in addition to markers of national pride and regional difference—and was strongly evident in the rise of the modern museum and library, which often grew up together, as in the case of the Reading Room at the British Museum.[13] Such displays of collecting were progenitors of a modernist collecting impulse that, as Jeremy Braddock has observed, was highly influential on modern poetry and other modern literature.[14]

Collecting had become such a popular practice that the prominent nineteenth-century book and print collector Daniel Tredwell could naturalize it as an innate and universal human characteristic: man was a collecting animal just as he was "a reasoning animal," "an animal who uses tools," and "a two-legged animal without feathers."[15] Turn-of-the-century book collecting can be distinguished from other kinds of collecting, however, in that it was also a particular reaction to the rise of nineteenth-century mass textual reproduction (itself a particular type of mass production) that facilitated mass print culture and that many collectors believed led to a corresponding cheapening of literature. Some blamed supply, arguing that "cheap literature means many books, and many books means superficial reading."[16] Others blamed the fickle new readership, where "the demand for light-hearted and marrowless literature is positively voracious, and novelists spring up and are forced down again like an army of jack-in-the-boxes, under the control of a still larger army of wayward children."[17] In any case, many critics agreed that a "great crowd of books is as destructive of the literary instinct, which is a highly delicate thing, as is a London evening party, of the social instinct."[18]

In an attempt to combat this cheapening of literature through the mass production of print, collectors hoped to conserve the rare and finely made book and by doing so to also preserve the privileged writing it expressed. As one collector exclaimed, books "are the opium of the West. They are killing us. Let us love them, but not for the things that they tell us. Let us love them, they are dear enough! But let them be well printed, well bound, beautiful in form. . . . They have a chance, then, to be eternal."[19] The book's potential for permanence, as a function of its material form, is privileged over what the book might say in the here and now. This bibliographical form is further fetishized by connoisseurs of the book's individual components, where "each unit, or step, almost, in the production of a completed volume, has its admirers, is specialized and collected. Bindings, first editions, uncut copies, large paper copies, tall copies, title-pages, colophons, unique copies, even errors become virtues, extra illustrated copies, and so on. The ramifications are endless."[20]

Books and their distinguishing features were collected not only because of their potential for permanence but also because they had already survived time's ravages. As J. H. Slater, one of the great book collectors and most prolific writers on book collecting of the late nineteenth century, explains, as mass-produced books became easier and cheaper to attain, there was an increased interest in old, scarce, handcrafted books for their own sake. In this climate, he argues, a "halo of romance encircles all things old, and if they be at the same time extremely scarce, very instructive, or for some special reason more than usually interesting, there can never be any fear of them being overlooked."[21]

Slater's suggestion that a text's instructiveness may add to the book's interest is, however, largely an attempt to strike a compromise between the privileging of either the material book or the literary text that often made bitter enemies of the collector and the gentleman scholar (the irreconcilable differences Eliot points to in his London Library address). In one corner, the true collector attacked the scholar for actually reading his books and marking them up. Exceptions were made, however, for signed and association copies kept by famous literary or historical figures, which inscribed some small personal aspect onto the page.[22] The collector compared the scholar to a bookworm—a dreaded bug who "loves books simply because he can cram his mind with them and literally and letterally gorge himself," his trail marked by "crumpled pages, dogears, nail marks, loose signatures, damaged binding, torn leaves and ruin generally."[23]

Many scholars, however, wore the term "bookworm" as a badge of honor, observing that for the bookworm "books are life, air, water, food, and, in fact, everything. If the two races of bookworms differ in point or degree of utility or otherwise, they are, at all events, identical in living a retired life, in being buried among books, and in following an occupation which is the one absorbing feature of life."[24] For them, the ideal book is the one in which the bibliographical features are most transparent and least valuable in their own right, since it is these features that are compromised in the name of knowledge as phrases are underlined, corners dog-eared, and spines broken. These readers maligned the collector as irrationally interested in material details such as the type of paper and quality of binding but ignorant of their books' textual meaning. As one bibliophile lamented:

> In vain might Homer roll the tide of song,
> Or Horace smile, or Tully charm the throng;
> If crost by Pallas' ire, the trenchant blade,
> Or too oblique, or near the edge, invade,
> The Bibliomane exclaims, with haggard eye,
> "No margin!" turns in haste, and scorns to buy.[25]

The collector is so preoccupied with the materiality of the book that he will sacrifice the wisdom of the ages if its physical presentation doesn't meet his precise specifications.

These contrasting emphases on the book and the text lead to a confusion of symbolic and cultural capital. As a key example of conspicuous consumption, book collecting expresses a subtle cultural capital where "mere reading of a rare book is a puerility, an idiosyncrasy of adolescence; it is the *ownership* of the book which is the matter of distinction."[26] This is evident in one of the best-known modern literary representations of such consumption: the library of uncut volumes that Jay Gatsby kept for his guests to admire. By contrast, the contents of books and other print offer a more obvious symbolic capital that is realized through the act of reading. There is, however, a complex conflation of these two categories in the gentleman's library, as well as a conflation of aesthetic and economic value that, as I argue in chapter 1, is foregrounded in the modern anthology.[27]

Confusion went beyond that of value, however. While the collector and the scholar emphasized different aspects of the book, many agreed with one turn-of-the-century collector that the "book beautiful is a composite thing made up of many parts and may be made beautiful by the beauty of each of its parts—its literary content, its material or materials, its writing or printing, its illumination or illustration, its binding and decoration."[28] Each of these parts, literary or bibliographical, contributes to the overall impression of the book or can be singled out as an exemplary characteristic, augmenting or detracting from one another in the process. While the collector's book and the scholar's text were frequently pitted against one another by collectors and scholars, treating the linguistic as one unprivileged dimension of the book among many allowed for some truce between the camps and even a potential resolution.

This understanding of the book as a harmonious arrangement of parts also models how the individual text and book can be incorporated into larger systems: the library and the book collection. As Tredwell understood, collecting was not merely hunting and gathering but also a creative act of synthesis: "It is genius which fabricates from these vast accumulations methods, and history in art, archaeology, and ethnology. It was the quarry-man, the stone-mason, and the iron-monger who collected the materials for the Brooklyn Bridge, but it was the synthetic intellect of Roebling that hung it from the air."[29] Like other collectors, connoisseurs of books and texts frequently aimed for such synthesis as well. Just as the material book and the linguistic text have differing aims and assumptions, so too do the collection and the library to which they contribute. The "collection of the collector" is an end in itself; the "gentleman's library" is a means to furthering knowledge. But just as the book and the text are closely intertwined, so too are the library and the collection.

The collection and the library are structurally similar in that they both aim for totality and completion. The ideal library contains all the texts necessary for a rounded education and cultural refinement and nothing but these texts (though the actual texts and aims are of course up for dispute), just as the ideal collection aspires to contain all the editions of a particular work or all the books in a series. As one well-known collector, Walter Benjamin, explains, what is decisive in collecting is that the object

> is detached from all its original functions in order to enter into the closest conceivable relation to things of the same kind. This relation is the diametric opposite of any utility, and falls into the peculiar category of completeness. What is this "completeness"? It is a grand attempt to overcome the wholly irrational character of the object's mere presence at hand through its integration into a new, expressly devised system: the collection. And for the true collector, every single thing in this system becomes an encyclopedia of all knowledge of the epoch, the landscape, the industry, and the owner from which it comes.[30]

The collection can strive for such completeness, in part, because it exists outside the progression of time, which becomes spatialized and fetishized in the bodies of the books themselves, bound and lined along the shelf.[31] As such, this collection, Benjamin notes, "stands to the customary ordering and schematization of things something as their arrangement in the dictionary stands to a natural arrangement."[32] As I argue in later chapters, this notion of indexed ahistorical completeness on display in the book collection would help provide the aesthetic justification for many modern poetry formations, including the objective anthology, the modern long poem, and the collected volume of poetry. If the collection posits a closed totality and strings items together according to an internal associative—one could say metonymic— logic, however, it would find its counterpart in the scrapbook, which can be likened to a thesaurus ruled by analogy as it strives to make meaning through a culture of mass print.

A Book of Scraps

A boy. A dog. The remains of a meal. A piece of trash. To quarrel. To throw away. The *Oxford English Dictionary* gives several definitions for the word "scrap." But the definition of a scrap as something to be retained as well as discarded is a relatively new one, being part of the compound word "scrapbook": "a blank book in which pictures, newspaper cuttings, and the like are pasted for preservation," citing its earliest instance in a book of anecdotes, *The Scrap Book*, from 1825.[33] Popular books on scrapbooking, though, tend to locate the origins of the phenomenon with the publication of John Poole's 1832 *Manuscript Gleanings and Literary Scrap Book, Original and Select*, designed "to supply the World of Literature and Fashion, and more especially the Fair portion of it, with an elegant and suitable Depository for those Selections which the reading of even the passing hour offers to its votaries."[34] Other scrapbooks quickly followed Poole's gleanings, and these were popular enough to be advertised as specialty items by the 1850s. Mark Twain, an avid scrapbooker, got in on the game by patenting a self-pasting scrapbook in 1872.[35] It was not at all unusual, though, for scrapbookers to paste onto the pages of a book already in their possession or to seek out hefty volumes, such as ledgers, dictionaries, and old government reports.

To understand scrapbooking's relationship to an emerging mass print culture, it is necessary to distinguish the scrapbook from three earlier, related constructions: the commonplace book, the product of artistic cutting and pasting, and the extra-illustrated book. Commonplace books, into which readers would copy choice passages and take structured notes, have been around since ancient Greece. They were important for such early modern writers as Francis Bacon and John Milton and for Enlightenment figures in Georgian England.[36] Such commonplace books have also challenged critical assumptions of originality, nationality, and periodicity on both sides of the Atlantic.[37] The scrapbook importantly differs from the commonplace book, though, in that it materially embodies mass print. The scrapbook contains not only the idea of the textual thing but also (as William Carlos Williams might put it) the thing itself. To the extent that accumulated scraps index the mass print sources and the wider print culture from which they came, they are a crucial means of marking the individual as a product of that culture.

Second, the cutting and pasting of paper and other textual objects into newly meaningful formations has a long history that precedes the scrapbook. Paper collage was practiced in the eighteenth century by such ladies of the court as Mary Delaney—pointing to a feminized origin for the découpage of the *avant-garde*, celebrated in the work of such artists as Juan Gris. Such constructions were primarily concerned with the materiality of the paper itself and were relatively empty of semantic meaning. One offshoot of such practices, coming into vogue at about the same time as scrapbooking, was Victorian photo collage, which offered a more linguistically rich assemblage of images growing out of new photographic technology.[38] Although, as I will show, the scrapbook was similarly used as a vehicle for assemblage and collage, it differs from these other forms in its heavy reliance upon mass-produced print.

Finally, although they both deal in bibliographical materials, the scrapbook differs from the extra-illustrated or grangerized book (named for James Granger, who popularized the practice): a book embellished through the insertion of additional prints and other items. Many book collectors, who were invested in the integrity of the book, lamented that for extra-illustrators, "books are mere receptacles of prints" and that "it was necessary to mutilate, or destroy altogether, many other books" to extra-illustrate a single volume.[39] Extra-illustrators, however, believed that their work was ultimately in service of the book, improving both its aesthetic and monetary value, and claimed that these volumes "are in such demand that they usually, though not always, sell for much more than the cost of their production."[40] Extra-illustrators exclaimed that it "is not to be supposed that such expensive volumes are made up like scrapbooks, with the letterpress and pictures pasted upon the sheets. That would be an inglorious ending for such a work of love and expense."⁴¹ Scrapbooks, by contrast, it was claimed, are "ephemeral publications that never will go into one's library; they are for the journey, the piazza, and the train."⁴² The two constructions are differently marked both by their processes of accumulation and assembly, and by their practitioners' relationship to mass print. It would be reasonable to claim, though, that extra-illustrators occupied a point on the collecting continuum somewhere between the book collector and the scrapbooker, sharing attributes with both.

The scrapbook proper—distinguished from the commonplace book, artistic collage, and extra-illustrated book—can itself be divided into three general and overlapping categories. The first is the professional scrapbook, which joined a number of diverse and imaginative repositories—including pigeonholes, envelopes, card catalogs, drawers, cabinets, and barrels—and evolved throughout the nineteenth century as a system for keeping track of, as well as negotiating, one's place within an increasingly bureaucratized print culture. Such scrapbooks were compiled by doctors and others who had newfound professional status and an exponential increase in information to sort through, as well as by such institutions as libraries, publishers, and businesses that increasingly saw the need to preserve and access records.

An important subset of these professional scrapbooks included those containing clippings or reviews of work from various newspapers and magazines, which frequently functioned as an author's portfolio. These scrapbooks were sometimes assembled by the authors themselves but were often compiled by the increasing number of clipping bureaus ready to do the job en masse. Such writers' scrapbooks are an important marker of a transforming mass print culture, underscoring the need to track such work in a culture of reprinting where a single story or poem may find its way into several of the proliferating periodicals, while at the same time highlighting the increased professionalization of the author that requires such a robust tracking of sources.

The second kind of scrapbook (and the one that has received the most scholarly attention) is the personal miscellany.⁴³ The nineteenth-century scrapbook has been described as a "material manifestation of memory," both of the individual compiler and of a cultural moment driven by an emphasis on reading, visual literacy, and mass consumption.⁴⁴ By the turn of the twentieth century, scrapbooks would also provide an overt psychological outlet for personal expression that was not easily attainable elsewhere.⁴⁵

Personal scrapbooks were often compiled over several decades by successive generations of scrapbookers, and were prized as a means of carving out identity within an increasingly complicated and impersonal world. As one scrapbooker remarks:

> Next to the Bible and Shakespeare, the book which should be on every family shelf is the Scrapbook. It is a thesaurus of the individual's life, and has that advantage over all other books which are made by other people. It is the best possible family record—for photographs, memoranda, documents, and everything else. It saves the vagrant verse and the material clippings which you wish to copy.... The scrapbook to those who know how to use it means more in the average household—more for culture, and more for comfort, and more for convenience than any other volume, except the Book of Books.[46]

The scrapbook is a treasured form of familial and cultural memory, as well as domestic comfort, second only to the key literary and theological texts of Anglo-American civilization. Additionally, the recognition that the scrapbook is a thesaurus to one's life underscores (in contrast to the book collection's dictionary-like metonymy) that the logic of the scrapbook is one of metaphor and analogy. Others' words spin a web of synonyms that point to meaning not written.

Although scrapbooks were kept by people from all walks of life, they were especially important outlets for individuals and groups who were marginalized by, and felt the need to negotiate, the codes of the dominant culture. A prime example of this is a volume on the "Negro Question" kept between 1883 and 1889 by the former slave William H. Scott.[47] In addition to being a teacher and ordained Baptist minister, Scott owned a bookstore in Washington, DC—a profession that gave him unusually wide access to newspapers and other periodicals from across the country, which he would draw upon to address civil rights issues and trace the emergence of Jim Crow laws during Reconstruction.[48] While not as formally inventive as some other scrapbooks of the period, and less concerned with personal expression, Scott's scrapbook manages to stitch together a postbellum virtual national print culture through common demonstrations of political, legal, and social injustice scattered across a wide geography.[49]

Women in particular used the scrapbook to important cultural and political ends as they embraced the popular side of an emerging "great divide" between high and mass culture.[50] While all types of scrapbooks were produced by both women and men, the *discourse* surrounding scrapbooking—evident in periodicals and other popular publications of the period—was overwhelmingly gendered feminine.[51] This was particularly evident in poetry scrapbooks.[52] Periodicals often encouraged the feminizing of poetic genre through such scrapbooks, as when John Brisben Walker, editor of *Cosmopolitan*, notes that "every magazine that went into the household should publish verse, since so many women kept scrapbooks filled, not with prose, but with lyrics and sonnets and ballads."[53] To recognize this dominant feminizing discourse does not, however, deny the fact that many women, such as women suffragists, used scrapbooks to challenge societal depictions of women or, as in the case of Marianne Moore, masculinized high modernism.[54]

In addition to seeing scrapbooks as a crucial means of negotiating mass print, some scrapbookers went so far as to see themselves emulating modern publishing practices, explaining that, in his own way, the scrapbooker "is doing what the trust magnate does, what the great publisher may do. He is commanding the brains of a multitude of men and women. They are working for him without knowing it. And permanently they are working for no one else."[55] This close connection between scrapbooking and publishing suggests a third kind of scrapbook that may be considered an extension of the second: the scrapbook specifically intended for clippings that would be incorporated into other writing. Even for those scholars who have recognized the scrapbook as an important diary of ages past and as a significant cultural form in its own right, this *productive* potential has largely been overlooked.[56] I am, however, keenly interested in how the scrapbook models processes of accumulation, selection, and preservation to new literary forms, as I discuss with respect to Marianne Moore's collage poetry, which I examine in chapter 3. But I also wish to extend my investigation beyond the individual poet, taking seriously the notion that the scrapbooker is doing essentially what the publisher does and entertaining another scrapbooker's claim that "all literature consists of snippets. Every book is but the record of a selection from the world of fact and thought."[57] Scrapbooking in this broad sense suggests ways that the selection and accumulation of ephemeral materials inform poetic modernism not only at the level of the individual poetic text but also at the level of such larger institutional forms as the magazine and the archive. The ways in which scrapbooks might mediate these aspects of poetic modernism become clearer when the scrapbook is seen not as an isolated and discrete object but as a particular manifestation of a robust turn-of-the-century snippet culture.

Clipping in Public: *Tit-Bits*, the *Scrap Book*, and Modern Snippet Culture

> I love the old fellow—together for years
>   We have managed the *Farmer's Gazette*,
> And although I am old, I'm his favorite shears,
>   And can crowd the compositors yet.
> But my duties are rather too heavy, I think,
>   And I oftentimes envy the quill
> As it lazily leans with its nibs in the ink,
>   While I'm slashing away with a will.
>
> —A. W. Kelly, "Soliloquy of the Old Scissors"

> This is the age of specialization, the hot-shot age, the fourteen-inch-gun age. The conventional magazine, with its smattering of illustrations, its smattering of fiction, and its smattering of special articles, is about as much like the fourteen-inch gun as a cat is like a locomotive. There is not enough of any one thing to make it convincing.
>
> —Frank A. Munsey, "To the Readers of the *Scrap Book*"

Although scrapbooks were often private affairs, chronicling intimate family histories and personal aspirations, they frequently drew upon a public print culture in their construction. Not only did they incorporate individual scraps from a variety of periodicals, but they also often formally mimicked the mass cultural texts from which their clippings were obtained. Nineteenth-century scrapbooks generally followed a strict multicolumn format that resembled straightlaced newspapers while (as I elaborate on later) by the first decade of the twentieth century they would begin to break through these columns, finding new freedoms in expressive collage techniques that resembled the form of many modern periodicals. This connection has not gone entirely unnoticed.[58] What has not been fully acknowledged, however, is the extent to which there was a symbiotic relationship between these private and public practices, made most obvious in the snippet journals and a more general snippet culture that helped redefine the individual's relationship to mass print.

Scrapbooking and popular print had in fact been explicitly interconnected throughout the nineteenth century. While scrapbookers took their cues from print, early magazines on both sides of the Atlantic, such as the *Scrap*

Book: A Manchester Weekly Publication (started 1822), the *Scrap Book of Literary Varieties, Entertaining and Instructive* (started 1831), and the *American Scrap Book and Magazine of United States Literature* (started 1861), were modeled to varying degrees on scrapbooks, even incorporating the term in their titles. The first significant publication to be self-consciously scrappy in form and not merely in name, however, was George Newnes's British weekly magazine *Tit-Bits from All the Most Interesting Books, Periodicals and Newspapers in the World* (1881-1984). In an oft-repeated story, Newnes explains the origins of the magazine: "One night, in 1880, when I was sitting at home reading the *Manchester Evening News* . . . I came across a story, or some interesting account, which very much pleased me. I read it to my wife and said, 'There, that's what I call a real "tit-bit."' This paper, but for it, is to-day decidedly dull, because there is absolutely no news to put in it. Now, why cannot a paper be brought out which should contain nothing but 'tit-bits' similar to this?"[59] From this initial insight—that one could simply reprint items of interest rather than commission original pieces—one commentator remarks that "eggs of an enormous brood of Tit-Bits, Answers, Scraps, Scrapings, Cuts, and the foundations of fortunes and reputations afterwards enhanced in other spheres were laid," forming a new "journalism of scraps" that includes such journals as Alfred and Cecil B. Harmsworth's *Answers* and Cyril Arthur Pearson's *Pearson's Weekly*.[60]

Tit-Bits carved out a space in the highly competitive publishing field of the 1890s by appealing to a growing reading public through casting off the piety of the religious press, resisting the impulses of the more unsavory juvenile crime and sporting papers, and encouraging a sense of "participatory journalism."[61] With the help of advertising, Newnes priced the paper at a mere penny, making it accessible to a wide cross section of society—especially the newly literate lower classes—and *Tit-Bits* reached an average weekly circulation during Newnes's tenure (from 1881 to 1910) of between four hundred thousand and six hundred thousand issues, helping to construct one of the key turn-of-the-century reading publics against which such critics as Hugh Kenner would later define literary modernism, noting that "by the turn of the century two reading publics at least were discernible, that of Everyman, that of *Tit-Bits*. The former thought the latter vulgar when they thought of them at all, and were themselves thought stuffy. And neither was the right public for Henry James or Joseph Conrad—or for James Joyce, for that matter."[62]

Tit-Bits appealed to this wide public through extending and potentially remedying what Meredith McGill has identified as a nineteenth-century "culture of reprinting" that depended on innovations in publication and distribution, in conjunction with lax copyright regulations, which promoted duplication and anonymity at the expense of original authorship.[63] Newnes is open about his reprinting, even when other periodicals frequently were not, and argues that (not unlike the clipping bureaus of the time) he is performing for his readers a necessary service in navigating the floodwaters of mass print. He explains that it is "impossible for any man in the busy times of the present to even glance at any large number of the immense variety of books and papers which have gone on accumulating, until now their number is fabulous," and to help combat this situation he offers "an organised system of extracting."[64]

The particular importance of *Tit-Bits* in literary modernism (contra Kenner) is hinted at in James Joyce's *Ulysses*. With a copy of *Tit-Bits* under his arm, Leopold Bloom famously heads to the toilet, where "quietly he read, restraining himself, the first column and, yielding but resisting, began the second. Midway his last resistance yielding, he allowed his bowels to ease themselves quietly as he read, reading still patiently that slight constipation of yesterday quite gone. Hope it's not too big to bring on the piles again. No, just right. So. Ah! Costive. One tabloid of cascara sagrada. Life might be so. It did not move or touch him but it was something quick and neat. Print anything now. Silly season."[65] This is easy reading, like a quick trip to the toilet. But it has its purposes. It's relaxing and relieving for the reader. And it allows Joyce to make some clever bibliographical puns, pointing to the journal's columns and the term *cascara sagrada*—"sacred bark" in Spanish, the bark of a shrub used to relieve constipation (alternatively called *chitticum*, "shit come")—that suggests the wood paper generally used by popular magazines. Moreover, it offers an effortless flow of money for the author. Bloom notes that a guinea a column has been paid to the author, making this story worth three pounds, thirteen and six, and thinks, "Might manage a sketch."[66]

Bloom's sketch would have been welcomed in the magazine. Readers were encouraged to participate in the production of *Tit-Bits* not only in writing original pieces (which would become more common as the magazine progressed) but also through entering weekly prize competitions, in which readers would scour the week's publications hoping to find a prized bit for submission. In this early form of crowdsourcing, contributors adopted an editorial role, which gave them a personal stake in the magazine, and this in turn boosted circulation.⁶⁷ Such contests made public the processes of accumulation and selection that many readers had already brought to their private scrapbooks, while privileging the manipulation and integration of information over the Romantic ideal of the original author and training contributors to read widely rather than deeply as they skimmed vast amounts of print.

Through such participatory journalism, *Tit-Bits* signaled for many turn-of-the-century British critics an emerging snippet culture in which "it is not to be denied that the Cult of the Snippet, though not yet the religion which it is in the United States, is strongly with us: so that it may very well ensue that there shall be no household without its literary rag-bags, and that the page shall be more to us than the chapter, the chapter than the volume, the volume than the book."⁶⁸ This anatomization of print, however—in which the illuminated part is privileged over the coherent whole—was often taken to be a negative condition, where such snippet journals as *Tit-Bits*, "cheaply illustrated and still more cheaply edited, with scissors and paste instead of independent thought, . . . are aiding in the mental deterioration of hundreds and thousands of young minds."⁶⁹

Several critics believed that such mental deterioration took its toll on the writing and reading of literature in particular. One critic laments that "this is an imitative and not a creative age; why? Partially because we debauch ourselves with flippant, flitting dips into the multitude of articles that appear in the newspapers, periodicals, and books of the day. Concentration comes before creation; reading daily upon a multiplicity of topics does not inspire thought, it merely dissipates the understanding."⁷⁰ Snippet culture even formally determined those literary works that still could be produced, so that the "flood of this pernicious hop-skip-and-jump style of literature is increasing to a most lamentable extent."⁷¹

Other critics of the time, however, praise snippet culture's potential for remixing and recontextualizing form and content in new ways, as well as for its promotion of literacy. As one observer remarks, from all the criticism of it,

> one might suppose that the fascination of *Tit-Bits* and its like had seduced serious minds from the immensities, that if the great public were not reading daily scraps and weekly snippets it would be sending into ever and ever new editions all the weighty books which now miss that felicity. But the fact surely is that the journalism of scraps is read to-day by people who in an earlier generation would have

read nothing at all. It is a delusion to suppose, when one sees, say during the luncheon hour in the City, boys and girls in St. Paul's Churchyard devouring their favourite *Scraps* or *Cuts* that they would otherwise be immersed in contemplation of the Cathedral or the study of philosophy.[72]

Any reading, so the argument went (and often still goes), is better than no reading at all. Functional literacy, so it is claimed, is a prerequisite to (and perhaps ultimately more important than) cultural literacy.

Although such snippet magazines as *Tit-Bits* were important vehicles for presenting a general snippet culture in which scrapbooking played a key role, the connection to the scrapbook was made unmistakable in an American magazine that carried the name, the *Scrap Book*. In its inaugural issue, the *Scrap Book* (1906-1911) declares that it would be "the most elastic thing that ever happened in the way of a magazine—elastic enough to carry anything from a tin whistle to a battleship," including "biography, review, philosophy, science, art, poetry, wit, humor, pathos, satire, the weird, the mystical—everything that can be classified and everything that cannot be classified."[73] An offshoot of the popular *Munsey's Magazine* (started by Frank A. Munsey in 1889), the *Scrap Book* reproduced items from "hundreds and hundreds of scrap books from all over the country, some of them a century old," which have yielded "an enormous number of gems, and facts and figures, and historical and personal bits that are of rare value."[74] The scrapbook's archiving of multimedia, heterogeneous genres, and multiple textual forms provides both the source material and inspiration for the magazine and, as such, offers snapshots of an evolving mass print culture.

This diverse content, which, like that of *Tit-Bits*, was designed to "appeal most forcefully to the human heart and human brain—to all the people of all classes everywhere," allowed for the first edition of five hundred thousand to sell out in three days.[75] Encouraged by this success, Munsey opted for a much better grade of paper than the one on which the first issue had been printed, believing that the *Scrap Book* "should be printed on a paper that will last, for it is these literary gems above all things that we most wish to preserve."[76] Like the scrapbooks it drew upon, the *Scrap Book* saw its role as one not only of immediate dissemination but also of historical preservation —a role played out in the material form of the paper itself (which has held up well to this day) and further evidenced in an offer to bind the first volume of the magazine. While it was common for magazines to provide binding services—inviting readers to return issues to be bound or exchanged for a different bound copy—it was unusual for a magazine to do much more than remove advertisements and slap on an index. The *Scrap Book*, by contrast, had decided to "reset the entire first six issues, eliminating the serials, which, after all, have no place in a scrap-book; enlarging the type, reassembling the very cream of the matter and altering the cumulative index which is part of Volume I, so as to facilitate research and make the book altogether a more attractive proposition."[77] As the magazine argues, "The best of the world's literature as offered in the last two thousand years occupy its pages. . . . In fact, THE SCRAP BOOK is a veritable encyclopedia of knowledge, a storehouse of information. The resetting of the entire volume is a considerable undertaking, but the completed work will be more desirable, better arranged, and easier to read than it would otherwise have been. The purpose is to make this work a reference volume for all classes and for all time."[78] Like *Tit-Bits*, the *Scrap Book* sought to provide a through line to mass print culture—not only a storehouse for mass print but also a means of accessing, evaluating, and manipulating its texts. Unlike *Tit-Bits*, however, the *Scrap Book* meant to do this not only synchronically at any given moment but also diachronically, preserving texts from over the long course of history that had often (largely by chance) survived only through their inclusion in the scrapbook.

The *Scrap Book*'s potential for reproduction and preservation was particularly evident in its recovering of individual poems and a necessarily changed notion of literary history:

> As one turns over the pages of scrap books of a quarter of a century ago he comes upon poems that appear to be common to all. Of these, some are the products of famous pens, while others are scarcely more than the poetical waifs which have remained unacknowledged by their parents. Some of these waifs are characterized by various degrees of interest that have caused them to attain popularity where more pretentious efforts have failed, and, in appealing to the heart rather than to the mind, they appear to be in a fair way to win a certain sort of literary immortality.[79]

This "literary immortality" was frequently secured by these scrapbooks themselves, which preserved poems until they could be reproduced in anthologies, collected works, or a magazine such as the *Scrap Book*. The magazine acknowledges this opportunity in reproducing a poem, "Fate," by Susan Marr Spaulding, noting, "Had it not been for the keepers of scrap books it doubtless would have disappeared a few years after it was written.

Instead, however, it has found a place in recently published collections of verse, and it is regarded as one of the most beautiful and expressive utterances in English."[80]

This scrapbook-based recovery was often necessary because of poetry's increasingly marginalized status within mass print culture. In "A Rescued Poem," the *Scrap Book* reprinted a poem that first appeared "in the middle of a page of want 'ads'! How it came to be buried thus some compositor may know. Perhaps a 'make-up' man was inspired with a glimmer of editorial intelligence to 'lighten up' the page." Slipped in among advertising (an accident in this case, perhaps, but for many magazines a placement quite by design), the poem could have been lost among the commercial, devoid of whatever aesthetic purchase it otherwise might have had. Fortunately, there were requests for copies and enough interest in the poem that the *Scrap Book* decided to take it on and "for the first time it is given to the public in a suitable position, with proper recognition—proof once more that the true spark cannot long remain hid under a bushel."[81]

The suitable position for such poems meant framing and centering them on the page (a process of aestheticization that I further discuss in relation to *Poetry* magazine in chapter 2), but it also meant appropriately placing them within literary tradition. While the *Scrap Book* would reproduce obscure poems throughout its run and sometimes print new poems, many of its poems, such as Whitman's "O Captain! My Captain!" and Tennyson's "The Eagle," were well known at the time and remain so today.[82] And while many of these poems were printed individually, they were also grouped into thematic minianthologies of two pages or so, as in "Autumn and the Poets," which reprinted William Cullen Bryant's "The Death of the Flowers," Keats's "To Autumn," Shelley's "Autumn: A Dirge," and Longfellow's "Autumn."[83] Some of the reproduced poems had even fallen out of a poet's known works, saved only by the grace of the scrapbook. After word got out that Rudyard Kipling had recited from "The Foreloper," a poem not in any of his collected works, the search was on, and "it was finally found in the scrap-book of an American admirer of Kipling."[84] Similarly, "An Irish Poem by Whittier," "which has never appeared in any edition of the collected works of Whittier was recently discovered by S. T. Pickard in a scrap-book kept by the poet's older sister" and subsequently reprinted in the *Scrap Book*.[85] Such anecdotes register the potential of the scrapbook and its periodical counterparts to negotiate and reconstruct poetic tradition by making chaos orderly, the ephemeral permanent.

Unlike *Tit-Bits*, however, the *Scrap Book* was a short-lived endeavor. Recognizing that "there isn't room enough within one cover to make a magazine big enough, and strong enough, to satisfy the reader of to-day," Munsey drew upon the scrapbook's logic of accumulation to simply create a larger magazine, giving it a curious two-section format midway through its second year.[86] In the process he introduced the first full-illustration magazine, which (hinting at the motives behind the change) "appeals most strongly to the advertiser, who not only helps to furnish sinews of war, but who presents, from month to month, facts which are most valuable, and I believe most interesting, to the reader."[87] Despite these commodified "facts," the experiment was a failed one, and after another year the *Scrap Book* had split into two magazines. The first section retained the name the *Scrap Book*, while absorbing another "scrap book" magazine, the *Live Wire*, and printing illustrations in color in its attempts to be "a pretty well rounded-out magazine for the American home."[88] In July 1910, the magazine returned to printing on the cheap newsprint of the first issue, and in January 1912 was absorbed by the all-fiction offshoot the *Cavalier*.

Despite its short run, the *Scrap Book*, like *Tit-Bits*, underscores the importance of the scrapbook for a turn-of-the-century clipping culture, which it both incorporated and informed through its privileging of the historically contingent, often anonymous, and heterogeneously juxtaposed scrap. Scrapping practices and a general scrapbooking ethos encouraged a negotiation of mass print culture—even for those who did not personally keep a scrapbook—in ways that differed greatly from book collecting's conservation.

Book Collecting, Scrapbooking, and the Modern Collecting Continuum

I have given sustained attention to book collecting and scrapbooking at the outset of this book not because I see them as the only responses to an emerging mass print culture but because they stand as extreme oppositions in a set of modern print-collecting continua, and I believe that close attention to their various formal, personal, and historical contradictions illuminates the many intermediate practices and forms that have helped condition poetic modernism. These continua range across several related axes that can help us locate modern collecting practices more generally. First, there is an axis of closure. On one end, book collecting conserves old and rare books into closed systems of meaning in the library and the collection. Scrapbooking, on the other end, offers a continual engagement with mass print that does not presume the possibility of closure. This axis of closure implies an axis of order as well. The closed collection is often intricately arranged, so that elements resonate with one another in meaningful ways; the open accumulation is less likely to be strung together in such a way, however, because the anticipated addition will necessarily disrupt the sequence. Likewise, closed ordering is often thought to be objective, existing independent of the collector. After all, if one believes that there is a finite number of elements in a collection and if some arrangements are thought to be more logically or aesthetically pleasing than others, then the ideal collection has very little to do with the personal whims of the arranger. By contrast, in an open-ended and haphazardly accumulated collection, a striving for such objectivity hardly makes sense, and one is driven to find meaning through personal association. The personal can't be divorced from the historical, however, so this open collection also tends to more deliberately engage with history's unfolding, while the ideal, objective collection retreats from such history in its attempts at a more abstract order—implying a historical axis to the collection as well. Given these attributes, book collecting can be thought of as symbolic, while scrapbooking corresponds to what Benjamin calls allegory, which he famously explains "is in the realm of thought what ruins are in the realm of things."[89] The allegorist, Benjamin argues, is "the polar opposite of the collector. He has given up the attempt to elucidate things through research into their properties and relations. He dislodges things from their context and, from the outset, relies on his profundity to illuminate their meaning. The collector, by contrast, brings together what belongs together; by keeping in mind their affinities and their succession in time, he can eventually furnish information about his objects."[90] Along these lines, the logical relationship among objects in the collection can, as I have previously suggested, also be thought of as metonymic, in which one object follows another in narrative succession. By contrast, in the scrapbook disparate items are brought together through their (often personal) metaphorical associations as they chronicle personal lives and negotiate individual identity through historical correspondences and previous contexts.

This is, however, a bit too schematic. In practice, the scrapbook's privileging of the individual scrap is not unlike the connoisseur's fetishization of the individual book, or feature of the book, before it is resolved into the larger collection. This fetishization, as Jean Baudrillard suggests, contributes to a fundamental tension at the heart of any system of objects, where "gratification flows from the fact that possession depends, on the one hand, on the absolute singularity of each item, a singularity which puts that item on a par with an animate being—indeed, fundamentally on a par with the subject himself—and, on the other hand, on the possibility of a series, and hence of an infinite play of practice."[91] Likewise, Benjamin identifies an unresolved dialectic between the collector and the allegorist, recognizing that in every collector "hides an allegorist, and in every allegorist a collector. As far as the collector is concerned, his collection is never complete; for let him discover just a single piece missing, and everything he's collected remains a patchwork, which is what things are for allegory from the beginning."[92] Nineteenth-century book collectors were all too aware of this fact, lamenting that that "there is no collection which is complete. The owner may boast that it is, but secretly he will harbor the fear that there is something he lacks. The completion of his collection is like tomorrow. It never comes."[93]

Just as the scrapbooker-allegorist points to the collection's necessary open-endedness, the collector suggests the extent to which the scrapbook often did have an internal associative and narrative logic. Many compilers limited their scrapbooks in accordance with subject matter (baseball, anatomy, travel) or genre (poems, photographs), purposely placing restrictions on the scraps they hoped to accumulate. In a more deliberate marriage of these two collecting practices, it was not uncommon for book collectors to keep scrapbooks, which often (quite naturally) took as their subjects bibliography and literature. This was the case with the *Old Corner Library Scrap Book* and *The Literary Junk-Book* (both housed at the Newberry Library in Chicago), which contain book plates, illustrations of libraries, and literature about books.[94] Likewise, while the *Scrap Book* drew upon the popular scrapbook to promote itself as a magazine for all classes of people, its advertising is largely pitched to an emerging middle-class readership, containing announcements for products that would appeal to the proprietors of gentlemen's libraries (if not true book collectors). The first issue, for example, contains in its front pages advertisements for such ready-made libraries as "The Library of Oratory: Ancient and Modern," "Library of Historical Romances," and "Shakespeare's Complete Works"; for "Partly Paid for Books: One Man's Loss Is Another Man's Gain"; and for a "De Luxe Odd Volume Sale: You Do the Selecting." Such examples suggest that even when it is useful to contrast idealized collecting practices, we must remain attentive to the specific historical examples—often marked by individual mediating activities—that productively complicate these extremes of openness and closure.

Additionally, an axis of permanence applies to the objects in the collection and to the collection itself. Book collectors frequently form libraries of old books as an act of conservation—not only of those individual books but of a body of knowledge or example of craft that is revealed in the aggregate. By contrast, scrapbookers contend with the flood of print in a wrestling with their contemporary moment, meticulously recording dates and sites of publication, even as scraps are cut, pasted, pasted over, written on, and painted—used and abused over time as they continue to index print sources. Whereas the book collector strives for the unity of timeless monuments in a transcendent moment outside history, the scrapbooker is primarily concerned with accumulating a scrap heap of paper ruins that mounts skyward like the wreckage encountered by Benjamin's angel of history—the piling debris of the day-to-day.[95]

This, too, must be complicated. After all, as the name implies, the scrapbook is a *book* of scraps. In contrast to many other clipping systems, the act of pasting newspapers, magazines, and other ephemera into a book helps to make them more permanent (and more rigidly placed in their possible associations with other scraps)—an attribute often hinted at in the care and elaboration of pages and bindings. A scrapbook page may be compiled over a span of years or even decades, so that scraps resonate with others from years hence, while the source of the scrap has long since crumbled in the landfill. Scrapbookers themselves speak to this power of preservation, noting that "what is worth reading once is worth reading again" and suggesting that "nothing should be preserved that does not bid fair to be interesting and intelligible after the lapse of years."[96] The act of scrapbooking itself helps to make the ephemeral permanent, the commonplace rare and valuable (and resistant to the reproducibility that characterizes the elements from which it is made). Even following its construction (which is never truly completed), the scrapbook may continue to be treasured and read for decades by its compiler, and then by successive generations—perhaps added to once again. The scrapbook (especially if kept by a person of historical interest) may find its way into the institutionalized archive, as is the case with the scrapbooks of Marianne Moore. More likely, however, it will end up—as was the case with Lucy Britton's scrapbook—in an old bookstore or antique shop, waiting for the right buyer to come along. The building blocks of such books might themselves be less ephemeral prints, and, as I've noted, the resulting object may come to be referred to as an extra-illustrated book. Conversely, the book collector may take as his object of collecting an ephemeral print object, such as an art catalog or a playbook, and, like the scrapbooker, engage in an act of making the ephemeral more lasting. Moreover, the open-ended nature of the collection reminds us that even if the individual objects are old and removed from their utilitarian nature, the collection of which they are a part may be in constant flux.

Finally, we might consider book collecting and scrapbooking as historical phenomena in themselves—examples of what Raymond Williams has referred to as residual and emergent cultural practices—in which the hegemony of a dominant cultural paradigm emerging through mass print is challenged by residual productions and positions (signaled by the book collection) that have not been sufficiently incorporated, as well as by emergent forms that challenge and may one day usurp the cultural norm (as suggested by scrapbooking).[97] If, as I have suggested, the book collection corresponds to the symbolic and scrapbooking to the allegorical, we might follow Fredric Jameson's explanation (rooted in his particular postmodern moment) that the symbol

> is the instantaneous, the lyrical, the single moment in time; and this temporal limitation perhaps expresses the historical impossibility in the modern world for genuine reconciliation to endure in time, for it to be anything more than a lyrical, accidental present. Allegory is, on the contrary, the privileged mode of our own life in time, a clumsy deciphering of meaning from moment to moment, the painful attempt to restore a continuity to heterogeneous, disconnected instants . . . [so that the] preference for symbolism is perhaps more the expression of a value than a description of existing poetic phenomena: for the distinction between symbol and allegory is that between a complete reconciliation and a mere will to reconciliation.[98]

As I trace the historical trajectories of print-collecting practices, I argue that such modernist constructions as the objective anthology, the aestheticized little magazine, and the totalized collage poem might more closely align with book collecting and be thought of as residual formations with a mere will to reconciliation, or, as Wallace Stevens would phrase it, an "idea of order" and a "supreme fiction" that ultimately cannot be attained. At the same time, I offer ways in which the allegorical accumulation evident in scrapbooking anticipates the logic of postmodernism, often characterized by a pastiche of heterogeneous multimedia elements and a proliferation of narrative meanings at the level of the poem and in larger social structures like the archive. But I don't wish to insert my own grand narrative here. Indeed, one of the reasons I focus my attention on modernism is that the distinctions between these residual and emergent forms often appeared messier in their relation to closure, permanence, and cultural priority than they do today. Like the evolutionary biologist reconstructing the past from a static fossil record, we must closely examine the texts that modernism has left behind in order to better understand this dynamic process.

Mediating Mass Print Culture

Even as book collecting and scrapbooking mark opposing ends of a collecting continuum that demonstrates myriad ways of engaging with emerging mass print, they also indicate larger societal shifts when viewed through the lenses of cultural studies, book history, and media studies. To consider book collecting and scrapbooking as modern cultural practices emphasizes that the term "mass print culture" carries within it the term "print" and serves to remind us that before cinema, radio, television, and the Internet, mass culture's first medium was print. Indeed, the growing hegemony of mass print in nineteenth-century mass-circulation magazines and mail-order catalogs clearly signals the beginnings of what the Frankfurt School theorists Theodor Adorno and Max Horkheimer dub the totality of the "culture industry," in which (drawing upon a telling metaphor of print) the "stereotyped appropriation of everything, even the inchoate, for the purposes of mechanical reproduction surpasses the general currency of any real style."[99] Similarly, as Benjamin notes in an often overlooked comment in his famous "Work of Art" essay, the "enormous changes brought about in literature by movable type, the technological reproduction of writing, are well known. But they are only a special case, though an important one," of the effects of technological reproducibility that are often attributed to such twentieth-century media technologies as film.[100]

Those who embraced these new cultural forms did not necessarily do so passively and unreflectingly, however. They were not mere dupes to an emerging industry of mass print as the Frankfurt School theorists might have feared. Scrapbooking's material manipulation of mass print culled from newspapers and magazines suggests the great extent to which many people sought to forge individual identity within and *through* mass culture, practicing subcultural identification and the bottom-up making of meaning through oppositional and negotiated readings of dominant messages that cultural studies theorists have generally associated with later decades and more recent media forms.[101] These contrasting reactions to an emerging mass print provide an early example of what Andreas Huyssen has referred to as the (gendered) "great divide" between mass and high culture that I problematize throughout this book.[102]

But even as book collecting and scrapbooking provide entrées into considering print as an early example of mass culture, they also underscore its specificity. To think specifically about print animates critical traditions in bibliography, print culture, and the history of the book that have tended to focus on two broad areas of inquiry. First, scholars are interested in the evolving bibliographical codes of textual objects, which are expressed in such things as the material substrate of ink and paper, the choice of typographical font, and the style of binding. Bibliographical elements may be read to determine the age of a book and clue scholars in to its likely producers and place of origin. These elements also serve to complicate a text's linguistic codes, marked by such attributes as literary form and style, which may migrate across different bibliographical contexts but are necessarily changed in the process. As I have already started to suggest, this core distinction between the linguistic and the bibliographic was foremost in the minds of collectors as they wrestled with the relationship between the book and the text (extended to the collection and the library) that helped lay the groundwork for bibliography as an area of study. An exploration of book collecting and the fetishization of bibliographical elements that I make throughout this book is important, therefore, not only as a lens through which to understand the text and its bibliographical manifestations but also as a means to uncover some of the origins of the bibliographical discipline itself. This consideration of linguistic and bibliographical codes is likewise central to an understanding of poetic form, which I address in greater depth below.

Second, scholars are attentive to what Robert Darnton has referred to as the "communications circuit" of the book (which can be extended to print objects more generally), running from the author to the publisher, the printer, the shipper, the bookseller, and the reader—who completes the circuit by becoming an author herself.[103] This model importantly traces how the economic and cultural conditions of print help determine that text's availability and potential for cultural impact: a physical book must be produced and distributed in order to be read, internalized, and potentially acted upon. In turn, the reader may choose to become a writer, producing a text that takes material form with the help of a printer/publisher as it repeats the communications circuit. While scholars have been attentive to various nodes of this circuit, focusing their attention on questions of authorship, printing and publications norms, the economics and legalities of book shipping and selling, and the history of reading practices, there has been a relative dearth of attention given to the collecting of books and print.[104] Indeed, one of the aims of this book is to more fully explore the practices and discourses of book collecting and print accumulation in order to complicate the communications circuit at the location of reception in ways that I hope will prove fruitful for other bibliographical studies.

Even so, *Poetic Modernism* resists being too closely boxed in by an exclusive attention to print and bibliography. Rather, I consider how mass print culture fits within a larger media ecology of its moment, how the printed text might be productively compared with other textual media, and how an archaeology of contemporary media formations might uncover connections to previously marginalized print forms. As Lisa Gitelman has suggested in her attention to the document as media form, we might be tempted to jettison the term "print culture" altogether in favor of a more general "scriptural economy" (a term borrowed from Michel de Certeau) that decenters manuscript and print texts even as it addresses their specific histories of production, distribution, and reception.[105] As the title of this books suggests, I am not quite prepared to give up on a term that I find to be central to my study, though I should stress that I see print not as an essentialized, transhistorical category but as an umbrella term for a host of material forms and practices that emerge and recede in particular times and places—and that must be understood through those particulars.

I do take Gitelman's point, however, that over the period I am considering, print interacts in a variety of nuanced ways with other media forms and can't be fully understood in isolation from those forms. The telegraph, for example, which was commercialized in the 1830s, facilitated information exchange through such organizations as the Associated Press (started in 1846) and fostered a national network of newspapers that allowed for the nineteenth-century snippet culture I have been examining. Likewise, while my focus is on print modernism, the age is marked by the rise of the cinema, the phonograph, and radio—and their attendant culture industries—as well as by print, and I appreciate the ways in which scholars have variously considered how such media forms have been articulated to poetic production. Some of these other media forms necessarily find their way into this work, as when I discuss the archive's mediating documentary forms in chapter 5.

Although I mostly focus on mass print as one of modernism's dominant media forms, I nevertheless seek to more precisely locate, as well as defamiliarize, such print within studies of media archaeology and comparative textual media. Throughout this book, and particularly in the coda, I draw on notions of media archaeology to consider how mass print forms might anticipate—and provide new ways of understanding—newer media forms, as when I locate forms of crowdsourcing and user interactivity in mass-market periodicals or when I liken the scrapbook to the electronic database.[106] In doing so, I am attentive both to the technical underpinnings of previously marginalized media, in the tradition of such scholars as Friedrich Kittler, as well as to the mediating social and cultural conditions that have framed that marginalization and subsequent recovery.

While I am interested in exploring the ways in which older print forms anticipate our current media situation, I don't want to see mass print culture as simply a means to another, more recent, end. Rather, I aim to better understand print's place among the other media of its own historical moment and in doing so approach what N. Katherine Hayles and Jessica Pressman have argued for as a general media framework. Such a framework offers opportunities to compare a variety of textual media, which helps to check critical assumptions about particular media forms that may be tethered to their own long histories and critical/institutional baggage (print studies being an obvious example here), to problematize assumptions about the roles of human and nonhuman actors in a given media formation (like the personified shears of the *Farmer's Gazette* referenced above), and to foreground specific technologies against their cultural backdrops.[107]

A comparative study of textual media also importantly emphasizes the role of mediation itself. "Failure to acknowledge mediation in cultural analysis," as John Guillory has argued in an essay that explores the long history of the media concept, "precipitates a theoretical regression into positivism, made all the worse by the implication of a 'magical' causality in the social realm," one that is inattentive to media dimensions I consider in this book, such as the material specificity of print forms (for example, the different technologies and economies of scale in the modern little and big magazines) and the interposition of long-standing categories of form, genre, and literary value.[108] In focusing on modern poetry and print within a larger media framework, I hope to take up Guillory's call that "scholars of culture strongly resist relegating the traditional arts to the sphere of antiquated technologies, the tacit assumption in the losing competition between literature and the new media. Moreover, scholars of a traditional art such as literature must take equally seriously both the mediation of literature by technologies such as print—as they already do in the context of book history—and the long-durational forms of writing, such as genre."[109]

Even as I am interested in how collected book and print objects mediate a larger mass print and textual culture, I am equally attentive to how those collections and scrapbooks can be mediating forms in themselves. As such, the present volume dovetails with Jeremy Braddock's focus on the art collection and the poetry anthology as key examples of a modernist collecting practice that offers both sociological and formal mediation for modernist literary and cultural production. As Braddock suggests, on the one hand, collections mediate between work and audience, occupying a space of determining influence in a field of cultural production; on the other hand, the collection is itself a cultural object and system of meanings that may formally represent social totality in ways that have been attributed to more autonomous aesthetic objects. As Braddock sums it up, "To recognize the collection as both an immanent (or formal) and a practical form of mediation is therefore also to recognize the collection's centrality both to the 'autonomous' work of modernism and to further-reaching questions of social practice."[110] I agree with this formulation, though (as should not be surprising at this point) I find it necessary to parse Braddock's notion of collecting practice—which I would largely identify with attributes and assumptions of book collecting articulated to a restricted notion of modernist production—into a more fluid continuum of practices, performed by a variety of people at all social levels and marked in their extremes by book collecting and scrapbooking.

While I engage in many ways with the material practices of book collecting and scrapbooking in the context of an emerging mass print culture that contributes to cultural studies, bibliographical studies, and media theory, this is more specifically a book about modern poetry. As such, it seeks to explain in particular how book- and print-collecting practices were articulated to the production, reception, and institutionalization of a robust poetic modernism that begins to account for the likes of both T. S. Eliot and Lucy Britton. To do so, however, it is necessary to more fully investigate this poetic modernism and how it informs the chapters to follow.

Making Poetic Modernism

Investigations into mass print culture and its attendant collecting practices would prove useful for studying an array of modern literary and cultural expressions, from the modern novel's various attempts at, or dismissals of, narrative resolution to developments in modern art (analytic cubism) and music (the jazz riff) that problematize the selection and arrangement of formal elements. I, however, focus specifically on the modern poem's capacity to formally mediate (and celebrate or critique) the material contradictions of mass print culture. In doing so, I demonstrate that, as a material and intertextual "palimptext," one of the modern poem's primary objectives is to "display the textual condition" and suggest how it allows for a "social philology" that enacts social conditions in the poem's deep structure.[111]

Poetic structure places particular emphasis on the interdependence of the linguistic and bibliographical codes that I have mentioned above, as formal features of the text (meter, rhyme, metaphor, quotation) are conditioned by and help give meaning to its material dimensions (font, margins, paper, binding), as the poem-object is mediated through both mass print and poetic genre. In the poem, the bibliographical code is often more clearly emphasized than it is in other texts—through such things as varying typography and the use of white space that draws attention back to the presence of the paper itself—and, as George Bornstein has argued, such emphasis corresponds to Benjamin's concept of aura that pinpoints an object's presence in time and space.[112] The poem can indeed often have a strong aura about it. As I suggest with my consideration of the manufactured first edition in chapter 1 and with my reading of *Poetry* magazine in chapter 2, however, it might be helpful to think of this aura in relative terms, in which some finely printed or deliberately framed objects can be said to have (or at least to strive for) a more auratic presence than do others.

Attention to the intricate interconnections of the poem's linguistic and bibliographical codes also suggests a materially inflected formalism that complicates a recent turn to New Formalism as the close study of literary form in reference to historical context.[113] As I argue throughout this book, a poem expresses different forms and meanings when published in the corner of a magazine page, reprinted in a collected volume of poems, pasted in a scrapbook, or traced to one of its handwritten drafts. None of these forms should be taken as definitive. Recognition of a poem's particular bibliographical expression, made possible through a series of authorial, printing/

publishing, distribution, and collecting decisions that are manifested in a host of media objects, thus tempers an embrace of too-abstract form as it emphasizes the ways in which the poem is materially and historically embedded.

In addition to complicating the formal features of poetic texts, attention to print objects and their arrangement in the collection also modeled ways for reading those texts. The book collection in particular suggested a new kind of systemic reading based less on traditional ways of making sense of a text—that is, relating it to history, biography, and authorial intention—than in positing the text itself to be a complex system of formal elements that cohere into a whole whose meaning is greater than the sum of its parts.[114] Such reading practices would culminate in the notion of organic form championed by the New Criticism of the mid-twentieth century, which I touch on in chapter 1 and return to in chapter 5, but was already anticipated by the end of the nineteenth century in criticism published in such outlets as the *Periodical of the Modern Language Association* (*PMLA*).

Though not to the same extent as the expressly bibliographical magazines of the time, *PMLA* underscores the connection between the material book and the literary text through its inclusion of articles on such bibliographical topics as the American editions of Shakespeare, which gave substantial attention to bibliographical elements, the "pseudo-science" of textual criticism and manuscript studies, the history of publication in Western Europe before the advent of the printing press, and the strategies of Elizabethan play publishing.[115] This engagement with bibliography and with a larger collecting culture would often bleed into more general discussions of aesthetics and literary form. One notable metaphor that critics would keep coming back to—and that has generally been associated with the New Critics of decades later—is that of organic form. In his 1891 essay "A Plea for the Study of Literature from the Aesthetic Standpoint," John P. Fruit draws on the work of the French naturalist and zoologist Georges Cuvier to argue that "in the constitution of an organic whole there are no unnecessary and insignificant parts. So art has been rightly termed 'the purgation of superfluities.' No integral part of a work of art is less necessary and less significant than such a part of a sentient creature. . . . Any part ought to be suggestive and significant of the whole. . . . If it is not, the work is not organic, not art."[116] The idea of organic literary form was widespread enough that another critic considered it necessary a decade and a half later to push back on the prevailing aesthetic studies of the day that were "directed to the end of establishing general principles whereby the rhythm of words and their position in a sentence are fitted organically to the feeling—tone of words and thoughts."[117]

The idea of organic form extended to pedagogy as well, where, as one critic explained—in a formulation directly combatting scrapbooking and snippet culture—the text

> should be studied not only for its beauty of style in details of composition, but more deeply in its artistic unity of construction, in the definite relation of the separate parts to the complete design. Thus, in the proper course of reading in literature and for literature, there must be, I think, the almost complete surrender of the too common practice of reading scraps and fragments. Volumes of such scraps are, I think, to be looked upon as almost the deadliest foe to the sense of literary form. A single poem, of course, if complete in itself, is an artistic unity, fit to be studied.... The work to be read, whether short or long, if worthy to be read at all as example of literature, should be read not in extracts nor in specimen, but in its organic unity of artistic composition.[118]

The invocation of scrapbooking is not merely coincidental, as scrapbooking models an alternative mode of reading to the systemic reading encouraged by the collection that is more clearly based in the historical contingency and personal connection that systematic reading was eschewing.

To fully understand poetic modernism, however, we must look beyond such formal reading strategies aimed at understanding individual poems and consider the mediating institutional structures that provided for the production, circulation, reception, and preservation of those poems. The poem in the corner of a magazine page was placed there according to particular editorial decisions and reader expectations; the poem reprinted in a collected volume is subject to the economics and legalities of book publishing; the poems made available in handwritten drafts or pasted in a scrapbook have been housed in the public archive or are made available for private ownership. By using the term "poetic modernism" in the title of this book, rather than a term like "modern poetry," I aim to draw attention not only to specific poem objects but also to what Lawrence Rainey has termed the "institutions of modernism," which often relied upon the selecting and collecting of bibliographical objects as a prerequisite for editing, publishing, and preservation activities.[119]

To foreground these dimensions of poetic modernism, I have organized chapters in rough chronological order and by textual and bibliographical sites—the anthology, the big and little magazine, the collage poem, the volume of selected poems, and the modern poetry archive—each of which highlights a long-standing and central question of literary value, genre, form, reproduction, and institutionalization. Chapter 1 locates the emergence of a new kind of modern objective anthology in Francis Turner Palgrave's highly influential *The Golden Treasury* (1861). In contrast to previous thematically driven anthologies, *The Golden Treasury* functioned much like a book collection in selecting the supposedly best poems and arranging them into a closed system according to what Palgrave calls "the most poetically-effective order."[120] This selection and arrangement influenced ideas of objective poetic value and a discernible poetic tradition embodied in many modern anthologies, including Cleanth Brooks and Robert Penn Warren's New Critical *Understanding Poetry*, and underpinned such notable essays as T. S. Eliot's "Tradition and the Individual Talent." By contrast, *The Golden Treasury*'s *Second Series* (1897) was an attempt to incorporate near-contemporary poems that was largely unsuccessful because it modeled literary worth on the manufactured value of the first edition book rather than on value accumulated over time through natural scarcity and historical consensus.

In chapter 2, I argue that Harriet Monroe's Chicago-based *Poetry: A Magazine of Verse* (1912–), one of the earliest and most influential of the little magazines, attempted to mimic the finely printed book in order to bibliographically, critically, and generically frame the modernist poem as an isolated aesthetic object. In doing so, I also emphasize the importance of bibliographical form for effectively studying modern periodicals as well as the importance of understanding little magazines within a diverse field of periodical production. *Poetry* aggressively opposed both the omnipresent newspaper status of poetry as "filler"—shoehorned into available space between news stories without surrounding white space, which served to make it an embedded discourse rather than one isolated for special attention—and the illustrated magazine poem that was given a page of its own but neatly contained within pictorial representation. For a certain stratum of elite reader, *Poetry* was a bulwark against the mass cultural appropriation of poetry in these periodicals that simply turned it into one discursive genre among others.

Poetry's isolation of the poem on the page, surrounded by a thick border of white space—coupled with critical essays and reviews that frequently compared the poem to painting, sculpture, and other fine-art objects—framed poems as discrete textual objects and the magazine as a gallery to display them in careful arrangement. This framing directed readings inward and helped promote poetry as a generic category separate from and superior to verse form. Such a redefinition was crucial for the magazine's showcasing of such modernist poetic movements as Imagism, exemplified by Pound's "In a Station of the Metro," and for its self-promotion as a collection of fine poetic objects. To better understand its particular influence on poetic modernism, I read *Poetry* against a variety of other magazines, arguing that it extended the format and generic assumptions of such "quality magazines" as *the Atlantic Monthly* (1857-), *Harper's* (1836-1919), and *the Century* (1882-1913) while standing in opposition to such magazines as the satirical *Life* (1883-1936) and the African American magazine the *Crisis* (1910-). These latter magazines encouraged intertextual, often socially engaged, readings of poems that offered interpretive alternatives to the dominant aesthetic criteria surrounding poetic modernism—for which *Poetry* was largely responsible.

Chapter 3 argues that scrapbooking modeled one of the most characteristic modern literary forms: the collage poem. Concentrating on Marianne Moore's early scrapbooks and mock scrap newspaper, "The Daily Scale," I claim that—contrary to the common critical assumption that the modern collage poem was a direct extension of the visual *avant-garde*—Moore's poetry invoked a long history of scrapbooking as a "feminized" negotiation of mass print culture. The scrapbooks not only provide Moore with source material (covering such subjects as animals, travel, and politics that would command her lifelong attention), but they also display material acts of importation, juxtaposition, assemblage, pasting-over, anchoring, and enjambment that would be translated into Moore's strategies of quotation and allusion and her general "scrappy poetics" on display in her collage poetry. Pointing to Moore's early influence on T. S. Eliot and her later exchanges with William Carlos Williams, I then argue that Moore's scrappy poetics challenges our conception of such long collage poems as *The Waste Land* and *Paterson* as collections of quotations and allusions that fail to cohere, suggesting instead that they should be understood as productive accumulations that need not strive for symbolic closure.

Chapter 4 focuses on Eliot's editing of the selected poems of Ezra Pound, Marianne Moore, and Rudyard Kipling for the London-based literary publishing firm Faber. In doing so, it highlights a crucial shift at the midpoint of the twentieth century from modernism's coterie mode of production (typified by the little magazine and the first edition book) toward a larger-scale reproduction that restricted the canon of modernist poems and poets as it consolidated transatlantic poetic modernism. The selected poems thus paradoxically emulated mass print culture's wider dissemination of books even as it made that dissemination available to only an elite list of writers and a carefully selected group of books. This consolidation was partly a function of Eliot's particular editorial choices, rooted in the logic of the collection, which shaped these poets' reputations as they substantiated Eliot's own notions of literary, cultural, and national coherence. It was also a function of literary publishing itself, marked by Faber's relationship to such periodicals as the *Criterion* (which Eliot edited), as well as to other book presses in both Britain and the United States, including smaller modernist presses (such as the Egoist Press) and larger presses (such as Macmillan) that necessitated transatlantic book production and a negotiation of international copyright law.

In chapter 5, I argue that, beginning in the late 1930s, the institutionalization of the modern poetry library and archive in such places as the Library of Congress, the University of Chicago, and the University of Buffalo provided a means to preserve and perpetuate a potentially much more wide-ranging modernism than was being enshrined in selected or collected volumes of poems. Libraries of little magazines and first edition books offer through their alternative poems, versions, and contexts critical roads not taken. Similarly, archives of letters, drafts, and ephemeral clippings may reveal authorial intentions or uncover unpublished work. As I show, however, while the modern poetry library and archive did indeed hold out the promise of a more comprehensive modernism than was available in selected and collected poems, they were frequently instituted under the influence of such New Critics as Allen Tate and relied upon the modern archive's general investment in objective aesthetic judgment and notions of organic unity. Although the modern poetry archive was in theory a democratizing instrument, it was in practice a product of its historical moment that denied many poets access to its privileged space. The archive thus often complemented and reinforced the modernist reaction against mass print culture's potentially democratized textuality.

In a concluding coda, I consider how investigations into mass print culture and its expression in poetic modernism might help us better understand not only our cultural past but also our contemporary moment characterized (somewhat paradoxically) by emerging digital media and a renewed attention to bibliographic form. As I suggest, a fuller understanding of poetic modernism informs our reception of contemporary literary texts indebted to that modernism.

In many ways, my approach exemplifies what Douglas Mao and Rebecca Walkowitz have pointed to as the vertical, geographical, and temporal expansion of the new modernist studies.[121] Although I discuss at length such well-known modernist figures as T. S. Eliot, Marianne Moore, William Carlos Williams, and Ezra Pound, I recognize that these poets do not occupy their own quiet retreats on the slopes of Parnassus but share the territory with numerous poets and popular "versifiers" who have long been neglected in studies of modern poetry. While critics have largely succeeded in breaking open the gates to the private estate, numerous poets have yet to receive their critical due.[122] They do not all necessarily need book-length or even chapter-length studies (though certainly some of them do), but in the aggregate they offer trenchant critiques of modernist assumptions (and our perpetuation of those assumptions) that result in part from focus on a few dominating figures. To help address this critical oversight, numerous scarcely known poets dot this study's landscape as both background figures and the focus of more sustained attention.

Just as I extend my consideration of poetic modernism beyond a restricted canon of modernist writers—even as I attempt to account for that canon—I also break rigid national frames to discuss a phenomenon that was decidedly transnational and transatlantic and that has been increasingly acknowledged in modernist study's recent global/transnational turn. Such a turn is exemplified by such collections as *The Oxford Handbook of Global Modernisms*, which argues for an analysis of modernism informed by comparative study of different world locations and attention to global systems of circulation, including essays on such topics as the global little magazine, that complicates my own attention to the modern periodical field.[123] Similarly, critics have been attentive to the ways in which poetry in particular foregrounds issues of globalism and transnationalism. Jahan Ramazani, for example, has argued for the ways in which modern and postmodern poetry's linguistic richness challenges national frames through the creolization and translocalization of the lyrical speaker, allowing it to both reflect and shape transnational experience.[124] Matthew Hart has identified the "synthetic vernacular" as a particular linguistic manifestation of this translocalization.[125] Rebecca Walsh has argued for the "geopoetics" of modernism, uncovering the ways in which poetic modernism and geographical knowledge coevolved.[126] Such studies, as well as attention to nineteenth-century transatlantic poetry by such scholars as Meredith McGill, productively complicate my own attention to modern poetic form.[127]

While this text is centered in a US and (to a lesser extent) British context, I am necessarily attentive to global and transnational circuits of production and reception. For example, I examine the influence of Palgrave's British *Golden Treasury* on modern American and British anthologies; I address the Jamaica-born Claude McKay as a key figure of the Harlem Renaissance; I consider how the American-turned-British Eliot edited poetry volumes by the American Marianne Moore, the American expatriate Ezra Pound, and the British-Indian Rudyard Kipling for the London-based Faber—a process that was itself steeped in transnational book production complicated by international copyright law; and I offer the Library of Congress's attempts to institute a national poetry archive as a counterexample to this transatlantic tendency (though one tinged by notable exceptions). I hope that the claims I make about poetic modernism and mass print might be further tested in other global contexts. Likewise, I hope that my particular attention to race in such places as the African American magazine the *Crisis* might be further expanded upon in other studies of readers, writers, and collectors.

Finally, I have sought to explore the history of an emerging mass print culture in what might be called a long modernism. Studies of literary modernism often begin in the first decades of the twentieth century, finding justification in such events as the rise of the modern little magazine and small literary press (both of which originated decades earlier), a pair of world wars that may have been extremely important for some writers and nearly meaningless for others, or (tautologically) at the moment of writing or reception or discovery of those texts one has deemed to be modern—be they representative of high modernism, the Harlem Renaissance, or some other literary-cultural formation. Many critics have seen modernism as simply a respectable version of the historical *avant-garde*, like a troublesome teen settling into middle age. Others have taken Virginia Woolf's startlingly pinpointed declaration at its word, that "on or about December 1910 human nature changed."[128] Critics have too rarely questioned the high modernists' often visceral reaction against, and subsequent marginalization of, mass print culture and the generations immediately preceding them, so that the writers of the late nineteenth and early twentieth centuries have remained largely underappreciated in studies of modern literature.

If, however, we understand modernism to be a cultural reaction to the material conditions of modernity, we should not be surprised that the mass print conditions that I am locating in the latter decades of the nineteenth century would encourage new cultural responses before the second decade of the twentieth. In choosing to label some of these responses "modern," I hope to uncover a more complicated relationship between modernist writers and their immediate predecessors than one of simple dismissal, while at the same time accounting for notions of modern poetic value and genre that have at times been naturalized through an occluded historical view. Likewise, as I am also investigating issues of reception, reproduction, and preservation, I have also found it necessary to look into the middle decades of the twentieth century to better understand the events that helped shape and consolidate the poetic modernism that we have come to most easily recognize. Additionally, it is my hope that a longer timeline and a more porous sense of modernism might help make this book more relevant to scholars who consider their interests to be largely outside modernism, especially to scholars of the nineteenth century, of postmodernism, and of our current digital age.

I present here a portrait of a capacious poetic modernism that begins to account for a variety of conflicting forms, practices, and critical assumptions that have not frequently been considered together, or sometimes at all—one that can address the likes of both T. S. Eliot and Lucy Britton and their respective cultural assumptions without making one figure secondary to the other. In doing so, I suggest how modern forms and institutions registered the deepest anxieties and most liberating possibilities of a culture of mass print through one of the most powerful tools at its disposal: poetry.

1 As Good as Gold

Palgrave's *Golden Treasury*, Poetic Value, and the Objective Anthology

The folio manuscript of Francis Turner Palgrave's *The Golden Treasury of Songs and Lyrics*, Second Series (1897), bound in red leather and tooled with gold lettering, has the external trappings of a finely made *édition de luxe*. Inside, however—as if to exemplify the old cliché about books and their covers—the volume more closely resembles a scrapbook or an object of extra-illustration. As the British Library's catalog describes the folio, "The poems are either copied by amanuenses or cut from printed books, only the notes," it explains, "being in Palgrave's hand."[1] The cutting and pasting of previously printed elements (augmented with hand-copied poems and original notes) is certainly done for reasons of efficiency and to help make typesetting more accurate by avoiding transcription errors. No need to copy out a poem if it can be quickly and easily attained in printed form. But the process through which Palgrave added to the perfectly ordered totality of the original *Golden Treasury* (1861)—and the resulting material contradiction between fine book and scrappy compilation—also strikingly illustrates the material manipulation at the heart of any objective anthologizing practice: the attempt to impose order on a heap of scraps, making the ephemeral valued, ordered, and permanent.

To better understand the modern anthology as a media form that registers many of mass print culture's contradictory values, I examine Palgrave's *Golden Treasury* as the objective anthology par excellence that drew upon the collector's principles of selection and arrangement in its efforts to gather the historically agreed-upon few best poems and in its ordering of these poems in the most poetically effective manner. These acts of selection and arrangement forwarded supposedly objective notions of value and tradition against more historically contingent ones held by politically and socially oriented anthologies of the day and would prove highly influential on the formation of later poetry anthologies.[2] Indeed, one of the reasons that a chapter centered on Palgrave's *Golden Treasury* belongs in a study of poetic modernism is that, through his collecting principles, Palgrave wielded a heavy hand in constructing the notion of objective literary value that modern poets, anthologists, and later scholars of modernism have often taken as a given, even as such modernist forms as the interventionist anthology would seek to challenge this value.[3] With the proliferation of mass print culture in the latter decades of the nineteenth century, however, Palgrave's collecting assumptions became increasingly untenable. This untenability prompted a turn to the manufactured scarcity of the modern first edition and ultimately led to what Palgrave and others have recognized as the failed patchwork of the Second Series that more closely resembled the scrapbooker's ephemeral accumulation than the book collector's treasured totality—and that unwittingly exposed a contradictory set of values and assumptions that might differently serve poetic modernism.

An Ideal Collection

In his 1901 essay "Concerning Anthologies," Arthur Waugh, the formidable turn-of-the-century scholar and father of Evelyn Waugh, explains the proliferation of poetry anthologies in the latter half of the nineteenth century, encapsulating much of the contemporaneous thinking on the subject. Far from being a literary fad, Waugh argues, such anthologies cut to the core of human nature, because "we are all collectors; and the desire to group together in a single volume our favorite passages of poetry and prose is at least as old as the illuminated manuscripts of the monasteries." In the preceding generation, Waugh claims, "taste was particularly luxuriant; and the first anthologies of the current fashion may be found in those albums of our grandmothers, of which every family preserves a few." These new anthologies, instantiated in the album, scrapbook, or commonplace book, "engrossed in the neatest and most angular of calligraphy," offer a capacious gathering of poems, thematically selected according to personal taste and brought together without any pretense to order or completion—a kind of anthologizing, practiced by grandmothers, generally considered to be feminine and genteel as opposed to masculine and professional. As Waugh notes, this gathering is conditioned by a pervasive print culture so that "nowadays, when everything that is written and collected seems to find its way sooner or later into print, nothing is more natural than that every man or woman of letters should be represented by his or her own particular anthology, as a sort of sign-manual of taste and erudition."[4]

Many late nineteenth- and early twentieth-century anthologies relied on this commonplace book model. Some anthologies, such as the *American Common-Place Book of Poetry, with Occasional Notes*, reflected this influence in their titles.[5] Others portrayed their affiliation through their presentation of such diverse subjects as gardening, religion, and train trips through the Rocky Mountains, through their interest in often-debased satire and *vers de société*, and through their hopes to chronicle (and sometimes intervene in) wars and revolutions.[6] Like personal scrapbooks, their private counterparts, these anthologies frequently embodied rich contingencies of value, made in accordance with the personal economy of the self in reference to particular historical contexts.[7] They gave credence to the popular poet Edwin Markham's assertion in the introduction to his 1928 anthology that it is not only the lofty bard who deserves an audience, but that "there is room also for the homely near-by poet, with his humbler ministries—for the wren that nests near the ground, as for the skylark that soars upward to dwell an immortal moment in the ecstatic 'privacies of light.'"[8]

As popular as many of these anthologies were (and continue to be), they were opposed by a mounting critical consensus—especially in those circles that would most directly influence modernist literary production and the institutionalization of modern poetry—that the best poems and less-best poems could be objectively distinguished and that it was the anthology's role to do so. To accomplish such a task, as Waugh notes (using a common pun on the gold standard of money), "Palgrave's standard, for instance—the measuring rod of 'The Golden Treasury'—could scarcely be improved upon."[9]

Palgrave also may have had the metal's objective economic value in mind when naming his *Golden Treasury* and proclaiming in its preface that this "little Collection differs, it is believed, from others in the attempt made to include in it all the best original Lyrical pieces and Songs in our language, by writers not living,—and none beside the best."[10] This is a marked contrast to those anthologies that selected poems in accordance with an overt or implicit thematic interest or political affiliation; rather, the *Golden Treasury* forwarded an idea of professional criticism based in objective, historically shared principles of taste that relied upon limited selection of individual poems and restrictions of generic scope that more closely paralleled the principles of book collecting.

As such, Palgrave professes impartial judgment in his selection. He explains that he passed his selection through two other readers (though merely hints at his heavy consultation with Alfred, Lord Tennyson, who has often been seen as a virtual coeditor), in order to ensure that "the volume has been freed from that one-sidedness which must beset individual decisions."[11] This "impartial judgment," which had the unfortunate effect of marginalizing, among others, women poets, was highly selective.[12] Waugh affirms Palgrave's principle of selection, noting that there is "a real responsibility in giving to the second-rate the popular currency of association with the first-rate, and that the general injustice which is done to the public taste by obscuring the distinctions of first and second-rate is even more to be considered than the individual injustice which may be done to a doubtful writer by excluding what might possibly have passed muster under a rather generous latitude of choice."[13] Such a selective logic distilled the whole of English poetry—from the Elizabethans to the Romantics—to 288 poems, covering 284 pages.

Palgrave also generically limits the scope of his collection. The decision to include only the lyric poem "has been here held essentially to imply that each Poem shall turn on some single thought, feeling, or situation. In accordance with this, narrative, descriptive, and didactic poems,—unless accompanied by rapidity of movement, brevity, and the colouring of human passion,—have been excluded." As a corollary to this decision, there is an emphasis on unity, where "passion, colour, and originality cannot atone for serious imperfections in clearness, unity, or truth,—that a few good lines do not make a good poem,—that popular estimate is serviceable as a guidepost more than as a compass,—above all, that Excellence should be looked for rather in the Whole than in the Parts."[14] As I explain below, New Criticism would later build on this distinction as it adopted a methodology demonstrating how excellence inheres in the relation of the parts to the whole.

Just as Palgrave foregrounds the poem's intricate interplay of constitutive elements, he explains that in the arrangement of the anthology as a whole, "the most poetically-effective order has been attempted." There is a rough chronology through the anthology's four books, with the first book encompassing the ninety years closing about 1616, the second book ending at 1700, the third at 1800, and the fourth at the midpoint of the nineteenth century, but the anthology is also meant to "present a certain unity, 'as episodes.' "[15] Waugh praises this order, explaining that the poems are "arranged with a sense of continuity and interrelation so delicate that the taste passes from poem to poem with perpetual refreshment and stimulation. . . . For by this juxtaposition of interests one poet is made to illustrate another, one poem to strike fire from its neighbor, and the splendid continuity of English verse is displayed in its perfection."[16] Such an arrangement shows that "the poet stands not alone, but as one of a goodly company, separated, it may be, by circumstances of time and event, but united in the maintenance of literary tradition and national character."[17] Collectively, poetic excellence promotes national and historical cohesion.

Palgrave's attempt to collect all of the best texts of a certain kind exemplifies the objective anthology's overall project and (as has been noted of the anthology form more generally) shares with the book collector the need to arrange objects into a coherent, internally consistent whole as the narration of an ideal tradition apart from lived history.[18] Far from the etymological meaning of the anthology as a gathering together of ephemeral flowers—budding, blossoming, wilting, decaying, and disseminating new seeds—or seeing the anthology as a vehicle for political or social intervention, *The Golden Treasury*, much like the book collection, posits a category of transcendentally fixed value and aspires to fossilize the best specimens for all time. But what if the poem has not had time to amber? What if it is produced by a recent—even a living, breathing—poet who has yet to join the pantheon? How does one objectively value and properly place a new poem into the objective anthology and, by extension, into a more abstracted literary tradition?

Manufacturing Value

"I am collecting first editions of American authors. I want to add your first book to my collection. Have you any copies of the first edition?"

"Yes," answered the author, "I have all of them!"

—"Nuggets," *New York Times*

In 1893, Herbert Stone, still an undergraduate at Harvard, published *First Editions of American Authors: A Manual for Book Lovers*. As the advertising circular for the book proclaimed, the wide-ranging 223-page bibliography of American first editions, with an introduction by the poet and book collector Eugene Field, "is a record of the works which go to make up American Literature,—together with the dates and places of publication, the size and number of pages, and the publisher's name. The value of such a volume to the Book-Lover, the Book-Collector, the Librarian, and the Student of Literary History will readily be appreciated."[19]

The book's value was indeed appreciated. The limited edition of fifty copies sold out before publication, and there was a general run of at least three thousand.[20] The success of the book encouraged Stone to go into publishing full time, where he and Hannibal Kimball—following in the Arts and Crafts tradition of William Morris (but with an eye fixed more to profit) and paralleling the work of Elkin Mathews and John Lane in London—would use the finest available papers, printing, and binding to "bring out books which will astonish most American book buyers in their beauty of manufacture."[21] The firm would go on to publish books by Eugene Field, Clarence Steadman, William Dean Howells, Henry James, and Robert Louis Stevenson, and to start an early little magazine, the *Chap-Book* (1894-1898).

The first book of its kind, *First Editions* tapped into a turn-of-the-century craze for first edition books, anticipating a later culture of fine printing in the early decades of the twentieth century that capitalized on the first edition's status to promote the beauty of the well-made book.[22] As the demand for old first editions outstripped its supply, this craze led to the manufacturing of a bibliographical form that in its contradictions embodied many of the anxieties over mass print: first edition books that were deliberately made to be rare and collectable, timely and timeless, expressing qualities of both old and new print media. *First Editions* gave collectors a roadmap to books of note and spurred on the publication of such guides as *Leon's Catalogue of First Editions of American Authors* (1885), *Early Editions: A Bibliographical Survey of the Works of Some Popular Modern Authors* (1894), *American Authors, 1795-1895: A Bibliography of First and Notable Editions Chronologically Arranged* (1895), and *A Record of First Editions of Bryant, Emerson, Hawthorne, Holmes, Longfellow, Lowell, Thoreau, Whittier* (1901).[23]

Many took the craze with a grain of salt. As one critic presciently observes, the collector "would have us believe that the text is purer, and so forth; but that is all nonsense. He buys the books because he admires the plates. The alleged reason, however, remains, and will some day be acted upon; and hence a demand will spring up for first editions which are not illustrated, as well as for those which are."[24] Others, who embraced the practice more wholeheartedly, argue that the first edition offered an intimate connection to the author that was frequently lacking in subsequent editions—a sentiment borne out by the fact that such writers as Walt Whitman and Mark Twain directly oversaw the initial printings of their works. As one collector claims, first editions "are nearer the author, being the primal embodiment of his thoughts in type and in the dress in which they first appeared to his sight."[25] Another elaborates the point, explaining that the first edition "is surely the author's edition, and this brings us nearer to him in every way, so that in a great measure, we enter into his hopes and fears for the success of his volume; for which end he carefully selects the type, the paper, the binding and all the other details of its make-up; carefully correcting; and possibly making many changes while it is passing through the press; watching its progress with mingled hopes and fears for its ultimate success." He goes so far as to suggest that due to these bibliographical decisions, "a favorite book always reads differently in the first edition—by which we do not mean an actual difference in the text, but only in the feeling with which the volume is approached."[26] This fidelity to authorial intention, with regard to both literary and bibliographical elements (though denying the possibility of authorial revision across editions notably practiced by such modern writers as Henry James, W. H. Auden, and Marianne Moore) suggests that, in an era of mechanical reproduction, a first edition expresses a personal, auratic quality not found in subsequent reproductions—one that is rooted in the author's control not only over the text she has written but over the manufacture of the material book as well. Whatever else it may have had, the frequently anonymous and reprinted poetry of mass print culture had little aura.

As N. N. Feltes has argued, auratic quality, which lends much of the value to the first edition, is a function not only of personal interest but also of relative rarity.[27] We prize those things that are hard to get. Rarity is not enough in itself to assure a book's value, however. As the turn-of-the-century collector and critic J. H. Slater explains, rarity, "irrespective of its merit or in spite of the want of it, sometimes works wonders, but not in the majority of cases. Rather should we regard scarcity as an auxiliary to recognized merit, and of little importance in itself. Some books are very scarce in the sense of being difficult to meet with when wanted, but if nobody wants them they are not in an improved position on that account."[28] Collectors, for example, were often encouraged to acquire books by the Romantic poets Keats, Shelley, and Byron, and by the more recent Victorian poets Tennyson and Browning, in large part because these authors were frequently listed in catalogs and their prices were somewhat predictable. Along with material ownership and association, the quality of textual authorship also became a determining factor in a book's bibliographical and economic worth. Within such collectively agreed-upon subjective preferences, the practices of the modern rare book market "introduced and sustained particular ideologies of singularity and uniqueness as components of literary value" within the rules of market exchange.[29] In its emphasis on the closeness to the author and on the relative scarcity of the book, the collecting of first editions was a particularly pronounced example of the general practice of book collecting as a reaction to increasing mass print.

While collectors understood this value to be the natural expression of first editions that had survived time's ravages, they also widely believed that it could be manufactured in modern firsts. This belief in such made value exemplifies what Elizabeth Outka refers to as the commodified authentic, which fuses the craft and the commercial, the old and the new.[30] This conflict was played out in the bibliographical features of the book itself, especially in those *éditions de luxe* issued with fine paper and hand-set type. Even those presses, such as Cuala Press and the Bodley Head, that strived for a sleeker, more "modern" bibliographical style than the cramped medievalism that was on display in books from Morris's Kelmscott Press, still largely relied on craft production rather than modern manufacturing techniques. The more costly process not only meant that books could fetch a higher price, but it also stressed a living connection between printer and book, meaning that even new books had something of the old intimacy about them. This artificial aging contributed to the logic of scarcity that allowed the collecting of first editions to fit into book collecting more generally. While fine craftsmanship kept these books from being made in the same numbers as mass-produced ones, their numbers were also deliberately restricted, so that, as one observer puts it, *éditions de luxe* were "scarce books, but artificially scarce, not naturally or historically."[31]

For many, the limited market dictated appreciation for the object itself, as when one collector notes of the Kelmscott books that "it was not until these books began to fetch high prices at auction that a full realization of their beauty and value dawned upon the world at large."[32] Just as the time-tested worth of the book or poem was both literary and material, so it was with the first edition, which—being new but old, rare but accessible to one willing to pay the price—provided a model for how new literature could be evaluated as well.[33] Without the test of time, however, collectors necessarily relied heavily on their own literary judgment for this evaluation. But just as the material value of the first edition was questioned, so too was its literary worth. As one collector warns, "The ideal collector should not build his library on the shifting sands of contemporary judgment; he should not follow the commercial vicissitudes of first editions of living authors, but rather plant a firm foot on the rock of literature that has been braced by the criticism of generations."[34] Such a strategy would ensure lasting literary and bibliographical value.

This complex negotiation of literary and material value at the heart of the collected book and the collection of which it is a part would help structure ideas of value and canonicity in Palgrave's *Golden Treasury* and modern poetry anthologies that followed in its wake. But just as collectors had difficulty pinning down the worth of manufactured firsts, Palgrave would struggle to produce a valuable, unified collection of more contemporaneous poets. The nugget one had discovered may very well turn out to be a fool's gold that could devalue tradition's more authentic specimens.

Seconding the Series

Some value my first for the sake of my second;
To some, though, its worth is by rarity reckon'd.
—L. G. Cresswell, "A Literary Double Acrostic"

One of the main reasons that *The Golden Treasury* could claim critical authority to collect all of the most valuable poems and arrange them in effective poetic order was that its chronology officially ended in 1850 but essentially concluded with the Romantics. As it did for the cautious book collector, historical distance allowed Palgrave to draw upon a general critical consensus of what were considered the best poems. Palgrave acknowledges in his preface that it would "obviously have been invidious to apply the standard aimed at in this Collection to the Living. Nor, even in the cases where this might be done without offence, does it appear wise to attempt to anticipate the verdict of the Future on our contemporaries."[35] Nearly four decades later, however, Palgrave does attempt to incorporate the near-contemporary Victorian poets into a Second Series, retroactively making the original *Golden Treasury* merely a First Series rather than the final word on English poetry as a whole. To justify this attempt, Palgrave draws upon the modern first edition collector's notions of manufactured scarcity to artificially inflate the value of contemporary poems. The Second Series was largely considered a failed project, however, and what could be seen as its structural failure calls into question the processes not only of selecting and collecting contemporaneous poems but of forging any definite sense of poetic tradition.

Rather than taking the Second Series as a sudden departure from Palgrave's earlier vow not to anthologize his contemporaries, it should be seen as a culmination of a long editorial process and evolution of editorial attitudes over several decades that was already beginning to challenge the critical authority of the original *Golden Treasury*. The Golden Treasury Series of books, for which Palgrave would edit volumes of verse by Shakespeare, Keats, Herrick, and Tennyson in addition to the *Golden Treasury* anthologies, and for which such renowned critics and poets as Matthew Arnold and Henry Longfellow would edit other volumes, would eventually publish ninety titles over the span of a hundred years. A precursor to popular ready-made libraries, such as the Everyman's Library (which began in 1904 and would be one of the first such libraries to reprint the original *Golden Treasury*) and Dr. Eliot's Five-Foot Shelf (which began in 1909), the uniformity of book size and binding suggested intellectual and aesthetic uniformity as well as uniformity of literary and intellectual tradition (such libraries were generally despised by collectors, however, because they were impersonal and denied the thrill of acquisition). Palgrave emphasizes the material dimension of these books in claiming that "I have endeavoured in this, as in three or four other little books, to provide companionship; these, methinks, are the true 'editions of luxury.'"[36]

The series suggests the mutual influence of the anthology and the book collection: just as book collecting helped structure the selection and arrangement of the anthology, the anthology modeled the new book collection. At the same time, however, it exposes the anthology's inability to bring together all of the best poems. If the poems are worth reading, why aren't they in the anthology? If they are less than the best, why reproduce them in a series? There is, of course, a finite amount of space for an anthology, and these may simply be the hoard of slightly less valuable poems—not gold, perhaps, but still poems of luster and worth. Such a formulation dredges up the possibility, however, that value is more subjective than Palgrave's original anthology would have us believe: that it involves history, biography, and the personal interests of the reader as well. In supplementing *The Golden Treasury*, the Golden Treasury Series points to what is always already missing in Palgrave's selection as well as to the more subjective criteria it has attempted to suppress.

In a similar way, this problem would be exposed in *The Children's Trea-*

sury of English Song (1875), the didactic implications of which were even more explicit than those of the original *Golden Treasury*. Modeled after *The Golden Treasury*'s objective selection, but only including about 80 of the 307 pages, while adding another 200, *The Children's Treasury* challenged in practice the theoretical premises of the original.[37] Are children necessarily learning less than the best? To what degree do the best poems depend on the audience at hand?

By 1890, as Palgrave was working on what would become the substantially revised and expanded edition of *The Golden Treasury* (1891), the problem of selection was becoming more pronounced. The new edition would consist of five volumes, the first four expanding on the territory of the first edition—that is, poems through the mid-nineteenth century—and the fifth volume incorporating poems from then to the present day. The edition again calls into question the integrity of the First Series, even as it refines it. As Palgrave explains in the preface, some poems, "especially in Book I, have been added:—either on better acquaintance;—or unknown to the Editor when first gathering his harvest," what he calls "after-gleanings." Further, the text "has also been carefully revised from authoritative sources."[38] Not only the selection and arrangement of poems, but also the forms of the poems themselves are altered in the revised edition.

The revised edition falls through on its promise of a fifth book, however. As Palgrave explains, it has "still seemed best, for several reasons, to retain the original limit by which the selection was confined to those then no longer living," though still maintaining the hope that a "complete and definitive collection of our best Lyrics, to the central year of this fast-closing century, is now offered."[39] Part of the problem with a fifth book was that (in large part due to the success of the original *Golden Treasury*) the lyric had simply become too popular. In response to an early suggestion by Macmillan that recently dead writers be included in the expanded edition, Palgrave replies that the suggestion was impractical, explaining that since 1850 (the date at which the first edition ended), "our poetry has definitely taken the lyrical direction: & to complete it on the plan of the last (viz. the best lyrics, but <u>all</u> of them) I roughly then would require a longer space,—probably a much longer space,—than the whole present fourth book" in the series.[40]

As Palgrave reasoned, to include a select group of six or eight recently or nearly dead writers would undoubtedly offend other living writers, a fact that he personally understood from his work as a book reviewer, as when, after receiving a bad review of his *Dramatis Personae*, Robert Browning accused Palgrave of "grubbing among my old wardrobe of thirty years accumulation, and, ripping off here a quaint button, there a queer rag or lapel, exhibiting these as my daily wear."[41] Things could quickly turn ugly if Palgrave included the wrong poets in a new volume—or even the wrong poems from the right poets.

But there were deeper critical concerns as well. First, there was the issue of selection: the poems—like modern first editions—had simply not been around long enough to guarantee lasting objective value. To include poems of unproven value may not only compromise the selection but could threaten the value of earlier poems as well, simply by placing them in bad company. There was also the issue of collection. Even if a cadre of poets could be identified whose poems would have lasting value, Palgrave would risk failing to include all of those poets and only those poets who forwarded the tradition of the original *Golden Treasury*.

Still, the idea of an expanded edition continued to weigh on Palgrave's mind. He wondered whether the preface to the expanded edition might be altered to say, "I return the rule of admitting nothing by writers alive in <u>1861</u>. My wish is however to add a fifth book, which would be as long as the 4th, & to add <u>two</u> to the 19th Century: meant to contain Arnold Browning & Tennyson if I outlive him." But at the same time he weighed whether he should "shadow forth the humility of a continuation, or say <u>nothing</u>." As he explains, a contemporary anthology had already been attempted in the United States a decade earlier, but it was "a rather clumsy looking affair." Palgrave was unsure as to whether the proposal "may keep others from <u>attempting</u> it: or may <u>provoke</u> them."[42]

Palgrave's increasing recognition that the 1891 *Golden Treasury* in particular would not extend the chronology of earlier editions, but that such an anthology was conceivable made him ambivalent as to whether the volume should be advertised as "revised and slightly enlarged." He originally suggested this option and then reconsidered because "this should impede the previous small edition, which I think may very well go on until that distant period when the fifth book (on which I profess an absolute silence) shall appear."[43] He would finally decide that "you will, I suffer presently advertise it as <u>revised & enlarged</u>: which it now truly is, to my best ability, & I think, to its considerable improvement."[44] Palgrave's wavering about how to advertise the 1891 edition suggests the extent to which he worried a later edition may eclipse, or at least compromise the integrity of, the original *Golden Treasury*.

Palgrave's meditation on the inclusion of contemporaneous or near-contemporaneous poetry was in large part due to the increasing importance of the modern first edition book, as is illustrated by his recognition of the book collector's market and his own insistence on making a limited edition of the 1891 *Golden Treasury*. Palgrave had suggested a limited edition for *The Children's Treasury* ten years previously, writing to Macmillan that "if you brought out a Prize Edition (or so named) of the Children's Treasury in the G.T. Series, printed on [finer] paper, it would probably have a fair sale & would, if so brought out, not interfere either with The Golden Treasury or with the School Edition of the Children's" and could be out by Christmas.[45]

As to the 1891 edition, Palgrave asks, looking "at the present fury for 'large' 'handmade' paper, would you think it likely to succeed (financially) if you were to issue a <u>Limited</u> edition of the proposed imprint in the same edition—maybe 200 <u>handmade</u> copies. To myself, the <u>Edition de Luxe</u> is the <u>handmade</u> form, but there is no library objection to pacifying the fancy of collectors of things rare."[46] He later questions whether Macmillan has "made arrangements for a fly leaf on which you will number the copies of the larger paper issue" and mentions that "I see the advertisement of the <u>Large Paper</u> of the G.T. only says 'Limited Edition.' It would be better to say 'limited to 25 copies' would it not?"[47]

This attentiveness to the modern first and limited edition market, where a finely made modern book could achieve some quality of the old and be thought valuable through its artificial scarcity, was instrumental in persuading Palgrave that he could finally produce an objectively valued anthology of near-contemporary poetry. Palgrave reasoned, as collectors of modern first editions did (and against his earlier better judgment), that because the material scarcity of the book helped lend value to the literary text, so that the first edition could be valued in the book collector's market, the new poem could be valued in the marketplace of poetic tradition. It would merely be a case of exercising critical judgment to determine which poems would best stand the test of time.

And so, with that conviction, Palgrave attempted a Second Series that would revisit the ground of the First Series, "beginning with a period nearly corresponding to what has been called the Victorian," with the aim to "include in the same volume the later risen of our stars." The anthology is not completely up to date, but it approaches the contemporary, with its inclusion of poems by Matthew Arnold, Robert Browning, Elizabeth Barrett Browning, Dante Gabriel Rossetti, Arthur Hugh Clough, and Alfred, Lord

Tennyson. As Palgrave admits, the selection "has been brought, near as I can venture, to our own day. But, especially in case of those later singers whose course is not yet run, it is all too soon even to attempt a valuation." As he progresses in the project, Palgrave comes to the conclusion that even to approach the contemporary has "proved impossible." He explains that a "decided preference for Lyrical poetry," which Palgrave himself helped cultivate, made it so that "despite this whole volume dedicated to a harvest of song more copious than even that famed Elizabethan outflowering, it has not been possible to renew the attempt made in the former book, wherein with but three or four exceptions on the ground of length, all our best lyrics (so far as I could judge) were gathered: and a selection only from the finest work of our greater Victorian poets (so far as my choice may have been happy) can alone be offered here."[48]

It wasn't simply that Palgrave was striking new veins of gold too rich to hold—a fortunate problem indeed—but there was also the problem of determining which works were truly golden to begin with. As Palgrave explains, the "second Treasury has cost thrice the labour of the first. For nothing, it need scarcely be said, is harder than to form an estimate even remotely accurate of our own contemporary artists, whatever the sphere of their art. This difficulty, in the former book, was far less. For its contents, the verdict of Time had been already largely given, and I had also that invaluable assistance which my Dedication acknowledges." That is, Tennyson. Without the corroboration of time and other critics, "a personal element always remains, too often refusing to be excluded; especially in case of early favourites."[49] Palgrave had come to realize what the detractors of first edition collecting claimed all along: that attempting an impartial judgment of the contemporary couldn't help but be like staking a claim in quicksand. Not only does the Second Series fail to gather all of the worthiest poems, as the First Series had supposedly done; it couldn't even declare that its selection was based on impartial principles.

The Second Series had its fair share of problems. As Megan Nelson explains, by the time Palgrave began work on the Second Series, his "failing judgment, readiness to bowlderise texts, and the many editorial idiosyncrasies and biases which had increasingly marred the expanded editions of the *Treasury* combined to undermine the quality of the book. Palgrave was also apparently constitutionally incapable of appreciating the work of the eighties and nineties, and the book includes scarcely anything after 1870. The book's quality is further impaired by his personal loyalties and, it must be admitted, his snobbery."⁵⁰ As formidable as its shortcomings were, I want to suggest that the biggest problem with the Second Series is structural, inherent in the flawed form of the objective anthology itself. And not just the objective anthology that tackles the contemporary but one that makes any claim to absolute historical judgment. The Second Series, and the editions leading up to it, violates the central tenets of the original *Golden Treasury*—the integrity of the individual poem, the selection of only the best poems, and the arrangement of those poems in the most poetically effective manner—and in doing so exposed the degree to which these had always been imperfect constructions.

Palgrave's Legacies

> We live in an anthological age; most of our literary instruction for the young, as also the urge to culture among the more advanced in age, is an adaptation of the phrase, "Say it with Flowers."
>
> —*The Golden Treasury* (1937)

> Dost thou laugh to see how fools are vex'd
> To add to golden numbers, golden numbers?
> O sweet content! O sweet, O sweet content!
>
> —*The Golden Treasury* (1911)

Palgrave's *Golden Treasury* exhibited a profound influence on the "outflowering" of objective anthologies that were published in its wake. Following the expiration of British copyright on the original *Golden Treasury* in 1904, cheap reprints and adaptations were soon being issued from multiple publication houses.⁵¹ Just as Palgrave's subsequent editions tried to uphold the general ideas of the First Series while simultaneously challenging many of its specific claims, these later anthologies acknowledged their debt to Palgrave and praised the original *Golden Treasury*'s perfection, even as they amended or augmented its selection—challenging it on historical, national, generic, and formal grounds—and ultimately succumbing to the questionable logic of the Second Series.

As Ernest Rhys claims in his introduction to *Palgrave's Golden Treasury*, issued as part of the Everyman's Library series, although the original edition had been amended "here and there, added to and considered again and again as it has been from time to time, its perfection was implicit in the first edition." The edition, Rhys asserts, was so perfect that, even when Bullen's

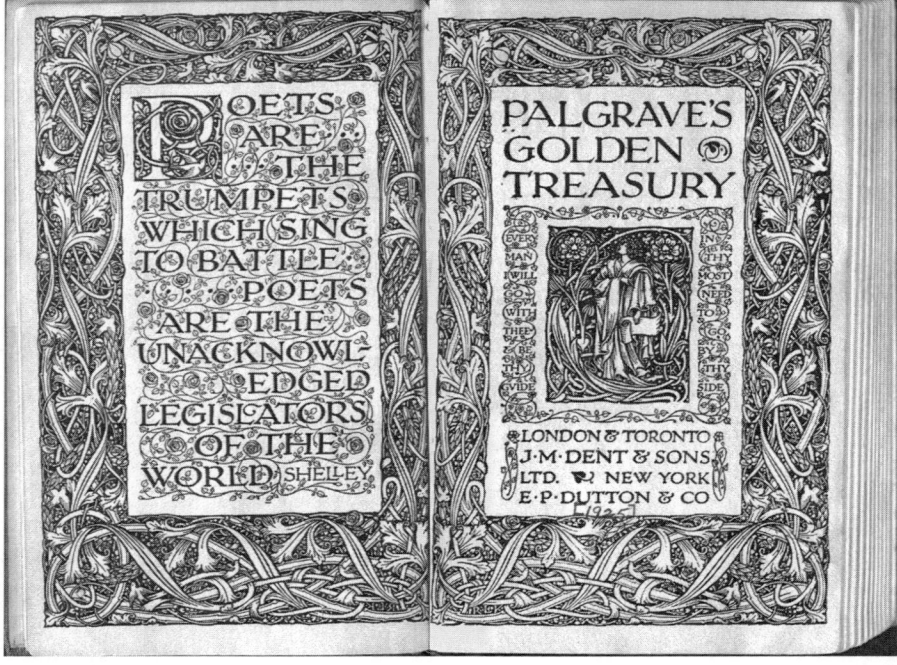

Figure 1.1. Ornate opening page to the Everyman's edition of Palgrave's *Golden Treasury*.

Elizabethan songbooks were discovered, "it was easy to put the best of those verses into the place that seems to have been waiting for them." Rhys goes on to emphasize the creative dimension of the anthology, explaining that while everyone will have his favorite poems, "no one has been able to make an anthology that has been more generally received by Englishmen as in itself almost a work of art."[52] Additionally, the woodcut title page of the Everyman's edition (fig. 1.1), recalling William Morris's Kelmscott Press, makes explicit *The Golden Treasury*'s connection to a culture of fine printing (an embellishment carried through later versions, such as the 1914 *New Golden Treasury*).

Nearly half a century later, C. Day Lewis would echo these sentiments in the introduction to his 1954 edition of the anthology, explaining that *The Golden Treasury* "commends itself, not only by the formal perfection, and therefore the durability, of the work it presents, but also by its arrangement.

To dispose poems of many different writers in such a way that each poem gains from its context and throws light upon those around it, is the supreme gift of the anthologist. In no other way do taste, sensibility, learning, and a fine ear for subtle shades of meaning so clearly reveal themselves. A satisfying arrangement of poems requires a special talent which can be fairly called 'creative.'"[53] Even in the aftermath of the modernist intervention anthology, an idea of the anthology based on a collecting logic that emphasizes perfection of the individual poems, their ideal arrangement, and the creative capacity of the anthologist-critic to bring it all together proved to be enduring.

Those anthologies that did not seek to reprint Palgrave's edition still borrowed his language of "golden" and "treasury," such as Louis Untermeyer's *A Treasury of Great Poems* (1942). Oscar Williams believed that his anthology had earned its title, *A Little Treasury of Modern Poetry* (1946), because "the modern period shows itself resplendent in its wealth of poetry . . . although the word connotes such riches that it has been applied before only to anthologies that draw their selections from centuries."[54] Some anthologies, including *A Treasury of Helpful Verse* (1896), *A Treasury of Humorous Poetry* (1902), and *The New Treasury of War Poetry* (1943), would adopt the title "treasury" even when it would seem to contradict its subjective theme and contents.[55] In addition to conjuring up thoughts of Palgrave, the use of such terms was shorthand for the presentation of the objectively best poems. But even if the terms weren't there, the idea of objective, permanent value often was. As Untermeyer explains in *The Book of Living Verse*, the poems in the volume "are living poetry in the sense that they have persisted in spite of changing times and shifting tastes. Thus (even in the section devoted to modern verse) they seem to possess the quality which implies permanence. They are, furthermore, 'living' since they contain that vitality which is independent of form and fashion."[56]

A curious byproduct of distinguishing the best poems is that now the lesser poems could also be determined and, rather than simply repeating the selection of a few choice examples, an anthology could give these runners-up their due. *The Cambridge Book of Lesser Poets* (1927) and *A Treasury of Minor British Poetry*, for example, were compiled to augment the best poems already collected in *The Golden Treasury* and *The Oxford Book of English Verse*.[57] And just as golden treasuries connoted the best poems, for the baser poems there were treasuries of "silver" and "bronze."[58]

Such modern anthologies as *The Golden Treasury of Longer Poems* and *The Shorter Golden Book of Narrative Verse* also questioned what constituted an anthologizable poem, challenging Palgrave's privileging of the lyric, which, as Frank Lentricchia has observed, would come to "shape a lyric canon, a list for all seasons, embodying the measure of literary value" that was often anathema to calls for originality and creativity that fueled high modernist poetic experimentation in the more restricted fields of modern literary production.[59] This challenge to the Victorian lyric (which, as I argue in the next chapter, was fueled by *Poetry* and other little magazines) encouraged the turn to *vers libre* in such modern anthologies as Pound's *Des Imagistes* (1914) and Yeats's *The Oxford Book of Modern Verse* (1936), which famously opens with Walter Pater's (lineated) prose.[60]

Although *The Golden Treasury* was distinctly English, many anthologies sought to apply Palgrave's principles to foreign bodies of poetry as well. Frederic Lawrence Knowles justifies the title to his anthology, *The Golden Treasury of American Songs and Lyrics* (1897), by declaring that the "verse of a single century produced in a new country should not be expected to equal the poetic wealth of an old and intellectual nation. But if American poetry cannot hope to rival the poetry of the mother country, it may at least be compared with it; and the fact of such a comparative point of view will aid rather than hinder the student of our native poetry in estimating its value."[61] Other national poetries were anthologized along similar lines, such as *The Golden Treasury of Canadian Verse* (1931) and Hugh MacDiarmid's *The Golden Treasury of Scottish Poetry* (1941).[62] A change of venue did not necessarily mean a departure from aesthetic detachment, however, as Yeats makes clear in his revised edition of *A Book of Irish Verse*, where he has endeavored "to separate what has literary value from what has only a patriotic and political value, no matter how sacred it has become to us."[63]

Some of the biggest departures from Palgrave's project came in anthologies incorporating more recent poems, marking their relationship to the original *Golden Treasury* with such titles as *The New Golden Treasury of Songs and Lyrics* (1914) and *Additional Poems to Palgrave's Golden Treasury* (1928), the latter expressing a common sentiment that the editors "have endeavored, as far as is humanly possible, to obliterate personal preferences and opinions and to reflect Palgrave's own viewpoint. We have tried to include those poems which he would have included were he living today, and to omit those which we feel he would have discarded."[64] Maintaining (or at least feigning) allegiance to Palgrave's supposedly infallible critical judgment, editors were more likely to blame history itself. As Williams writes in his preface to the modern revised edition of the *Golden Treasury*, modern readers "still take pleasure in *The Golden Treasury* and find its only serious flaw that of the incompleteness made apparent by the passage of time." The inclusion of new poems in book 5 that supplemented the first four books of *The Golden Treasury* "is not meant as an adverse criticism of his taste, but rather as a guess as to what that taste might have become if he had lived on into our own time." Williams muses on what Palgrave would think of such modern poets as Hopkins, Yeats, Eliot, Robinson, Frost, Auden, and Thomas: "massively shocking to a Victorian sensibility, yet incontestably great with their new techniques, richness of vocabulary and depth of understanding in areas considered outside the scope of poetry."[65]

But even as they continued to praise Palgrave, these supplemental editions pointed to the limitations of Palgrave's own Second Series and more generally to the inability of anyone to make a contemporary anthology based in objective critical judgment. As William T. Brewster explains in his revised and enlarged *Golden Treasury* (1937)—which would replace 201 of the poems written after 1850, keeping only 27 from Palgrave's selection—the Second Series "is usually thought to be inferior to the original; and, being largely Victorian, is, at the moment, obviously under a special curse. With this inferiority the natural limitation imposed on the anthologist has much to do . . . and they lie in the unlikelihood of fifty years producing more excellence than three hundred preceding years."[66]

Beyond the question of which poems were to be included, anthologists wrestled with the impossibility of managing the comprehensiveness that Palgrave achieved in his original *Treasury*. As Laurence Binyon explains, *The Golden Treasury of Modern Lyrics* (1924) is designed to continue the historical trajectory of the first *Golden Treasury* through the present day, but "it cannot make quite so comprehensive a claim as its predecessor. Even in the case of work which has been sifted by time a wide diversity of opinion, as to what is best, persists: the diversity is accentuated the nearer we approach to contemporaries."[67] Likewise, as A. S. Collins explains in *The Treasury of English Verse New and Old* (1931), "No volume of manageable size could contain all that may be regarded as 'best,' and so the present Editor has been compelled to omit much that is undeniably immortal poetry."[68]

Williams seems to have been able to work within the confines of Palgrave's original arrangement, noting that the "half thematic, half chronological sequence of the poems has always given a special charm to *The Golden Treasury* and has been retained for the supplementary matter."[69] Others, however, believed that no one but Palgrave (and Tennyson) could have grouped the newer poems in "the most poetically-effective order" and added their selections chronologically.[70] Henry Van Dyke's *Little Masterpieces of Poetry* (1905) abandoned the chronological through line, arranging poems according to poetic form and claiming that this method of grouping "not only brings together the poems which are most alike in their effect (a matter of the first importance to the reader's comfort and pleasure), but also serves to show how significant and how vital the element of form is in poetry." Emphasizing the pedagogical implications of the anthology, Van Dyke suggests that this arrangement will also "enable the reader to follow, without effort, the development of the various forms of verse."[71]

While Palgrave's Second Series had particular shortcomings, the fact that later editors so consistently abandoned the hope of objectively selecting and arranging a few best poems that had been the hallmark of the original *Golden Treasury* suggests that the problems were rooted in the form of the objective anthology itself. The objective anthology was severely limited with respect to questions of history, nationality, genre, and form. Even within these constraints, it would seem that contemporaneous poems could not be judged effectively and included without question in an anthology of the best poems.

Such a critique would culminate in the 1928 *A Pamphlet Against Anthologies*, in which Laura Riding and Robert Graves argue against the professional, public anthology, claiming that the role of the anthologist "is to make a single book out of clippings from many books; to create a composite author who shall be a mean struck between all the poets included."[72] This results in an anthology that can't help but be a kind of uniform, muddied gray. Jeremy Braddock has pointed to this pamphlet as a condemnation of thematic "trade anthologies" that resemble the modern interventionist anthology.[73] It is important to note, however, that Riding and Graves single out Palgrave in particular, writing that they "would not go so far as to say that every poem in *The Golden Treasury* is uncharacteristic of the author, but we do say that even positive poems lose their character by being anthologized." Their point is that not only may an anthologist fail to choose the best possible specimens from what is available but that the objective anthology form itself encourages a mediocrity where nothing stands apart as exceptional. Riding and Graves offer a prescription for the popular anthology-piece: "It must be fairly regular in form and easily memorized, it must be a new combination of absolutely worn-out material, it must have a certain unhealthy vigour and languor, and it must start off with a simple and engaging statement of a sentimental character. Somewhere there must be a daring poetical image. . . . It must have as many 'subjects' as possible, so that it can be easily shifted about by the anthologist from one section of his book to the other wherever fattening is required." Although Palgrave's rejoinder would likely be that harmony is maintained if everything is of the highest quality— if everything is brilliant, nothing outshines the rest—the list does in fact seem to apply to many poems in *The Golden Treasury*, which are indeed well known and easily memorized. The multiplicity of subjects (so that subject ultimately becomes an alibi for form) and the combination of "vigour" and "languor" (the new among the traditional) can be read as an indictment not only of the poorly made anthology but of any anthologizing impulse (whatever critical form it may take) that seeks to value poems as a function of their place in the context of the anthology or in an abstract literary tradition, rather than as a particular poetic expression. Riding and Graves make their point through scathing close readings of poems that, through the validation of anthologies, have come to be seen as perfect modern lyrics. Such a lyric, they claim, is W. B. Yeats's "Lake Isle of Innisfree," explaining that the "ordinary reader is inclined to take 'Innisfree' for granted as a 'perfect lyric' on the assurance of the critics, and will be surprised, when he examines it out of its anthology setting, to see what a misery it really is."[74] This emphasis on how the anthology itself could color a poem's meaning and reception would, rather ironically, directly inform the more decontextualized close reading practices of the New Critics.

Riding and Graves condemn the modernist interventionist anthology not because it has gone too far to question notions of objective poetic value and tradition but because it has not gone far enough. They champion instead what amounts to a private, purposeless collection, recalling the kind of grandmotherly albums that Waugh locates as historically prior to *The Golden Treasury*. Such an anthology offers deliberate acts of aesthetic, social, and political retaliation against an old regime of objective poetic value and tradition as it signals the structural impossibility of such a regime that nevertheless continues to dominate critical understandings of poetic modernism.

Understanding Poetry

> It is absurd to think that the only way to tell if a poem is lasting is to wait and see if it lasts. The right reader of a good poem can tell the moment it strikes him that he has taken an immortal wound—that he will never get over it. That is to say, permanence in poetry as in love is perceived instantly. The proof of a poem is not that we have never forgotten it, but that we knew at first sight we never could forget it.
>
> —Robert Frost, *The Book of Living Verse*

Although it has often been taken as a textbook, Cleanth Brooks and Robert Penn Warren's *Understanding Poetry* (1938) betrays its anthological lineage with the subtitle *An Anthology for College Students*. One of the key founding documents of New Criticism, *Understanding Poetry* extends the role of the objective anthologies that sprang up in *The Golden Treasury*'s long shadow, drawing upon modernist notions of objective value and tradition espoused by such poet-critics as T. S. Eliot (which were themselves largely shaped by assumptions underpinning the objective anthology), as it provided the objects and criteria for studying modern poetry.

Affirming Palgrave's placement of poems to maximize poetic resonance and Van Dyke's arrangement according to poetic form, *Understanding Poetry* organizes poems "first, on aspects of poetic communication, and second, on pedagogical expediency." Poems are placed into formal categories—narrative poems, descriptive poems, metrics, tone and attitude, imagery, statement and idea—allowing poems to resonate with one another through particular poetic elements while at the same time being "arranged in a scale of increasing difficulty" in order to offer the student a continual challenge. Within this arrangement, "the editors feel that disagreement and debate may be healthful in sharpening the critical instinct of the student, so they feel that the study and analysis of bad and uneven poems will contribute to the same end." Therefore, "it is hoped that the juxtaposition of good and bad poems, and of new and old poems, will serve to place emphasis on the primary matter of critical reading and evaluation."[75] *Understanding Poetry* goes beyond even those anthologies that seek to gather the second-best or third-best poems by also distinguishing what it has determined to be the objectively worst poems, contending that discriminating between the best and worst poems can itself serve to refine critical judgment and taste.

In their "Letter to the Teacher" that prefaces the anthology's first edition, Brooks and Warren make clear that their rationale for such an arrangement is to counter what they see as a tendency to study poems in strictly biographical and historical terms. Instead, they argue, "one must grasp the poem as a literary construct before it can offer any real illumination as a document" (though they would dial back their antibiographical and ahistorical rhetoric in subsequent editions).[76] Focusing on the specificity of the poetic text, they famously forward the idea that a poem "should always be treated as an organic system of relationships, and the poetic quality should never be understood as inhering in one or more factors taken in isolation."[77] *Understanding Poetry* confirms the poetic harmony that Palgrave saw as characteristic of the lyric (though stretching the limits of this genre) while also inverting Palgrave's ideal selection and arrangement of poems within the objective anthology in order to lay a cornerstone of New Critical orthodoxy: the poem itself is an ideal selection and arrangement of elements that can only be fully understood in its totality.

While these concepts of poetic value, tradition, and organic unity owe much to the rise of the objective anthology, so that their appearance in a textbook-anthology is entirely appropriate, such concepts were similarly being explored in other New Critical texts as well, such as Cleanth Brooks's *Modern Poetry and the Tradition*, with its opening assertion that every poet that we read "alters to some degree our total conception of poetry."[78] Additionally, as I argue in chapter 5, they would also provide a governing logic for the institutionalization of the modern poetry archive at such places as the Library of Congress. This orthodoxy should therefore be seen as extending a more general critical conversation on poetic modernism, which was itself greatly influenced by Palgrave.

One of the loudest and most authoritative voices in this conversation belonged to T. S. Eliot, although he would never produce an anthology of modern poetry. Perhaps the closest Eliot would come would be to write a preface for Anne Ridler's *A Little Book of Modern Verse*, in which he concedes that, within its narrow limits, the little book of verse "has endeavoured, not to find a place for every distinguished name—which would be impossible—but to provide an illustration of the various styles of poetry which are generally acknowledged to be 'modern.'" This shared condition of modernity, Eliot explains, "can be perceived by a sensibility, but not defined in words."[79] Such a sense of the modern is a localized instance of what Eliot famously calls the "historical sense," which is a sense "not only of the pastness of the past, but of its presence; the historical sense compels a man to write not merely with his own generation in his bones, but with a feeling that the whole of the literature of Europe from Homer and within it the whole of the literature of his own country has a simultaneous existence and composes a simultaneous order. This historical sense, which is a sense of the timeless as well as of the temporal and of the timeless and of the temporal together, is what makes a writer traditional."[80] This understanding of the present, mingled with the past, is an anthological one, recalling Palgrave's episodic logic of arranging poems poetically and periodically in order to reveal, as Waugh put it of *The Golden Treasury*, "literary tradition and national character."[81]

Eliot furthers this connection to the objective anthology in his contention that the existing literary monuments "form an ideal order among themselves, which is modified by the introduction of the new (the really new) work of art among them. The existing order is complete before the new work arrives; for order to persist after the supervention of novelty, the *whole* existing order must be, if ever so lightly, altered; and so the relations, proportions, values of each work of art toward the whole are readjusted. . . . The past should be altered by the present as much as the present is directed by the past."[82] Like those anthologists who claim that the selection and arrangement of the original *Golden Treasury* was perfect and the addition of some lost or forgotten poem would merely confirm that perfection through alteration, Eliot argues that the new poem confirms the perfection of literary tradition even as it modifies that tradition.

For perfection to occur, however, the new poem must be "really new." This "really new" expresses a historical sense that for Eliot is paradoxically a sense of both the temporal and the timeless that, as I have argued, characterizes the manufactured scarcity of the first edition in an increasingly ephemeral mass print culture. Just as the first edition is admitted into the collection, the really new poem is admitted into tradition. Eliot explains that "we do not quite say that the new is more valuable because it fits in; but its fitting in is a test of its value." Recognizing the pitfalls of evaluating the contemporary, however, Eliot explains that this test "can only be slowly and cautiously applied, for we are none of us infallible judges of conformity."[83] Often, as in Palgrave's Second Series and subsequent modern anthologies, the test was haphazardly applied, penning a cautionary tale for the application of tradition to the contemporary while stressing the importance of precise critical reading.

But even if the most valuable poems could be selected, their introduction disrupts the arrangement of the anthology and confirms the fact that tradition is never complete and perfectly ordered. While Eliot, like anthologists before him, claims that tradition is a perfect whole both before and after the incorporation of the new poem, this is at best the temporary illusion of completion. As the scrapbooker has demonstrated to the collector, behind this façade are the cracks that keep the past present and the ordered always in shambles. A new poem can always be added; completion is fleeting. As I argue in chapter 3, this acknowledgment helps to clarify the haphazard composition of the modern collage poem, including Eliot's own *The Waste Land*.

Even if compromised in practice, however, Eliot maintained a lifelong commitment to notions of literary and poetic tradition that (as I demonstrate in chapter 4) would, among other things, undergird his editing of selected volumes of poetry by Ezra Pound, Marianne Moore, and Rudyard Kipling. Eliot's critical commitment would also help supply a necessary fiction for the New Critical understanding of modern poetic value and tradition that would inform such texts as *Understanding Poetry*. These texts in turn would have a profound influence on poetic pedagogy and a resulting modern poetic canon, since they were often the basis of the syllabus and the college curriculum.[84]

Palgrave's original *Golden Treasury* demonstrates how the impulses for selection and arrangement that governed book collecting practices were embodied in the form of the modern poetry anthology and were central to its promotion of a supposedly objective literary value and tradition. By the time Palgrave released the *Golden Treasury*'s Second Series, an increasingly dominating mass print culture that allowed for a proliferation of the lyric poem exposed the anthology's original form as a structural impossibility. To combat this, Palgrave turned to the logic of the manufactured first edition book, which is itself a new media form registering anxieties over the value and permanence of print. But even in light of such difficulties, many modern anthologists and critics who espoused a definitive literary tradition helped naturalize notions of objective value and tradition. These notions would often be taken as stable categories by the first decades of the twentieth century and subsequently challenged by the modernist interventionist anthologies (closely resembling in form and function the earlier contingent anthologies against which Palgrave had initially been reacting and uncovering a long, if at times concealed, contingent-interventionist tradition). This objective valuing had the effect of critically marginalizing not only certain kinds of anthologies but many of the poems that found their value in primarily social and political realms—a marginalization that largely remains to this day.

2 Making Modern *Poetry*
Format, Form, and Modern Poetic Genre

A slender volume, this little magazine. Small enough to put in a jacket pocket and pull out on a lunchtime break or on the long train ride home from work. In its spatial dimensions looking more like a "well-printed book," as one advertising circular would later put it, than like the popular magazines of the day.[1] Before even glancing at the contents, a reader is struck with a number of bibliographical impressions of *Poetry*'s allegiances and clues as to what lies within. Its slate-gray cover, double-bordered in thick black lines, brings to mind a painting by Mondrian or a window by Frank Lloyd Wright. Within these lines, leaves of black and red recall the lush bibliographical codes of medieval manuscripts and such rare turn-of-the-century *éditions de luxe* books as those from William Morris's Kelmscott Press—which would usher in a "renaissance of printing" that included such poets as W. B. Yeats and this magazine's "foreign correspondent," Ezra Pound.[2] The quill and parchment at the top, nestled in a bed of leaves, reinforce this connection and underscore the importance of individual authorship in an age of mechanical reproduction. The title of the journal, synonymous with its demarcation of genre: Pegasus in flight bursts through the big, red, ornate *P* of *Poetry*. And dropping down for further clarification or redundancy or contradiction: *A Magazine of Verse* (fig. 2.1).

Literary and cultural historians have long recognized the importance of little magazines such as *Poetry* in disseminating modernism. A notable early study, *The Little Magazine: A History and a Bibliography*, argues that the little magazines were founded for two reasons: "rebellion against traditional modes of expression and the wish to experiment with the novel (and sometimes unintelligible) forms; and a desire to overcome the commercial or material difficulties which are caused by the introduction of any writing

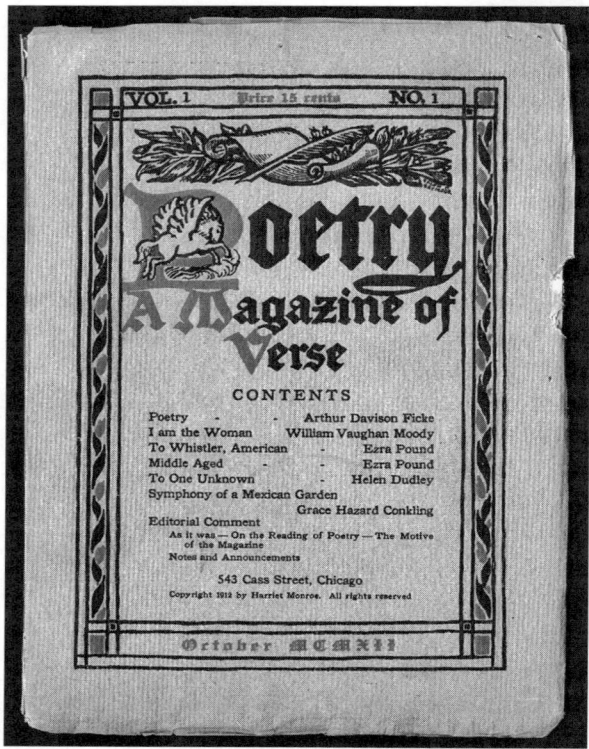

Figure 2.1. Cover page of *Poetry* 1, no. 1. The Modernist Journals Project, Brown University.

whose commercial merits have not been proved."[3] This traditional critical formulation, which suggests that modern little magazines occupy a place of maximum autonomous aesthetic value and minimal commercial value with respect to other periodicals—when those periodicals have even been considered at all—has been challenged on multiple fronts in recent years, however, with a rise of modern periodical studies that has more seriously considered little magazines in relation to mass-circulation magazines, newspapers, and other materials.[4] Scholars have also recently been more attentive to how little magazines' promotion of aesthetic experimentation (in terms of both form and content) were often caught up in negotiations of race, gender, class, international politics, and mass culture, as well as to how previously neglected women editors and publishers, such as *Poetry*'s founder, Harriet Monroe, were instrumental in modernist literary production.[5]

Scarce attention, however, has been given to the role that the bibliographical and generic framing of texts played in the making of modernism. In focusing on these concerns, I argue that *Poetry: A Magazine of Verse*, one of the most influential modern literary magazines, helped turn the poem into an aesthetic object by isolating it on the page, framed by a border of white space, and thereby cut poetry off from some of the more complex and potentially significant social and political meanings it could acquire within mass print culture. *Poetry* encouraged a detached close reading of the modern poem that was reinforced by essays, reviews, and publication circulars that frequently compared the poem to fine books and objets d'art. These various framings opened up a space for such formal experiments as *vers libre* and polyphonic prose, and were instrumental in promoting Imagism as a key modernist poetic movement. The publication of such poems, I suggest, was part of a larger effort to redefine modern poetic genre against traditional verse form that extended efforts of earlier little magazines and middle-class "quality" journals against a dialogic reading of the poem made available in such popular magazines as *Life* and the *Crisis*.

This attention to bibliographic and aesthetic framings of modern poems, and how such framings served to distinguish poetic genre from verse form, highlights another dimension of collecting in an emerging mass print culture. *Poetry* functions like the book collection and like the objective anthology in its selection of similar textual objects—all of which need to be generically defined as poems despite their formal differences—so that they can be brought together into a coherent system based on that similarity. By contrast, the more dialogic magazines suggest a public parallel to scrapbooking (that I explored in the introduction) in its more subjective bringing together of disparate texts and multiple kinds of media that index their historical and textual origins. Moreover, while these mass magazines recognize and often celebrate their ephemerality (even as they are subsequently preserved in the archive), *Poetry* strives for the book collection's permanence in the face of its undeniable status as a periodical.

Framing Modern Poetry

The first issue of *Poetry* opens with a group of poems by Ezra Pound, including "To Whistler, American," with the explanatory subtitle, "On the loan exhibit of his paintings at the Tate Gallery":

You, also, our first great,
Had tried all the ways;
Tested and pried and worked in many fashions,
And this much gives me heart to play the game.

Here is a part that's slight, and part gone wrong,
And much of little moment, and some few
Perfect as Dürer!

"In the Studio" and these two portraits, if I had my choice!
And then these sketches in the mood of Greece?

You had your searches, your uncertainties,
And this is good to know—for us, I mean,
Who bear the brunt of our America
And try to wrench her impulse into art.

You were not always sure, not always set
To hiding night or tuning "Symphonies"
Had not one style from birth, but tried and pried
And stretched and tampered with the media.

You and Abe Lincoln from that mass of dolts
Show us there's chance at least of winning through.[6]

The poem introduces a number of concerns that would be important for both Pound and *Poetry*. In commenting on the reception of an American's work abroad, it points to Pound's transatlantic aspirations and to the rising stock of American modernism. It values experimentation and working "in many fashions," which would come to define so much of Pound's writing and modern poetry more generally. In lauding Whistler and Lincoln, it betrays an early interest in great figures who would become central to such later poems as *The Cantos*, and it intervenes in the not-so-old Whistler/Ruskin debate, siding with the former's championing of art for art's sake.

The poem is also important in the ways it hopes to learn from a visual artist. Rather than find inspiration in Whitman or Poe—both of whose reputations were strengthening via Baudelaire and the French Symbolists and both of whom could be said to have "stretched and tampered" with their media—Pound locates his precursor in an American Impressionist painter.[7] As Pound later explains in *Gaudier-Brzeska*, his interest in Whistler had a definite political dimension: "Whistler was almost the first man, at least the first painter of the last century, to suggest that intelligent and not wholly ignorant and uncultivated men had a right to art."[8] "To Whistler, American" goes beyond analogizing poetry and painting, though. In an early example of modern poetic quotation, Pound places the titles of the paintings themselves in the poem, mimicking the gallery presentation of artworks in a manner conveyed by the subtitle to the poem: "On the loan exhibit of his paintings at the Tate Gallery." The parallel suggests that the poem can go beyond commenting on the presentation of paintings to itself become a work of art physically placed on the page. And, of course, with its final dismissal of a "mass of dolts" and its celebration of "winning through," the poem sets high art against mass culture and the class interests of readers that other poems might serve.

Although critics have often cited "To Whistler, American" as an example of Pound taking advantage of Monroe and her magazine to advance his own aesthetic agenda, it also suggests how Monroe was using Pound to forge an overtly *avant-garde* position for her fledgling magazine.[9] Additionally, Monroe uses the poem to announce *Poetry*'s systematic turning to the visual arts as models for poetry that foreground the magazine's collecting and exhibition practices—which would help it to fulfill its stated mission of being a Chicago cultural institution not unlike a museum or gallery. Comparisons to the visual and plastic arts would be made more explicit in such early editorials as "The Motive of the Magazine," in which Monroe argues that painting, sculpture, and architecture are given a place of privilege, while poetry alone "has been left to shift for herself in a world unaware of its immediate and desperate need of her, a world whose great deeds, whose triumphs over matter, over the wilderness, over racial enmities and distances, require her ever-living voice to give them glory and glamour."[10]

As Monroe makes clear, *Poetry* is motivated to reflect and engage with the social issues of its day. I contend, though, that the isolating format of the magazine makes such engagement difficult. The logical extension of poem-as-art-object was that *Poetry* would systematically house these pieces of art, so that it would become, as one circular put it, like "the ideal art exhibition."[11] The magazine would further claim that the "existence of a gallery for poems and verse has an especially attractive social value in its power of recalling or creating the beautiful and clarifying pleasure of truly reading poetry in its broad scope and rich variety. The hospitality of this hall will have been a genuine source of happiness if somehow it tells its visitors, either while they are here, or after they have gone to other places, what a delight it is to enjoy a poem."[12] *Poetry* did not want merely to supplement the presentation of poetry as a journal on painting might comment and reproduce paintings, or as the bibliographical magazines of the nineteenth century would discuss book bindings, however. Instead, it aspired to present a gallery of the poems themselves, a hall through which the reader could wander from poem to poem in his verbal flânerie.

One of the key differences between a poem and a painting, though, is that the painting exhibits what Walter Benjamin famously refers to in his "Work of Art" essay as "aura": "a strange tissue of space and time: the apparition of a distance, however near it may be." The printed poem, by contrast, falls prey to Benjamin's observation that "technological reproducibility emancipates the work of art from its parasitic subservience to ritual. To an ever-increasing degree, the work reproduced becomes the reproduction of a work designed for reproducibility."[13] This absence of the auratic is a dissatisfaction that Monroe herself admits to in her lament that printed books "soon begin to seem unresponsive to an editor, strangely remote and cold. For manuscripts, even the modern kind beaten into type, are alive; each one is charged with personality, it comes hot from the author's hand."[14]

Poetry attempts to get around this problem of making a poem both accessible and auratic by promoting a sense of what we might call "relative aura" derived from the scarce, finely printed book.[15] This allegiance to the fine book and its efforts to distinguish itself from mass print culture is readily evident on its cover, as I have suggested, and continues inside the magazine. As the magazine declares in an October 1917 circular, sent out to encourage further support for the magazine at the end of its five-year experiment, all of the poems "are printed not for page ends as in most magazines, but in leisurely, well-spaced pages, that make for your enjoyment like a well-printed book."[16] This isolation of the poem on the page, framed by a border of white space, has the effect of directing the reader's attention to a discrete poem, encouraging a self-contained and detached reading in which meaning is derived from the interplay of textual elements (such as image and sound) without distraction from surrounding texts. It also encourages a reading of the poem as an objectively valuable text, marked by wide margins and a liberal use of white space. As one nineteenth-century collector explains of such margins:

> In the olden times, when books were rare and readers few, the chief part of a volume was its interior, and the chief value its literary contents. . . . For this reason books were printed with margins more or less wide, according to circumstances, which depended almost entirely upon the amount of cash at the disposal of the publisher. . . . Thus it came to pass that a wide margin had a peculiar charm of its own, for there was something substantial and aristocratic about a wealth of paper of the finest quality, just as there was about the castellated mansion which looked contemptuously down upon the labourers' cottages on the slopes.[17]

To demonstrate its commitment to poetic framing, there are many instances in the early issues in which poems run slightly onto the next page, allowing enough room for another short poem to be published (which would in fact happen in later volumes, probably due to financial considerations), but these pages are largely left blank or are ornamented with a small woodcut emblem.[18] Such framing reduced the number of poems that could appear in any given issue, but that was precisely the point. As Pound would remark to Monroe, nobody "does *much* good work, in the sense in which I use the word. I think your format is big enough as it is. Few people want more or can stand more than 20pp. of poetry at once."[19] Format provided a built-in mechanism for selectivity, supporting *Poetry*'s mission to only publish the best verse and perpetuating an idea of scarcity that, as I explained in the previous chapter, provided a basis for modern poetic value. Framing had the double effect of encouraging the reader to give sustained attention to the intricate specificity of the poem while simultaneously pledging that the poem was of sufficient quality to be worth the reading effort.

The poem's positioning and the comparison of the poem to the auratic arts affected to some degree how all poems were read in *Poetry*, but it was crucial for the magazine's showcasing and disseminating of Imagism—a free verse form that was deliberate in its use of white space and conscious of its placement on the page.[20] While Imagism has generally been traced back to the work of Henri Bergson and T. E. Hulme, and locates its transnational roots in Japanese verse and visual culture, and while it had been hinted at in other publications such as Harold Monro's *Poetry Review*, it was in the pages of *Poetry* that the movement really took hold.[21] Pound is generally credited with bringing the Imagists to the magazine and to an American audience, through promoting the work of Richard Aldington and H.D. and through penning "A Few Don'ts by an Imagiste," which, along with F. S. Flint's "Imagisme" editorial (itself based on "A Few Don'ts"), critically framed the movement.²² It should be noted, however, that while Pound was one of the first poets to exploit the format of the magazine and its framing of the poem for formal experimentation, Imagism is not simply a case of Pound using Monroe to forward his particular poetic agenda. Monroe was also taking advantage of an *avant-garde* movement that would best illustrate the magazine's bibliographical and poetic possibilities. This fact is confirmed by the number of Imagists or Imagist-inspired poets published in the magazine who had tangential, contentious, or nearly nonexistent relationships with Pound. Amy Lowell, who spun her verse into what Pound would denounce as "Amygism," is perhaps the most obvious example. But *Poetry* was also the first magazine to publish such quasi-Imagists as Carl Sandburg and Wallace Stevens, and it was the first to publish William Carlos Williams in the United States.

Just as it argued for the poem as art object, *Poetry* would claim that the Imagist poem also required a bibliographical format that could present it as a textual object for contemplation. Alice Corbin Henderson, the assistant editor of the magazine, would compare the carefully wrought Imagist lyric to the visual and book arts, claiming that it is "essentially a graphic art, and, like the finest etching, print or wood-cut, depends upon a highly cultivated state in the observer."²³ The reader becomes a connoisseur, admiring the poem not so much for its content as for its image and its play of sound, just as a connoisseur of the book admires etchings and end papers.²⁴

The importance of *Poetry*'s format on Imagism can perhaps best be seen in one of its most famous poems, Pound's "In a Station of the Metro" (fig. 2.2). Published as the last poem in "Contemporania," "In a Station of the Metro" takes up the remaining two-thirds of the final page of the April 1913 issue of *Poetry*.²⁵ The poem, one of the most famous examples of Imagism, has been republished in hundreds of anthologies and critical texts and has been taught in countless classrooms. Its composition is steeped in mythology, much of which Pound generated himself. Pound famously recounts the composition of the poem:

> I found it useful in getting out of the impasse in which I had been left by my metro emotion. I wrote a thirty-line poem, and destroyed it because it was what we call work "of second intensity." Six months later I made a poem half that length; a year later I made the following *hokku*-like sentence:—
>
> The apparition of these faces in the crowd:
> Petals, on a wet, black bough.²⁶

Making Modern *Poetry* 79

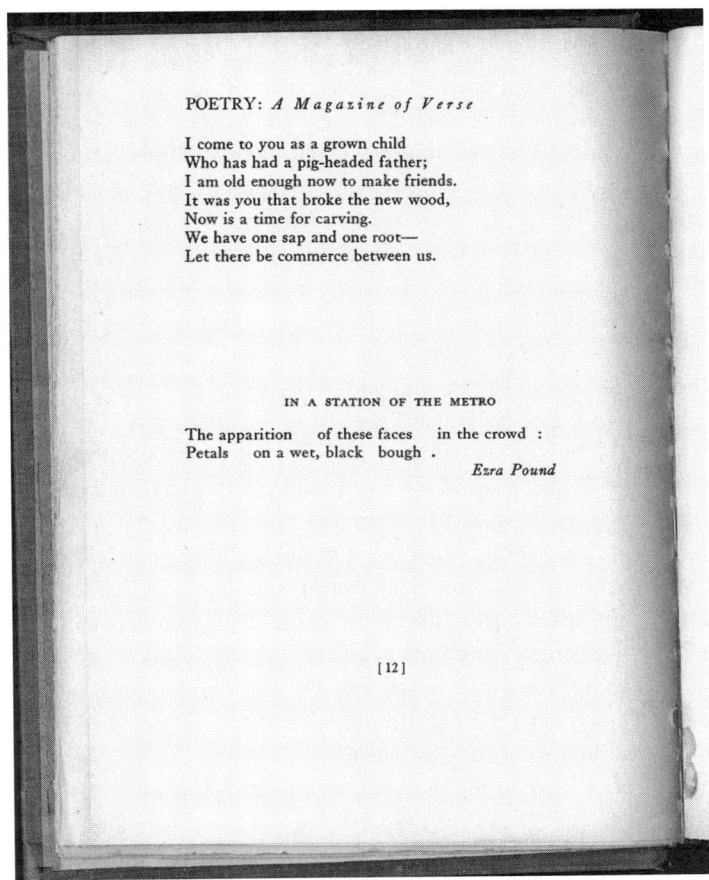

Figure 2.2. Ezra Pound's "In a Station of the Metro," *Poetry* 2, no. 1 (April 1913): 12. The Modernist Journals Project, Brown University.

But this is not an entirely accurate recounting. The poem Pound reproduces here is not the one that first found its way into print. It is, rather, a Vorticist rerendering of the poem—Pound's deliberate severing from his Imagiste past. The poem in fact took on many forms, being subsequently printed without the spaces between the words and phrases, with and without the comma after "Petals," with a semicolon replacing the colon—decisions that Pound himself made in subsequent reproductions, so that the composition time of "In a Station of the Metro" is considerably longer than even the eighteen-month trajectory Pound provides.[27] In addition, I haven't found a single reprinting of the poem in a book collection, textbook, or anthology, by Pound or anyone else, where the poem was given its own page.

This first printed version, however (itself one of multiple versions Pound was considering), quite self-consciously exploits its spacing and isolation on the page.[28] Pound had indicated in a letter to Monroe, "In the METRO hokku, I was careful, I think to indicate spaces between the rhythmic units, and I want them observed."[29] He would write in a follow-up letter: "The Station in the METRO: give this whatever space there is left on the page, i.e. set it in the center of whatever white space there is, and group the words" as they would eventually be grouped in the printing.[30] These letters suggest that both Pound, who made the request, and Monroe, who followed through on it, saw the centering of the poem within the white space of the page and the breaking up of the words and phrases (shown in the reproduced *Poetry* page in fig. 2.2) as integral to its meaning.

It is worth considering, then, what meaning this original publication of the poem held that has often been lost in subsequent reproductions. For one thing, the spacing gives the reader pause. Similar to enjambment, the space after "apparition" prompts us to ask, What apparition? What is this apparition doing? We are answered only with the modifying clause "of these faces" and are given a moment to peer into these individual faces before they are lost "in the crowd." We take the line itself as a unit of meaning but then confront the colon and recognize that another line will follow in some relation. With the "Petals" of the next line, we see this relation is one of metaphor (the later substitution of a semicolon for the colon suggests a move from the metaphorical to the metonymic). But these petals are further qualified by being "on a wet, black," producing a striking visual contrast; then the noun, "bough," which is the object of the "wet, black"; and finally a period terminating the relationship and the poem. Beneath this, off to the side, reminding us of the poem's maker: "*Ezra Pound.*"

Just as it emphasizes the syntactical construction of the poem, isolating these words, phrases, and marks of punctuation foregrounds the visual and musical features of the poem—what Pound would later call phanopoeia and melopoeia—where phrases are taken as individual units of meaning but also as material fragments, traces of ink that call attention to their place on the page. They become musical phrases as well, where, rather than conforming to the tick of the metronome, each grouping carries its own time: like quarter notes, the four syllables "of these faces" take the same time to read as the half notes of "Petals" and the whole note of "bough." The words may also be taken as clusters of meaning that become legible with each stop of the Metro train, a modern reading phenomenon related to and predating the "automobi*ll*iteracy" connected to Burma Shave billboard verse and the poems of William Carlos Williams.[31] At moments, the spacing works against other poetic conventions, such as alliteration, where the phrase "black bough" is aurally linked but must traverse a gulf of white space. Framing the poem within a border of white space gives the reader room to contemplate these formal features—without other writing competing for attention—and contributes to the isolation of the poem as a whole.

Looking back on the composition of "In a Station of the Metro," Pound writes that "my experience in Paris should have gone into paint. If instead of colour I had perceived sound or planes in relation, I should have expressed it in music or in sculpture. Colour was, in that instance, the 'primary pigment'; I mean that it was the first adequate equation that came into consciousness."[32] In this first incarnation of the poem, however, with its close attention to typographical and formatting possibilities, Pound does largely succeed in placing planes in relation and making words into music—in painting with ink. It is only in subsequent reproductions that these qualities are lost or muted. Just as much of this meaning was lost as the bibliographical code was changed and the gaps patched in subsequent revisions and reproductions, "Station" could originally have been effectively presented only in a little magazine such as *Poetry* that framed the poem for contemplation apart from discursive distractions.

The Open Door Shuts: From Magazine Verse to Modern Poetic Genre

Poetry's presentation of "Station," along with Imagism and *vers libre* more generally, depended not only on an aestheticization of the poem through bibliographical isolation and comparison to art objects but also on the recognition that this textual construction was indeed a poem in the first place, to be distinguished from mere "verse." For many critics today, the distinction between poetry and verse may be an obvious, or even natural, one. As I argue, however (much like notions of objective poetic value I discussed in the previous chapter) this distinction is historically produced through a definition of poetry as less a *form* governed by traditional features of verse (such as rhyme and meter) than a *genre* that was discursively, bibliographically, and institutionally determined. These determining forces combine to produce what Tzvetan Todorov refers to as generic "horizons of expectation" for readers and "models of writing" for authors who write in the function of (though not necessarily in agreement with) existing generic systems.[33] This definition of poetic genre can be traced to a variety of origins, such as the writings of the French Symbolist poets at the end of the nineteenth century, but, as a central publishing organ for a burgeoning poetic modernism, *Poetry* was particularly influential in solidifying the distinction between "poetry" and "verse."

For *Poetry* these were receding horizons and elastic models, where expectations of what constituted poetry were continually being transcended in the pursuit of uninhibited excellence. As Monroe explains, "The Open Door will be the policy of this magazine—may the great poet we are looking for never find it shut, or half-shut, against his ample genius! To this end the editors hope to keep free of entangling alliances with any single class or school. They desire to print the best English verse which is being written today, regardless of where, by whom, or under what theory of art it is written."[34] The magazine was largely successful in this policy. As Monroe would reflect in 1918 upon the magazine's first five years: "*Poetry* has frankly tried to widen the poet's range, to question conventional barriers, whether technical or spiritual, inherited from the past, and help to bring the modern poet face to face with the modern world. We have printed not only odes and sonnets, but imagistic songs, futuristic fugues, fantasies in *vers libre*, rhapsodies in polyphonic prose—any dash for freedom which seemed to have life and hope in it—a fervor for movement and the beauty of open spaces—even if the goal was vague and remote, or quite unattainable in the distance."[35] Aside from its investment in Imagism, which could be seen to relish in the "beauty of open spaces" within and between poems on the page, *Poetry* would make a substantial commitment to pushing formal conventions and the boundaries between verse and prose. In its first two years, the magazine would publish about half a dozen substantial narrative poems,[36] about half a dozen prose poems,[37] and nine poem sequences.[38] Such long forms (in contrast to the short lyric that Palgrave and others had seen as the dominant mode of Romantic and Victorian poetry) underscore *Poetry*'s willingness to devote a significant number of pages to a single poet in a way that was generally impracticable in mass-circulation magazines.

Breaking barriers posed some difficult questions, though. If these new forms abandoned the strictures of rhyme and meter and if prose paragraphs

Making Modern *Poetry* 83

and dramas were suitable for publication in a magazine devoted to the poem, just where were the lines to be drawn? Just what was modern poetry? Edgar Lee Masters would attempt to answer the question, What is poetry? by claiming that "the complete artist" is not bound by inherited ideas of form but "must accept whatever forms are necessary to achieve the poetical effect," going on to claim that the vibrations that truly matter in poetry are not sonic or visual, but the "vibrations of the soul." In what would seem to be an inescapable tautology, the poet proves his soul by what he writes, and the reader recognizes this writing as poetry because it is the true expression of the poet's soul. Through this formula, Masters trusts, "someone may construct a definition of poetry—a definition that will include all poetry worth including and will exclude all writing which is only verse."[39]

This definition that privileges "poetry" over "only verse" appears throughout *Poetry*. As Monroe points out in one of her editorial "Reviews," many books of verse make it to the magazine, "of which a few are poetry. Sometimes the poetry is an aspiration rather than an achievement; but in spite of crude materials and imperfect artistry one may feel the beat of wings and hear the song. Again one searches in vain for the magic touch, even though the author has interesting things to say in creditable and more or less persuasive rhymed eloquence."[40] Again, the poet is not defined by her achievement, the material she wishes to work with, or her level of artistry; rather, she is a poet because she has a touch of indefinable magic and because she aspires to some elusive music. The distinction being made here is ultimately one between objective (and, hence, more difficult to dismiss) formal accomplishment—the ability to write a sonnet in accordance with certain historically held standards of rhyme and meter, for example—and a more elusive, subjective notion of genre that need not meet those standards.

As many of these forms were potentially encroaching on the realm of prose, the delineation of poetic genre was at the same time necessarily distinguished from prose, a form that had become the basis for most other types of writing—the news, the narrative, the essay—that were dominant throughout mass print culture. The enlargement of poetic genre offered the possibility that prose, that great usurper, both in the popular press and in the universities, could itself be usurped.[41] Thus, while the magazine went to great lengths to define poetic genre, it seemed to go out of its way *not* to delineate these other genres. Those who wrote in them were generally lumped together simply as prose writers, or, as Monroe terms them, "paragraphers."[42] Prose was simply one means of writing the narrative or the drama, which could also be effectively done in verse, a conviction that served as the basis for the early promise to contributors (and a response to Palgrave's dominating lyric) that all kinds of poems "will be considered—narrative, dramatic, lyric—quality alone being the only test of acceptance."[43]

Through this dual distinction—the poem becomes that which is neither formally verse nor generically prose—*Poetry* attempted to redefine the scope of poetic genre. Beyond offering individual instances of innovation and usurpation, however, the magazine promised an entire forum for poetic contemplation that grew out of and helped contextualize the individual instance. As one circular would claim, "*Poetry* offers a chance to be heard by their audience, in their own place, without the limitations imposed by the popular magazines. And to lovers of poetry it offers each month a sheaf of new verse in delicate form uninterrupted by prose demanding a different mood."[44] The magazine as a whole requires a different strategy of reading than that used for news items, opinion pieces, or even narrative prose typical of the mass-circulation (and, it should be noted, many little) magazines.

This reading strategy was encouraged not only by the magazine's editorials and other critical discourse but also through the bibliographical framing of the poem that encourages isolated contemplation and helps condition *Poetry*'s generic horizons of expectation. The frame both creates a space for certain kinds of texts and keeps them from radiating outward to other texts, so that they retain generic integrity.[45] *Poetry*'s thick framing allows for individual texts to express a poetic function with minimal contamination from, or confusion with, other extrapoetic texts (which are themselves ancillary to poetic texts). *Vers libre*, polyphonic prose, and other textual constructions are understood to be poetic because they convey an aestheticized poetic function outlined in the magazine's critical discourse and because there is little chance that they will be called upon to function in this particular context (as they well might in other periodical contexts) as social or political texts. Not only does framing allow for individual texts to be taken as poems, regardless of their formal construction, but—much like books arranged in a collection or paintings organized in a gallery—the combinations of these poetic texts provide an expansive notion of poetic genre through "family resemblances" that link traits so that texts as diverse as a two-line poem and a verse play can both be labeled poetry.[46] These texts may have relatively little in common with one another, but their relationship can be traced through a succession of intermediate texts, such as the dramatic monologue.

The ordering of poems into a genre is not merely a formal matter, how-

Making Modern *Poetry* 85

ever. It is also an institutionally determined one. These texts are thought to be generically similar—members of the genre of poetry—in part because they are published in a magazine called *Poetry*. It is difficult to read the editorials (or the circulars or correspondences, or this chapter for that matter) without recognizing an emphasized connection between the genre of poetry in general and this particular instantiation of it, *Poetry*. The connection is doubly metonymic. While poems will differ in terms of subject matter and form, any (noncritical, paratextual) writing is poetic simply by virtue of its appearing in *Poetry*'s pages and—like the book in the collection or the valued poem in poetic tradition—the poem in the magazine is interchangeable with any other insofar as it exemplifies the genre of poetry instantiated in *Poetry*. At the same time, the addition of each poem widens the scope of both *Poetry* and the poetic genre that *Poetry* stands in for (but in doing so calls that generic definition into question).

Poetry magazine is also discursively and institutionally framed within a larger field of periodical production, so that poems are understood to function differently within this magazine than they do in others less dedicated to exploring the contours of poetic genre.[47] To fully understand this framing, it is necessary to examine a wider field of periodical production than that which literary scholars have generally considered, accounting for *Poetry*'s relationship not only to the other modern little magazines but also to the varied terrain of mass-circulation magazines that includes the "quality journals," such satirical magazines as *Life*, and such race-conscious magazines as the *Crisis*. This will serve to underscore alternative poetic configurations and functions to those offered in *Poetry* and often privileged in studies of poetic modernism.

A Cinderella Corner in the Ashes? *Poetry* and the Journals of Quality

He: One of my best poems went all over the country.
She: And was it finally accepted?

—*Book Lover*

In the editorial "The Motive of the Magazine," coming at the tail end of the first issue of *Poetry*, justifying the writing that preceded it and the many years of writing to follow, Harriet Monroe complains of the plight of the poem in the current publishing scene. She explains that the "popular magazines can afford her but scant courtesy—a Cinderella corner in the ashes—

because they seek a larger public which is not hers, a public which buys them not for their verse but for their stories, pictures, journalism, rarely for their literature [and, almost as an afterthought], even in prose."[48] Such laments would continue throughout the early years of *Poetry*, both within the magazine and in its correspondences and advertising circulars. "The popular magazines are printing continually less verse," one circular complains, "and rarely verse beyond page-end length and importance. Their editors blame the public, asserting that there is no demand for poetry. We believe that there is a public for poetry, but that it is scattered and unorganized. Poetry has no organ to speak for it, and its public does not know where to find it."[49] In a letter to Monroe, Ezra Pound would go so far as to claim that these magazines were deliberately suppressing modern poetry, as he erratically and unabashedly names names:

> I have said , in print , and I can not repeat it too often that "The Atlantic," "Harpers," and the "Century" have done more harm to american letters than the worst and yellowest of journals. They had some virtue in 1870 and they have tried to chain american letters to the year of and style of the Philadelphia Centenial. And they have fought tooth and nail against every living manifestation of the art, against every progress and against every discovery. . . . How any lover of poetry with blood in his veins can stand the state of stodge artificiality and woodenness Is past my comprehension , and if it is any consolation to those who don't , and as it is proper to say so for the instruction of the public , let it stand , that I have never heard an american artist speak of these publications with anything save the most scathing contempt , and that the letters from the editors of these periodicals to the english authors by virtue of whose names they maintain their position , these letters are passed bout and quoted here as matter for side splittin mirth and ridicule , and they and the public may as well know it.[50]

Pound's rants against magazine verse, while venomous, were nothing new. A sonnet published in 1898 in the Chicago-based the *Chap-Book*—the first American little magazine and a formidable influence on *Poetry*[51]—admits to the poet writing poems that are stale and unimaginative:

> But, since laboriously in them I've brought
> The trite old names from "Cynthia" to "Pan:"
> Because I've used big words and not a thought,
> Because they will not parse, nor rhyme, nor scan:
> Methinks by *Harper's*, or by *Century* they'll be bought.[52]

It's not surprising that magazines such as *Harper's Monthly Magazine* (1836-1919), the *Atlantic Monthly* (1857-), and the *Century Illustrated Monthly Magazine* (1882-1913) would be singled out by proponents of the little magazines. As Richard Brodhead has noted, in the years between 1860 and 1900, these big monthlies were identified as the three "quality journals," aimed at a high-cultural audience.[53] If the little magazines were to make a bid for their own small plot of the productive literary field, they would need to slay their personal Goliaths, as Pound was attempting to do.

Monroe's claim that these magazines are printing less verse, however, is more suspect and called into question by distantly reading the number of poems in these magazines. Taking the long view, we find that the number of poems published in these magazines between 1880 and 1920 fluctuated greatly, between about twenty and eighty a year (fig. 2.3).[54] The *Atlantic Monthly* shows a peak at the turn of the century and a smaller spike on or about 1910. *Harper's* similarly peaks at the early years of the century, though not as dramatically.[55] The *Century Illustrated Monthly* reaches its apex a decade earlier, in the 1890s, though the drop-off remains relatively consistent in the decades to follow. On average, the *Century* was publishing about twice as many poems as *Harper's* or the *Atlantic*.[56]

A quick quantitative analysis of these three major quality magazines suggests that not only was there not a radical drop-off in the number of poems published in the first decade of the twentieth century, but that—at least for two of the magazines, the *Atlantic* and *Harper's*—there was actually an *increase* in publication at the turn of the century, dovetailing with John Timberman Newcomb's assessment that there was an increase in the books of verse produced during the 1890s and 1900s.[57] This analysis calls into question *Poetry*'s long-accepted claim that there was a dearth of modern verse being produced in other periodicals, thus necessitating the magazine's existence in the first place. More fundamentally, it suggests that *Poetry*'s emergence was not so much a reaction to verse production in the bigger magazines but a particular extension of it: enough verse was being produced and consumed that specialized venues could be supported.

Poetry's call for a Cinderella corner does, however, underscore the poem's long history of marginalization in popular periodicals. Those twenty to eighty poems were, after all, out of more than fifteen hundred pages. A liberal estimate would place poetry at somewhere around 5 percent of these magazines' total output. Although these numbers hadn't changed significantly in half a century, *Poetry* capitalized on the *perception* that the poem

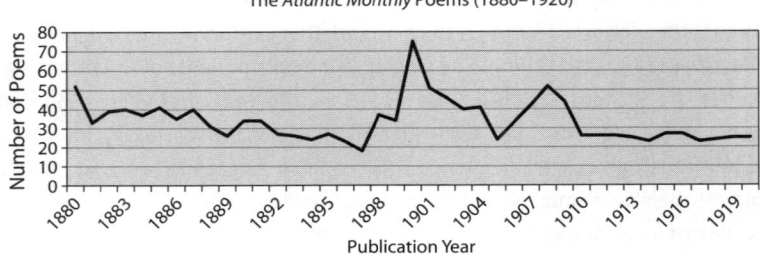

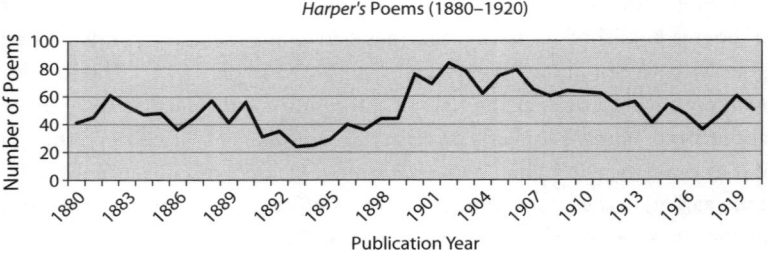

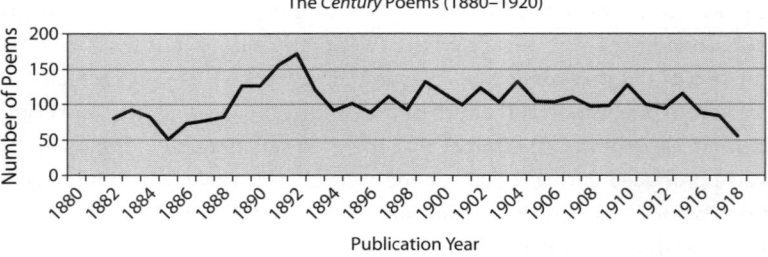

Figure 2.3. Charts showing the number of poems published in the *Atlantic Monthly*, *Harper's*, and the *Century* (1880-1920).

was losing ground in these magazines to encroaching prose (both nonfiction articles and fictional stories), as well as to illustrations, advertisements, and that increasingly pervasive modern text, the photograph.

Even this, however, was an old argument. In the first year of its publication (1836), *Harper's* published two articles on the marginalization of poetry, "Have Great Poets Become Impossible?" and "Lack of Poetry in America," in its own attempt to stake out a place for poetry.[58] Nor was this marginalization lost on the poets of previous generations. As one poet put it more than a decade before *Poetry*'s inception:

> Prose now usurps our Magazines; we find
> That poetry holds there no lofty seat,
> But, to two small lines, or four at most, confined,
> "Sings small," low crouching at the usurper's seat.[59]

This slight lyric, stuck in the corner of a magazine page, speaks to the increased marginalization of poetry at the usurpation of photographs, illustrations, and especially prose in its fictional and nonfictional forms (the very usurpation that, as I have suggested, *Poetry* was combatting in its disparaging of "paragraphers" and its attempts to expand the poem's generic role, though in the process severing the genre from the rich networks of association that other print culture venues often embraced). These slight lyrics were the mainstay of such weeklies as *Collier's*, which placed poems directly in their three-column format alongside prose, relying upon formal verse features to distinguish it as poetry. In these magazines, poems do seem to be an afterthought, plugging a hole or rounding out a page. As the poem suggests in its own slight size, the importance of poetry could be seen not only in its fewer numbers but also (challenging Palgrave's lyrical notions) in the shortened form of the poem itself—which, unlike the Imagist poems in *Poetry*, lacked the presumption that big poems can come in small packages.

One important way to increase the length and importance of the poem was to give it a frame of one's own. As one poem, "Wide Margins," published in the *Atlantic Monthly* in 1902, exclaims:

> Print not my Book of Days, I pray,
> On meager page, in type compact,
> Lest the Great Reader's calm eye stray
> Skippingly through from fact to fact;
>
> But let there be a liberal space,
> At least 'twixt lines where ill is writ,
> That I with tempering hand may trace
> A word to dull the edge of it.
>
> And save for me a margin wide
> Where I may scribble at my ease

> Elucidative note and guide
> Of most adroit apologies!⁶⁰

Wide margins do not only bibliographically distinguish the poem from surrounding prose but offer both writer and reader a space for contemplation as well as a forum for commentary through marginalia. This is a point that *Poetry* would pick up on, liberally deploying white space as an aid to critical reading.

Many magazines—including those magazines Pound castigates—heeded this call for wide margins. Although they typically printed prose in two columns, they used the full width of the page to print poems. There is an obviously practical reason for this: the line may not fit in the column. Many magazines did not necessarily prize the integrity of the poetic line, however, as is evident in the frequent indenting of the ends of Whitman's long lines. Likewise, such magazines as *Collier's* simply tended to select poetic forms, such as ballads, with inherently shorter lines. As is the case with *Poetry*, there was a deliberate decision to take the poem out of the column and frame it within a wide margin or an ornate border.

This framing signaled an effort to make poems into aesthetic objects for contemplation. Although prose texts frequently reinforced one another in topic or theme, poems were to be taken as self-contained texts intended more as respite from the other writing on the page than as something to be read alongside it and integrated into the magazine as a whole. If, as William Carlos Williams famously remarked, it is difficult to get the news from poems, this was in part because poems often lacked news and many readers had learned not to look for it there anyway. This aestheticization of the poem in the popular magazines is ultimately less sure than it is in *Poetry*, however, because, although there is a thick frame surrounding the poem, there are also more varied genres and discourses that place greater interpretive pressure on the text's edges, so that some poems, especially those deeply engaged with issues of social modernity, may find resonance in other texts.⁶¹

Amy Lowell's "The Starling," published in the July 1912 *Atlantic Monthly*, three months before *Poetry* brought out its first issue, provides an example of white space as a means of poetic framing (fig. 2.4). The poem is bibliographically and thematically isolated from the accompanying article entitled "The Aesthetic Value of Efficiency" and taken as a thing in itself. One would be hard pressed to argue that "the small / Barred window of my jail"

Making Modern *Poetry* 91

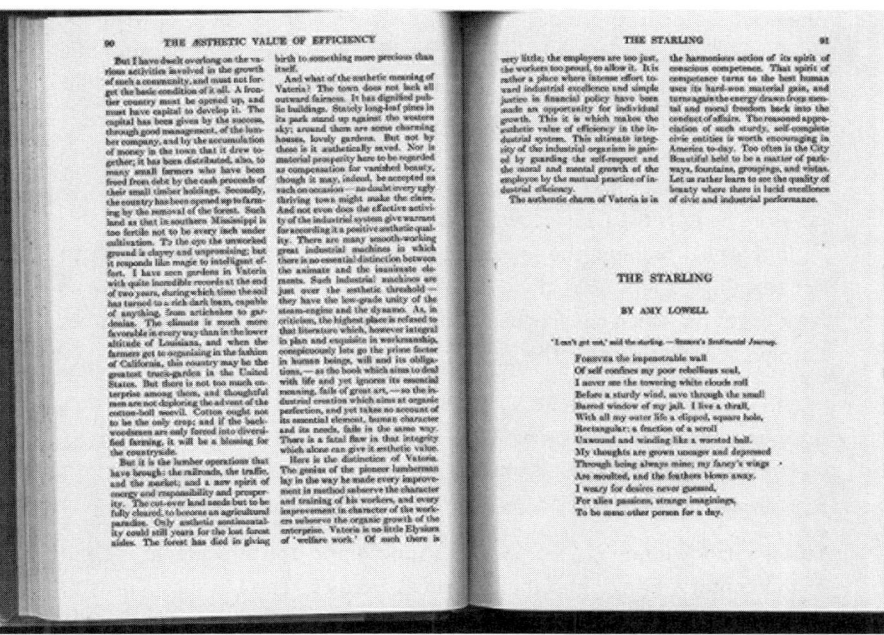

Figure 2.4. Amy Lowell's "The Starling," *Atlantic Monthly* 110, no. 1 (July 1912): 91.

refers to actual incarceration as a result of social protest or political unrest, or that "fancy's wings" refers to recent innovations in aeronautics, let alone to make some direct connection to the beauty of working towns that is the subject of the article. Rather, these images work in a different register, contributing to the metaphor of the starling that extends and combines long ornithological and astral literary traditions to comment on the sorrow of the soul. An invested reader, however, could—in a way altogether unavailable in *Poetry*—attempt to forge a connection between the texts, perhaps seeing the loss of the starling as the cost of industrial efficiency, although this would not appear to be the authorial or editorial intent.

A logical extension of this framing of the poem on the page is the relegation of the poem to the magazine's back pages, alongside jokes, cartoons, puzzles, and stories for children, where it was frequently taken as "light verse." The *Atlantic Monthly* didn't use such pages, but other quality journals, such as the *Century*, did. For many, this was not a place of honor. As one contributor to these pages warns, the poet who chooses to write for this "special column" must be willing to suffer embarrassment because of a changed letter or missing word of a minimally invested editorial staff, "but let the stricken poet or humorist, whichever he is pleased to think himself, take heart, nobody but himself is likely to notice it, and if any one does chance to see that the verse or sketch is meaningless, he will forget all about it before he puts the paper down."[62]

In this environment, the serious poet couldn't help but feel the pinch. In her seemingly slight lyric, the 1900 "Fin de Siècle," satirizing the *Century*'s back pages (in which she frequently published), the much underrated poet Carolyn Wells claims that the loss is more than just the poet's:

> They say the age is frivolous.
> The reason to me seems plain;
> 'Tis because the end of the Century
> Is always "In Lighter Vein."[63]

This is a darkly punning poem (with its apocalyptic overtones set at the end of the century, bringing to mind Thomas Hardy's "The Darkling Thrush") that warns of the dire consequences when poetry—even (or especially) the pithy brand of poetry that Wells herself practices—is not taken seriously. How, after all, can an age be anything but frivolous when some of its most trenchant criticism is kept as far away from the political and social observations of the front pages as possible? Beyond sticking a poem in a corner or isolating it on the page, these back-page poems—conveniently labeled light verse—are kept away from the magazine's more serious work. The next logical step would be to remove the poem from the concerns of the quality journals altogether, giving it exclusive presentation in a magazine called *Poetry*. Alternatively, these so-called light poems could be more fully integrated into a magazine's larger social concerns, as was the case with the satirical magazine *Life*.

Of *Life* and Poetry

> What is Life?
> Life's a whirl of drums and parties, till the nervous frame breaks down.
>
> —*Life*

Life magazine (1883-1936), the popular American weekly humor and general interest magazine produced in the vein of the US-based *Puck* (1871-

1918) and the long-running British *Punch* (1841-2002), presents a scrappy alternative to the book-based form and function of the poem in such modern little magazines as *Poetry*, and to the quality magazines that preceded them. Although *Life* would feature well-known writers such as James Whitcomb Riley and Brander Matthews and would include multiple covers by Norman Rockwell, it also cultivated in such sections as Aut Scissors Aut Nullus a populist participatory journalism akin to that of *Tit-Bits* and the snippet journals I discussed in the introduction, and includes many unattributed (often reproduced) works in its pages.

Life frequently dwelled on rather trivial topics, devoting entire issues to such popular themes as baseball and the Fourth of July, but its status as a humor magazine also allowed it—like the brazen court jester—to make scathing social critiques without losing its head. The magazine had recognized its critical potential from the beginning, noting in its opening issue that "while we do not pledge ourselves to invariable jocularity, we shall try to domesticate as much as possible of the casual cheerfulness that is drifting about in an unfriendly world."[64] Working in a long and subversive satirical tradition, which would be extended in such self-avowed leftist magazines and newspapers as the *New Masses* and the *Daily Worker* (although it was more popular than progressive, cutting across the political spectrum), *Life* mined a vein of jokes and political cartoons to take social issues head-on with the disclaimer that it was all in good fun. At the same time, its many full-page realistic illustrations belie this humor, providing a pathetic counterpoint, so that reading through an issue demands a coming to grips with various competing texts that tread a surprisingly wide affective terrain. These texts, being thematically connected and generically disparate, are not taken as discrete units, however, but are read together in affirmation, redundancy, and contradiction in a heteroglossic mishmash of jokes, cartoons, and illustrations that contribute to a novelization of the page, the issue, and the magazine run as a whole.[65] This novelization not only anticipated many elements of *avant-garde* collage that would break onto the scene a few decades later but also (as I argue in the next chapter) influenced the construction of modern scrapbooks that increasingly adopted a collage aesthetic.

Alongside these texts—taking up many of the same topics and often prominently placed on the page—were numerous poems. If *Poetry* imposed a thick bibliographical frame and a critical discourse that encouraged the close reading of the poem as an aestheticized textual object, and such quality journals as the *Atlantic Monthly* and the *Century* presented a more generically and thematically varied textual terrain but nevertheless largely quarantined the poem from these potentially contaminating texts through its framing or relegation to inconsequential back pages, *Life* placed poems in thin, porous bibliographical and generic frames that encouraged radical intertextuality. This thin framing shattered the aura of the poem, giving it a potential social purchase that it was unlikely to realize in the quality journals or little magazines.

The poem's potential for social purchase that is largely denied through *Poetry*'s format and generic assumptions is illustrated in *Life*'s "Outcasts Number" (fig 2.5).[66] Published October 10, 1912, the month of *Poetry*'s debut, the issue is devoted to the members of society marginalized economically (and, to a lesser extent, by gender). As with many of *Life*'s issues, this one prominently displays a poem on the front page. "The Beneficiary," heroic in its couplets, stages an address from a worker to his boss (who likely isn't listening):

> I am as large a man as you, as strong;
> I feel as much as you and love as long;
> Your face is fine, your hands are soft and white,
> But I am scarred and gnarled with toil of day and night;
> Yet, since I do your work while you make song,
> You are Powerful Right and I the Wrong.
>
> Once you and I by preordaining Fate
> Were helpless, just alike, just animate;
> Left here to live and love, to grow and breed—
> Yet something makes you flower and makes me struggling weed;
> And I, your workingman, must labor late
> That you, secure, may be compassionate![67]

The laborer laments that, although the two are naturally equals, through a twist of social circumstances, the worker is subordinate to his boss and "I, your workingman, must labor late / That you, secure, may be compassionate." The poem is confident in its iambic pentameter, employs the assonance of "scarred" and "gnarled" to good effect, and puns on the political Right and Left. In an act of poetic gender bending that is rather unusual for the time, the poem, written by a woman, Ruth Kauffman, has a male persona. Closer reading shows a cognitive dissonance between the poet and the speaker as well that suggests a leftist ideology at work. While the laborer

Making Modern *Poetry* 95

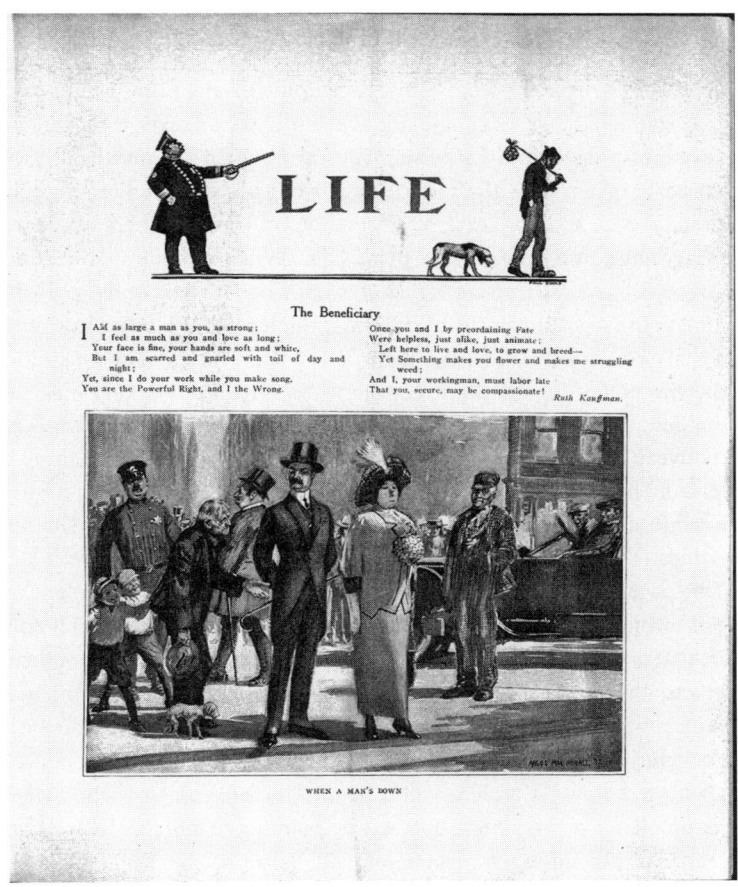

Figure 2.5. *Life* 60, no. 1563 (October 10, 1912): 1945.

begs to benefit from his boss's compassion, the poem suggests that it is, ironically, the employer who is truly "the beneficiary" of his worker's exploited labor, and perhaps even the poem itself, this beneficiary's song. Relying on the typical tricks of the critical trade—reading closely for formal elements, speaker, tone, points of contradiction, and paradox—one finds that "The Beneficiary" hangs together as an object of close critical scrutiny, and, without too much stretching, we could imagine the poem having found its way into *Poetry*.

But a contextualized reading of the poem doesn't stop here. To get a fuller sense of the poem, we need to consider how it contributes meaning to—and adopts meaning from—its interaction with the other elements on the page (which is true, of course, for all the magazine's texts, though I have centered my analysis on the poem). Set just beneath the masthead, "The Beneficiary" resonates with the cartoon of a cop on the beat directing away a "scrappy" man and dog. And, as affirmation or negation, there interposes the magazine's title, as if to say "that's Life." While the plump officer and handkerchief-toting tramp are caricatures, they nonetheless underscore and legitimate the legal apparatus of the state, reinforcing the poem's observation that "You are the Powerful Right, and I the Wrong." The illustration below the poem depicts the spectrum of society: the working man in a flannel suit, the developing middle class in an automobile, the necessary cop, the nouveau riche, and again the man and his dog (older now and taunted by children). The scene is much less funny. "When a Man's Down" is a pageant play reinforcing the poem's lesson not to disrupt the social order. The man who doesn't thank his beneficiary may find himself without benefit.

This page and this poem also resonate with the issue as a whole. Even before turning to this first page, the reader is confronted with a full-color cover that presents a realistic illustration of a naked Christ-like figure thrust up as a torch into the cosmos by "The Hand of Fate." Further into the issue is an illustration of a downtrodden man escorted by St. Peter through the pearly gates while the rich, who have become "the outcasts," look on from a dark abyss below.[68] Carolyn Wells's poem, "Ifs for Women," supplements the issue's focus on economic outcasts by pointing to women outcasts and the force of the suffragist movement.[69] "A Ballad of the Times" cautions against radical change, claiming that

> each of us clings to a "movement"
> That seems to him clearly the best
> To further our social improvement
> In spite of the rest.[70]

A full accounting of the issue necessitates an examination of its advertising alongside those other kinds of texts that have more frequently received critical attention. Advertisements for cameras and perfume, encouraging personal conspicuous consumption, seem to thwart any raising of class consciousness that may have occurred elsewhere in the issue. Indeed, the automobile—one of the most prominent signs of class disparity depicted in the front-page illustration—is the subject of five separate advertisements.[71] In the context of the issue as a whole, the meaning of "The Beneficiary" is increasingly complicated. While the St. Peter illustration may encourage the meek to shut up about their situation, lest they not inherit a place in heaven, and the poems caution against too radical reaction, the advertisements quietly feed the consumerist desires and reinforce the capitalist system that allows some to benefit while others are cast out. A reader may be variously attentive to these complicating and contradictory texts, but it is difficult to imagine she doesn't to some degree bring them to bear on her reading of "The Beneficiary."

There is also resonance from issue to issue and across the magazine's run. This is perhaps truer for a weekly magazine such as *Life* than for the monthlies: one may have just finished reading through one issue before receiving the next. As part of its subscription campaign, *Life* would frequently print teasers for upcoming issues. The "Dramatic Number" issue announces, "Next week will usher in the Outcast Number of Life. In order to avoid this superlatively sad, but intensely human number, be careful and do not send in your subscription at once."[72] "Sad" and "intensely human" have already set affective expectations. Similarly, later issues would resonate with the "Outcasts Number." The "Debutante's Number" presents a social regime that is itself largely dependent on reeling some people in and casting others out.[73] Soon there would be a whole "Auto Number" devoted to the automobile that had already become a focus of the advertising.[74] At a time when people are perhaps more disposed to remembering the outcasts among us, the "Christmas Number" returns to the theme.[75] In two full-page pictures, it contrasts two kinds of hunger: men in the stock market hungering after money and men in a line hungering after bread.[76] Similarly, "Skinny's Christmas Dream" depicts a frail, hungry boy at a banquet.[77] Another pathetic illustration presents a girl digging a doll out of the trash for what is presumably her little brother, with the caption, "There, now, Jimmy! Didn't I Tell You There's a Santa Clause?"[78]

To fully understand the significance of "The Beneficiary" requires not only a close reading of textual elements but also a telescoping outward to other contextual frames: the page, the issue, the run of the magazine, the larger culture of mass print. It may be that we have in our daily lives largely become accustomed to employing cross-genre, multimedia, and radial reading strategies with newer electronic media forms, such as websites, but— although mass magazines share many structural affinities with this newer media—this is not the kind of reading that critics of literary modernism have typically practiced. In part, this is because critics still tend to privilege an individual author function (even while acknowledging that the author lacks a firm grip on intentionality) that is confirmed in the reading of discrete texts. Indeed, the fact that *Life* did not publish many of the poets who often have come to define the canon of poetic modernism—those figures who found their way into *Poetry* and the other little magazines—discourages us from relying too heavily upon authorship as a primary marker of literary quality or meaning. Rather, we are better able to toggle between critical methods: we can perform close readings when we seek to better understand the aesthetic achievement of particular poems and poets; we can turn to more contextual readings when we are primarily interested in how those same poems reflected and informed the social and cultural conditions of modernity. While I do not think these twin approaches can be divorced even for those poems, such as "The Beneficiary," that we may be tempted to place in the secondary poetic ranks or altogether cast out of our critical ken as "verse," the inclusion of highly regarded poems in magazines that beg for such contextual analysis points even more directly to a necessary negotiation of aesthetic and political value in our charting of poetic modernism, as is often the case in the African American magazine the *Crisis*.

Poetry and the *Crisis*

The *Crisis* exemplified in its early years the multiple roles that a poem could play as it often encouraged both aesthetic and socially engaged readings. From its beginning in 1910, the *Crisis* would reach a national audience, with a circulation in its first decade of approximately one hundred thousand subscribers (as compared to *Poetry* numbering in the hundreds and low thousands, and *Life* hovering around one million). Like *Life*, it did not pretend to the status of a fine book in the way that *Poetry* did; rather, its cover art and larger format resembled that of many other mass-circulation magazines. Unlike many of these magazines, however, the *Crisis* was targeted at an African American readership (or one sympathetic to the African American cause) and had an explicit agenda of social justice. What was an occasional concern for *Life*, as depicted in its outcasts issue, pervaded every issue of the *Crisis*.

This agenda is evident in a "Woman's Suffrage Number," published in September 1912, a month before *Poetry* magazine began. Along with a number of news and opinion pieces, the issue included a poem, "Brother Baptis' on Woman's Suffrage," by Rosalie Jonas. In contrast to how the poem was isolated and framed for contemplation in *Poetry* magazine, this poem here is placed at the bottom of a page concluding "A Woman's Suffrage Symposium," where it reinforces the long-standing (at times vexed) connection between African American and women's voting rights that is stressed in the symposium and throughout the issue as a whole. As "Brother Baptis'" recognizes:

> When hit come ter de question er de female vote,
> De ladies an' de culled folks is in de same boat.[79]

"The Foundling Hospital," one of the best-known poems by Jonas, a leading figure in the Harlem Renaissance, would be published in *Poetry* the following year.[80] Such publication suggests the extent to which the Harlem Renaissance would be recognized as an important movement for aesthetic as well as political reasons, expanding beyond a specifically African American circuit of publication and readership. It should be noted, however, that while "The Foundling Hospital" has a general message of social justice, it is not written in dialect in the way that "Brother Baptis'" is—a linguistic convention that has long been taken as a (frequently problematic) marker of race—and it is difficult to locate the poem in a specifically African American context. Likewise, *Poetry*'s framing of "The Foundling Hospital" isolates it from the kind of immediate political impact it may have through juxtaposition to other texts, as is the case in the *Crisis*.

Less immediately contextualized is Jean Toomer's poem "Banking Coal."[81] The poem, giving a slice of life in blank verse, suggests Robert Frost, especially in the concluding lines:

> I'd like to tell those folks that one grand flare
> Transferred to memory tissues of the air
> Is worth a life, or, for dull minds that turn in gold,
> All money ever saved by banking coal.

While the poem is concerned with "banking" and spending, perhaps implying a subtle critique of capitalism, this is the kind of poem that easily could have appeared in *Poetry*. And, while not framed in the way that it would be in that magazine, the poem seems to have little to do with anything else on the page.

A careful reader of the magazine, however, will recall the "Opinions of W. E. B. Du Bois" on coal from ten pages earlier, in which Du Bois explains that coal "is not yet scarce but it is made artificially scarce so as to raise prices. . . . More mines are opened than are needed and in these mines men are kept at work on part time, so that when the demand for coal is highest all may work, and when it is lowest, some may starve. And this is done to support with high profits the largest number of coal operators."[82] Du Bois goes on to exclaim that "the great coal and iron and steel companies centering in Philadelphia and Pittsburgh, with their stock owned by good and simple Quaker folk who preach sweetness and light, and their policies dictated by metal-hearted bandits, own West Virginia." Toomer's poem is not explicit on these points—and it may well be that he did not intend them to be in his poem—but its selection for inclusion in this issue of the *Crisis* necessarily highlights these concerns, encouraging one to read them into "Banking Coal" and foregrounding the role of the editor (alongside the author) as an agent for making textual meaning.

The case is similar with "America," by Claude McKay, which appeared in the same issue, anticipated by a review of McKay's first collection, *Harlem Shadows*, in which Jesse Fauset notes, "The first thought that will flash into the mind of the reader of 'Harlem Shadows' will be: '*This is Poetry!*' . . . Mr. McKay possesses a deep emotionalism, a perception of what is fundamentally important to mankind everywhere—love of kind, love of home, and love of race. . . . He has dwelt in fiery, impassioned language on the sufferings of his race. Yet there is no touch of propaganda. This is the truest mark of genius."[83] Aside, perhaps, from pointing out the love and sufferings of race in particular, the review could appear in any number of magazines, with its celebration of universal themes, its rejection of "propaganda" (which we might also read as "verse"), and its embracing of "genius."

This reading of McKay has continued through the present day. As William J. Maxwell explains, because the poem "America" is "lushly allusive, semantically knotty, imagistically dense, hooked on conceptual tension, the sonnet's refusal to liquidate iambic pentameter and other high modernist enemies nonetheless begs for high modernist interpretive protocols."[84] The presentation of "America" in Maxwell's *The Complete Poems of Claude McKay* certainly encourages such deep textual interpretation, with a standard bibliographical framing not unlike that of *Poetry*'s that emphasizes the individuality and generic distinction of the individual poem. And it serves the critical aims of Maxwell and others, who have attempted to recover McKay as a poet deserving of the kinds of close readings long reserved for the likes of Eliot and Pound. Within such bibliographical and critical contexts, Maxwell highlights the sonnet's juggling of the Petrarchan and Shakespearean forms, arguing that the poem is a discordant verbal mirror—with rhymes divided against stanzas and the first block against the second—so that courtly love becomes courtly intrigue and the speaker a revolutionary secret agent. From these linguistic cues, Maxwell attempts to place the text within a more general historical context of government surveillance and leftist political movements that were often connected to a radical black agenda and included such figures as McKay and Langston Hughes.

Direct evidence for such a historical connection is not, however, readily evident in the text of the poem. As with many of McKay's poems, "America" is hardly textually marked with race at all and depends on context for such meaning. The clearest suggestion of race in the poem comes in the line beginning "Darkly I gaze," which hints at the race of the speaker, though "darkly" in fact modifies the act of gazing and, as Maxwell and others have noted, alludes to 1 Corinthians 13:12: "For now we see through a glass darkly."

This line would have particular resonance, though, with the reprinting of "America" in the *Crisis*. The sonnet is the lead-off item in "The Looking Glass," a section that gathered together news items and editorial pieces on race relations from around the world, functioning as telescope and microscope as well as social mirror.[85] Included in the section are "Notes on Lynching" that highlight the passing of a national antilynching bill that gives the federal government jurisdiction in places where lynching may be a threat, references to the American intervention in Haiti and the Dominican Republic, and a story on a Jamaican regiment that refused British orders to sail for colonized India. The section also details an article, "Without Honor," that McKay wrote for the *Liberator*, in which he criticizes Marcus Garvey's Back to Africa movement. As McKay claims, Garvey's "spirit is revolutionary, but his intellect does not understand the significance of modern revolutionary movements. . . . The most puzzling thing about the 'Back to Africa' propaganda is the leader's repudiation of all the fundamentals of the black worker's economic struggle."[86] McKay further notes that Garvey never urged African Americans to organize in industrial unions, denounced Socialists and Bolshevists for placing black workers under the banner of white labor, and derided the NAACP for including white leaders and members in its cause.

As with the inclusion of Toomer's "Banking Coal," the placing of "America" in close proximity to McKay's critique of Garvey's movement provides an immediate context for the radical politics that Maxwell and others have located in McKay's poetry, offering a very different lens for reading the poem than that which Fauset gives earlier in the magazine (which, it should be noted, the reader may or may not have encountered—we should not assume that a reader consumes all of a magazine or does so in a linear fashion). The periodical presentation of the poem, therefore, asks the reader to choose between—or somehow bring together—two seemingly contradictory interpretive strategies: one that is based in a historically detached, supposedly objective sense of aesthetic excellence; and one that breaks frames and depends upon porous bibliographical, historical, and political context for its particular meaning. There is not one right answer here. The individual must decide for herself how to take the poem—and in doing so must interrogate her own allegiances to the political and the aesthetic, the historically contingent and the bid for permanence.

Such presentation deeply challenges the aesthetic and political assumptions that undergirded a little magazine such as *Poetry*. But while the *Crisis*, like *Life*, encourages a dialogic reading of the poem into its larger periodical and social contexts, and offers an opportunity for contemporary critics to reconsider poetic modernism as more deeply interconnected with a widespread modern print culture than has previously been assumed, *Poetry* and its ilk largely won out in presenting a strain of poetic modernism invested in the aestheticized text, a notion of poetic genre as apart from verse form, and an emphasis on the individual author. This became the dominant (or only) available dimension of poetic modernism for many poets at the time and for many critics since.

Poetry's Legacy

Poetry's influence on the production and evaluation of poetic modernism could be felt from the beginning, although it was not without its controversy. As one critic writes of T. S. Eliot, an early contributor to the magazine, the curious cataloguing of such things as cigarettes and female smells "certainly have no relation to 'poetry,' and we only give an example ["Rhapsody on a Windy Night"] because some of the pieces, he states, have appeared in a periodical which claims that word as its title."[87] Similarly, the *Dial* writes that the typographical arrangement of Sandburg's "Chicago," first published in *Poetry*, "creates a suspicion that it is intended to be taken as some sort of poetry, and the suspicion is confirmed by the fact that it stands in the forefront of the latest issue of a futile little periodical described as 'a magazine of verse.'" *Poetry*, looking to escalate the argument, circulated the state-

Making Modern *Poetry* 103

ment widely with the retort that "THE DIAL recoils from the 'hog-butcher' school. Our Sandburg is not a Milton any more than Schönberg is a Beethoven."[88] Just as the celebrated composer's free atonality cannot be restricted by the traditional octave, Sandburg's poetry cannot be judged by outdated conventions of metrical verse.

The literary public both in Britain and America eventually did side with *Poetry*, recognizing its importance in the promotion of a certain privileged strand of poetic modernism.[89] A contributor to the *Writer*, for example, remarks in what was by 1921 a critical commonplace (and an echo of Masters's earlier declaration):

> The difference between poetry and verse? Poetry is the language of the soul. . . . External features, such as meter, may be overlooked. Meter is not essential to true poetry. Almost anyone can write verse, but we have very little poetry. Too many verse-writers are trying to be poets, instead of leaving the writing of real poetry to those who are inspired. Of course, it is pleasing to think you are a poet, but if you have n't the divine gift, it is better to seek some other endeavor and thus be one less misfit in the world.[90]

This passage reflects the modernist distinction between poetic genre and verse form that, while not new to *Poetry*, had been vigorously argued for in its pages—both explicitly in its critical discourse and more implicitly through its format. It also emphasizes the scarcity of the poem (not unlike the scarcity that Palgrave and other anthologists had imposed on poetic tradition) and the notion that the writing of poetry (as opposed to verse) is an elite activity, available only to the privileged few.

Poetry's contribution to the redefinition of poetic genre helped to both limit the objects of study and determine the ways in which those objects have been studied. While the demarcation of genre elevated certain figures that found their way into and out of *Poetry*'s pages, it also provided a way to denigrate and eventually ignore those poets and sites of publication that did not fit this restricted definition. No matter how formally accomplished and technically proficient a text may be, it could be relegated to the realm of verse if deemed lacking in some elusive, subjectively determined poetic spirit. As I show in subsequent chapters, these prevailing poetic assumptions fueled the New Critical reading of the poem as an organically connected whole, would govern the politics of poetic reproduction, and would color criteria for the institutionalization of poetic modernism.

We must keep in mind, though, that as much as it sought to model issues on well-made books and to collect poems according to generic similarity, the magazine is in the end just that—a magazine. Certainly, with its paper cover and relatively cheap binding, *Poetry* is more materially ephemeral than a book (a fact further attested to in now-yellowing copies from these early years), and its textual endurance depends in large part upon publications of anthologies and individual volumes of poems, including volumes of selected and collected poems (which I examine in chapter 4), in order to maintain the book collector's hope for permanence. Reading *Poetry* into a wide bibliographical field helps remind us of this fact. As a number of little magazines—notable ones such as the *Little Review* and *Others*, along with countless magazines that scarcely went beyond their first issue—had a format that resembled *Poetry*'s, we might investigate the extent to which *Poetry*'s aestheticization of the modern poem holds true for the little magazine more generally. We might also ask how *Poetry* is different from its larger cousins but how (to a lesser degree) it too is subjected to the porous textual frames and historical contextualization that govern other presentations of poems—even against its stated aims. Finally, we might reconsider *Poetry*'s many formal poems by relative unknowns that resemble those poems commonly found in *Life*, the *Crisis*, and many other periodicals of the time and that have not garnered much critical attention. In doing so, we might continue to problematize the generic assumptions of poetic modernism even as we expand our poetic horizons.

3 Scrapping Modernism
Marianne Moore and the Making of the Modern Collage Poem

> When a thing has been said so well that it could not be said better, why paraphrase it? Hence my writing is, if not a cabinet of fossils, a kind of collection of flies in amber.
>
> —Marianne Moore

In "A Crystal for the Metaphysical," her review of Marianne Moore's 1966 poetry collection *Tell Me, Tell Me: Granite, Steel and Other Topics*, the poet Muriel Rukeyser meditates on the strategies of what has generally been called poetic collage:

> The poet who believes in the materials of the world—written material—in such a way that his desire to include drives him to use them selectively, but in their own voice, is at once faced with questions. How to claim, to make the material one's own, and still leave it to walk among its origins? The traditional assertion that all materials belong to the artist is true in a sense. This is actually an assertion that the artist does not want to own the world but to use the world. It includes the entire range of life in horror and love.[1]

Rukeyser offers various methods and metaphors for this poetic collage, such as that of the scholarly footnote or the film splice (which may characterize her own poetry more than it does Moore's), but her observation is initially prompted by Moore's own depiction of her hybrid poetics. Rukeyser quotes from Moore's famous description of her compositional methods in "A Note on the Notes" in her collection *What Are Years?*:

> A willingness to satisfy contradictory objections to one's manner of writing might turn one's work into the donkey that finally found itself being carried by its masters, since some readers suggest that quotation-marks are disruptive of pleasant

progress; others, that notes to what should be complete are a pedantry or evidence of an insufficiently realized task. But since in anything I have written, there have been lines in which the chief interest is borrowed, and I have not yet been able to outgrow this hybrid method of composition, acknowledgements seem only honest. Perhaps those who are annoyed by provisos, detainments, and postscripts could be persuaded to take probity on faith and disregard the notes.[2]

Not to be deterred by such disclaimers, scholars have often acknowledged the importance of quotation in modern poetry and its distinction from the long tradition of poetic allusion—Shelley to Dante, Dante to Virgil, Virgil to Homer—in its incorporation of not only previous ideas but the precise wording of those ideas (in their original languages) as well, which gives the poem a rich amount of what Leonard Diepeveen refers to as "texture."[3] Likewise, Moore has frequently been recognized as one of the key practitioners of this modern poetic quotation, drawing on a range of high literary and popular texts.[4]

Moore's hybrid method of composition, and modern poetic quotation more broadly, has generally been seen as an exclusive and unproblematic extension of the masculinized visual *avant-garde*, characterized by the aestheticized assemblages of Picasso and Braque, as opposed to the personal realization of the intertextual relationships available in mass print culture. As Marjorie Perloff, one of the most famous proponents of the establishment position, has asserted, "Collage, perhaps the central artistic invention of the *avant guerre*, incorporates directly into the work an actual fragment of the referent, thus forcing the reader or viewer to consider the interplay between preexisting message or material and the new artistic composition that results from the graft."[5] The collage techniques of the visual *avant-garde* are the shining example for the verbal artist looking to subvert tradition and authority, bringing the "real world" into the realm of the poem, just as the visual artist frames it and hangs it on the wall.

Perloff's account is less persuasive, however, when she specifically addresses poetic collage. She argues that collage is "by definition, a visual or spatial concept, but it was soon absorbed into the verbal. . . . But perhaps because verbal, as opposed to visual, collage must be understood metaphorically (words and phrases are not literally pasted and glued together)."[6] To say that poetic collage must merely be understood metaphorically, however, concedes too much ground, denying the spatial dimension of language and severing poetry from its particular material history. Nevertheless, this has remained the dominant view of poetic collage, and it has held even when other, perhaps more fitting, models are available.[7] I don't mean to deny this influence altogether. Moore circulated in a modern New York scene that included notable painters and photo collage artists, such as her good friends Alfred Stieglitz and Joseph Cornell, whose work undoubtedly impacted her developing notions of poetic collage (though, as Moore's exchanges with Cornell suggest, the influence was mutual).[8] I am nevertheless suspicious of the argument that Moore developed a verbal collage technique that can be distinguished from the rather different aims and evidence of cubism and yet is primarily indebted to *avant-garde* visual collage.

Against the critical history that has taken Moore's collage poetry to be a direct extension of the visual *avant-garde*, I suggest that Moore developed what I call a "scrappy poetics" that is largely indebted to the scrapbook as a popular and "feminized" alternative to this formulation—an alternative that calls into question the major assumptions of the historical *avant-garde* (and the modernist understandings of poetry that stem from this *avant-garde*) while foregrounding the material dimension of language that Perloff and others are quick to dismiss. The two scrapbooks that Moore kept in the five years between her graduation from Bryn Mawr and her publication in the little magazines, along with a scrap publication, "The Daily Scale," not only highlight the print sources that would find their way into Moore's poems through quotation and allusion, but they also showcase her various material manipulations of scraps that would be translated into formal techniques in her later collage poetry—offering some of the most salient examples of how scrapbooking's long negotiation of mass print is formally embodied in poetic modernism. With its attention to quotation from popular and distinctly nonpoetic sources, Moore's poetry frequently establishes intertextual relationships comparable to those in popular magazines that I examined in chapter 2 even as it assumes a more contingent value than that posed in the objective anthology. Beyond its particular importance for her own poetry, though, Moore's scrappy poetics offers a way of reading the scrappiness of the modernist long poem more generally, exemplified in such poems as T. S. Eliot's *The Waste Land*, Ezra Pound's *Cantos*, and William Carlos Williams's *Paterson*.

Scrapping Modernism

In an effort to better explain Moore's poetic collage, and her complicated relationship to the visual *avant-garde*, scholars have increasingly recognized the importance of Moore's collecting practices in relation to print ephemera and her gathering of quotations in her notebooks.[9] Until now, however, there has not been a sustained focus on Moore's scrapbooks and material acts of scrapbooking that I believe contributes to a fuller account of the formal structuring of her collage poetry and the basis for her scrappy poetics. It is here that both the source materials for Moore's poetry and her manipulation of those materials are most strikingly on display.

Moore's scrapbooks are typical of modern scrapbooks, which, as Jessica Helfand has argued, "would migrate away from the realm of the domestic, toward a new, often socially alienated and arguably more internalized sense of self" than was exhibited in their nineteenth-century precursors.[10] These scrapbooks point to a historical coincidence between modern scrapbooking and collage as well, in which scrapbookers and visual artists both "grasped the idea of a fragmented world and expressed it through a scrap aesthetic. The arrangement of items in both collage art and scrapbooks functioned in much the same manner."[11] To extend these insights: the long historical trajectory of domestic, feminized scrap collage that I have been tracing throughout this study challenges the long-held assumption that visual (and poetic) collage is the product of a masculinized *avant-garde* that burst onto the scene in the first decades of the twentieth century. In the realm of modern poetry, this is the logic, perpetuated at least from Pound onward, that has either denigrated the feminine or labeled women poets (including Moore, along with H.D. and Mina Loy) as "masculine," in a near-sighted attempt to redeem them for the literary *avant-garde*.

Uncovering the buried connection between the scrapbook and *avant-garde* collage also emphasizes that scrapbooking, like book collecting, is an important *productive* practice that extends beyond private anthologizing or the chronicling of reader response. The scrapbooker is an active participant in reshaping and re-presenting mass print content, highlighting and exploiting thematic or formal connections and differences, and providing key heteroglossic sites where different scraps are brought together, retaining their individual distinctions but adopting new meanings through juxtaposition and recontextualization. The awareness of this productive potential—which often infiltrated the turn-of-the-century discourse surrounding scrapbooking and the debate over snippet magazines that I discussed in the introduction—is a central theme in Moore's early poetry and prose writings that derive from and instruct readings of her scrapbooks and scrap publications.

Pack Rats and Poem Scraps

> An over-fondness for quotations may betray a superficial rather than a thorough reader,—as if one had been, so to speak, at a literary banquet and brought away only the scraps.
>
> —J. Henry Hagar, "A Word about Quotations"

While a number of modern poets—including E. E. Cummings, Edna St. Vincent Millay, Hart Crane, Amy Lowell, and H.D.—kept early scrapbooks foregrounding subjects and ideas they would later tackle in their poetry, Moore was particularly conscious of the formal influence scrapbooking had on her developing poetic sensibilities. Perhaps alluding to the magazine *Tit-Bits*, she would write to her brother John Warner Moore, for instance, that this "is a letter of scraps in the interior of the literary rat's nest. If you must, hire a literary magpie, to select and expound the virtues of its various tid-bits, but don't go away angry."[12] Another time she remarks that "between sorties I work on my poems. If some of them don't materialize this time in breakfast food, I'll kick my scrapbasket to California."[13] Tellingly, she also relays her mother's cautious advice to not publish her early poems because "they're ephemeral."[14] Of the early poems that did "materialize," a great many are about mass print culture and the act of scrapbooking itself (fitting into a long, undiscussed tradition of "scrapbooking poems" that were popular from the mid-nineteenth century onward, which I have previously referenced). As Moore writes in "Holes Bored in a Workbag by the Scissors":

> A NEAT, round hole in the bank of the creek
>   Means a rat;
>   That is to say craft, industry, resourcefulness:
>   While
> These indicate the unfortunate, meek
>   Habitat
>   Of surgery thrust home to fabricate useless
>   Voids[15]

"Rat," the nickname Moore would claim for herself after reading *The Wind in the Willows*, carries the connotation of "pack rat," doubling with the scissors as a means of opening a gash (in the body, the bank, the bag). The scissors, like claws in burrowing and the scalpel in surgery (the subject of "Those Various Scalpels," another early poem concerned with the cleaving of language) become an instrument of (re)making.[16] They craftily fabricate ("fabric" being here a key root word suggesting both textile and text), but what they fabricate are habitats, spaces apart from the useful, places that can be lived in only through the force of habit. Similarly, the poet carves a space for poetry out of and apart from everyday language and materials. As one of Moore's early elaborate free verse constructions radically manipulating the white space on the page, the void points to the importance of the formal employment of spaces as well.

"Apropos of Mice," the poem originally published beneath "Holes Bored in a Workbag by the Scissors," implores:

> Come in, Rat, and eat with me;
> One must occasionally—
> If one would rate the rat at his true worth—
> Practise catholicity.
> Cheesepairings and a porkrind
> Stock my house—good of their kind
> But were they not, you would oblige me? Is
> Plenty, multiplicity?[17]

Inviting Rat into her own neat space, the speaker encourages him to develop more catholic tastes, to find nourishment in different sources, just as the poem and Moore's overall aesthetic are nourished with both the high literary and the popular. Both cheesepairings and porkrinds—markers of high and low culinary culture, respectively—become discarded scraps for the rat. The invitation to partake in these scraps is a constant one: eating cannot be done once and for all time; one needs to do so "occasionally," frequently making an occasion of it and making it ephemeral. Plenty is not multiplicity; it is sufficient to satisfy a need or get a point across, but it doesn't allow for variation, contradiction, proliferation. Reading this poem in conjunction with "Holes Bored in a Workbag by the Scissors" suggests how to draw on sources as well as the catholicity with which sources must be drawn upon, so that, as Moore writes in another early poem, "Diligence is to Magic as Progress is to Flight," "aesthetic procedure . . . dubs them poetic necessities —not curios."[18]

Composition is itself a material act of pasting, as Moore suggests in an early (much rewritten) poem, "Leaves of a Magazine":

Scrapping Modernism

They open of their own will to the place
Where Captain Kidd stands with averted face
And folded arms, as solid as an oak,
His loosely knotted sash and scarlet cloak
Encircling him, and flapping in the breeze
That lines the withered, undulating seas.
Upon the page across from him, a frame
Of knives lie point to point about the name
Of a dim verse fantastically made
In praise of him,—a ragged block of shade;
A block of shade, with blurs and puckers where
Admiring hands have often brought to bear
Their pressure on the picture and the rhyme
Of buccaneering in the olden time.[19]

The poem conflates the historical Captain Kidd and this particular representation of Kidd, collapsing the two into a single referent that is juxtaposed to the verses in praise of him—a kind of second-order representation that confirms the conflation as it points to both the historical figure and the "ragged block of shade." To further complicate things, Moore's lyric encompasses this dialogic interaction in its own representation of the assemblage as a whole—an early attempt to bring mass cultural heteroglossia into her work—so that the poem itself becomes a made thing, confirmed by the (supposedly) actual magazine leaves to which it refers.

The poem can be read as a commentary on the popular collage already evident in snippet culture, which Moore would access through such magazines as *Tit-Bits*, *Life*, and *Punch* that she was reading at the time. The "admiring hands" that have brought their pressure to bear on the relationship between picture and rhyme extend beyond passive reception, however, to also suggest an active material process, such as scrapbooking, that literally presses leaves together as a means of reinforcing textual connection. These early poems grow out of and help inform Moore's scrapbooking practices that would anticipate her most characteristic collage poetry.

Making Marianne

Moore produced two major scrapbooks during the formative years 1909–1914, now housed at the Rosenbach Museum and Library in Philadelphia.[20] These correspond to and illuminate what Patricia Willis has called a "rather hidden life for Marianne, the years between college and her first appearance in a little magazine," although, it should be noted, this time has been made much more visible through Linda Leavell's biography of Moore, *Holding On Upside Down*.[21] The scrapbooks not only helped chronicle the major moments of Moore's life, but, as this was the time when Moore was developing her literary sensibilities and finding her characteristic poetic voice, they are invaluable as a *Künstlerroman* as well, exposing subjects, themes, source materials, and stylistic innovations that would inform much of her later poetry.

In many ways, however, these scrapbooks are quite typical. Moore used modest, commercially produced matte-black books, labeled "Scrap Album" front and center. The construction-paper pages are crumbling and have become detached from their binding. Some clippings have come loose and are now preserved individually in cellophane sleeves. Like many scrapbookers, Moore preserved materials of sentimental value. Her scrapbooks contain various personal items: letters of invitation to Bryn Mawr social events; photos of Lake Placid where Moore worked a stint for Melvil Dewey; a Library of Congress reading card requesting Willard Fiske's *Dante*; correspondences from William Alexander of the *Ladies' Home Journal*; the letter from the US Civil Service Commission, Washington, DC, explaining that her "request providing for an examination for business teacher (male)" for the Carlisle Indian School could not be accepted. And—tucked into a homemade envelope with a watercolor painting of a sparrow and a tree in spring—a copy of a short biography and follow-up letter sent to Harriet Monroe of *Poetry*, regarding her early accepted verses.

Moore also kept in these pages little mementos: sketches of skunks and wolves, construction-paper cutouts of butterflies and birds, a Valentine's Day owl—mementos suggestive of the many animal poems she would later write. The vast majority of the pages, however, are made up of clippings from a handful of newspapers and magazines, as well as a few pamphlets and other printed ephemera.[22] As such, the scrapbook exemplifies what Willis points to as Moore's "life-long habits: a choice of subject matter close at hand and conservation of poetic material for later use."[23] It is certainly tempting to read these clippings against specific poetic lines. Did Moore think back to the article "Hobs vs. Creepers for Ice Work" when she conjured up "An Octopus/of ice" in her long collage poem "An Octopus"?[24] How much did she return to those newspaper pictures of abbeys and cathedrals as she reconstructed her "England?"[25] These are questions certainly worth investigation, some of which I will do here. But beyond tracing the bibliographic genealogy of any particular poem, I aim to show more generally how Moore's scrapbooks stage a process of textual accumulation that importantly illustrates a poet thinking deeply about her poems, meditating on a subject or image, for years perhaps, before it emerges in writing.

The scrapbooks reveal the myriad subjects that Moore would return to throughout her life, limning the contours of a developing artist who worked, as Elizabeth Bishop would put it, like a bird obsessed. Moore pasted in a menagerie of animals, from elephants and tigers to camels and frogs. She included an article on baseball in Japan. References to biology, psychology, and religion. She made anthologies of flower poems such as "A London Flower Show."[26] She clipped pictures of the Brooklyn Bridge, Gibraltar, and Trafalgar Square.

The scrapbooks reveal Moore's early artistic and literary allegiances as well. She kept reviews of plays and ballets as well as news items on Sarah Bernhardt and Marcel Duchamp. The scrapbooks show that from very early on Moore was conversant with the various -isms of the day, including Post-impressionism, Cubism, Futurism, Imagism, and Vorticism—movements she would speak to with such authority in her many articles and reviews. Likewise, the scrapbooks suggest early literary influences, with clippings of poems and reviews of the title figures in her poem "To a Cantankerous Poet Ignoring His Compeers—Thomas Hardy, Bernard Shaw, Joseph Conrad, Henry James," who were key figures in an emerging literary modernism.[27]

At the same time, the scrapbooks demonstrate engagements with social and political contexts that Moore's critics are only beginning to fully appreciate.[28] The scrapbooks illustrate Moore's commitments to women's suffrage in its inclusion of articles, fliers, and pamphlets for the National American Woman Suffrage Association. They present portraits of Presidents Teddy Roosevelt and Woodrow Wilson and pictures of zeppelins that portend a looming world war. Many of these clippings come in the form of political cartoons, a discursive form often containing some of the most trenchant critiques of the status quo. The scrapbooks are likewise riddled with jokes, some taking prominence in the middle of the page, some wedged into corners, turned on their sides, placed anywhere there is a little bit of space. Moore's gathering of these cartoons, jokes, and caricatures not only reveals her interest in the popular as a key adjudicator of the political, but it also displays Moore's ethical humor rooted in identification.[29]

Moore's interest in the possibilities of expression went beyond humor. She clips an article from *Life*, "He Cabled Every Word (except the *the's* and

and's)," writing in pencil "Everybody's Way," implying that this is how everybody does it, while simultaneously recognizing the benefits of such a pared-down language.[30] At another point, Moore clips an article about a children's dictionary that confuses the star fish and—the subject of one of her early poems—the jelly-fish, betraying her obsession with taxonomy while demonstrating the need to be precise in description as well as language.[31]

The scrapbooks provide a rich, underutilized resource for studying Moore's personal development at this crucial point in her life—as well as the mass cultural expressions, social concerns, and historical events that helped shape her development. Scholars would do well to further investigate them as archival sources illuminating many of her lifelong interests and commitments. But it is also important to consider the ways in which the scrapbooks provide valuable clues as to *how* Moore was developing her characteristic forms of poetic expression, a development demonstrated in her material manipulation of printed scraps.

A Scrappy Poetics

Just as the scrapbooks preserve and present the images, themes, and sources that informed the subject matter of Moore's poems, they also illustrate her processes of poetic composition. The scrapbooks are roughly chronological from front to back, suggesting that one of the key principles of organization, as with many scrapbooks, is temporal: clippings are placed together because they were published at the same time, and often in the same publication. This organization is important, in that it allows one to trace Moore's general poetic development over these crucial five years. But while many pages follow this chronology, others appear to be more deliberately assembled over a longer span of time. There are several examples of unfinished pages and pages where the dates of clippings are separated by weeks or months, suggesting that Moore often thought of the page as a site for long-term selection and incorporation, and was willing to wait a while to elaborate a subject or complicate a theme. These clippings generally come from several different sources and genres (photos, cartoons, articles, poems), staging an interplay of different media and discursive registers, often resembling the pages of magazines from which they were culled. Sometimes the connections are obvious; at other times they require a leap of logical association, much as the poems do.

With this in mind, it is one of my guiding contentions that Moore's scrapbook pages need to be examined with the same close attention we would give to her poems. Such a close bibliographical reading shows not only how the scrapbooks illuminate Moore's principles of selection, displaying the scraps she chose to rescue from the flood of mass print, but also how the presentation of these scraps demonstrates processes of bibliographic manipulation that would be translated into the formal manipulation of her poems. This manipulation is most evident in the incorporation and juxtaposition of clippings, often in full-page assemblages, as well as in processes of pasting-over, anchoring, and enjambment.

These processes are dependent on the dual status of the individual clipping. Clippings are taken out of their prior contexts (these clippings themselves often reproduced from still earlier contexts as newspapers and magazines liberally borrowed from one another in a pervasive culture of reprinting) and placed into the new context of the scrapbook, exhibiting markers of date, place, and name of publication (which Moore meticulously recorded) in an effort to maintain some connection to the previous contexts from which they were removed. In this way, the scrap indexes both a prior mass print cultural context and a new private aesthetic one (that may in turn be articulated to another public) and exhibits, as has been argued of Moore's poems, "a precision that not only takes physical objects seriously but operates by appeals to indexicality and by proliferating detail."[32] Individual clippings adopt new meaning as they are incorporated into this scrapbook context, and through this incorporation the page as a whole takes on new meaning at the intersections of clippings.

Moore exhibits a principle of juxtaposition throughout the scrapbooks, two examples of which I consider here. One assemblage (fig. 3.1) juxtaposes an article on biologically modified tadpoles, "Pigmies and Giants by Feeding," to "At the Aquarium," a poem by Max Eastman that compares the wanderings of fish to that of people, who may be in for a "pale and cold surprise."[33] The two clippings are connected through a water metaphor (artificially constructed—be it aquarium or laboratory) and through taxonomy: both fish and tadpoles are classified as water creatures. But just as Eastman's poem draws a connection between the wandering people and the wandering fish, the pigmy and giant tadpoles take on human connotations so that distinction between the social and the natural is, like the fish themselves, slippery.

Beneath Eastman's poem is an editorial cartoon, "A Consultation," that (through a composition similar to that of the tadpole image) caricatures the Balkan Wars. The relationship between the cartoon and the poem is difficult to establish at first, but once we think about Eastman's own socialist com-

Figure 3.1. Full-page assemblage from Marianne Moore, "Scrapbook One," 96. Rosenbach Museum and Library.

mitments and the radical stance of the *Masses*, where the poem was originally published, the poem becomes deeply connected to the cartoon. War is the ultimate outcome of a people caught off guard; revolution is the potential in the wandering masses. Whereas the connection between the tadpoles and the fish is a formal one, this connection is more complex—it requires knowledge of history and biography to understand the formal juxtaposition. The meaning is not merely present on the page; the individual clippings must be traced back to their (historical, ideological, biographical, bibliographical) sources to make sense in this immediate coming together. This meaning beyond the page, manifested in a radical labor politics, is also necessary to understand the point of the juxtaposing joke "'How many people work in your office?'/'Oh, I should say about a third of them.'" Funny, yes, but as with so many of Moore's jokes, this one illuminates a serious social issue as it addresses the problem of professional labor. Beneath the cartoon of the Balkan states is an article entitled "Whitman's Siege of Europe." The reference to Europe and the term "siege" suggest aesthetic revolution as a corollary to the Ottoman revolution that was a key contributing factor to the Balkan Wars (bringing to mind the militaristic connotations behind the term *avant-garde*). The placement of the article against that on tadpoles also makes Whitman a giant among poet-pigmies. And he too had a commitment to the masses.

Beyond a simple binary juxtaposition, we start to see a triangulation of multiple sources as they pertain to Whitman (and to the other clippings on the page as well). In an open-ended additive process, as opposed to a closed-off intersection of meaning, Whitman becomes a figure of cultural influence: a giant, a conqueror, a laborer, a wanderer. The clippings on the page—representing a variety of discursive forms, including the joke, the poem, the illustration, the photograph, and the journalistic essay—contribute to the complex meaning of the assemblage as a whole. The page thus foregrounds issues of artistic and political influence, the line between the social and the natural, and the relationship between the great individual and the will of the masses.

In another assemblage, Moore constructs a page as material embodiment and criticism of a divided Ireland (fig. 3.2).[34] The "Irish Question" of independence and unification that faced the country in the first decades of the twentieth century is a subject that Moore takes up at other points in the scrapbooks. Indeed, it is a topic particularly suited to being presented in a scrapbook, where form mimics conflicted content and the bringing together of different clippings contributes to a complex pastiche on the page that cannot be reduced to a single idea or resolved into unity—much like Ireland itself. As in the previous assemblage, the uneasy integration of clippings encourages a reconsideration of integration—and even conflict—in the social context that the clippings metonymically represent.

Moore places side-by-side two copies of sketches by John "Jack" Butler Yeats that help literally divide the page down the middle. The first is a "Scene

Figure 3.2. Full-page assemblage from Marianne Moore, "Scrapbook Two," 63. Rosenbach Museum and Library.

at an Irish Fair" glorifying the traditional Irish peasantry who remember their brothers fallen in battle. The second is a self-portrait, "The Goya of Ireland," which praises the artist who has the abilities and the sensibilities to produce a work like "Scene at an Irish Fair." Beneath the self-portrait, above the caption, Moore has penciled in "Padraic Colum," the name of the Irish poet and playwright who—like another well-known Yeats, William Butler—was a key literary figure in the Celtic Revival, writing in Gaelic and collecting folklore. Importantly, though, while W. B. Yeats was a booming voice in the fight for independence, later producing such influential and often-anthologized poems as "Easter, 1916," he was Protestant and increasingly identified with the Anglo-Irish aristocracy. Colum, by contrast, was Catholic, and more clearly shared the religious and class sensibilities of the majority of the Irish people. For these reasons, Moore may see him as a more fitting descendent of Goya's populist aims. At the very least, Moore challenges the notion of a single inheritor of the Goya tradition and the idea that this tradition is necessarily perpetuated through a particular art form, implicitly making the case for her own aesthetic inheritance as a poet as well. The lateral juxtaposition of the two images also suggests the tension between the artist's need to represent the people and the external world more generally and the need to accurately depict one's self.

Beneath these sketches, Moore quotes lines from Shakespeare's *Measure for Measure* in response to the notion that Ulster was an inevitable spoil of war:

> But man, proud man,
> Drest in a little brief authority,
> Most ignorant of what he's most assured,
> His glassy essence, like an angry ape,
> Plays such fantastic tricks before high heaven
> As make the angels weep.[35]

The quotation points to the theatricality of the war and the importance of there being a poet to chronicle historical events, but it is also a potent example of how Moore would often read clippings in opposition to their intended meaning. Even as the excerpt suggests the role of the literary and references poets such as Colum and Yeats, it underscores the cultural imperialism of honoring an English Shakespeare in an Irish land (an issue that would vex, among others, Joyce's cerebral hero, Stephen). While the quotation is meant to be read against the British conquering of Ulster, the source makes the meaning ambiguous. Beside this quotation is a passage on Wu Ting-Fang and Tang Shou-Yi, two revolutionaries who were educated in British-controlled Hong Kong and who were instrumental in establishing the Republic of China. The clipping suggests one political response to imperialism, with its reference to an "admixture of birdlike curiosity for new ideas and political experiments," though without making explicit endorsement.

Looming above these clippings, covering the full top third of the page, is a photograph of a man wrestling a shark. The literal meaning of the picture is disconnected from the issues of Irish tradition and political division presented elsewhere on the page, but its placement in this political climate charges it with metaphorical significance. The image connects the otherwise divided page but does so through violent struggle, just as violent struggle connected an otherwise divided Ireland. While the shark may be personified to some degree, as the tadpoles and fish are in the previous example, it still retains its status as a creature of brute force with the clear advantage. It is hard not to identify the shark with Britain. To invoke Shakespeare once again, the image figures for Ireland the "sea of troubles" that foreshadows the sea image in Moore's most politically charged poem on the question of Ireland, "Sojourn in the Whale."[36]

These two examples of Moore's full-page assemblages suggest the many ways in which the incorporated text can take on new meaning through its association with other texts, while at the same time encouraging a connection to earlier social and bibliographical contexts. This accumulation of clippings, adopting many forms and coming from many sources, can add up to complex, often politicized, statements greater than the sum of their parts. Such possibilities, and the dangers of discouraging such possibilities, are central to Moore's poem "Novices," where a mature poet reflects on fledgling attempts to "anatomize their work" ("their" referring to both the poet presenting the work of others and the ones whose work is being combined) in a manner mimicking the anatomized page that discourages intertextuality.[37] Set against a background of marine metaphors that is integral to both examples, the poem makes explicit the connection between the natural and the cultural—perhaps looking back to the first assemblage—as it points to authors as "the masters of all languages, the supertadpoles of expression."[38]

More generally, incorporation, juxtaposition, and assemblage provide a bibliographic basis for what has often been recognized as the dominant formal strategies in Moore's poems. These processes help explain her complex associations of tropes and images, and—perhaps most obviously—her use of quotations. With Moore's scrapbooks in mind, we can see her quotations not only as linguistic negotiations of identity, voice, and context but also as material manipulations, where quotation marks impose real bibliographical barriers to words and phrases.

In some poems, a quotation is simply imported from another source and placed in the poem, like a pasted scrap. The surrounding text may then help illuminate the quotation's meaning, as Moore's marginalia often does in the scrapbooks. "In This Age Of Hard Trying, Nonchalance Is Good And," for example, begins with the phrase "'really, it is not the/business of the gods to make clay pots.'"[39] The phrase is read not only through the preceding title-phrase, which makes both the ancient gods and clay pots contemporaries of "This Age," but also through the negation in the next sentence that undercuts the possibility that the gods would change their minds as it reinforces that this instance is not unlike any other. Critics have long pointed out that Moore's readings of quotations are not merely explications but are often powerful *mis*readings, where quotations are taken radically out of context in order to challenge the integrity of that context or the possible meanings of the text itself—but, then, this is true as well in the scrapbooks that often supplied such quotations.

Although several of her poems incorporate only a single quotation, Moore would frequently juxtapose quotations as well. In such cases, meaning derives not only from the original text surrounding the quotations but also from the interplay of different quoted texts and, by extension, their sources. Often, these quotations are mediated by original phrases, as in the conclusion of "Sea Unicorns and Land Unicorns," where "the unicorn 'with pavon high,' approaches eagerly;/until engrossed by what appears of this strange enemy."[40] At other times, these quotations are directly juxtaposed without mediation, as in "To a Snail," where the phrases "'a method of conclusions';/'a knowledge of principles'" are placed, with the help of a semicolon, in metonymic series.[41]

This logic of poetic juxtaposition structures Moore's most rhetorically complex poems, "Marriage" and "An Octopus." These poems, premiere examples of Moore's collage poetry, and of modern collage poetry more generally, most closely parallel the full-page assemblages. Quotation—marking itself as quotation—retains some fidelity to the book or magazine from which it came but with its meaning changed in relation to the other textual elements in the poem and the poem as a whole making meaning through these assembled elements. In the notes to "Marriage," for example, Moore explains that the lines where Eve is "able to write simultaneously/in three languages—" with what would seem to be automatic hand are derived from *Scientific American*, January 1922.[42] In doing so, she points to a recent, popular-scientific source, rather than a poetic one, as she challenges and expands the assumed sources for poetic allusion. At the same time, she underscores the process of drawing on the ephemeral, repositioning it to illuminate the mythic figure of Eve and making it more permanent—just as ephemeral scraps are made more permanent in the scrapbook.

In addition to juxtaposing clippings and constructing assemblages, Moore would often paste one image over another. Sometimes she would do this completely so that only the new image is visible. At other times, she would literally "enjamb" one edge of the new image, pasting only the top, bottom, or a side, so that both images are still available for consideration— the clipping swinging open as a door does on its jamb. Recognizing this process as enjambment reminds us that a term generally reserved for the carrying-over of poetic meaning, allowing a word or phrase to be read in relation to both the preceding and subsequent line, is etymologically rooted in a material process. In this way, the term is representative of Moore's general project to translate the material into the formal.

Through pasting-over and enjambment, the image is no longer anchored to its original caption, or—to privilege the word over the image—the original caption is made to function in new contexts as it is placed against new images. The page is not restricted to a finite set of clippings that produce a limited number of associations; rather, another clipping can always potentially be added in this open-ended accumulation. Moore uses this strategy throughout the scrapbooks, as when she pastes a cartoon of Kaiser Wilhelm II over a cartoon of two people in an intimate scene.[43] The underlined caption, "In the Sentry Box," changes from being a lighthearted commentary on displays of public affection to critical scrutiny of the Prussian emperor largely responsible for the onset of the Great War. The trace of the earlier context is not completely erased, however, so that there is an affective carrying-over from the lovers, encouraging a consideration of the sexual and fraternal intimacies of war often bred in the trenches.

There is a double example of this pasting-over (fig. 3.3) as Moore brings together two reviews of George Bernard Shaw's Christmas pageant play, pasting over photographs of two separate scenes.[44] "Where the Romans Trade" is enjambed with a market scene, possibly taken from Rome, but at the very least from a recognizably exotic location. The availability of both images—the photograph of a "realistic" market scene and the absurd staging of Shaw's play—encourages a reading of the real and the absurd as two sides of the same coin. The second example is more politically explicit. Moore pastes a portrait of Dean Conant Worcester, the secretary of the interior of the Philippine government who fought against Filipino slavery, over a still

Scrapping Modernism 123

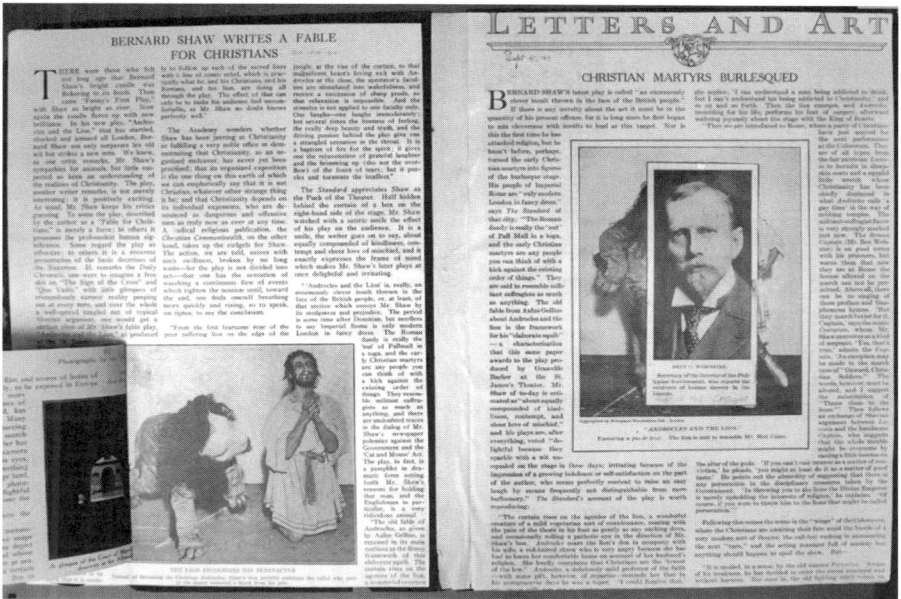

Figure 3.3. Pasting-over and enjambment from Marianne Moore, "Scrapbook One," 88–89. Rosenbach Museum and Library.

partially visible scene of Androcles fighting a lion. As a result, Worcester takes on the title "Christian Martyr." The absurdity of the play and the title of the review, "Christian Martyrs Burlesqued," however, suggest the ways that Worcester was himself "burlesqued" for his actions, charging his Christian martyrdom with irony.

This pasting-over and enjambment of texts suggests strategies for reading many of Moore's sentence-level formal innovations that critics have largely failed to consider. We get something akin to pasting-over in poems such as "'The Bricks Are Fallen Down, We Will Build with Hewn Stones./The Sycamores Are Cut Down, We Will Change to Cedars'" where the phrase "'defeated ourselves with/false balances'" is a quotation within a longer quotation that makes up more than half of the twelve-line poem.[45] One quote frames another within the poem as a whole just as one clipping frames another in the scrapbook. But this example is only a particular meta-instance of how Moore often wields quotation: as a precise wording, with a particular texture, which overlays a more general or abstract idea. The quotation may not be a translation of the idea—indeed, it may mask or expressly contradict it—but it comes to stand in as an alibi for that idea. That is, quotation may not only be the point to discourse but the point *of* it—the destination as much as the departure.

Enjambment is also significant in many of Moore's poems. In "The Steeple-Jack," a pun at the end of the line allows for "waves as formal as the scales" (a trope I will return to more fully below) to anticipate the run of a musical scale before unexpectedly landing "on a fish."[46] In "The Jerboa," people gave to boys playthings "and made toys for them-/selves: the royal totem"—so that "themselves" cleaves along its phonemic break, where an altruistic gesture turns to self-worship.[47] These strategies of pasting-over and enjambment promote the kinds of concealment, multiplicity, and contradictory readings that are often associated with Moore's poetry as well.

In addition to pasting-over and enjambing, Moore would on occasion cut out only the captions or other short phrases from previous sources, severing them from their original contexts altogether and allowing them to be radically recontextualized. These phrases, like the one-liners she was so fond of, can be inserted into various constellations to punctuate a point or complicate a theme. This is perhaps the most easily spotted (though often misinterpreted) use of quotation in Moore's poems, especially evident in poems such as "'He Wrote The History Book,'" where the title is itself a quotation and the function of the poem is to explicate that quotation (which is also often enjambed with the title).[48] One of the adverse effects of excising phrases or short verbal exchanges, however, is that while some of these phrases have been pasted in new places, many are now loose in the scrapbooks, free-floating, completely cut off from both their old and new contexts, never pasted or having long fallen out of place, presenting a host of scholarly conundrums. The same could be said for the many untraceable phrases in Moore's poems.

There are, however, striking examples of how these phrases do function in new contexts. "The Coon That Won't Come Down," originally a caption for a cartoon of a raccoon stuck on a pole, becomes critical commentary on the 1908 ascendancy of Mulai Hafid as sultan of Morocco, an act that consolidated tribal regions and threatened French and Spanish imperial interests (though Moore's presentation of this position does not necessarily constitute acquiescence; fig. 3.4).[49] Moreover, the upside-down Arabic script (an error in orientation Moore may or may not have been aware of) suggests a dangling raccoon and an upside-down political situation. There are do-

Scrapping Modernism

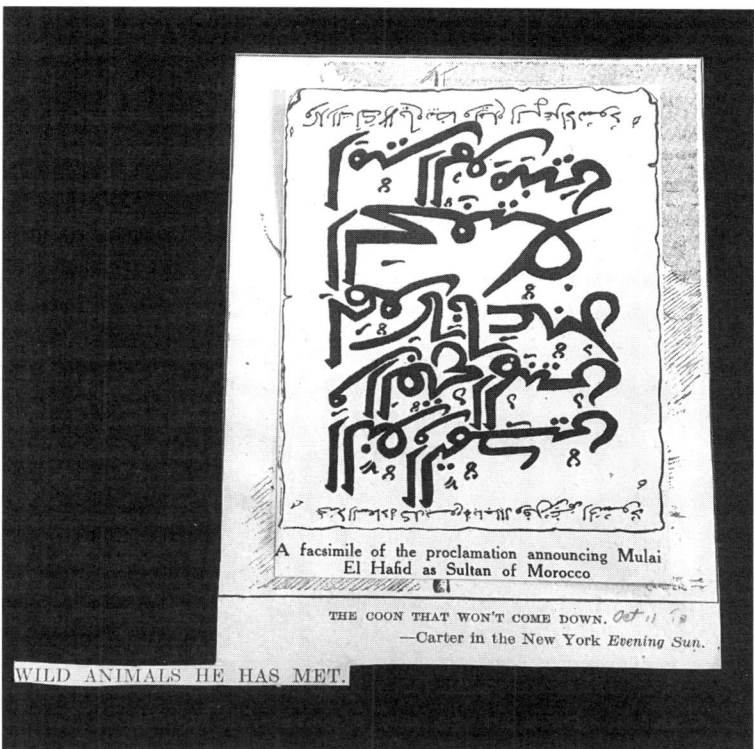

Figure 3.4. Aestheticized collage from Marianne Moore, "Scrapbook One," 87. Rosenbach Museum and Library.

mestic racial overtones in the phrase as well, as a slur for African Americans comes to designate the Moor and, by way of the pun, implicates Marianne Moore herself.[50] The collage differs from the previous examples of pasting-over and enjambment, however, in being anchored with the phrase "WILD ANIMALS HE HAS MET," so that meaning is shaped by connection both to an image and to another verbal text. The phrase may refer to the sultan and the difficulties he overcame to declare himself the rightful heir to the throne, but, as the sultan has already been dehumanized in his comparison to the raccoon, the phrase more properly refers to the witnessing of the sultan's rise.

The collage also differs from previous examples in that it is pasted directly onto the matte paper of the scrapbook and not onto another newspaper or magazine page. This has the effect of isolating and framing the assemblage (though now with black space rather the white space that I argued in the previous chapter helped isolate and frame the poem in the modern magazine). The page, most likely dating from November 1913, is the closest that Moore's scrapbooking gets to artistic collage, and one may be tempted to point to this example as a clear case of her learning from the visual *avant-garde*. But even this assemblage can be traced to Moore's previous scrapbooking practices. The collage exhibits the same processes of cutting and pasting, and draws on the same kinds of sources, as any other page in the scrapbook (the same kind of ephemera that visual collage artists would draw on, for that matter). For Moore, at least, *avant-garde* collage is not a radical departure from, but a peculiar subset of, the scrapbooking that she (and many others) had long been practicing.

While some of these examples do include scraps of poems along with a variety of other texts, it is near the end of the second scrapbook that Moore directly manipulates previously published poems, pasting the stanza of one poem over another, to make new meanings. She clips out a stanza from Walter Conrad Arensberg's "Out of Doors":

> I hear the wings, the winds, the river pass,
> And toss the fretful book upon the grass.
> Poor Book, it could not cure my soul of aught,
> It has itself the old disease of thought.[51]

This is enjambed onto the first four lines of a stanza from another, unidentified poem:

> No angel is so high
> But serveth clowns and kings,
> And doeth lowly things.
> He in this serviceable love can see
> The symbol of a heavenly mystery,—
> So labor grows white wings.[52]

The resulting stanza becomes:

> I hear the wings, the winds, the river pass,
> And toss the fretful book upon the grass.
> Poor Book, it could not cure my soul of aught,

> It has itself the old disease of thought.
> He in this serviceable love can see
> The symbol of a heavenly mystery,—
> So labor grows white wings.

The two poems hinge on "wings," an image that shows up in other poems pasted in the scrapbooks as well as in several poems Moore would write throughout her career.[53] In the first fragment, the wings, metonymic of birds and of nature in general, are contrasted with the book, which stands in for cultural production (history, literature). Tossing the effete book in the grass becomes for the speaker an act of relinquishing culture to nature. In the second fragment, by contrast, wings are a symbol of work; they are not simply endowed by nature but must be earned—like an angel's wings. The conflated poem negotiates these stances on nature and labor, making a more rhetorically complex, dialogic poem, where the wings become the mark of one who has worked her way back into a natural, spiritual state. This poetic pasting-over emphasizes the nature/culture dialectic that is central for much of Moore's work. It is one of the clearest examples of how Moore's scrapbooking practices had direct, specific application to her emerging poetic processes—and how scrapbooking practices in general were articulated to the production of poetic modernism—where bibliographic manipulation is translated into formal poetic meaning and quotation is incorporated into original compositions. But just as the personal scrapbook was in continual dialogue with snippet journals, satirical magazines, and other public expressions of mass print, exchanging both content and form, Moore likewise recognized the importance of periodical culture for her own work and explicitly spoke back to these periodicals in her crafting of such scrap publications as "The Daily Scale."

Weighing In on "The Daily Scale"

While the scrapbooks present textual materials important to Moore's poetic development, along with examples of the numerous ways in which those materials were put together, "The Daily Scale" brings the voice and "original" writing of the compositor into the mix as well (fig. 3.5). As opposed to the scrapbooks, which were intended primarily for Moore's private use, even as they provided models for her more public poetry, Moore's scrap publications were objects intended for (albeit very limited, family) circulation. As such, "The Daily Scale" gives Moore an opportunity to deeply con-

128 Poetic Modernism in the Culture of Mass Print

Figure 3.5. Front page of Marianne Moore's scrap-publication "The Daily Scale." Rosenbach Museum and Library.

sider the cultural form and function of the mass print sources she has borrowed from as she underscores and problematizes the relationship between the private scrapbook and the public periodical that inform her scrappy poetics.

"The Daily Scale" is a twenty-one-page mock newspaper, a scrap composition that integrates newspaper clippings with original passages using the relatively new technology of the typewriter—a technology that Moore, along with other modern poets, including E. E. Cummings, T. S. Eliot, and

Ezra Pound, exploited in their writings while at the same time voicing their frustrations with the newfangled contraption.[54] The newspaper was a joint venture, "published" with her mother. It is difficult to ascertain precisely what work belongs to which writer (or, indeed, whether this is even a productive line of inquiry), but I will err on the side of attributing the linguistic and poetic constructions that follow to Marianne, as they prefigure much of her later poetry—though reserving the possibility that the interaction between daughter and mother on display here was itself a key factor in Moore's poetic development.

The "Scale" in the title is a complex pun with a number of associations. It most obviously suggests an instrument for evaluating relative weight, or the act of evaluating—especially the weight of legal arguments with the scales of justice and economic weight with golden scales. In this sense, it suggests quantifiable objective value and definitive judgment that, as I argued in chapter 1, helped delineate modern poetic tradition. Moore supplements and challenges these notions with other meanings of "scale" that are explored throughout the publication: a specific observational framework akin to point of view (such as "global scale" or "atomic scale"), a musical scale, a verb closely aligned to the act of climbing, the skin protuberances of a reptile or fish, or the act of removing these protuberances. Such possibilities are suggested in some of Moore's most celebrated poems, as in the lines "with waves as formal as the scales/on a fish" that concludes the first stanza of "The Steeple-Jack," the first poem in Moore's *Selected Poems* and *Collected Poems*, or in the opening lines of "The Pangolin," that describe "Another armored animal—scale/lapping scale."[55]

The first edition of "The Daily Scale" is also its last—a point made at length in the opening pages that suggests its own belatedness while at the same time questioning what it means to make a periodical that is not produced periodically and to generate an ephemeral object that is not meant to mark a series of historical moments (and in this way acting as an inverse to the manufactured first edition that I discussed in chapter 1). The newspaper generally resembles the newspapers and magazines of mass print culture from which Moore gathered many of her clippings; it is broken into four columns and, like the column-constructed *Tit-Bits* and *Colliers*, texts generally carry over from one column to the next. Occasionally, as in the quality magazines *Harper's* and the *Century*, an illustration may break out of the column's confines to take up the greater part of a page or contribute to a full-page collage.

"The Daily Scale" contains a front-page section and sections on sporting news, drama, yachting news, and fine arts. There are editorial pages, a column on book reviews, and—the focus of much of my attention here—a column on poetry. There are also a number of advertisements, suggesting Moore's attention to the market forces that help determine the dissemination of any discursive production, "literary or otherwise," within mass print culture (as the first page announces, "There are 6693 Lines of Advertising in Today's SCALE"). Indeed, these advertisements are folded into the overall aesthetic of the paper, but they do, at least in the abstract, retain their economic function—and, as they point to actual products advertised in the papers from which Moore made her selection, they retain to some extent their real-world advertising function as well. Just as the scrapbooks call into question the typical critical narrative of *avant-garde* collage by displaying instances of collage rooted in the popular, the mock-newspaper highlights the print sources of collage themselves.

Not surprisingly, "The Daily Scale" is filled with much of the same subject matter found in the scrapbooks, including a preoccupation with animals and jokes. There are many playful, linguistically thick passages, as when the "Editor" is asked, which is correct, "But the teeny weeny Duckbill" or "And the teeny weeny Duckbill"? The answer is simple enough: "Either is correct (it depends on what you want to say, Mouse)."[56] Is a quotation used for confirmation? Contradiction? Both? Beneath this jocular surface is a deep consideration of the linguistic context for such a speech act and the importance of highlighting the logic of Boolean operators, as Moore's poems frequently do in prominently placing such words as "but" and "and" at the ends of lines and stanzas.

In addition to engaging in such linguistic play, "The Daily Scale" incorporates and complicates the presentation of the lyrical poem in popular periodicals in a manner paralleling her conflation of the "wings" poem in the second scrapbook. Examples of these lyrics abound throughout the paper. For example, in a section entitled "The Inquiring Dormer," when the Kangaroo Rat requests (with an assumption of maleness that Moore has by now come to expect), "Will the Editor of *The Scale* be kind enough to tell me what he considers the very best poem in the world," the Editor replies with the poem, "To a Bandoliera":

> Sing a song of summer,
> Sing about the Scale.

Make your boat a hummer,
Rival to the Whale.[57]

The poem appears to be a trifle—quickly dashed off. As the Editor considers it to be the very best poem in the world, however, far be it from me to discount it too quickly. On closer examination, we see that this poem (which, as far as I can determine, is Moore's original composition), in addition to shamelessly promoting the context of "The Daily Scale" in which it is placed, stresses the musical connotation of "scale." One becomes a virtuoso, singing from its depths to its summits. The poem encourages the reader to make her boat hum, an action close to singing, though without an articulation of referential meaning. But it also implores the reader to make the boat a "hummer" (to use the popular slang of the time): a thing of extraordinary excellence. The boat is a small thing, like the poem or a hummingbird. It's not a cruise ship or transatlantic vessel. In being a well-made thing, however, it collapses physical scale and (drawing on a familiar image) becomes a rival to the whale—as Jonah was, or Ahab—anticipating the sojourn through the bellies of New York and Ireland that Moore would later depict.[58]

While there are snippets of such verse throughout the publication, "The Daily Scale" includes, in the manner of a magazine such as the *Century*, a specific "Poetry" section near the back, containing the single poem "Spider Song."[59] Not unlike the "wings" poem in her second scrapbook, the poem is constructed from two different stanzas, one typewritten and one pasted in. The first stanza:

> The East has yielded, yet the day
> Makes splendid fight
> Who weaves his web so steadily
> Between the mountains and the sea.

is taken liberally from Rollo Britten's "Was It Not Day Just Now?," published in the *Harvard Monthly* in December 1911. Britten's complete poem is a quasi-Imagistic free verse construction that reads at least in part as an ominous response to Wordsworth's "Composed upon Westminster Bridge" in its accounting of the shadows that fill the darkness before the dawn:

> Was it not day just now?
> These shadows: towers, steeples, roofs were they.
> The East has yielded, yet the day
> Makes splendid fight

Who weaves his web so steadily
Between the mountains and the sea.
Was it not day just now?
Was it not day?⁶⁰

The second stanza in Moore's conflation is the opening stanza of Julia Fletcher Carney's popular nursery rhyme, "Little Drops of Water":

Little drops of water,
Little grains of sand,
Make the mighty ocean
And the pleasant land.

The history behind this reproduced fragment is a revealing one, underscoring the ways in which scraps often carry historical associations that (intentionally or not) can be animated in new literary contexts. A turn-of-the-century newspaper article tells sentimentally of how the child Carney was forbidden to write verses, but there would be found at housecleaning time "rolls of rhyme hidden in every nook and corner of the attic. Some of these were so touching and pathetic as to melt the heart of the loving, though anxious, mother, and the law was repealed."⁶¹ The famous verses, written when Carney was a schoolteacher, were actually an experiment in shorthand, "penned in stenographic characters," a curious expression of modern efficiency that anticipates the standardization of the typewriter and the deindividualized automatic hand. Upon returning home, Carney found "a young man waiting for some scraps, as the editor called them," to be published in the local paper, and Carney quickly composed some additional stanzas to augment her stroke of genius:

So the little monuments,
    Humble though they be,
Make the mighty ages
    Of eternity.

So our little errors
    Lead the soul away
From the path of virtue,
    Far in sin to stray.

Little deeds of kindness,
    Little words of love,

> Help to make earth happy,
>   Like the heaven above.⁶²

The additional stanzas mimic the structure of the first, so that the multiple "little" instances accumulate to grand effects, progressing to the possibility of a great happiness. As popular as the poem was, it is unclear whether Moore knew of its fabled origins, but the story of a child poet turned schoolteacher certainly would have resonated with her.

Carney's popular poem sounds suspiciously similar to William Blake's "Auguries of Innocence," a poem by a poet who was relatively unknown during his lifetime but who has since become central to the English literary canon. This is a point that Moore has not missed. Blake's poem is, in fact, quoted at length earlier in the publication, as a supplement to a snippet pasted in with a saccharine illustration of a girl (fig. 3.6). The Editor of "The Scale" reminds the reader in a comically understated passage that the author of this poem "was an artist (or draughtsman) as well as a poet and illustrated his own works." Blake's poem itself makes reference to a spider, as "The wanton boy that kills the fly / Shall feel the spider's enmity." The image of the spider and the incorporation of Carney's poem—as well as, through the text, the surrounding historical context—allows Moore to make arguments about poetic accomplishment (do we take Blake's poem to be the superior one?), about the importance of sentimental verse and mass culture (how can the ideas in what was at the time Blake's much less widely circulated poem appeal to a mass audience?), and about poetic cribbing itself (is there a productive political and aesthetic project behind allusion and quotation?).

The reference to Blake's poem encourages direct comparison between Blake and Carney, although their poems are separated by eleven pages. It also points to the missing metaphor of the spider that links Carney's poem with Britten's observation that the day "weaves his web so steadily" into the shadows of the night. Likewise, Carney's "little monuments" become Britten's now obscured "towers, steeples, roofs" (obscured in Britten's original poem by the shadows and by Moore in her choosing not to quote the line in "Spider Song"), though Carney seems to offer an optimistic answer to Britten's dark question, in which deeds of kindness can combat sins and errors, so that the earth becomes like the (shining) heaven above. Beyond problematizing the subject matter of each of the poems, Moore's conflation foregrounds dialogic form and dependence upon contextual interaction that

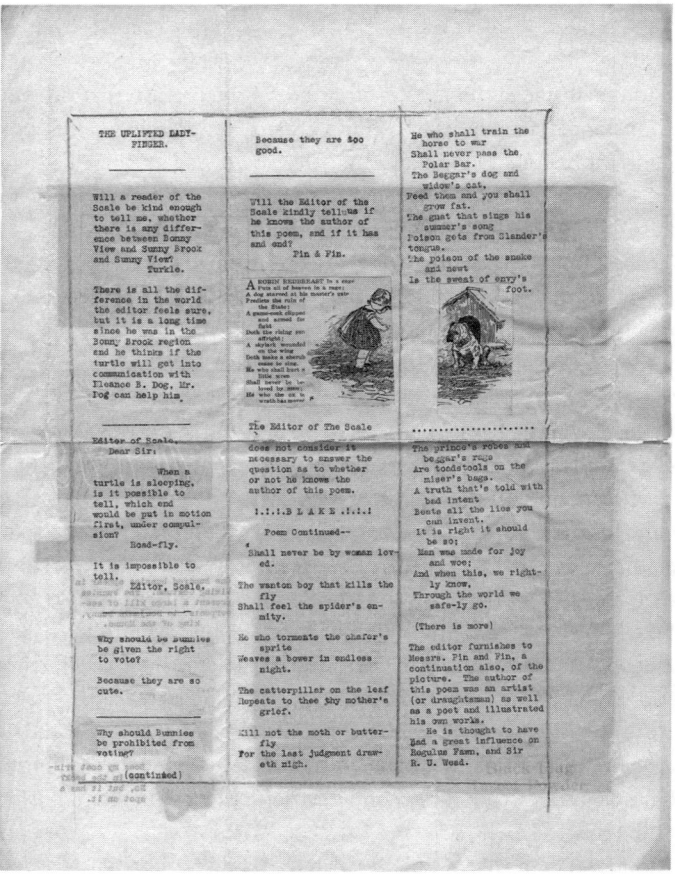

Figure 3.6. Reproduction of Blake's "Auguries of Innocence," "The Daily Scale," 6. Rosenbach Museum and Library.

requires a reading across "The Daily Scale" in order to understand its full meaning.

This encouragement to accrue associations across the length of the whole publication suggests an act of radial reading, in which meaning does not collapse centrifugally into an image or trope but radiates centripetally as it encounters other texts and textual frames—not dissimilar to the contextualized reading of poems in such periodicals as *Life* and the *Crisis* that

I pointed to in chapter 2. Such radial reading is difficult and unpredictable and demands attention to a number of competing elements, which may have their payoff elsewhere . . . or not at all. It transcends the complex page associations of the scrapbooks and suggests the degree of extended association that Moore would achieve in her longer poems "Marriage" and "An Octopus." It also provides strategies for reading across Moore's oeuvre as specific images and tropes (the whale, the rat) change or remain consistent from poem to poem. It would be wrong to think, though, that all of the textual pieces click into place and "The Daily Scale" ultimately resolves into symbolic unity. Rather, the scrap publication, like Moore's scrapbooks, accrues its meaning through a series of chance textual encounters—offering another material precursor and model for understanding Moore's complex and allusive collage poetry.

Although she would still keep less experimental noncollage photo albums recording her personal accomplishments and would continue to extra-illustrate books all her life—often interleaving them with newspaper articles over the course of several decades—Moore would stop producing such involved scrapbooks and scrap constructions at about the time she started to write her characteristic collage poems and began to be published in such well-known modern little magazines as *Poetry*. The scrapbooks and scrap publications were not exclusively responsible for Moore's poetic material or for the development of her formal innovations, but they are some of the best evidence we have. They point to an array of interests and allegiances that Moore would wrestle with throughout her career, while at the same time displaying material acts of importation, juxtaposition, assemblage, pasting-over, anchoring, enjambment, and radial reading that would be translated into her later collage poetry. In doing so, they underscore the long tradition of scrapbooking as a feminized negotiation of mass textual culture and challenge the long-held assumptions that the modern collage poem was simply a translation and extension of a masculinized visual *avant-garde*. They also underscore the opportunities for incorporating the material evidence of a mass print culture into new textual constructions, while being mindful of the historical contingency of the material being snipped. Such formal innovations were not, however, achieved in isolation. Beyond underpinning her own writing, Moore's scrappy poetics can help us better understand the role of mass print culture in the formation of the modern collage poem more generally.

Scrapping Modernism

Academic feeling, or prejudice possibly, in favour of continuity and completeness is opposed to miscellany—to music programs, composite picture exhibitions, newspapers, magazines, anthologies. Any zoo, aquarium, library, garden, or volume of letters, however, is an anthology and certain of these findings are highly satisfactory. The science of assorting and the art of investing that assortment with dignity are obviously not being neglected, as is manifest in "exhibitions and sales of artistic property," and in that sometimes disparaged, most powerful phase of the anthology, the museum.

—Marianne Moore

As I have suggested, Moore's scrapbooks and such scrap publications as "The Daily Scale" provide a material basis for what I am calling Moore's scrappy poetics. This scrappy poetics poses a radical critique of the impulse to arrange like textual objects into a symbolically closed collection of the (often long) collage poem that critics have frequently identified with the high modernism of such poets as T. S. Eliot.[63] In promoting Moore as a key modern poetic figure against Eliotic tradition, however, critics have often turned Eliot into a high-modernist straw man (a stuffed man, a hollow man . . .) without considering his own complicated relationship to unified poetic form. It may have at one time been necessary to stress the differences between the two poets in order to give Moore the critical recognition she deserves. Now that Moore has become a more central figure in accountings of poetic modernism, however, it is easier to see the extent to which she does not simply present an alternative to Eliotic high modernism but in fact exposes the scrappiness of such core modernist achievements as *The Waste Land*—even against a critical privileging of tradition, organized and unified by an individual poetic talent.

As Lawrence Rainey has noted, the idea of *The Waste Land* as a narratively coherent, myth-driven work can be traced in large part to Eliot's own publication strategies and references to the poem's book-like qualities.[64] Eliot's mythological scaffolding is perhaps most clearly (or convolutedly) expressed in *The Waste Land*'s notes. The general critical rationale for Eliot's strategy to add notes—which were more or less dashed off and have famously become somewhat of a red herring in the poem's interpretation—was that he needed to get ink on enough pages to publish the poem as a book. The notes were not, however, his only option; Eliot had written other poems at the time that he could have included. Not to include these other poems but to still insist on book publication suggests that it was important for Eliot that the poem "The Waste Land" map directly onto the book *The Waste Land* in order for it to make its most pronounced cultural impact (though the notes being separate from, and a commentary upon, the main text necessarily undercuts this attempt, having long provided the loose threads for critical unraveling).

Indeed, the modern first edition book had become so ingrained in the structural makeup of high modernism that Eliot first attempted to publish his poem as a limited edition book with the Cambridge publisher and bookseller Maurice Firuski, and, even after it was published by the commercial house Boni and Liveright, he published a limited edition of 460 copies ten months later with Virginia Woolf's Hogarth Press. There are two key reasons that Eliot sought to map his poem onto the first edition book. First, by striking a one-to-one correspondence with the book, rather than merely being part of it, the poem could latch onto the book's status as a discrete object and symbolically closed whole, even as it is part of a larger collection of bibliographical objects. Second, as I argue in chapter 1, the first edition book modeled a particular kind of modern poetic value, based in manufactured scarcity, which would allow *The Waste Land* to make a bid for both the new and the old as it fit snugly into literary tradition.

Eliot would emphasize the bibliographical dimension of the poem later in life, as when he explains that "I am not ungrateful to the British Museum: but when I installed myself there after lunch on a Saturday, it often happened that I had hardly opened the essential volume for which I had been waiting, when there sounded the familiar warning which corresponded to the phrase 'Hurry up, please, it's time.'"[65] The description, likely conjured up in retrospect, turns the intrusively repeated line that closes the second section of *The Waste Land* into both a last call for alcohol interrupting the discussion of an abortion and an annunciation of the end of days that will be fulfilled in the poem's final section—suggesting the importance of the collected book housed in the museum's reading room as itself a lifeline against aborted tradition.

As much as Eliot underscored the bookish nature of *The Waste Land* through his publication practices and bibliographical references, the actual composition of the poem was decidedly messier, compiled through various scraps of paper over several years.[66] The resulting incoherence was noted even by its earliest critics. As Conrad Aiken notes in a 1923 review in the

New Republic, "I think we must, with reservations, and with no invidiousness, conclude that the poem is not, in any formal sense, coherent," and in fact Aiken sees this as a source of the poem's power.[67] Similarly, in a review in the *Dial* two months earlier, Edmund Wilson remarks of *The Waste Land*, and of Eliot's verse more generally, that it is sometimes "much too *scrappy*— he does not dwell long enough upon one idea to give it its proportionate value before passing on to the next—but these drops, though they be wrung from flint, are none the less authentic crystals. . . . The poem is—in spite of its structural unity—simply one triumph after another."[68] Or, one could argue, the poem triumphs *because* of its disunity.

Such readings serve to remind us that *The Waste Land* only vaguely puts into practice Eliot's notions of literary value and tradition that he forwards in such essays as "Tradition and the Individual Talent." In fact, as Rainey has shown, at the time he was stitching the poem together "Tradition" was not as central to Eliot's thinking as has often been supposed, noting that as late as 1921 Eliot "praises the metaphysical poets because in their works 'the most heterogeneous ideas are yoked by violence together.' A few months earlier he praises Baudelaire over Dryden because he 'could see profounder possibilities in wit, and in violently joined images.'"[69]

This violent assemblage of texts approximates Moore's own conflation of poems and other textual materials in her scrapbooks and in "The Daily Scale," which help give rise to her scrappy poetics and its yoking together of quotations in her collage poems. As I have argued, Moore effectively drew upon and negotiated periodical culture in these constructions. That Eliot was doing the same should not be surprising and is suggested by *The Waste Land*'s working title, "He Do the Police in Different Voices," a title taken from Dickens's novel *Our Mutual Friend*, where the old widow Betty Higden describes the orphan Sloppy's reading practices: "You mightn't think it, but Sloppy is a beautiful reader of a newspaper. He do the Police in different voices."[70]

That Moore's own methods of composition, rooted in a negotiation of mass print culture, paralleled Eliot's is evident in Eliot's review of Moore's recently published "Marriage" as well as her *Poems*, which she had published two years previously.[71] Eliot had promised to review the earlier work, a promise that "for one reason or another, I never fulfilled," but he makes a point to mention that "I have read Miss Moore's poems a good many times, and always with exactly the same pleasure, and satisfaction in something quite definite and solid." He would tell Moore that her writing interested him more than that of anyone then writing in America and, foreshadowing his eventual editing of the *Selected Poems* for Faber and Faber that I discuss in the next chapter, mentions, "I wish that you would make a book of it, and I should like to try to get it published here. I wish you would let me try."[72] In his essay, Eliot points to what he sees as at least three elements that are innovative in Moore's work: "a quite new rhythm, which I think is the most valuable thing"; a "peculiar and brilliant and rather satirical" use of the learned American vernacular; and "an almost primitive simplicity of phrase."[73] He also gives Moore the backhanded "'magnificent' compliment: Miss Moore's poetry is as 'feminine' as Christina Rossetti's, one never forgets that it is written by a woman; but with both one never thinks of this particularity as anything but a positive virtue."[74] As if one were predisposed to think that this "particularity" is not necessarily a plus. Eliot adds in cryptic understatement, "There may be more."[75] That "more" should certainly include Moore's scrappy poetics, clearly evident in both *Poems* and "Marriage," putting on display the kind of "haphazard accumulation" that characterizes Eliot's own book collecting practices and negotiation of mass print.

A similar scrappiness to that of *The Waste Land* can be found in *The Cantos* of Ezra Pound. As Michael O'Driscoll has argued, Pound saw himself acting in his long poem as a kind of cultural archivist, incorporating textual fragments that serve to metonymically index the historical documents (and embedded contexts) from which they were derived.[76] In doing so, Pound exhibits an "archival consciousness" (about which I say more in chapter 5) that "signals both an awareness of the archive as a force of history and memory and a paradigmatic movement towards a kind of intertextual mindset that is evident in the formal and thematic properties of much twentieth century literature."[77] To enact such a consciousness, however, Pound finds it necessary to employ a principle of exclusivity (as many archivists have done) so that a long but in the end thuddingly finite poem might indeed be said to contain history (if you can't expand the poem, collapse the past). No matter how restricted the focus, however, this indexical project cannot ultimately bring about a symbolic whole, leading to Pound's admission in his late Canto CXVI: "I cannot make it cohere."[78] But, as O'Driscoll notes, there is also a principle of equivalence at work among the images and allusions that places fragments in personal, metaphoric relationship. It is this principle, closely resembling Moore's own accumulative logic, which allows Pound to revise his statement to claim that "it coheres all right/even if my notes do not cohere."[79]

Likewise, Book IV of William Carlos Williams's *Paterson* recognizes its own haphazard accumulation as it presents through the guiding trope of the library a collage of prose and verse (and questions this generic distinction as both are subsumed into poetry). Upon completing Book IV (which, for a while, Williams believed to be the end of *Paterson* as a whole), Williams wrote to Moore:

> If the vaunted purpose of my poem seems to fall apart at the end—it's rather frequent that one has to admit an essential failure. At times there is no other way to assert the truth than by stating our failure to achieve it. If I did not achieve a language I at least stated what I would not say. I would not melt myself into the great universal sea (of love) with all its shapes and colors. But, if I did not succeed on one level, I did cling to a living language on another. The poem, as opposed to what was accomplished in the story, came to life at moments—even when my failure was most vocal and went above that to a different sort of achievement. Or so I believe.[80]

Like Pound, Williams admits that his long collage poem fails to cohere as a symbolic whole (the kind of wholeness that Eliot also encouraged through mythic scaffolding and the integrity of the book object). Nevertheless, it achieves another kind of success that resembles Moore's own scrappy compositions.

Read in the context of Moore's scrappy poetics, the long collage poems of Eliot, Pound, and Williams demonstrate the achievement of open-ended accumulation against what is often taken to be an assumed good of symbolic closure. As I argue in the next two chapters, however, this scrappy poetics has largely been obscured by the reproduction and institutionalization of a particular kind of poetic modernism characterized by Eliot's editing of selected and collected volumes of poems for Faber and Faber and by the mid-century rise of the modern poetry archive. It is important to keep in mind, though, that these processes solidified only one possible trajectory for modern poetry—even if it is the story with which critics are most familiar—and that Moore's poetry points us to other open-ended interpretive strategies for reading the many collage poems that were central to poetic modernism and to the poetry that would follow in its wake.

4 Selecting Modernism

Eliot, Faber, and Poetic Reproduction

The House of Faber, standing at 24 Russell Square, is an understated Georgian structure nuzzling up to the greenery of Russell Square, flanked on one side by University College, London, and on the other by the imposing British Museum. Until recently, it had been the long-standing home to the publishing firm of Faber and Gwyer, and then Faber and Faber.[1] Surrounded by profound academic and cultural institutions, it inhabits the geographical heart of Bloomsbury—a location that parallels Faber's situatedness within a modern field of literary and cultural production in London and on a grander transatlantic and transnational stage. As an upstart, midsized literary publishing firm, Faber would help promote poetic modernism as it reproduced work from the more ephemeral periodicals and the smaller *avant-garde* presses while simultaneously legitimating the movement for the larger presses and a more general reading public both at home and abroad.

T. S. Eliot would step into these stately offices as he joined the Faber and Gwyer board of directors in September 1925, entering a new phase of his literary career. Although Eliot had distinguished himself in the teens and twenties through both his poetry and criticism, a great deal of his critical authority during the thirties derived from his private role as mentor and publisher, where he became known as the "Pope of Russell Square" in search of (as he put it) poetic "genius."[2] Eliot was more than a literary luminary deigning to deliver his opinion from time to time to a few worthy apprentices, however. He was a workhorse and throughout the whole editorial process was an important policy maker for Faber.[3]

Eliot's influence on a second generation of poetic modernism is evident in Faber's poetry list during his tenure with the firm, which included such notables as W. H. Auden, Robert Lowell, and Ted Hughes.[4] Likewise, Eliot helped shore up earlier generations of poetic modernism through the issuing of selected and collected volumes of poetry by Ezra Pound, Marianne Moore, and Rudyard Kipling. These volumes would serve (somewhat belatedly) to identify these as Faber poets—reinforcing Eliot's claim that "I consider that the publishers of a poet are the firm who publish his Collected Poems."[5] In editing volumes by these poets, Eliot recognized that consolidating modern poetry's institutional status and its distinction from mass print culture would require more than promoting an alternative poetics. The book itself would need to acquire something of the unity and independence that an emerging New Critical hegemony was granting to the individual poem—minimizing politics and contingency through an ordering based less on chronology than on unities of feeling and value. In doing so, volumes of selected and collected poems extended a privileging of objective literary value that I considered in chapter 1 and a stabilization of poetic genre over verse form that I discussed in chapter 2.

If, as I argued in the previous chapter, Marianne Moore's scrappy poetics —based in the scrapbooker's negotiation of mass print—points to the disunity of such quintessential long collage poems as *The Waste Land*, Eliot's editing of selected and collected poetry volumes would serve to thread a sense of unity across a poet's career. Apart from Eliot's personal investments in the poets he edited, such volumes underscore an increasingly dominant print media form that frequently registers modernism's impulse to consolidate a canon of the best poems and poets as it simultaneously betrays anxieties over doing so within an increasingly crowded market of mass print.

As I suggest, especially with Eliot's editing of Kipling, poetry volumes are not merely self-contained aesthetic objects, however, but can themselves function as instruments of cultural politics—not unlike the contingent anthologies or socially embedded periodical verse—though often of a very different sort from the political and mass cultural engagement that occupied many other writers in the 1930s. In editing Pound's *Selected Poems*, Eliot was in fact drawing on aims evident in the several collections Pound himself had published, but with his volumes centered on Moore and Kipling one begins to see how a high cultural modernism could be severed from mass publication and gain a distinct identity. And, as Eliot's editing of Kipling in particular suggests, in the emerging postimperialist age in which Eliot was working at Faber, the unity and coherence of a poetry collection might begin to offer a model for the nation-state, not merely through its intertextual relationships but through its presentation of a unity emblematic of national culture—a cultural unity that Eliot was also arguing for in some of his most influential essays of the period.

Resounding Pound

Eliot first uses a selected volume of poetry as a vehicle for critical collecting in his editing of Pound's *Selected Poems*, initially issued by Faber in 1928. With Eliot's introduction preceding even the table of contents, the reader encounters Pound's poems through a critical prism that confirms this as Eliot's particular selection. Eliot is up front about this fact, acknowledging that his is "rather a convenient Introduction to Pound's work than a definitive edition. The volumes previously published represent each a particular aspect or period of his work; and even when they fall into the right hands, are not always read in the right order."[6] Underscoring the integrity of each discrete volume as a punctuated moment in Pound's poetic development, Eliot selects and arranges the *Selected Poems* to get the right poems in the right order, making the point that Pound's work "is not only much more varied than is generally supposed, but also represents a continuous development, down to *Hugh Selwyn Mauberley*, the last stage of importance before the *Cantos*."[7] This continuity in variety is confirmed with a "Bibliography of the more important volumes of verse and prose by Ezra Pound" that provides the textual touchstones for the *Selected Poems*.[8] Only some of these books are actually named in the table of contents as subheadings for Eliot's selection: *Personae* (1908, 1909, 1910), *Ripostes* (1912), *Lustra*, *Cathay*, Poems from Lustra (1915), and Hugh Selwyn Mauberley (Life and Contacts).[9]

This structure closely parallels that of *Personae: The Collected Poems of Ezra Pound, including Ripostes, Lustra, Homage to Sextus Propertius, H. S. Mauberley*, published in New York by Boni and Liveright two years earlier. Eliot concedes this fact in his introduction, mentioning that he "made a few suggestions for omissions and inclusions in a similar collection to be published in London; and out of discussions of such matters with Pound arose the spectre of an introduction by myself."[10] That the Faber *Selected Poems* would so closely parallel *Personae: The Collected Poems* suggests the extent to which Eliot and Pound were already on the same page with regard to how to best frame Pound's poetic development.

Indeed, Pound had been wrestling with issues of how to select from and arrange his poems almost as soon as he had books to select from. The dust jacket to the 1910 *Provença* advertises Pound's volume as "the first American edition of his work, and contains the best of the two volumes, *Personae* and *Exultations* . . . with new poems which are to be issued in England separately under the title of *Canzoniere*."[11] Notably absent are references to the earliest poetry books, *A Lume Spento* and *A Quizane for this Yule*, poems from which had already been folded into *Personae*. Pound's next major attempt to frame his earlier work came in the 1917 American edition of *Lustra of Ezra Pound with Earlier Poems*, in which he revised and supplemented the *Lustra of Ezra Pound* published in London by Elkin Matthews (in both an abridged and unabridged printing) the previous year to include "Poems Published Before 1911," "Canzoni, First Published 1911," "Ripostes, First Published 1912," and "Three Cantos of a Poem of Some Length."[12]

Following this was the publication of what could be called the first true selected edition of Pound's early work, *Umbra: The Early Poems of Ezra Pound*, published by Elkin Matthews in 1920. The volume included sections entitled *"Personae," "Exultations," "*From *'Canzoni,'* " "From *'Poetry and Drama'* for February 1912," "Ripostes," "Translations" of Guido Cavalcanti and Arnault Daniel, and *"The Complete Poetical Works of T. E. Hulme*." The volume signals a consolidation of the earlier poetry as separate from the later work, as further suggested by the publication the following year of *Poems, 1918-21*. It contains the longer poetic sequences *Langue d'Oc, Moeurs Contemporaines*, and *Homage to Sextus Propertius* previously published in *Quia Pauper Amavi*, along with the previously published *Hugh Selwyn Mauberley*, and early versions of *Cantos* IV-VII.[13] With its emphasis on the multivocal, longer poetic forms, *Poems, 1918-21* suggests less a summation of where Pound's verse had been, as was the case with *Umbra*, than a proposal of where it was going.

The 1926 *Personae* would similarly separate the earlier and more mature poetry, but it would conclude prior to the *Cantos*, now including poems from the volumes gathered in *Umbra* as well as *Homage to Sextus Propertius* and *Hugh Selwyn Mauberley*. There were also notable additions and subtractions. The "Ripostes (1912)" section cut nine poems from the original *Ripostes* volume, including the five poems from "The Complete Poetical Works of T. E. Hulme" that Pound had been sponsoring.[14] Two poems—"The Cloak" and "The Alchemist"—were actually added to the "Ripostes (1912)" section, although they had never appeared in *Ripostes*.[15] *Cathay*, first published in 1915 and reprinted as part of *Lustra* in 1916, is given its own section, to emphasize that it had initially been its own volume, but it is placed after the later-published *Lustra*. To complicate things further, these sections precede the sections "Poems from Blast (1914)" and "Poems from Lustra (1915)." The fact that these sections are dated and the "Lustra" and "Cathay" sections (following the "Ripostes [1912]" section) are not gives the erroneous impression that the volume has been arranged according to publication chronology, constructing a more coherent narrative for Pound's poetic trajectory of self-modernization than had actually been the case.

This narrative coherence was reinforced by Pound's own collecting impulse, in which he encourages his critics to "think of the book as a whole, not of individual words in it. Even certain smaller poems, unimportant in themselves, have a function in the book-as-a-whole. The shaping of a book is very important. It is almost as important as the construction of a play or a novel."[16] That Eliot was also deeply interested in relaying Pound's narrative of modernization and his notion of the book as a closed form is evident in the fact that the Faber *Selected Poems* would be closely patterned after *Personae*, which itself was the product of a long history of editorial decisions in which Pound had played a decisive role.

It is fair to say that Eliot had less editorial work to do, and had less of an impact on Pound's poetic reception, than he would have in editing Moore and Kipling. It would be a mistake, however, to take at face value Eliot's claim that he had merely made "a few suggestions" for the new volume. These changes were in fact much more substantial than he let on or that critics have generally acknowledged.[17] Aside from the six additional poems that Eliot chose to highlight by gathering them together at the end of the book, the Faber *Selected Poems* also cut twenty-three poems from *Personae*.[18] Eliot acknowledges in his introduction the most blatant excision, that of *Homage to Sextus Propertius*, stating that he thought the poem "would give difficulty to many readers: because it is not enough a 'translation,' and because it is, on the other hand, too much a 'translation,' to be intelligible to any but the accomplished student of Pound's poetry."[19] He also points out that he omitted "Ballad of the Goodly Fere," because it has become more popular than it deserves and has obscured some of the better work of the period (a claim that, likely due in part to its exclusion from the *Selected Poems*, does not seem to hold today).[20] The next most obvious excisions, which Eliot does not call attention to but which a cursory glance at the table of contents for both volumes makes clear: the entire section of "Poems from Blast (1914)" has been cut, which had included "Salutation the Third," "Monumentum Aere, Etc.," "Come My Cantilations," "Before Sleep," "Post Mortum Conspectu," and "Fratres Minores." This excising, no doubt due in part to Eliot's confessed inability to fully appreciate Pound's epigrams, has the effect of removing the entire Vorticist phase of Pound's career.

These excisions are in large part justified by Eliot's tracing of Pound's ideal poetic trajectory in a way that mostly, but not completely, resembles Pound's own account—neither of which entirely corresponded to the actual history of poetic publication. Eliot outlines this trajectory in the introduction, explaining that "a poet's work may proceed along two lines of an imaginary graph; one of the lines being his conscious and continuous effort in technical excellence, that is, in continually developing his medium for the moment when he really has something to say. The other is just his normal course of development, his accumulation and digestion of experience" in all its varied forms.[21] When these two lines converge at their apex, we get a masterpiece. In what seems to be a corrective to his famous call for impersonality (or a mistaken understanding of that call) in "Tradition and the Individual Talent," Eliot further explains that "an accumulation of experience has crystallized to form material of art, and years of work in technique have prepared an adequate medium; and something results in which medium and material, form and content, are indistinguishable."[22]

Eliot admits that this is an idealized diagram. Valuing only "perfect" poetry would rule out all but a few of the "greatest" poets. Rather, if we seek to know poetry in all of its degrees, the distinction between technique and feeling, "a distinction necessarily arbitrary and brutal," will not bother us: we shall be able to appreciate what is "good of its kind" (interestingly echoing the comparison of cheesepairings and porkrinds in Moore's "Apropos of Mice" that I discussed in the previous chapter) and "the fusion of matter and means, form and content, on any level"—examples of which can be found throughout the *Selected Poems*. This problematic separation of technique and experienced content suggests the distinction between verse and poetry that had (largely through such venues as *Poetry*) come to govern dominant notions of poetic modernism. Eliot relies on this distinction to explain Pound's interest in epigrams, translations, paraphrases, and the "lighter forms of serious verse," explaining that one "cannot write poetry all the time; and when one cannot write poetry, it is better to write what one knows is verse and make it good verse, than to write bad verse and persuade oneself that it is good poetry."[23]

There are times, however, when Eliot revises his own critical judgment, as when he embraces *Homage to Sextus Propertius* in his postscript to the

Selecting Modernism 147

1948 edition of *Selected Poems*, perhaps understanding its Classical underpinnings and polyvocalism differently in light of *The Cantos*. In justifying his original excising of the poem (which he does not alter in later editions), Eliot makes the general point that "in the work of any major poet who does not repeat himself, the later part is necessary for understanding the earlier."[24] Not only is the early work necessary for understanding the poet's trajectory and how he has prepared to write the later work, but—like the new poet altering the literary tradition that has preceded him—the later work highlights themes and tendencies in the early work, the significance of which may be seen only in retrospect. This formulation suggests that, for Eliot, one of the primary responsibilities of a selected volume of poems is to select and arrange poems not from the perspective of their writing or initial publication but from the standpoint of a poet's most realized poetic production. Eliot would expand upon this principle in his editing of Moore and Kipling.

Less Is Moore

In 1935, seven years after the first printing of Pound's *Selected Poems*, Faber would issue the *Selected Poems* of Marianne Moore. Seeing that by the mid-1930s her reputation in Britain was beginning to wane, Eliot suggested to Moore that "your poems ought to be collected, or at any rate selected and put upon the London market again."[25] This was a significant moment in the consolidation of poetic modernism, and, as Celeste Goodridge has noted, Moore's "dependency on Eliot—her 'strange parent'—has much to do with the enormous role he played in publishing this collection of her poetry."[26] Eliot saw the volume as much more than a business venture, however, or even a vehicle for increasing Moore's popularity in England. In publishing the volume, Eliot was making good on an old promise to see that Moore's work received the exposure it deserved—a promise that through life's little distractions had been compromised up to this point.[27] It was not only that Eliot felt a responsibility to disseminate the work of a modernist poet he deeply admired, however; his selection and arrangement of Moore's *Selected Poems* would also afford him an opportunity to address some of the anxieties that Moore's scrappy poetics had posed for his own poetry as he selected, arranged, and critically framed individual poems in accordance with his own aesthetic criteria of permanence, unity, order, and masculinity.[28]

Although Moore would eventually acquiesce in the publication of a volume of selected poems, recognizing it as a necessary vehicle for solidifying her poetic reputation within certain modernist circles, she also understood the ways in which such a volume might compromise a poetic project characterized by constant revision and accumulation—a recognition that accounts for what seems to be a willed misunderstanding, deep ambivalence, and profound indifference to Eliot's editing of her *Selected Poems*.[29] Initially, Moore seems to not even understand Eliot's request to edit such a volume. She believes that he is looking for a collection of new poems, which she has already promised to the New York-based Macmillan, though she says of Faber that "there is no house where I should like more to be allowed to feel at home."[30] Eliot explains to Moore, however, that what he has in mind is an edition of all of her work to date, making a point to single out the poem "Marriage," one of the long collage poems that he had previously reviewed and that parallels much of his own collage poetry.[31] After realizing Eliot's intention, Moore remains hesitant to compile a selected or collected works at all, not wanting to revive *Observations*, which she saw as a thing of the past, preferring to concentrate on more recent work.[32] Eliot could hardly put together a volume of selected poems without the most substantial book by a poet who didn't let too many poems see the light of day in the first place. Again, he explains that what he envisioned was a complete volume, minus only a very few poems she might wish to suppress.[33] Eliot suggests that, as with the previously issued volume by Ezra Pound, the book should simply be titled *Selected Poems*. A more subjective title might suggest to those unfamiliar with her work that Moore is a new author rather than an established figure worthy of a selected volume, and this would give ignorant reviewers a chance to be patronizing. The straightforward title also emphasizes supposedly objective processes of selection and arrangement rather than a particular subjective take on the work that might be suggested by a catchier phrase.

Moore would eventually agree to the *Selected Poems*, adding that "if you would care to introduce the book, or preface it with comment, I should be grateful," though characteristically insisting that "you must safeguard yourself in any way that seems best, against permitting this venture to be a bugbear."[34] Eliot claims to be not altogether happy with the introduction (or with such introductions generally), writing to Moore that "one feels something of the fatuity and superfluity of the chairman in after dinner speechmaking."[35] Moore was apparently overjoyed with the essay, however, responding that one "could scarcely be human and not wish your Introduction might have the effect of a tidal wave, on the public, that it has had on me," as it conveyed its energy of thought with sobriety and fine dignity.[36]

As with the Pound volume, Eliot's introduction to Moore's *Selected Poems* is an important critical intervention underscoring what he wishes others to see as central in Moore's poetry. First, Eliot points to "genuineness" as a key attribute of Moore's poetry and admits that "what I call *genuineness* is a more important thing to recognise in a contemporary than *greatness*," though genuineness is a prerequisite to greatness.[37] Such genuineness is to be contrasted against the poet who is popular for "extraneous reasons," and whose "effect upon contemporary readers may be a legitimate and proper result of some great poetry, but it has been also the result of much ephemeral poetry."[38]

The genuine for Eliot roughly corresponds to what he sees as the sense of "experience" behind Pound's best poetry that may intersect with, though is separate from, technical mastery. Moore certainly would agree with the importance Eliot places on genuineness; she does, after all, reserve a space for it as the word that concludes and in many ways justifies her radical revision of her poem "Poetry."[39] But Eliot (not unlike Palgrave before him) invests in the genuine as the basis for poetic value that accrues over time as a part of literary tradition, rather than as a function of history. As such, Eliot's pitting of the genuine against the "ephemeral" bristles against Moore's scrappy poetics and the ephemerality that characterizes so much of her source material. Moreover, ephemerality is not only a basis for Moore's subject matter and formal innovation, as I argued in the previous chapter, but is also demonstrated in her lifelong visions and revisions, which, as George Bornstein has observed, exhibit "not merely a series of variants but, more importantly, a physical enactment of the process of transmission of modernist poetry."[40] This process is a radically unstable one, however, and contrasts with transmission through a volume of selected or collected poems, which often aims to preserve and perpetuate poems (and, by extension, a larger canon of poetry) through stabilizing textual variation—printing only one version of a poem, for example. To drive the point home, Eliot argues that, far from being ephemeral, descriptive poetry is "really one of the permanent modes of expression," so that even on the level of technique, Moore's poems fit neatly into long-standing tradition.[41]

Beyond linking the genuine with the permanent, Eliot further defuses Moore's scrappy poetics and its engagement with mass print culture by attempting to resolve her contingent and serendipitous production into textual unity. He suggests that the first aspect of Moore's poems that is likely to hit the reader is "that of minute detail rather than that of emotional unity"—seemingly recognizing Moore's illumination of the particular without a desire for resolution.[42] Eliot is quick to recover from this position, however, arguing that "the detail has always its service to perform to the whole."[43] Not allowing for a lack of coherence, his reading strives to find unity in what seems to be "a very wide spread of association" that tests the bounds of an easy metonymy. To come to grips with this observation, Eliot claims only that the poet's choice of subject matter is a personal affair and need not be too closely scrutinized.[44] Privileging the unity of the poem over its individual (and, through revision, interchangeable) components further calcifies the poetic text that would be made widely available through reproduction in the *Selected Poems*.

This editorial principle is writ large as Eliot attempts to forge unity across the collection as a whole. Such unity comes about by placing poems into a web of connections that suggests more than the sum of its parts. As Eliot writes to Moore, who was concerned as to whether she had enough poetry to justify a volume of selected poems, the point at which one has enough poems for a collection is not merely a quantitative matter but also "a question of form. One only has not enough, when one feels that the poems written require the cooperation of certain poems not yet written, in order to be themselves quite."[45] As a microcosm of literary tradition, the later work in a volume of selected poems can serve to justify the earlier work and the poet's canon as a whole.

To enact this cooperation among poems in an effort to achieve this formal unity, Eliot would radically alter the collection's arrangement, though he would claim in his introduction that "I have hardly done more than settle the order of the contents."[46] Having received Moore's blessing to arrange the volume as he saw fit, Eliot imposed a reverse chronological ordering, moving the newer poems that Moore had written since ceasing editing of the *Dial* to the front and the older poems, many of which had been published in her 1924 *Observations*, toward the end.[47] As Eliot explains to Moore, even at her simplest she baffles those who love "simple" poetry, so she may as well begin with the more difficult work and make a bid for those readers willing to tackle such difficulty. It is also likely to sell more copies.[48] As Andrew J. Kappel has observed, placing these post-*Dial* poems first presented Moore as a writer of longish, syllabic, descriptive poems, crystallized by the decision to begin the volume with "The Steeple-Jack," a poem that is concerned with the dynamics of observation and description and that has foregrounded for many critics those elements of Moore's poetry.[49]

In addition to highlighting particular features of Moore's work, the rearrangement also obscures much of Moore's poetic development and poetic commitments. The insertion of free verse poems (1920-1925) between the shorter early syllabics (1915-1919) and longer early syllabics (1915-1919), rather than after both groups, where they chronologically belong, artificially separates the short and long syllabic poems into different formal categories and downplays the fact that Moore experimented heavily with *vers libre* just before the poetic hiatus she took while editing the *Dial*, though she would ultimately be unsatisfied with the less structured form.[50]

Further, the arrangement also depoliticized Moore's poems by taking them out of their earlier print contexts. For example, the relegation of "Sojourn in the Whale" to the end of the volume removes the poem from the political context of a divided Ireland that Moore meticulously chronicled (among other places) in her scrapbooks.[51] Similarly, although the original publication of "The Fish" in the August 1918 issue of the *Egoist* encouraged a politicized reading of the poem as commentary on the horrors of war (connotations that were somewhat muted in the more baroque rendering of the poem in *Poems* but that Moore again emphasized in *Observations* by juxtaposing it to an overtly militaristic poem, "Reinforcements"), its placement in the *Selected Poems* immediately following a poem about aesthetic objects, "Nine Nectarines and Other Porcelain," encourages a reading of the poem as primarily concerned with formal features rather than with social commentary.[52] This depoliticization of the poem is reinforced by Eliot's suggestion to Moore that the prominent placement of "The Fish" will likely frame it in such a way that it "will figure in anthologies of the English Association. Do not misinterpret this remark, I like the Fish very much, but I think it will frighten anthologists less than some."[53] As with his comment on booksellers, this remark suggests that beyond being attentive to the *Selected Poems* as a repository for Moore's poems and a formally coherent textual object in its own right, Eliot (rightly) saw the volume as a concrete means of shaping her reputation.[54]

This radical reordering and eschewing of an autobiographical poetic seems to be at odds with the emphasis Eliot placed on poetic trajectory in Pound's *Selected Poems*. Pound's was an ideal and highly contrived trajectory that only loosely mapped onto biographical reality, however, and in this respect Moore's *Selected Poems* closely resembles in its manipulations of publication history Pound's own volume. The reconstructed trajectory is perhaps more profound in Moore, though, because her collection consists of a number of unpublished poems that Eliot wished to foreground—so that it functions more as a cross between an original volume and a selection— and because there had not been previous attempts to select and arrange her work as there had been with Pound. As much editorial control as Moore relinquished to Eliot, the *Selected Poems* was, like Pound's volume, intended as an intermediate step to a full accounting of the poet's oeuvre, confirmed by Eliot's editing of Moore's *Collected Poems* a decade and a half later, which leads off with the *Selected Poems*. This can be contrasted with Eliot's choice of Kipling's verse, which would present not only a settling of poetic contents but also an unsettling of a reputation.

Reclaiming Kipling

It is not surprising that Eliot would edit the *Selected Poems* of Pound and Moore, given their formative influence on his own poetic identity and his genuine desire to help expand (as well as shape) their reputations. Less obvious, perhaps, is his rationale behind editing *A Choice of Kipling's Verse* (1941). As with the volumes of Pound and Moore, this "choice" says as much about Eliot's critical collecting and his relation to his poetic predecessors as it does about Kipling himself—a point commonly acknowledged by reviewers of the volume. Eliot's editorial role is foregrounded in the book's paratextual features: as opposed to the *Selected Poems* of Pound or Moore, the front cover displays Eliot's name prominently beneath Kipling's and the rear dust jacket flap lists critical works by Eliot rather than poems by either Eliot or Kipling (fig. 4.1). Beyond his editing of Pound and Moore, however, the editing of *A Choice* allows Eliot to relate the act of critical collecting to the conservation of an increasingly postimperialist and insular Britain—paralleling the concerns of his contemporaneous critical essays.

Kipling provided more than a convenient opportunity to muse on the current state of the nation, however. As Eliot would later reveal, "Traces of Kipling appear in my own mature verse where no diligent scholarly sleuth has yet observed them," explaining that "The Love Song of J. Alfred Prufrock" would not have been called a "Love Song" were it not for "The Love Song of Har Dyal" and that "The Hollow Men" owes its title to "The Broken Men" (the latter an acknowledgement that further complicates the colonial politics of a poem that takes its epigraph, "Mistah Kurtz—he dead," from

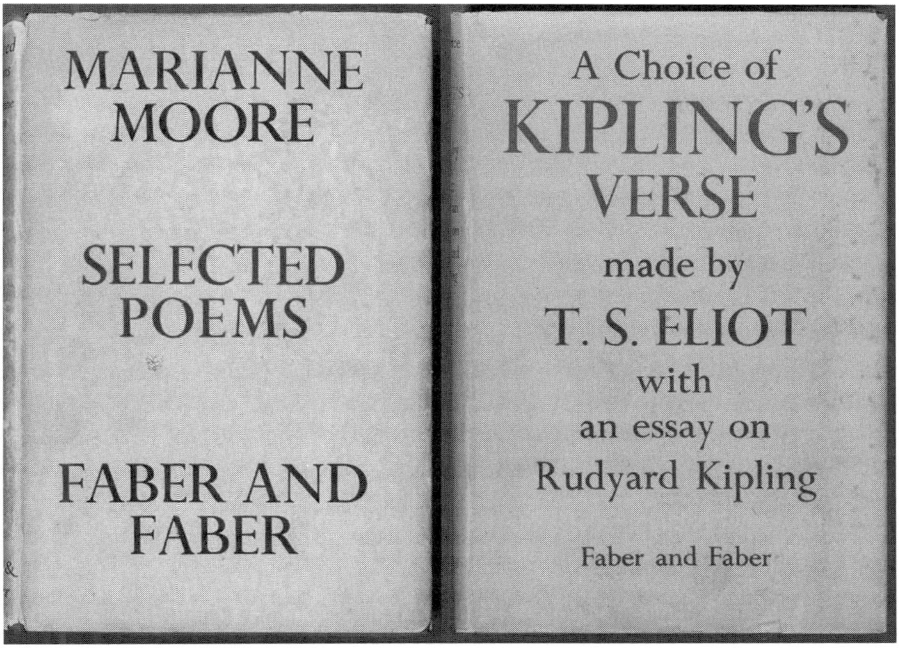

Figure 4.1. Comparison of Marianne Moore's *Selected Poems* and *A Choice of Kipling's Verse*, showing similarities in jacket design and relative prominence of Eliot's name.

Joseph Conrad's *Heart of Darkness*).[55] Nevertheless, Eliot acknowledges that *A Choice*

> aroused considerable astonishment in the world of letters, that Kipling should be championed not only as a prose writer but as a writer of verse, by a poet whose verse was generally considered to be at the opposite pole from Kipling's. Whereas my poems had appeared too obscure and recondite to win popular approval, Kipling's had long been considered too simple, too crude, too popular, indeed too near the doggerel of the music hall song, to deserve from the fastidious critic anything but disdain. I was suspected, if not of insincerity, at least of a mischievous delight in paradox.[56]

Arguing that Kipling's and his own work have merely *appeared* to be at opposite ends of the poetic spectrum, Eliot entices us to consider how his own writing might express popular sentiment in ways that had been (and largely remain) downplayed or ignored.[57] At the same time, he calls upon us to take Kipling's verse more seriously, as perhaps being invested in some of the same cultural questions that had driven his own poetic production.

It should be noted, however, that Eliot himself had not always recognized this dimension of Kipling's work. As he explains in an early essay, "The Defects of Kipling," "There is one fatal weakness penetrating and marring almost everything to which Kipling sets his hand; accounting for several of the minor blemishes; it is his restless and straining immaturity."[58] The statement is ironic not least of all because it was written in 1909 when Eliot was a Harvard undergraduate, in an essay for which he would receive a B+. Eliot would go on to suggest in the same essay that especially through his use of "local color in outlandish and unknown places," "Mr. Kipling was always more anxious to be striking than to be convincing."[59] Despite his obvious technical mastery, Kipling lacks sincerity and therefore fails to be a great writer. Eliot would later remark that he was not impressed by this early criticism, which he thought unduly harsh—though he did find his handwriting at the time to be surprisingly good.[60] Still, the essay is interesting for the way that it previews Eliot's lifelong interest in Kipling and his early attempts to separate the technical achievements of verse (and more general literary) form from biographically informed poetic experience and intention that Eliot would trace (among other places) in the *Selected Poems* of Moore and Pound.

Eliot would refine these impressions with particular reference to Kipling's poetry a decade later in his review essay, "Kipling Redivivus," on Kipling's collection *The Years Between*, remarking that "Mr. Kipling is very nearly a great writer" and that there is "an unconsciousness about him which, while it is one of the reasons why he is not an artist, is a kind of salvation."[61] Interestingly, Eliot compares Kipling to Swinburne, arguing that both poets register the "sound-value of oratory, not of music. . . . They persuade, not by reason, but by emphatic sound" that exhibits the emotion of the moment rather than tapping into some emotional reservoir independent of artist or audience.[62] They are poets of a few simple ideas without a coherent viewpoint, and it is only by historical happenstance that Swinburne is a poet of liberty and Kipling is a poet of empire, but, Eliot believes, "the alteration would be unimportant."[63] It is this lack of a coherent point of view around which tropes and images can orbit that makes the verse of Swinburne and Kipling "appear to lack cohesion—to be, frankly, immature."[64] Such a critique contrasts with Eliot's celebration of the "genuine" in Moore and his seeking to read her poems as unified forms, and even with his lifelong devotion to Pound, who—although a harbinger of some very bad ideas—would remain a man with a singular point of view, tossed between his better and lesser angels.

Extending the question of cohesion from individual poem to poetry collection and to a complete canon of work (that itself adds to literary tradition), Eliot is emphatic that the volume of Kipling's work under review at least "ought to be consistent with itself. . . . But the poems no more hang together than the verses of a schoolboy."[65] In this way, he importantly qualifies his previous critique of Kipling's work as an immature production, explaining that this immaturity is ultimately rooted in what appears to be a lack of symbolic coherence. The attempt to recover Kipling as an important, "mature" poet requires uncovering or constructing this coherence—in a way not unlike his editing of Moore's *Selected Poems*—and relying upon modernist ideas of genre and formal unity to make his case.

In the years preceding his editing of *A Choice*, however, Eliot had started to reconsider the implications of Kipling's verse. He would, for instance, favorably explain in a Faber reader's report of David Jones's *In Parenthesis* that there are aspects of the book "which give it somewhat the same kick that you get from something by Kipling, and I almost think that Kipling himself might have liked it. I don't mean that it is full of ordinary jingo or empire sentiment, but that the author has a kind of sense of history and a sort of sense of glory in the relation which is somewhat Kiplingesque."[66]

No doubt due in part to his thinking deeply about the relationship between poetry and verse with respect to both Pound and Moore, Eliot is able to confidently claim in his introduction to *A Choice* that "Kipling does write poetry, but that is not what he is setting out to do."[67] Rather, as Kipling works in the often critically debased ballad form, his "poetry, when it comes, owes the gravity of its impact to being something over and above the bargain, something more than the writer undertook to give you; and that matter is never simply a pretext, an occasion for poetry."[68] This easy divide between poetry and verse is complicated, however, by the volume's title, *A Choice of Kipling's Verse* (not unlike *Poetry*'s undercutting subtitle, *A Magazine of Verse*).

Admitting that much of Kipling's writing is "occasional," Eliot nevertheless stresses its lasting value and induction into literary tradition, noting that "the question is not what is ephemeral, but what is permanent: a poet who appears to be wholly out of touch with his age may still have something very important to say to it; and a poet who has treated problems of his time will not necessarily go out of date."⁶⁹ As it had been with both Pound and Moore, Eliot's solution to the problem of occasional verse production (which Moore, for one, would not necessarily find problematic) is not to recognize the importance of its historical contingency and the ways in which the poem may mean differently in a new time and place (even, as was the case with Moore, necessitating textual modification as well as a change of context). Rather, it is to find the least common denominator of historical meaning so that some permanent significance can be salvaged from the largely ephemeral.

Moreover, as in the case of the *Selected Poems* of both Pound and Moore, Eliot strives to find "unity in variety," acknowledging that "no part of Kipling's work, and no period of his work, is wholly appreciable without taking into account the others: and in the end, this work, which studied piecemeal appears to have no unity beyond the haphazard of external circumstances, comes to show a unity of a very complicated kind."⁷⁰ Eliot confesses that the critical tools that have customarily worked in analyzing poetry do not seem to work for Kipling, but he is unable or unwilling to conceive of a Kipling whose works do not form a unified whole, only that this whole must be a very complicated one.

The importance of *A Choice of Kipling's Verse* for a late modernist audience is announced by a blurb on the front dust jacket flap (which very well may have been written by Eliot himself⁷¹), claiming that the book is "something of a landmark in the history of English literature," taking a true account of Kipling's stature as a great English poet. And just in case we missed Eliot's name on the cover, we are told that we

> need not labour the significance of the fact that it has been made by a distinguished modern poet and critic at a time when all that Kipling prized is in danger. Mr. Eliot's long introduction will be read with manifold pleasure—the pleasure which all discriminating admirers of Kipling will derive from so true and fine an estimate of his poetry, the pleasure to be got from a major critical essay by Mr. Eliot, and, beyond all this, the very special and intense pleasure of seeing two periods of English literature join hands. "He, being dead, yet speaketh."⁷²

Echoing this praise for editor as much as poet, the back cover of the paperback reprint would reproduce a review from the *Spectator*, exclaiming that "Mr Eliot's essay is an admirable example of the finest type of criticism. He succeeds in making us look at his subject's work with freshly opened eyes and he is at once sober, illuminating and sound."⁷³

Other reviews are more critical of Eliot's introduction. The loudest complaints, curiously enough, are not that Eliot had ventured to find poetry in Kipling's verse but that he failed to recognize that some of this verse was really, truly poetry. As one reviewer asks, "Does one altogether agree that Kipling was only a great writer? Can we not disengage from his verse a number of true poems—not verses only that occasionally deviate into poetry?"⁷⁴ George Orwell, in his review of the collection, echoes this same critique, exclaiming that "apparently Kipling was a versifier who occasionally wrote poems, in which case it was a pity that Mr. Eliot did not specify these poems by name."⁷⁵ Orwell pushes Eliot's logic to its extreme, arguing that "one can, perhaps, place Kipling more satisfactorily than by juggling with the words 'verse' and 'poetry,' if one describes him simply as a good bad poet."⁷⁶ That is, rather than hold out exceptional cases of poetry within a general field of verse, all of it can be taken as good bad poetry. Orwell's formulation threatens to dismantle the very dichotomy of poetry and verse that has undergirded Eliot's critical assumptions not only about Kipling but also about modern poetry more generally, which (as I discussed in chapter 2) can be traced in part to such little magazines as *Poetry*. The separation of poetry and verse—based in the pervasive modernist division of technique and feeling in which the latter trumps the former—presents a false distinction for Orwell. For him there is only poetry, be it good or bad.

Orwell understands these terms as a matter of taste derived from lived experience. He explains that Mr. Eliot "thinks it worth while to edit [Kipling], thus confessing to a taste which others share but are not always honest enough to mention. The fact that such a thing as good bad poetry can exist is a sign of the emotional overlap between the intellectual and the ordinary man."⁷⁷ Good bad poetry (as opposed to good *good* poetry) could be described as the marriage of technical proficiency and base experience, and it could be said that Eliot enjoys reading Kipling in the way that he enjoys reading detective novels—not as a high intellectual pursuit but as a common (guilty) pleasure.

This good/bad distinction involves not only such personal experience but also political and moral judgment—rooted in communal experience—as well. In this context, the phrase "all that Kipling prized" from the *A Choice*'s jacket blurb should give us pause. It necessarily encompasses both Kipling's literary priorities and his political ones, especially a commitment to Indian colonialism that was increasingly marginalized with the shrinking of an empire and the realization of a new British provinciality. Orwell addresses this political dimension at the outset of his review, finding it his duty to remind us of Kipling that for "five literary generations every enlightened person has despised him, and at the end of that time nine-tenths of those enlightened persons are forgotten and Kipling is in some sense still there. Mr. Eliot never satisfactorily explains this fact, because in answering the shallow and familiar charge that Kipling is a 'Fascist,' he falls into the opposite error of defending him where he is not defensible."[78] Orwell acknowledges that Kipling is not a Fascist because he could never condone the hubris of a Hitler or a Mussolini but stresses that he "*is* a jingo imperialist, he *is* morally insensitive and aesthetically disgusting" and "has a definite strain of sadism in him."[79]

It is worth noting that Orwell's critique of Kipling's imperialism recalls Eliot's own earlier criticism of the poet. But this dimension of Kipling's work is downplayed in the introduction to *A Choice*. Eliot acknowledges that "the majority of readers do not want either imperialism or socialism in verse," but suggests that if one is to think of Kipling's writing as "political jingles," that the word "jingles" be emphasized rather than "political."[80] It is, however, too easy to simply chalk this statement up to an increasingly Right-minded critical negligence or an expunging of Kipling's record for literary posterity; rather, Eliot's downplaying of the imperialist themes in Kipling's work speaks more broadly to Britain's identity shift from an imperial power to a nation preoccupied with its own domestic history and culture.

As Jed Esty has argued, for Eliot, imperialism "supplied the cultural meaning around which modern Britain organized and justified itself: empire building was not just one feature of the post-Revolutionary nation; it was the nation's central mission."[81] Imperialism "animates and drives the centrifugal culture of post-Revolutionary England, extending and prolonging the social fragmentation of modernity, while poetry (in what Eliot would identify as a broadly romantic mode) provides it with representations of—and aesthetic compensations for—its fallen state," exemplified by such high modernist works as *The Waste Land*.[82] Eliot offers a partial solution to this dilemma in *The Idea of a Christian Society* (which he delivered as a series of Cambridge lectures in 1939, three years before editing *A Choice*), arguing that Britain's waning imperialism provides an opportunity for a renewed investment in insular domestic culture in which art and literature are not merely compensatory but also reflective of a unified people.

It is hardly surprising in this context that Eliot would celebrate Kipling's late poetic turn away from imperial themes and toward an insular England. As Eliot notes, in taking rural Sussex as his subject, Kipling is "concerned with the problem of the soundness of the *core* of empire; this core is something older, more natural and more permanent. But at the same time his vision takes a larger view, and he sees the Roman Empire and the place of England in it."[83] Eliot has found a kindred spirit in the late Kipling, who reimagines Britain as a domestic nation and as merely one thread in the European linguistic and cultural tapestry—ideas that Eliot would more fully articulate and complicate in his 1948 *Notes towards the Definition of Culture*, in which England has a familial relation to the nations of Europe and encompasses the Celtic subnations of Scotland and Wales.

For Eliot, the "Celtic fringe" provides England with an "other" through its lyrical poetry, which provides a manageable source of cultural difference that is nevertheless subject to English's linguistic hegemony.[84] This investment in regional difference coincides with Eliot's contention in "The Social Function of Poetry" that, while part of a larger tapestry of culture, poetry should be local and "every people should have its own poetry."[85] This investment in particularity serves to account for the great number of regional and colonial-born poets published by Faber, including Louis MacNeice (Ireland), Roy Campbell (white South African of Ulster descent who moved to North Wales), Idris Davies (Wales), Ronald Duncan (Southern Rhodesia), Keidrych Rhys (Wales), A. L. Rowse (Cornwall), and Vernon Watkins (Wales). Eliot makes this connection explicit in his preface to the *Selected Poems* of Edwin Muir, noting that while Muir is among the poets who have added glory to the English language, and of whom Scotland should be proud, there is something essential in his writing that is specifically Orcadian. There is "the sensibility of the remote islander, the boy from a simple primitive offshore community who then was plunged into the sordid horror of industrialism in Glasgow, who struggled to understand the modern world of the metropolis in London and finally the realities of central Europe in Prague."[86] Muir embodies the Celtic fringe as England's proximate other and becomes a conduit for a larger European context.

These developing ideas of the nation certainly colored Eliot's selection of Kipling's work and his emphasis on the late Sussex verse. Beyond highlighting the late poems, however, the act of choosing and arranging from all of Kipling's work is itself a circling of the wagons, turning Kipling's colonizing logic inward to poetic insularity. Freewheeling verse is circumscribed within the horizons of poetry, and the discrete object of the selected volume becomes a unified poetic whole. In this way, poetic and bibliographical form model the diversely unified and insular form of the English nation itself. To actually have an effect on that nation, however, *A Choice*, like the *Selected Poems* of Pound and Moore, needed to be made accessible through publication—an act that required Faber to negotiate a complex bibliographical field of print production in its solidification of poetic modernism.

Faber and the Modern Publication Field

Beyond promoting and helping shape individual reputations, the selected poems of Pound, Moore, and Kipling combine to form a picture of modernism as transnational, formally diverse, and steeped in a long literary tradition. Eliot was able to effectively promote this vision through his role as editorial director at Faber, where he negotiated a complex field of modern poetic production and reproduction that included other Faber titles, various periodicals, smaller and larger presses, and the vagaries of transatlantic publishing and international copyright law.

Connections among these individual poets are made evident in their being part of a publishing series marked by shared bibliographical codes. The second edition of Pound's *Selected Poems*, for example, was issued in 1933 with printers changed from Butler & Tanner to Kimble & Bradford. This provided the now-named Faber and Faber an opportunity to make the dimensions of the book and the size of the font slightly smaller than those of the first edition, while keeping pagination and lineation the same. An almost imperceptible change in itself, this effort made the book bibliographically consistent with the Faber Library Series, in which it was labeled number 17. In its new incarnation, the volume existed not only as a record of Pound's early poetry but also as part of Faber's larger claim on contemporaneous literature, which included such diverse books as Siegfried Sassoon's *Memoirs of an Infantry Officer* (1930, number 2 in the series) and *The Endless Furrow* by A. G. Street (1938, number 40 in the series). Similarly, Moore's *Selected Poems* advertised Faber's poetry list on its back cover, so that Moore could be read against other Faber finds and the criteria that promoted these poets.

The paperback reprint of *A Choice of Kipling's Verse* points to the ways in which Eliot's editing of Kipling had kick-started a series of projects in which well-known poets and other literary figures would edit works of their distinguished predecessors, including *A Choice of Dryden's Verse*, edited by W. H. Auden; *A Choice of Shelley's Verse*, edited by Stephen Spender; *A Choice of Shakespeare's Verse* and *A Choice of Dickinson's Verse*, both edited by Ted Hughes; and *A Choice of Whitman's Verse*, edited by Donald Hall. This series suggests the importance of choosing verse as a means of recovering and reconstructing a particular literary tradition that reinforced the linguistic and cultural legacy of contemporaneous British literature. The edited volumes of Pound, Moore, and Kipling—which owe their principles of selection and arrangement in large part to the act of book collecting—help materially manifest this collecting as the basis for dynamic tradition as they configure the book series of which they are a part and gain significance in relation to these series.

These volumes (and Faber's list as a whole) would also need to negotiate a larger field of print production, including the diverse field of periodical production, with which Eliot and the firm had a close, symbiotic relationship. Periodicals often supplied the poems that would be included and made more permanent in Faber books. They would also cultivate the reputations of Faber poets through the reviewing of books after their publication. This symbiotic relationship is most evident between Faber and the *Criterion*. Eliot had joined Faber in 1925 after having been the editor of the *Criterion* for three years, and from the beginning of his tenure promoted editorial compatibility between the periodical and the publishing house. Eliot explained to Geoffrey Faber at the time that he "did not have in mind an exact correspondence between the publishing and the review. That would limit both too narrowly. I should think it only desirable to avoid any gross inconsistency—ie publishing a book by some writer who had been consistently and steadily damned in the review."[87]

As Jason Harding has explained, however, the relation between the two print outlets became increasingly intertwined over the years as Faber came to financially support the *Criterion*, seeing it as a breeding and recruiting ground for such authors as W. H. Auden, Stephen Spender, Louis MacNeice, and Charles Madge, as well as a means of publicizing Faber's list through multiple reviews of such books as *The Faber Book of Modern Verse*, edited by Michael Roberts under Eliot's watchful eye.[88] In this sense, the *Criterion*—as opposed to both the earlier modernist *avant-garde* little magazines that existed largely on an economy of patronage and the more popular magazines driven largely by advertising to the masses—was a curious throwback to those nineteenth-century magazines such as *Scribner's* and *Harper's* that primarily functioned as vehicles for promoting their associated book publishing firms.

Beyond the specific connection to the *Criterion*, facilitated largely by Eliot's multifaceted editorial identity, Faber had a more general structural relation to the field of periodical production. In its publication of poetry books—whether originally issued volumes or the selected volumes I have closely examined—Faber frequently reproduced poems that had initially appeared in periodicals. In the case of a poet such as Moore, the texts of these poems could change significantly from magazine publication to its first publication in a book to its reproduction in a selected, collected, or complete volume of poems, complicating any version's claim to primacy or authority. This radical revision complicates the status of the *Selected Poems* as it foregrounds the question of not only which poems to choose for reproduction but which poems can legitimately be considered "finished" in the first place and therefore valid for inclusion. Moreover, the periodical foregrounds the poem's ephemerality, in which (even in relatively stable texts) meaning is made in accordance with historically contingent, and continually shifting, contexts. Such mutability flies in the face of the *Selected Poems'* relatively decontextualized and static presentation of the permanently valued poem, and its bid to be placed into literary tradition.

These textual and contextual issues between the book of poems and the periodical are also at play (perhaps to a lesser degree) in the *Selected Poems'* relationship to the field of book production. During the midcentury institutionalization and consolidation of poetic modernism, New Directions in the United States (which, started by James Laughlin in 1936, in many ways stood as Faber's counterpart across the pond) occupied an emerging intermediary place between an earlier dialectic of smaller and larger presses. This place was roughly analogous to what Lawrence Rainey has argued for as the location of the limited edition book at the height of modernism, which "occupied the middle position in the larger tripartite structure of avant-garde and modernist publishing (between journal and commercial edition)."[89] Private *avant-garde* presses, such as the Egoist Press and Hogarth Press, had stood on the front lines of modernism, publishing experimental work in small editions for select audiences. Larger commercial presses, such as Macmillan, appealed to a more mainstream readership and helped popularize the work of the smaller independent presses as they brought the coterie to the wider public. Faber (along with New Directions) would synthesize a position be-

Selecting Modernism 163

tween these extremes by constantly juggling market value and aesthetic value in its promotion of the literary.⁹⁰

The extent to which Faber was attempting to distinguish itself from both the smaller modernist presses and the larger commercial ones is evident in Eliot's initial inquiry into publishing Moore's *Selected Poems*, in which he notes to Moore that the run of her initial *Poems* was very limited and that Harriet Shaw Weaver, who had published the book, was not as well positioned to get books advertised or reviewed.⁹¹ Faber, by contrast, was capable of producing and distributing a larger run and (through its negotiation with such periodicals as the *Criterion*) had developed a network for publicizing and reviewing modern poets. At the same time that he points to Faber's capacity to get Moore's work the exposure it deserved, he emphasizes the cultural capital the firm's list had started to accrue as distinct from the more strictly financial motives of the larger presses, noting that there is not much money in poetry for anyone but she would be joining a very select poetry list.⁹²

Even as it jockeyed for position in the publishing field, however, Faber was aware of its debt to the small presses that had incubated poetic modernism and made a point to not entirely edge them out of the marketplace. After agreeing to publish in the *Criterion* a short notice of the Egoist Press's publication of Dora Marsden's *The Definition of the Godhead*, Eliot asked Harriet Shaw Weaver whether her press had other intentions for publication and offered to help in any way, including recovering volumes that had been entrusted to the *Criterion* and subsequently controlled by Faber.⁹³ Eliot's motives for the most part appeared to be altruistic (though Eliot and Marsden were never the best of friends and he was perhaps not too keen on publishing her work in the first place), but his continual support of the Egoist Press also allowed for the possibility that more cutting-edge or obscure work could be tested in a small press run before Faber committed to a larger edition.

Faber would also give bigger jobs to the larger commercial firms, which often relied upon Eliot's experience and recommendations. Eliot, for example, writes to the British-based Macmillan that Hugh MacDiarmid's long poem *Mature Art* seems to be "a remarkable work" and deserves to be published, but, because it is of considerable length and because Faber had made financial commitments to other volumes of verse, they were unable to fund the project and hoped that Macmillan would consider it.⁹⁴ While Faber lacked the capital to bring MacDiarmid's work into print, Eliot acts as critical intermediary, delivering a seal of approval for the artistically admirable, though commercially questionable, book (though, perhaps for economic reasons, Macmillan likewise declined to publish the poem in its entirety). The letter suggests the extent to which Eliot believed the commercial firms might heed his advice and reminds us of the lengths he would go to in order to help publish a poet of promise—even if it wasn't with Faber.[95]

As much as Eliot was invested in fashioning through *A Choice* and elsewhere a particularly British identity, his and Faber's interactions with commercial publishers were not limited to those within Britain. In many ways, Faber's success depended on a transnational network of publishing that would help define poetic modernism in Britain and on the larger global stage. Faber's dependency on this network is evident in its issuing of Moore's *Collected Poems* a decade and a half after first publishing the *Selected Poems*, where, rather paradoxically, Moore's reputation in Britain depended largely upon the volume being published in the United States as well.

After overcoming renewed concerns about collecting her more recent work, Moore finally acquiesced to the *Collected Poems*, which Eliot would once again have a heavy hand in editing.[96] Concerned with both the costs of publication and with Moore's standing in America, Eliot wonders whether some New York publisher might go in on publishing the *Collected Poems*, as had been done with the *Selected Poems*, preferably importing printed sheets from Faber.[97] Moore explains that she was contractually bound to offer the collection to Macmillan, but she was disappointed that the *Selected Poems* had languished in America without a reprinting and didn't want Eliot to count on Macmillan's interest.[98] In the hopes of securing a more enthusiastic firm, Moore gave Macmillan an opportunity to bow out gracefully.[99] Not surprisingly, however, Macmillan was interested in issuing the *Collected Poems*, and its vice president, H. S. Latham, notified Peter du Sautoy of Faber that the house would wish to publish the book, either through manufacturing or importing sheets or bound books.[100] That is, Macmillan was weighing the options of importing complete books published by Faber, importing pages manufactured by Faber and binding those pages together under the Macmillan imprint, or printing its own pages altogether. Macmillan saw the economic incentive for printing its own sheets and, as a large publishing firm, was fully capable of doing so. This likely would not have threatened an edition at home (although, given Moore's dependence on Eliot's advice for selection and arrangement, it may have been a very different version from the one we are familiar with). But it may well have kept an edition from being issued in Britain.

Faber, a midsized publishing firm without Macmillan's vast resources (made evident in Eliot's willingness to give up publishing MacDiarmid's *Mature Art*), would have been taking a big risk in publishing an American author without a guarantee that another publisher would use its sheets. It would have done so at significant financial cost, which in turn might affect which other projects could safely be taken up. Faber was in a difficult situation: if its sheets were too expensive for Macmillan to purchase, the firm would manufacture its own; if the sheets were too cheap, Faber would lose money on any transaction. As a result, Eliot, who encouraged the enterprise in the first place, could end up not being able to issue the book in Britain or would have to do so at a substantial loss. The agreement would not only secure Moore's reputation in her home country but also would keep Faber on surer economic footing than if it ventured alone.

There were, however, convincing reasons for importing the sheets. As evidenced in exchanges over her *Selected Poems*, Eliot was an editor whose judgment Moore deeply trusted (perhaps too much at times), and Faber did good presswork. Moore reminds Latham that her Faber *Selected Poems* did not contain the misprints that had made their way into the New York edition and mentions to du Sautoy that she still felt slighted that Macmillan had chosen not to import from Faber sheets for the *Selected Poems*.[101] With help from Moore, Faber and Macmillan were eventually able to make arrangements, where Macmillan would import sheets from Faber with a Macmillan imprint and would pay Moore ten cents royalty per imported copy.[102] In manufacturing a cheap edition of the book, Macmillan would need to pay a smaller royalty, but the firm recognized that, as with any book of poems, the limited readership meant that the situation was unlikely to occur.[103]

As much as the Macmillan publication of Moore's *Collected Poems* in the United States had facilitated its publication by Faber in Britain, the fact that Moore was a foreign author made her, as she recognized, a bit of a clerical inconvenience.[104] This inconvenience extended to both sides of the Atlantic, and, shortly after the Faber sheets were printed, Latham writes to Moore that her status as an American had led to some peculiar publishing problems.[105] Macmillan had presumably been denied the use of a legal loophole that allowed an American publisher to import up to 1,500 copies of a foreign edition, securing interim copyright protection until an American edition could be made, but Latham found the situation to be a ridiculous one, as the word "foreign" had always applied only to manufacture, and now it was to include foreign authorship as well.[106]

While it is difficult to pin down the rationale, the confiscation likely followed from the 1909 US copyright law, which states that, when a book is imported, "such a privilege of importation shall not extend to a foreign reprint of a book by an American author copyrighted in the United States."[107] The clause, designed as it was to protect US manufacturing interests, may have been enforced on the radical assumption that the *Collected Poems*, with its inclusion of previously published poems, itself constituted a kind of reprinting. From a materially minded legal standpoint (in this case, at least), it seems that there is no difference between a book of selected or collected poems as a fundamentally new aesthetic object and original piece of intellectual property, and an earlier book of poems that had simply been reprinted. This lack of legal distinction underscores the extent to which selected and collected volumes of poems are seen not as individual creative acts of synthesis but as the material embodiment of objective collecting practice made independent of any individual collector.

Eventually, everything worked out for Faber, Macmillan, and Moore. Most of the imported sheets were stopped, but, because some of the stock had already been released, Macmillan took a chance on distributing the forty-odd copies of the English edition that Moore had inscribed and that had already been distributed to reviewers in advance (a very rare true first American edition). Faber had already printed the sheets and taken the money, so the British edition was secure. Moore, characteristically, offered to forgo her royalties to absorb the loss, but Macmillan printed the sheets at its own expense, and, because they were manufactured in the United States, Moore actually received a larger royalty than she otherwise would have.[108] Still, nearly 1,500 copies is a lot to be refused. It is a lot for a book of poetry; it would have been even more so for a poet who had not become as celebrated as Moore. And it would have been a greater burden if the importing publisher had been a medium-sized American firm like New Directions, with its own more limited resources.

The incident exposes the extent to which, by the middle of the twentieth century, international copyright proved to be a legal constraint that inhibited the free flow of a global modernism based in the transnational distribution of publishing capital and the cheap reproduction of texts. Nevertheless, the fact that Moore's *Collected Poems* was produced relatively inexpensively in both the United States and Britain also suggests that the material grounds on which US international copyright had been based since the passing of the Chase Act in 1891 were eroding in the presence of an increasingly dematerialized text. Paradoxically, through mass reproduction the modern poetic text becomes more pervasive and permanent while the book through which it is materially embodied approaches the cheap and ephemeral.

This reproduction allowed Eliot and Faber to significantly impact the transnational consolidation of poetic modernism. In his editing of the *Selected Poems* of Pound and Moore and *A Choice of Kipling's Verse*, Eliot drew upon the book collector's notions of selection and arrangement that had throughout poetic modernism been defined and complicated along lines of objective and permanent poetic value, a distinction between poetic genre and verse form, and a sense of textual coherence. Eliot's position at Faber meant that his acts of critical collecting were not merely theoretical but also helped determine—within a highly negotiated field of modern print—how the work of modern poets was to be received. Other figures, however, would realize alternatives to this reproduction and consolidation through the preservation of books, drafts, versions, and contextualizing documents in formally institutionalized modern poetry libraries and archives that structurally resemble the gatherings of the scrapbook—though these would in practice often rely on New Critical notions of selecting and collecting that owed much to Eliot and to modernist notions of critical collecting.

5 Instituting Modernism
The Rise of the Modern American Poetry Archive

A letter from Allen Tate, the second Consultant in Poetry at the Library of Congress, to Archibald MacLeish, the librarian of Congress—a *Report of a Dada Conversation in the Division of Manuscript on September 29, 1943 at 10:30 AM*:

> TATE (closing the box of Henry James letters to Pearsall Smith—which letters incidentally are folded across the middle and are still in the original envelope in which Percy Lubbock returned them to Smith): I will have to see how many of these letters Lubbock used in his <u>Letters of Henry James</u>.
>
> MARTIN (worried): Yes, the finest collection of historical material that we have here is the Andrew Jackson collection.
>
> Interval
>
> TATE: I would like to see the letters of Virginia Woolf to Logan Pearsall Smith.
> ANON. (small with red hair): Who was she?
>
> Interval
>
> TATE: Don't you think that the literary manuscripts in the general Collection should be separately cataloged and perhaps merged with the poetry archives?
> 2ND ANON. (slender, grey): We are waiting for Mr. Auslander to return before we decide whether to break up the archive and distribute it into a general collection.[1]
> TATE: But don't you think there should be a separate catalog of literary material?
> 2ND ANON.: There is so much overlapping it would be difficult to tell what is literary.

I submit that the point of view and the facts indicated above point to an intolerable situation as regards literary material in the Division of Manuscripts. I predict that there will be resistance to any attempt at reform. A closely documented survey of these conditions would take the entire time of one person over many months. Mr. Mearns tells me that for some time he has been in favor of filling the first vacancy in this division with a literary man.[2] This would seem to me to be the real solution of the problem.[3]

Labeling the above exchange a Dada conversation, Tate mocks what he sees as a jarring cognitive dissonance between the literary and historical uses of manuscript materials and between the roles of the literary researcher and the librarian-preservationist. The gap can be bridged, Tate offers, through the employment of a "literary man," who will institute a specifically literary collection of rare books and manuscripts. Such a collection would make public the acts of acquisition, assessment, and arrangement that have long guided the private collecting of books and ephemera and that conditioned notions of modern poetic value, genre, and form.

In this final chapter, I examine the rise of the modern poetry archive as a mechanism for the preservation of poetic modernism and as a particular instance of the institutionalized public archive that helped make possible the archival turn across the humanistic disciplines. It is worth pausing for a moment, however, to consider just what we mean by the term "archive." As Marlene Manoff has noted, the term tends to be ambiguous, governed by two institutional and theoretical forces: "One is the conflation of libraries, museums, and archives; and the other is the inflation of the term 'archive,' which has become a loose signifier for a disparate set of concepts" related to information management and technologies of memory.[4]

To take the second part of this definition first, archival thinking in its most expansive sense has tended to follow definitions set out by the likes of Michel Foucault and Jacques Derrida. For example, in *Archaeology of Knowledge*, Foucault takes the archive to mean not the sum of documents used to attest to the past and a continuing presence, nor the institutions for preserving such documents, as we might mean in a more restricted sense. Rather, he claims that the archive is "the law of what can be said, the system that governs the appearance of statements as unique events" without flattening out the history of those events.[5] The archive, for Foucault, "is that which, at the very root of the statement-event, and in that which embodies it, defines at the outset *the system of its enunciability*.... [I]t is that which defines the mode of occurrence of the statement-thing; it is *the system of its functioning*.... [I]t is that which differentiates discourses in their multiple existence and specifies them in their own duration. . . . It is *the general system of the formation and transformation of statements.*"[6]

In a similar vein, Derrida argues in *Archive Fever* that the archive, "as printing, writing, prosthesis, or hypomnesic technique in general is not only the place for stocking and for conserving an archivable content *of the past* which would exist in any case, such as, without the archive, one still believes it was or will have been. No, the technical structure of the *archiving* archive also determines the structure of the *archivable* content even in its very coming into existence and in its relationship to the future. The archivization produces as much as it records the event."[7] The archiving process—which, in its expansive sense, may take the form of an institutional archive or a published one—not only marks the past but charts the future as well. It limits the horizons of interpretation in accordance with individually subjective, historically contingent criteria.

Such definitions of the archive and archivization run the risk of abstracting the concept to the point of near meaninglessness and are open to critiques of material and historical specificity, such as those by Carolyn Steedman, who responds to Derrida's "archive fever" with an accounting of actual fevers and maladies as occupational diseases brought on by working in the archive and then proceeds to write a cultural history of the archive, its space, and its constitutive objects.[8] While such consideration of the material archive serves to direct attention to the specific sites of inquiry that have formed the basis of the humanities' archival turn, it is important, as Dominick LaCapra reminds us, to not fetishize the archive and place in dubious opposition the written text of history and those texts the archive has preserved. We must recognize that one dominating force of the archive is "the prior 'constructions' of the archive itself, which render it something more than a stock of raw material or a series of mere facts, in that the material it contains is preselected and configured in certain ways, for example, in terms of state interests or the interests of other institutions (such as religious institutions) that create and manage archives, often suppressing and getting rid of embarrassing material."[9]

While it is indeed the case that archives have been subject to deliberate acts of suppression, the winnowing of archival materials has also often been seen as a practical necessity in an age of bulk print documents, so that only a small percentage of what is produced ever makes it to the archive. Still, as David Greetham notes, even conceding the necessities of such selection, "the practical, taxonomic, and ontological question remains: what is the *everything* from which those few select shards will be saved, and how do we identify the documentary limits of a body of material which is then to be winnowed?"[10] This question is central to general archival practice, prompting us to consider the principles of selection that governed the construction of the archive in the past and our own principles that may be upheld or challenged in the future.

This question is also central to the literary archive in particular. As Wilhelm Dilthey argued in his 1889 talk at the newly founded Gesellschaft für Literaturgeschichte (Society for Literary History), the literary archive occupies an uneasy space between the library and the archive proper in that it receives its authority both from the archive administrator and from the originating author: "Just as the state archive receives its character and particular governing spirit from the nature of political papers, so, too, a genius loci will emerge in these rooms, and from the estate of eminent authors and its nature will develop the character and the law of the archive" that determines its principles of selection and organization.[11] For Dilthey, the literary archive offers a way out of the hermeneutics of the text, in which we "understand a work in its relationship to its coming into being in the spirit of its creator, and we understand this living, spiritual relationship through individual works. We fully escape the circle of this hermeneutic operation only where drafts and letters produce an inner, fully living relationship between isolated and cold printed works."[12]

Dilthey anticipates much of the genetic and historical criticism of the twentieth century that would depend on the institutionalization of the literary archive, but he also points to how the literary archive suffers the same concerns over selection and organization that plague the state archive. As we turn our attention to the rise of the modern poetry archive in particular, we might ask, to what extent did the modern poetry archive and manuscript collection merely mimic the priorities already set forth in the treasured library of first editions and other rare books that offered one image of the past, privileging objective value and definitive genre? Even as it offered possibilities for genetic and historical criticism through the preservation of manuscripts, drafts, notes, correspondence, and records of collateral reading that looked and acted much more like the scrapbooker's accumulation than a collection of books orderly arrayed along the shelf, was the assumed scope of the modern poetry archive still those poets whose careers followed a familiar trajectory of little magazines, individual books of poems, and volumes of selected and collected works? Would such an archive merely demonstrate how the genius and coherence of the finished poem gradually coalesced? Or would it place the poem in fundamental dialogue with mass print culture by documenting influences, references, inspiration, and contemporaneous contexts that alter our understanding of the poem itself? In what ways, if any, did the archive expand upon or challenge the assumed *everything* of modern poetry?

As Jeremy Braddock has noted, the struggle to promote and define the modern poetry archive was taking place in such public poetry collections as the Poetry Collection at the University of Buffalo and the James Weldon Johnson Memorial Collection of Negro Arts and Letters at Yale during the very decades in which the restricted modern poetry canon was being consolidated through literary scholarship, especially New Criticism. The public modern poetry collection provided through such printed materials as little magazines and first edition books alternative poems and versions of poems to those in volumes of selected and collected poems, which have frequently been the basis for New Critical close readings. These documents—along with letters, drafts, and ephemeral clippings—have helped further reveal authorial intention and context, expanding the canon of poetic modernism and uncovering possibilities for historical and genetic scholarship that complicated New Critical attention to the text itself. As Tate's call for a "literary man" suggests, however, the relationship between the modern poetry collection and New Criticism is not an entirely oppositional one. The overlapping agendas of Allen Tate, Conrad Aiken, and Randall Jarrell, all of whom consulted for the Library of Congress on how to build its print and manuscript collections, while simultaneously arguing for the coherent meaning of the literary text, point to the ways in which literary criticism at the midpoint of the twentieth century—particularly as it congealed into what has come to be known as New Criticism—has helped justify the preservation of particular poets and texts while privileging notions of formal and cultural unity.

At the same time, the building of modern poetry libraries and archives, influenced by New Critical assumptions and by a more general archival logic of selection and collection, restricted the poets and texts made available for critical investigation. In this vein, the modern poetry library and archive can be read into more general debates on the form and function of the midtwentieth-century archive, even as they specifically demarcate genre, tradition, and the definition of the literary itself. As a response to an increasingly fractured and dispersed culture of mass print, the modern poetry library, archive, and manuscript depositories exhibited new methods of selection, preservation, and classification that privileged the supposedly objective, organic unity of the collection.

This emphasis on organic unity coincided with New Criticism's renewed interest in the organic unity of the poem. It was not a historical accident that Tate, MacLeish, and other New Critics or New Critical fellow travelers were such powerful players in one of the most important literary and cultural institutions in the country. New Critical emphases on critical selection and formal closure correspond to general ideologies of the archive that not only affected what and how materials were preserved in the modern poetry collection but—even in those collections ostensibly most dedicated to expanding literary history and new avenues of scholarship—also helped create a particular canon of poets that did not significantly differ from that enshrined in volumes of selected and collected poems. The general failure to recognize this fact has left us to trust the objectivity of the institutionalized modern poetry library, archive, and canon in ways that scholars are only now beginning to seriously reconsider. Such reconsiderations are rooted not only in traditional literary questions but in conceiving of the modern poetry archive as a bibliographical form selecting from and mediating the ever-increasing bulk of mass print.

The Modern Archive in the Age of Bulk

The modern poetry archive is a particular manifestation of the more general modern archive, whose origins in the United States can be traced to the first decade of the twentieth century as a response to the rise of mass print in what archivists frequently referred to as "the age of bulk." As one such archivist explains the "machine age has brought to the student the problem of dealing with a volume of manuscript sources such as to appall all but the less careful and the less scrupulous. From the typewriter, the dictaphone, the mimeograph machine, and other instruments devised to produce or duplicate the document on paper and on film have issued a mass production comparable to any other machine-made product of this industrial age." This machine-made archive—created by specific technologies, such as the typewriter, that sped up textual production, and by a rise of bureaucratic and corporate organization that demanded a constant interchange of memoranda among departments and reports issued in triplicate—resulted in a "situation of over-abundant source materials."[13]

Archivists approached this supposed overabundance in much the same way that bibliographers and book collectors had done before them: by selecting from the flood of mass print and attempting to organize it into coherent unity. It has been argued that in our contemporary context archivists are "no longer regarded as the neutral guardian of historical source materials—the 'raw materials' of history, as the traditional industrial manufacturing metaphor depicted archival records—but as active agents in the process of shaping our knowledge of the past."[14] It is clear, however, that at least since the 1940s, archivists have not pretended to this neutral status either. As the archivist Renée Doehaerd bluntly puts it, the problem of the modern archive is not preservation or classification "but the necessary task which faces us all, and which becomes increasingly urgent, of destroying a large part of them. And by destruction, I do not mean the necessary destruction of documents which duplicate others, but pure destruction, which will relegate certain facts to oblivion by eliminating the written evidence of things that might have been remembered. . . . This work of destruction places us in a position to choose the picture which our contemporary world will leave to the men of the future through the written document."[15] To help them sleep at night and wake refreshed for another day of slashing and burning, modern archivists devised numerous principles of selection that would allow them to "refine" much of the historical record, including the destruction of (supposed) duplicate or "overlapping" documents, privileging a document of general scope over one of particular scope, preserving types of information and at least one representative from each type, preserving statistical information that itself has been culled from numerous other documents, and (with an air of presumption not to go unchallenged) "eliminating documents which lack historical interest."[16] Some archivists attempted to shift blame to the document creators themselves, arguing that their administrative or historical intentions, and the physical origin of the document, "which may include a paper mill, an ink factory, or a quarry where graphite is obtained for pencils," are the most important factors in determining what is to be kept in the archive—all but absolving the archivist of her stated responsibilities.[17]

This selection led in part to the notion of the catalogable unit as "a collection of mutually related items, such as the letters comprising the correspondence of an individual or the single manuscript unrelated to any other item in the collection."[18] This concept of the unit has been used in defense against the notion that records should be broken up and arranged according to subject matter or in some other manner that would facilitate research. Solon J. Buck, in his capacity as archivist of the United States from 1941 to

Instituting Modernism

1948, explains that the archival document, "although it may be physically separate from all other documents, is not an independent item as are most books and pamphlets. It is, as a rule, a part of a file or a dossier, which in turn is part of a series, which is a part of the body of records or archives of an agency; and much of its significance depends upon its relationship to the other documents in these categories."[19]

These relationships were often naturalized, where "records have meaning only insofar as they are kept together and their organic relationship to each other retained. As long as that relationship is retained, that body of records has harmony, symmetry, and significance. In short, it is alive. To dismember it, and to distribute the chopped-up parts to the four corners of an archival depository is to destroy the life which makes the content of that body of records meaningful." In this respect, the archive was frequently compared to the book, where "the physical dismemberment of an organized body of the archives of an agency is as outrageous and destructive an act as the physical dismemberment of a book, and it is only because some librarians have fallen into the misconception of thinking of a single document in an archival collection as being analogous to a book that they would even propose such a practice. It is rather the record group which is the true archival analogue for the book which constitutes the indivisible unit with which a librarian deals."[20]

It's difficult to square this concept of the archival unit with the fact that much of what goes into this unit has already been destroyed. If the archival unit is indeed like the book, it's like a book in which pages have been torn out, the binding broken, and the cover ripped off so that it can more easily fit on the shelf—bringing to mind the extra-illustrated book or scrapbook rather than the pristine first edition.[21] But it is the fiction of this archival unit that serves to justify the destruction of records in the first place. In this sense, the record *does* function like some books such as the objective anthology, which claims coherence based on the selection and arrangement of its privileged parts, or like the volume of selected poems that limns the contours of a poet's career.

Although initially placed in opposition to the archive, manuscript collections would also by midcentury succumb to this archival logic that privileges fidelity to the documents over fidelity to the user, provenance and chronology over subject classification, the whole record over the individual illuminating detail, and organic unity over artificial construction. Historically, the archive, with its parallel in the library's collection of books, had frequently been placed in opposition to the haphazard accumulation of unique, historical manuscripts. Archives were thought to be better organized than were manuscripts, continuous whereas manuscripts are sporadic, and arranged according to provenance rather than chronology or subject matter—loyal to the original documents rather than the demands of the researcher.[22]

The institutionalization of the archival profession itself had been in part a reaction to the study of manuscripts. The establishment of the Public Archives Commission in 1899 was in direct response to the founding of the Historical Manuscripts Commission in 1895, and the "existence side by side of these two standing committees indicates that the distinction between historical manuscripts and archives was roughly understood." A primary reason for the creation of a separate archival profession in the United States was a "failure in this country to distinguish clearly between public archives and miscellaneous collections of historical manuscripts and to provide for the systematic preservation of public archives in central depositories, under the care of trained officials."[23]

By the time the Society of American Archivists was founded in 1936, however, there was "never any question but that the term 'archives' was to be used in a broad sense to include private and business archives and collections of historical manuscripts."[24] By 1943, 41 percent of individual members were in official archive agencies, 29 percent in the historical societies or manuscript collecting agencies, and 16 percent in federal agencies other than the National Archives.[25] Of the 226 founding members of the society, 19 were state archivists, 83 were on National Archives staff, 56 were curators of historical manuscripts, and 20 were academic historians, although the curators of historical manuscripts "harbored some very artificial collections with nothing organic about them except perhaps some silverfish not yet removed."[26]

As this last colorful comment suggests, although manuscript curators were welcome in the society, it was recognized that (as opposed to the organic archivist) the manuscript curator often collected manuscripts artificially, acquired collections that were themselves the artificial constructions of private collectors, and incorporated documents displaced from their original records. If, however, the curator has developed a plan of collecting with a sound historical basis, "his richest material consists of bodies of organic papers of persons or families, organizations, or institutions, in their original order of arrangement, as the hypothetical archivist of any one of them would have preserved them." In this case, each group "is an organic entity and will be filed as such, but their interrelationship is fully as important historically as that between record groups within a larger corpus of archives." When the manuscript curator is most deliberate in his collecting and mindful of the organic connections among his materials, he most closely resembles the archivist. And as a practical point, "many librarians, especially those in charge of manuscript divisions of libraries, are also archivists in that they have accepted the responsibility of administering bodies of official records."[27]

Responding to this shifting sense of responsibility, the 1948 report from the American Historical Association's ad hoc committee on manuscripts confirms the close ties between modern manuscripts and the archive. Echoing those who saw the modern archive as a response to the rise of mass print, the committee recognizes that "the invention of the typewriter and the gradual increase in its use has, by now, made necessary what amounts to a revolution in archival practice with regard to the handling of manuscript materials of recent origin" that are not subject to the same careful arrangement and cataloging that was given to manuscripts in the past. Although not explicitly stated, it would seem that those documents generated by the instruments of mass culture hardly deserve the term "manuscript"—which, after all, connotes a document that is handwritten. Although the committee does recommend that manuscript materials be arranged chronologically rather than retain their original ordering as generally advocated by public archivists, it also stresses a sense of periodicity that likewise governed the objective anthology and a modernist sense of tradition, where relatively short periods are to be "treated as sub-groups, and within these groups [items are to] be alphabetically arranged." While given as pragmatic advice rather than a point of orthodoxy, the committee also recommends that the "indexing of individual items, however ideally desirable, be considered for practical purposes the exception rather than the rule" and that "certain ephemeral types of material . . . are not in the long run, worth the time it would take to put them in usable shape."[28]

It is evident that by the middle decades of the twentieth century archivists and manuscript curators had established principles of selection and arrangement, as well as the practical limits of those activities, that helped dictate how meaning was made through the collecting of personal papers and other ephemeral materials—whether they originated from an individual or an institution. These general principles would be adhered to in the emergence of the modern poetry archive, as particularly evident in Tate's work at the Library of Congress and key collections at the University of Chicago and the University of Buffalo.

Collecting Modernism

The Library of Congress's lack of a literary collection or a stated policy for building one provoked Tate to propose in 1943 a tentative policy for enhancing the American literary manuscripts collections. Tate notes in his proposal that the Library of Congress had the beginnings of collections by only nine writers, some of whom are of dubious distinction today: Maxwell Anderson, William Rose Benét, Heywood Broun, Robinson Jeffers, Elizabeth Madox Roberts, Edwin Arlington Robinson, John Steinbeck, George Sterling, and Elinor Wylie. In line with general thinking on the modern archive that I examine later in this chapter, Tate expands the definition of the literary manuscript to mean "any holograph or typewritten paper or corrected proof sheet, which illuminates for the scholar or critic an author's process of composition. This definition includes letters to and from the author and miscellaneous papers which reveal the writer's relation to his society and his art. Publishers' archives should be one of the chief sources of this material. A 'literary' writer is a poet, novelist, historian, scientist, or any person who functions primarily in the medium of books." In addition to swelling the definition of "literary" beyond books and "manuscript" to also include typewritten materials and the institutional archives that have been left behind by bulky mass print, Tate further notes that even if the library were to decide to collect American literary manuscripts, it would have to start "virtually from scratch. With the exception of the Whitman collection the 19th century material is negligible. In the contemporary field, as I have indicated, we have, with the exception of the Roberts papers, only a few feeble beginnings, and beyond these there are only 'token' manuscripts."[29]

Tate outlines three possible courses of action. The library could continue to collect nineteenth-century material not deposited in other libraries: "The result of this would probably be unsatisfactory, even ludicrous, unless we were willing to accumulate second and third-rate materials." Alternatively, the library could continue to emphasize historical materials, though Tate believes that if it chose to do so it should have a coherent acquisitions policy and reject literary materials as a matter of course. Finally, the library could compete with other libraries to gather contemporary literary manuscripts and potentially collaborate on a collections policy. Though there would be keen competition, especially from prestigious academic libraries, the Library of Congress would have a distinct advantage in being able to construct a nationally representative collection.

This last option is the one that Tate favors adopting, writing to thirty-four college, university, and public libraries to get a better sense of poetry holdings throughout the country with the aim of improving the Library of Congress collections.[30] Librarians were asked to submit any information regarding collections and bibliographies in progress on an accompanying checklist of sixty modern American poets that Tate had produced.[31] The list includes such obvious heavy hitters of poetic modernism as E. E. Cummings, Hart Crane, and Robert Frost but also such rather obscure figures as Kimball Flaccus, Frederic Prokosch, and Marya Zaturenska that rarely make it into contemporary anthologies of the period or onto the undergraduate syllabus today. Meanwhile, Paul Laurence Dunbar, Claude McKay, Edna St. Vincent Millay, Lola Ridge, and Jean Toomer (to name a few) fail to make the cut.

As Tate explains the reasoning behind his choice of poets in *Sixty American Poets, 1896–1944*, a bibliography produced from the checklist, sixty poets "make a good round number." The bibliography ostensibly begins in 1896 with the publication of E. A. Robinson's *The Torrent and The Night Before*. In actuality, however, the period covered is even shorter: "At least fifty of our sixty poets have published about nine-tenths of their books since 1912, the year taken as the renascence in American poetry." A period marked, it should be noted, by the beginning of *Poetry* magazine, which (as I argued in chapter 2) had a heavy hand in showcasing and redefining modern poetry. With a rather large number of poets plucked from a span of about thirty years, Tate admits to "something like a wild liberality of choice, and even to the librarian's omnivorous impartiality, which scarcely reflects one's critical estimate of the period."[32]

Tate goes on to explain that he could imagine a different sixty poets, or even ninety poets ("but save us from more"), if the list contained what he sees as a "central thirty" poets, though he "shall not pause to name all the thirty poets whom I should place at or near the center, since not more than half a dozen could stand within reaching distance of it." He does, however, venture to suggest that among the most central would be Ezra Pound, T. S. Eliot, Wallace Stevens, John Crowe Ransom, Hart Crane, and Marianne Moore.[33] Tate's canon—as materially embodied in his bibliographical checklist and the actual volumes to which that checklist refers—can be thought of as a set of concentric circles with a core of six or so figures, surrounded by a shifting mantle of another couple dozen, and these encrusted by another thirty or sixty (but no more) lesser modern American poets.

The problem with calcifying an array of poets into such a structure, however, is made evident in Tate's own selection. While most of these poets are still objects of close critical scrutiny, Tate's New Critical compatriot John Crowe Ransom would now by most critics' accounting not be in such distinguished company as Stevens, Eliot, and Moore (though perhaps still in a list of thirty), his place perhaps taken by William Carlos Williams, much of whose poetry Tate says "is casual and half-finished; more of it is solid and brilliant," or by Langston Hughes, who Tate says "will probably remain the best Negro poet of the period between the two great wars."[34] But a *Negro* poet nonetheless.

Such possibilities for critical reassessment doubtlessly factored into Tate's decision to include a round sixty. He hedges his bets so that his choice thirty are likely to remain *somewhere* within a canon of top sixty modern poets, and asterisks those volumes that seemed to be the most important or available or both. He doesn't distinguish among these asterisks, however, so that there is an odd confusion of quality and popularity—attributes that may at times intersect with one another but frequently will not. The Library of Congress is itself cautious in this respect as well. David C. Mearns confirms the point that the bibliography "is not an objective selection based upon a poll of public esteem or even upon the agreement of a particular school of letters, but, quite the contrary, it represents the distinctly personal choice and taste of the compiler."[35]

If *Sixty American Poets* were merely a distillation after the fact, the list could be taken in stride. There is, after all, no accounting for taste. It would have remained an important New Critical document, but only one, albeit privileged, interpretation of poetic modernism. The fact, however, that Tate had established the list from the outset, rather than soliciting libraries for opinions on what they considered to be their strongest modern poetry collections, is much more problematic. It means that the literary collections at the Library of Congress and to a lesser extent the libraries that Tate contacted—as well as those librarians, critics, and general readers that would go on to read *Sixty American Poets*—were likely unduly influenced by Tate's subjective criteria of selection. While the literary collection potentially offered a wider and more complicated picture of poetic modernism than that made available in anthologies or volumes of selected and collected volumes, it severely limited this potential by prescribing at the outset which poets were worthy of admittance.

Even allowing for such critical subjectivity, *Sixty American Poets* as bibliography and checklist does expand the material possibilities of poetic modernism. First, it lists volumes of poetry (including selected and collected volumes), privileging the breadth of a poet's work over a particular selection and arrangement. Oversights occur and volumes are missing from the list, but there is no obvious attempt to deliberately suppress a particular volume for aesthetic or political reasons.[36] Second, it points to published bibliographies and criticism of the poets, sketching out a critical tradition for the study of modern American poetry and presenting a view of poetic modernism that ranges beyond the collected volume of poetry. Prose works are included because "they are indispensable to the study of a poet's mind."[37] For presumably the same reason, translations and edited works are included as well. Finally, *Sixty American Poets* lists collections of manuscripts, correspondence, and other ephemeral materials that may lead to a fuller portrait of a poet and a better understanding of the poems. The inclusion of manuscripts and correspondence suggests the extent to which these were coming to be seen as important materials in their own right, and as a means of potentially complicating the printed record of poetic modernism—an importance already being recognized in such places as the *Poetry* archives at the University of Chicago and the Poetry Collection at the University of Buffalo.

Archiving Modernism

When making your Will, please remember
   The cats and the dogs have enough;
When your life has attained its December
   Leave the Library some of your stuff.

—H. D. O'N., "To Moribund Members"

Tate's checklist and subsequent bibliography, while admittedly subjective, helped gauge the extent to which the private strategies of book collecting and scrapbooking—which helped condition notions of modern poetic value, genre, and form—had been publicly institutionalized in a national library, especially with respect to modern and contemporary poetry. With a couple of notable exceptions that I consider below, responses to Tate's query suggest a generally sorry state of the modern American poetry library and archive at the midpoint of the twentieth century. Yale had few good collections to speak of, and published writings were kept in the main library stacks with no modern poets set aside as individuals to be collected separately.[38] The University of Texas at Austin noted that its poetry collection is largely based on an extensive purchase made in the latter part of the nineteenth century—a focus that would shift dramatically in the next decade with the establishment of the Humanities Research Center in 1957.[39] Several libraries had a collection or two from a poet associated with the institution. Williams College expected to receive a gift of a collection related to Edwin Arlington Robinson.[40] Both Dartmouth and Amherst were collecting materials on Robert Frost, and Amherst pushed for the inclusion of Emily Dickinson on Tate's checklist as well (which did not occur).[41] K. D. Metcalf replied that Harvard College Library had manuscript materials as well as relatively complete collections of work for about a dozen modern poets but no bibliography manuscripts in progress for any of them.[42] Nelson W. McCombs of New York University noted that there are modern poetry collections at both the Washington Square and University Heights Libraries, but both were aimed at getting representative works of certain favorite modern poets, and there were likely fewer than three or four volumes from any one poet, including some nice first editions.[43] The Newberry Library in Chicago, echoing McCombs's reference to first editions, responded that it would be focusing its acquisitions on "first trade editions of English and American poets from about 1900," hoping to eventually amass a sizable and representative collection of published works.[44]

Such responses were typical. In general, libraries did not collect materials related to modern poets, and to the extent they did they focused on printed books. Tate did receive responses from two librarians in particular, however, that underscore the extent to which some institutions had been actively collecting modern poetry books and manuscripts (if not in such a nationally coordinated way) as the Library of Congress was now attempting to do: the University of Chicago and the University of Buffalo. When Tate inquired into the state of poetry collections at the University of Chicago, he was told that the library contained 3,360 volumes, centered on the Harriet Monroe Collection, which included 2,350 volumes of poetry, as well as letters, manuscripts and typescripts of poems, and a collection of little magazines—all of which had been gathered by Monroe during her years as editor of *Poetry*.[45]

This was a much larger and more comprehensive and systematically assembled collection of modern poetry than in most other libraries—due in large part to Monroe's belief that an archive of materials related to *Poetry*'s production and reception should, like the magazine itself, be a Chicago institution. George Dillon, editor of *Poetry* from 1937 to 1949, explains at the dedication of the collection in 1938 that, although the collection includes volumes of verse, criticism, and anthologies (some of which are inscribed first editions), the books are for the most part those that were considered worth reviewing in *Poetry*: "They represent only a minor proportion of the number of volumes sent in; the collection is therefore a selective one, reflecting the critical standards of the magazine."⁴⁶ The collection also contains the corrected proofs of each issue along with manuscripts of poems by such poets as Vachel Lindsay, Rupert Brooke, Edna St. Vincent Millay, Rabindranath Tagore, and James Joyce. Recognizing the importance of correspondences, Dillon notes that, "by far the most valuable part of the collection, from the standpoint of research students and literary historians, is the complete file of poets' letters accumulated during the first twenty-four years of the magazine."⁴⁷ These correspondences add to and complicate the history of poetic modernism depicted in bound books.

Several poets similarly praise the collection. Relying on a common standard of poetic value popularized in large part by Palgrave's anthology, Lew Sarett writes that Monroe "saw the literary gold in her possession. Today her books and MSS are of extraordinary value and interest. A century from now they will be doubled in value and interest." John Hall Wheelock remarks that "the New Testament uses the strange beautiful phrase, 'the Word made flesh.' One might, in writing of a library, reverse the phrase, for in inspired books the flesh is made word again." And Eunice Tietjens simply exclaims that "*Poetry* now has two homes, the office and the library of the university."⁴⁸

Not all of the responses were positive, however. Ezra Pound, who had been instrumental in building *Poetry* in its first few years, aims his rancor at American institutions of higher education:

> It is my belief that loyalty to Harriet's memory does NOT include a willingness to let the criteria in *Poetry* decline NOR to let it get stuck at a given PAST date.
>
> A group of people too cowardly to face CONTEMPORARY thought and knowledge can NOT maintain Harriet's living spirit. . . .
>
> The sloth of American universities is UNSPEAKABLE. The unwillingness of these institutions to mention contemporary discoveries and activities of contem-

porary thought is vile. If it be largely unconscious it is for that very reason all the more dangerous and all the more demands that we fight it to the last limit.

Are the "Friends of the Library" really GOOD friends to it? Do they want it dead or do they want it alive? *Poetry* is or shd/ be H.M.'s living monument.[49]

Monroe herself sees the importance of such a library, having willed it away five years previously.[50] Indeed, she had announced in *Poetry* on the occasion of its nineteenth birthday in 1931 her intentions to house a "library of modern poetry" at the University of Chicago as a permanent Chicago institution and gift to the city.[51] As prescient as such a decision was against a backdrop of what was still largely a national indifference to publicly collecting poetry, Monroe had in fact already planned to donate the *Poetry* papers a full decade before that. In an earlier will from August 19, 1921 (updated April 21, 1922), Monroe singled out the manuscripts, letters, photographs, and books that had come into her possession as editor of *Poetry*—materials that she believed would increase in value and that should be preserved as a literary and historical memorial to the city.[52]

This belief was shared by Charles D. Abbott, director of libraries at the University of Buffalo. When Tate wrote to Abbott about Buffalo's holdings, he was told that the Poetry Collection intended to include every book and pamphlet from the poets that Tate had listed, which they were well on their way to doing.[53] Along with a catalog of the collection, Abbott submitted a list of the collection's extensive holdings in modern poetry manuscripts and correspondence and reminded Tate that his own worksheets had previously been requested.[54] Aside from being a gentle reminder that Buffalo had been actively collecting modern poets for half a decade before Tate appeared on the scene, Abbott's request for worksheets underscores the nature of this collecting: that the library, like Monroe's *Poetry* collection, was interested not only in printed works but also in the material that informed the making and understanding of those works that up until that point had generally been considered ephemeral and worthless. This interest in draft materials is, as Braddock rightfully points out, Abbott's "most remarkable invention" in terms of his immediate collecting strategy and his eventual impact on literary scholarship.[55]

As Abbott explains, his goal is to attain "the genuine work-sheets which the poet has used in the making of his poem—preliminary notes, the first rough draft, the various transitional stages, everything up to and including the final version, with proof sheets if textual changes are there recorded: a complete *dossier* on the composition of that particular poem.... Such a *dossier* is not only a history of a particular poem; it is also a factual biography of the poet's mind at work. It is the most nearly perfect tangible exhibit of poetic creativeness we can ever present."[56] Abbott is after "the rapid and often chaotic notes that show the first impulse towards creation; the rough draft in which the material begins to take shape; the intermediate versions, however many there may be, through which the composition progresses towards its final form; the proof-sheets, if they contain revisions; and the final form itself as seen in the printed text."[57] He argues that, while such a request may have been impractical in earlier times, it is not too much to ask of the modern poet. He believes that, almost invariably, "the young poet who has lived the whole of his life amidst the tensions of twentieth-century striving comprehends without effort the ultimate usefulness of worksheets. Oftentimes he has begun to save them long before knowing that such a project as ours was in the offing—irrefutable testimony to the project's roots in the immediacy of demand."[58] Abbott argues that the use and preservation of ephemeral materials is a characteristically modernist phenomenon—one that, as I suggest, other contemporaneous archivists generally identified with the rise of mass print—and that one of the purposes of the Poetry Collection is to make this private process public.

Abbott recognizes as well that poets often attempt to conceal this modern textual condition in an effort to emphasize the final product. "Sometimes we have to accept incomplete records because important parts have disappeared or have been destroyed. The wastebasket or fireplace has been too tempting to the orderly mind. But these *fragmentaria* we are delighted to acquire, if they include, clearly, a significant fraction of the process."[59] At the same time, Abbott maintains the scrapbooker's sense of accumulation, recognizing that "there is no end to what remains still to do, since the ideal of completeness will always beckon. That impossible ideal cannot be achieved but it can be stoically sought.... We would keep constantly in front of us the goal of completeness, that desert mirage, forever vanishing to reappear in the distance."[60]

To attain such manuscript materials, Abbott would travel throughout the United States and Britain to personally speak with poets.[61] He also sent poets letters (and frequent follow-ups), requesting whatever drafts they were willing to part with. In such letters, he explains that while there has been a great deal of progress in the library's acquisition of first and variant editions of books as well as files of little magazines (the kind of acquisition Tate would be engaged in), the Poetry Collection was particularly interested in the rough drafts and false starts that might suggest the poet's mind at work and be of particular interest to future scholars. Of the first fifty letters he sent out in search of manuscripts, Abbott received three complete silences, twenty-five fair copies, seventeen true documentary histories, four promises, and "one thunderous rejoinder from Rapallo, a mettlesome volley aimed not at our purposes but at the whole structure of American education" in which Ezra Pound claims that "I don't give a damn about storing mss/ in a safe" and, echoing his diatribe against the *Poetry* collection at the University of Chicago, couches his response as an attack on an ineffectual university system and effete intellectual culture in America.[62]

Another somewhat perplexing rejoinder, given her own investments in the ephemeral and an endless dedication to revision, came from Marianne Moore, who explains that with the possible exception of a Shakespeare or Dante, an author gives enough in what she wishes others to read and, besides, Moore has heard that libraries now have too much manuscript to curate anyway. Moore does admit that letters may be of interest, if not aimed at posterity, and notes that she keeps some of her translations around to humble her, but she cautions against overvaluing such things.[63] Moore would, however, give Abbott copies of "Festschrift" and "Then the Ermine" along with a handwritten draft of "See in the Midst of Fair Leaves" and versions of "The Pangolin" (corrected version for *Selected Poems*, 1935) and "The Frigate Pelican" (version for *Selected Poems*, 1935).[64] She would also largely succumb to Abbott's point of view, eventually selling much of her manuscript material to the Rosenbach Library in 1968, to which she would bequeath the rest upon her death in 1972.

The poet who most directly heeded Abbott's call, however, was William Carlos Williams (a poet who, as I pointed out in chapter 3, drew heavily upon archival materials and meditated on the importance of the library in his long poem, *Paterson*), demonstrating one poet's evolving appreciation for the modern poetry collection. Williams is initially driven to the archive by the threat of the Second World War and an immediate need to secure his working drafts, writing to Abbott that "if this becomes a combat area later on I'd like to feel that the few pieces of work I have in progress are being somewhat protected for the time being. I have no illusions as to their intrinsic value but they do represent a lot of time put in so that if I should go on living I'd like to feel that that had not been entirely lost."[65] Williams (with a bit of false modesty, perhaps) is skeptical of any lasting value of his manuscripts but does recognize the importance of protecting them and sees the library as a convenient sanctuary. He continued to deliver materials and, two months after their first correspondence, sent Abbott a batch of early letters containing, among other things, references to Pound and H.D. He cautions, however, that

> the tone of them all is so very immature that I am astonished. Certainly they are not for general investigation. You may keep them all, though I should prefer it if you selected a few and destroyed the rest. There is nothing much of good in them and much that is close to infantile. I can assure you that the letters do not by any means reflect what I was thinking in those days. The probability is that I did not have the courage or the ability to place my most intimate actions and reactions on paper for anybody's eyes. I can distinctly remember many, many details of those times that the letters do not even adumbrate. Well, they are letters. Do what you please with them. The best might be to burn them.[66]

An understandable case of the old master judging the young buck and looking to expunge his record, but then these early remnants were exactly what Abbott was looking for. Williams, over time, would also come to recognize the importance of literary correspondence. At one point he writes to Abbott on the subject of Ezra Pound's treason and possible hanging, remarking that "I'm glad you have the letters from my file which Pound sent me over the years. It would be a fascinating thing to put them together chronologically, should a catastrophic occasion arrive, and publish them—not as a defense for the man but to show how his mind wobbled and veered."[67]

Williams would continue to send Abbott material, though still doubting some of its worthiness for preservation. He offered books and magazines in which his work appeared; duplicates of prints, published and unpublished; and "junk—original scripts on odd pieces of paper, early forms of work since greatly altered—all in disorder—parts of scripts—anything I find lying around. Everything I send is yours to file or fling out as you please, to hell with it."[68] Junk, perhaps, but Williams thought it important enough to save at the time and now it is preserved in the archive. Slowly coming around, Williams would write a year later that "if I'm any good as a writer the stuff's valuable, if I turn out to be a so and so it's just so much waste paper. That's a chance you take and must take. I wish you luck. . . . I've left you instructions to give you everything," lamenting, "What tons of it I've thrown away!"[69]

Despite the earlier Rapallo rejoinder, Williams also suggested that Abbott write to Pound in St. Elizabeth's Hospital, asking him what he was doing with the mail that he was receiving and that Abbott would wish to preserve.[70] And in 1947 he encouraged Abbott to buy from James Laughlin the existing material up to the completed *Cantos* (the library had already acquired material related to a few cantos).[71] Regrettably, Abbott did not make the purchase. Laughlin's attempt to sell Pound's manuscripts (beyond depicting the hubris or desperate state of a poet who had previously discounted such an institutional collection) does, however, point to the extent to which a poet's manuscript materials—which a decade previously were thought by many to be worthless in every sense of the word—had, in large part due to Abbott's collecting, accrued not only literary and cultural value but monetary value as well.

Beyond whatever the collection may have gained in price, it was certainly of great creative and scholarly value, as attested to in the contributions to Abbott's 1948 edited collection of essays, *Poets at Work*. Picking up on Abbott's own interest in tracing the poet's process, the critic Rudolf Arnheim argues for the collection's importance not only as reliquiae or as a means of retracing the poet's path to Parnassus but also "primarily for the study of the creative process, that curious end-product of a long phylogenetic development, during which the refinement of the organism's reactions to its environment has finally led, in man, to the capacity of producing interpretive images of what is exciting, puzzling, desirable."[72] W. H. Auden suggests in "Squares and Oblongs" that the collection would be important not only for scholars but also for poets:

> Until recently the concern of critics and public alike was a reader's concern with the final published product, the questions of value they raised, readers' questions. "Is it good or bad? Why do I like it or dislike it?" But the existence of this collection seems to me a sign—there are plenty of others—that, today, more and more people are coming to look at poetry, for instance, not primarily as readers but as actual or potential poets, to be raising therefore quite different questions. "How is poetry written? Could I write it? Is writing poetry a valuable occupation? Would I like being a poet?"[73]

The availability of worksheets and correspondence allows readers to take a peek under the hood of a poem and to see the kinds of tinkering the poet had done to keep it humming. Such materials do not only spur interest in textual variants and alternative readings but also act as a kind of how-to manual for the aspiring poet on how and why certain poetical choices were made.

In a similar vein and echoing Dilthey's earlier observations, Donald Stauffer sees the collections as enabling a genetic criticism and a "historical criticism which few could consider irrelevant, since it will use solely the materials which the poet himself used in bringing his finished work into shape." Directly invoking a scrapbooking metaphor as negotiation of urban modernity's deluge of mass print, Stauffer wonders whether "epigrammatic verse is the natural poetry of the modern cities partly because there is time to compose only in scraps." Stauffer goes on to claim that as much as reproduction in a volume of collected poems may petrify it, a poem is "a living organism of thought. Its final version is no more than the fiat of its creator that here, now, it possesses its highest, fullest life, ready to be gathered, at last changeless forever, into the artifice of eternity. Its life as a finished poem may be realized more fully in the history of its earlier life, in its generating seed, its transmutations, its persistent sap, its buds that withered as well as those that flowered on full branches."[74] Stauffer helps to confirm Abbott's earlier declaration that with "so much corroborative evidence at their disposal individual critics will find it somewhat more difficult to read into a poem two quite different meanings."[75]

In this sense, the modern poetry archive does indeed offer academic scholarship as a powerful corrective to New Criticism's wilder flights of interpretive fancy. It should be noted, however, that even Buffalo's Poetry Collection is governed by subjective criteria that blunt historical scholarship's ability to cut through the tangle of proliferating (often contradictory) acts of close reading. As Abbott admits, because of financial and storage considerations, the Poetry Collection had a restricted sense of the poets worthy of preservation, claiming that "the only reasonably safe criterion for inclusion was the imprint of a reliable publisher, one whom common knowledge accepts as above the deceits of promotional chicanery, whose name is sign that this book is a legitimate contribution to the poetry of its time." Exceptions could be made later, if necessary, though later additions could prove costly as first editions (and later manuscripts) rose in price.[76] To make such an imprimatur the basis for inclusion meant buying into many of the same aesthetic assumptions, based in objective value and stable genre, that underpinned the editing of selected and collected volumes of poetry, as well as the New Criticism itself—criteria that would become even more evident as the critic-consultants of the Library of Congress began to systematically gather manuscripts.

Modern Poetry and the Archival Nation

More than a decade after Tate's call for a literary collection—and long after such materials were being gathered at Chicago and Buffalo—the Library of Congress set out to systematically collect manuscripts by contemporary poets and other writers. The 1957 leaflet *Literary Papers and Manuscripts*, pointedly subtitled *A Plea for Their Preservation in the National Archives*, promises American authors that their "papers will survive, here, as long as the seat of government survives; they will be available to critics, cultural historians, and other scholars; they can help to give the man who wrote them the place in our cultural history to which he is entitled. Such papers are an essential national resource," and as part of this national collection, "an author can be remembered with fidelity." Reflecting the degree to which the conception of what should be included in the poetry collection (and the literary collection more broadly) had evolved in just a few years, the leaflet explains that the library "is interested in all of a writer's papers, even in those that may seem intimate, trivial, or fragmentary—in successive drafts, trial lines, corrected galleys, unpublished works, notebooks, journals, memoranda, scrapbooks, and correspondence (both letters received and retained copies of letters sent)."[77]

The leaflet assures authors that their papers will be safe in this collection with "fireproof and airconditioned stacks" along with an expert staff of conservationists and reference librarians. Likewise, their papers will actually be used: "Historians, literary scholars, and critics continually avail themselves of the resources of the Manuscript Division. It is seldom possible to write scholarly studies on any phase of American civilization—political, military, social, economic, religious, or artistic—without recourse to these great national collections."[78] At the same time, researchers will be closely observed, donors may still reserve copyright, and if they wish they may place further restrictions on their materials for a time.

Promises of preservation and accessibility were nothing new. Chicago and Buffalo could also offer a safe (if smaller) haven for manuscript materials and emphasized the importance of their collections for both scholarly and creative work. The Library of Congress, however, attempted to trump these lesser institutions through an appeal to patriotism and investment in the nation:

> You are invited to perform a service to the Nation by making your papers and literary manuscripts, or those you hold in trust, a part of this permanent record.

Instituting Modernism

> In the manuscript collections of the Library of Congress are the rough draft of the Declaration of Independence; the notes on the proceedings of the Constitutional Convention; the first and second drafts of the Gettysburg Address; the manuscripts, letters, and assorted papers of our Presidents, statesmen, jurists, soldiers, artists, scientists—of the men and women who, throughout the centuries, have profoundly influenced the lives and destinies of their countrymen.[79]

Such patriotism extends beyond political figures such as Thomas Jefferson and Benjamin Franklin, "men who were both statesmen and authors," to include such writers as Walt Whitman, Edwin Arlington Robinson, and A. E. Housman, as well as other persons of cultural and historical importance. As the leaflet claims, "It has become customary for American statesmen, scientists, soldiers, for public figures of every kind—to give their papers to the Library in order that they may be kept as a living, evocative, and enduring memorial."[80]

The appeal to national pride distinguishes the Library of Congress from other literary and cultural institutions. While other libraries may offer safekeeping in the ivory towers of academe or in a local museum dominated by local concerns, the Library of Congress offers an opportunity to be part of a nation and its unfolding history. How, exactly, does one turn down the chance for one's work to be placed beside the Declaration of Independence or the Gettysburg Address? Like an unknown soldier's grave or a marbled monument, the archive becomes a memorializing repository for what Benedict Anderson has called an "imagined community" of citizens stitched together by a national print culture.[81]

Even with such patriotic promises, however, it did take a while for the library to get its act together. Conrad Aiken, as Consultant in Poetry from 1950 to 1952, solicited the current and past Poetry Fellows (an advisory panel consisting of many of the most distinguished modern poets), inquiring as to whether they "have any manuscript, work-sheets, or whatever, whether fragmentary or of book-length, which you would care to present to the Library for such a collection," hoping that each fellow "would constitute himself a committee of one to persuade such other authors as he knows to do likewise," and with an almost desperate plea repeating: "Correspondence, corrected galley-proofs, <u>anything</u>."[82] Aiken concedes that the library has even at this time come late into the field and doesn't want to conflict with other chosen repositories but in a call to literary patriotism hopes that "even in these cases it might be suggested that for the purpose of a nationally representative collection the writer might be prepared to make an exception, and to give the Library of Congress at least one complete and typical manuscript, preferably of book length. Better still, to be sure, where writers are not yet committed, if they would consider making the Library of Congress their chosen or sole repository: it is the logical place for such a national collection."[83] Through an appeal to a national collection, Aiken encourages a dispersal of manuscript materials that, beyond compromising the unity of any particular author's collection, makes scholarship that much more difficult—though he would of course be ecstatic to have the Library of Congress be the sole repository for some authors' papers without in turn sharing the spoils.

Randall Jarrell would take up Aiken's mantle five years later, outlining a program for gathering manuscripts, from which the 1957 leaflet would derive. Jarrell's description of poets suggests the continued close connection between literary criticism and collecting practices at the Library of Congress. Without equivocation, Jarrell states that the "greatest generation of American poets begins with Robert Frost, who was born in 1874, and ends with T. S. Eliot and John Crowe Ransom, who were born in 1888. It is, naturally, important to try to get their manuscripts as soon as possible." He concedes that there is little chance of acquiring Eliot's manuscripts, many of which are at Harvard, but observes that Eliot "is an extremely dutiful and conscientious man who could never, as he says, refuse an invitation to serve on the committee—there is a fair chance that the invitation of the Library of the Congress of his own country would arouse all the conscientiousness in his nature."[84] Jarrell doubts as well that Pound will give up any materials (an astute observation, considering Pound's vitriolic correspondence with both Chicago and Buffalo). Frost is collected out, but because Jarrell is on good terms with him (having written perspicaciously on his poems) he thinks he might be able to secure something.[85] Moore's materials would be a coup if not already promised, as would be those of William Carlos Williams—though Jarrell doubts the possibility of acquiring the latter (much of which had been given to Buffalo at this point). Although there is little chance of claiming Ransom's poetry (Ransom having written only one poem since 1934), the library may be able to acquire prose manuscripts or general papers. Jarrell also suggests several other middle-aged poets[86] worth the attempt as well as younger poets[87] that he believes the library has an excellent chance of acquiring. The inclusion of these latter poets, many of whom have come to be seen as the most significant midcentury American poets, suggests the importance of having a literary critic at the helm of a progressive acquisitions program.

Jarrell's scheme was met with general approval by the library's higher-ups. Mearns mentions, however, that the list (of prose as well as poetry) "includes the names of several distinguished foreign writers whose papers would be excluded by our acquisitions policy as presently enunciated."[88] The response from Roy Besler of the Reference Department clarifies, however, that most of the persons listed under the heading "Foreign Writers" are actually naturalized citizens: "In some instances the problem might emerge if the country of the writer's nativity or nationality might be expected to have an interest in opposition to our own which we should respect," but he notes that this is currently not the case. In other instances, "foreign nationals of permanent or quasi-permanent residence in the United States might be considered on an individual basis for solicitation."[89] The exchange underscores the fact that—as opposed to the collections at Chicago and Buffalo that gathered together the materials of poetic modernism without being constrained by geography or nationality—the Library of Congress, in its appeals to patriotism and national memory, sought to build a specifically *American* collection. Exceptions for foreign nationals (such as Auden) and those who have changed nationality (such as Eliot) only served to prove the rule.

Aside from working within the restraints of national identity and being relatively late to the collecting game, one of the primary obstacles to the Library of Congress acquiring a substantial collection of poetry manuscripts was the general archival principle, outlined earlier, that collections should be kept together whenever possible. Mearns notes that Jarrell "should emphasize the fact that we want all or nothing—that is to say that we do not knowingly accept collections which are now (or later will be) divided among several repositories. Fragmentation imposes intolerable burdens upon research."[90] Although Aiken had floated the idea of poets donating a representative sample of their work from another collection—thereby denying the possibility of a complete collection at any given institution (a possibility that, as Abbott had already recognized, was itself a necessary fiction)—the principle of archival coherence was more or less adhered to even during his tenure. Karl Shapiro, then editor of *Poetry*, had suggested to Aiken that the library might be interested in the complete collection of manuscripts and correspondences that had been held by *Poetry* since the death of Harriet Monroe in 1936, cunningly noting that the Newberry Library was also interested in the materials.[91] While the Library of Congress got the impression that $1,000 or $1,500 might secure the collection, it was unable to obtain the funds, and, as Aiken explains to Shapiro, the library believed that, as the earlier materials were in Chicago, these materials should be as well in order to maintain the integrity of the collection as a whole.[92] Shapiro had the same idea, having already approached the University of Chicago, which he also believed had priority.[93] Aiken concurs, writing that "I kind of agree with you that Chicago is the place—always a pity to divide these things."[94] Through an anonymous donor, Chicago was able to secure the later papers, doubling the size of a long-prized collection.

As Besler suggests (perhaps out of some sense of desperation), however, Mearns's "all-or-nothing" principle is "considered perhaps too restrictive if rigorously applied in soliciting literary manuscripts and papers. The literary field, it was felt, has somewhat different conditions than the ones that describe the papers of public figures in other fields. These possibly unique conditions do not question the basic policy that we desire total collections, but do suggest that we should not push the all-or-nothing approach at the time of first contact," although it should still suggest such desires.[95] This exception, of course, works to the Library of Congress's advantage in affording it an opportunity to pick up a stray manuscript or a string of correspondences, but it seems to have little respect for other institutions' similar attempts to build complete collections.

Another obstacle to the library acquiring manuscript materials was the fact that in the decade and a half since Abbott had started convincing authors of the scholarly worth of their manuscripts, correspondences, and other ephemera—and that they should donate these materials to his burgeoning collection—these papers had also increased dramatically in monetary value. Authors were becoming more attuned to this fact. The Library of Congress leaflet, recognizing that authors are increasingly looking to get paid for their manuscripts, concludes by mentioning rather off-handedly that "the Library will, upon request, submit for tax-deduction purposes an appraisal of the value of gifts received." Jarrell takes the liberty of translating the phrase for potential donors, explaining that the papers are valued by the library when they are deposited, and an amount equal to 20 percent of the author's income is transferred outright to the library each year, making 20 percent of his or her income for that year tax-free: "This is the first tax-provision I have heard of that trusts a writer almost as kindly as if he were an oil-well owner; it's odd that most writers have never heard of it."[96]

Instituting Modernism 195

Although the library is able to use a potentially lucrative tax loophole to its advantage in a way that other institutions cannot, it emphasizes historical and cultural value over monetary value—evidenced in Mearns's public exchange with Shapiro, who complains that American libraries were engaged in a competition to build up poetry collections without having to pay for them. Shapiro argues that American libraries

> are among the richest institutions in the country, and it is their business to purchase materials for the use of readers and scholars. Why they make a distinction between published work, which they pay for, and manuscript, which they seem to feel entitled to, is hard to determine. The writer, and especially the poet, has no other property of any financial value, aside from his published books, except the paper he has written on. As everyone is aware, a writer of reputation is sometimes able to sell his manuscripts to collectors for hard cash. The writer obviously deserves whatever remuneration he can get for this material. American libraries are devoted to service, and it is incredible that they should engage in such high-handed practices as this.[97]

Giving libraries the benefit of the doubt that they know not what they do, Shapiro offers the case of Dylan Thomas as a parable of this "practice of filching the writing of living authors." He explains that Thomas donated the bulk of his manuscripts to an American library at a time when he believed them to be worthless. When Thomas found himself impoverished a few years later, but with a reputation that had grown considerably, selling these manuscripts would have solved his financial difficulties (and as a result, perhaps, would have kept the poet alive and writing). Shapiro condemns the notion that libraries should "speculate in the personal property of authors" and calls for poets to "refuse to donate their manuscripts without adequate payment, and that they register a protest to any library engaged in this unfortunate practice."[98]

Mearns replies that "you sustain your indignation by munificently ascribing to them vast financial reserves which they simply do not possess." His defense, though, ultimately relies on cultural value rather than monetary value. Mearns argues that libraries extend "the most cordial and realistic hospitality to the manuscripts and other papers of those men and women who variously contribute to the cultural and intellectual life of our time. The invitations by their issuance imply an acknowledgment of value and distinction." He claims that libraries are up-front about their acquisition policies. There is "no duplicity, no misrepresentation, no stealth, no miserliness, certainly no picking of pockets," and if a writer can find a public or private collector willing to pay him for the material he is encouraged to make the sale (those collectors would presumably later be encouraged to donate their collections). In return for their generosity "beyond their capacity for on-the-spot monetary remuneration," however, libraries offer other benefits.[99] Aside from a lightening of tax burdens, which is particular to the Library of Congress, these include the promise of permanent preservation, restoration, and protection against loss or dispersal; expert handling and service by qualified specialists; congenial surroundings; critical recognition and attraction to inquiry; and the assurance of an appropriate and enlivened memorial.

These benefits privilege the material and cultural value of the manuscript materials over their monetary value, a value that would directly benefit only the author who has deposited them. As this debate suggests, however, it is now not only the monetary value derived from collecting rare first editions and other books that helps to structure literary value. The unique manuscript materials (items of the most extreme rarity) have also become financially valuable and this value carries over into other registers. Beyond being useful for scholars and future poets as indicators of a writer's state of mind or examples of where a manuscript could have gone but didn't, these manuscript materials—individually and as part of a coherent national collection—structure literary worth and add to the stores of the nation's symbolic value.

Ultimately, the building of a national modern poetry collection was a mixed success. Concurrently, however, a virtual national collection was being stitched together through the national register of manuscripts—an initiative led by the Library of Congress that in some sense was an extension of Tate's *Sixty American Poets*. As one archivist notes, a national register of manuscripts would be even more valuable than the union catalog of books (a record of publications held in libraries throughout the country), because books "usually exist in several copies and are likely to be found by a little searching; there are mighty few unique books. But every manuscript collection is unique; it exists in but one place."[100] A national register would inform librarians not only of materials at other institutions but also of the collections that they already possess. It would additionally have the advantage of persuading librarians who are uncomfortable with manuscripts to examine their collections in order to transmit the desired information to the central catalog, countering the tendency by which library-science training, in its emphasis on books, has bypassed manuscripts as mysterious bundles to which the orthodox rules will not apply; or that, their public being predominantly a book-seeking throng, the demand for manuscripts is so slight that they can be stuffed in boxes and closets and forgotten; or that, since most of our bibliographies are based on printed works, manuscripts need not be organized for research; or that the extra equipment, needed for shelving manuscripts is the flexible item in the budget that can always be withdrawn or postponed.[101]

A dozen manuscript repositories—Cornell, Duke, Harvard, Princeton, and Virginia Universities; the Bancroft, Clements, Huntington, Morgan, Newberry, and New York Public Libraries; and the Historical Society of Wisconsin—expressed "great interest" in implementing a national manuscript register.[102] This eagerness highlights some degree of success in forging a virtual archival nation based less in a tangible collection of poets' papers than in a kind of meta-archive pointing to the many distinct and local places across the country where American poetry could be found—resembling more recent digital projects with a similar mission.[103] Such a registry was not solely the product of modern poetry acquisitions; it reflected more general conceptions of the modern archive and the archive's relationship to the manuscript collection, though having particular resonance with New Criticism and the critical reception of modern poetry.

Closed Reading: Archive, Text, and Total Social Form

Although the modern poetry collection offered possibilities for historical scholarship beyond what was available through closely reading volumes of selected and collected poems, it too was a product of a historical moment that tended toward a preservation and consolidation of poetic modernism, rather than an expansion of its central canon. This was partly due to direct New Critical intervention at such places as the Library of Congress. But it was also the result of a more general archival logic that had become dominant by the middle of the twentieth century—at precisely the time modern poetry archives and collections were coming into being. This frequent depiction of the archive as a harmonious, organic whole that I have pointed to in discussions of the modern poetry archive and the modern archive more generally is strikingly similar to the New Critical conception of the poem (which itself was a throwback to a turn-of-the-century critical formulation).

As Tate explains, "The meaning of poetry is its 'tension,' the full organized body of all the extension and intension that we can find in it."[104] This simultaneous pushing out and in—the poem (and its context) pushing inward on a symbolic core of meaning and that core radiating outward—gives the poem its dynamic wholeness. Likewise, Cleanth Brooks and Robert Penn Warren instruct teachers in *Understanding Poetry* that the poem "should always be treated as an organic system of relationships, and the poetic quality should never be understood as inhering in one or more factors taken in isolation."[105] Not only did the New Critics have a practical influence on the modern poetry library and archive through their work at such institutions as the Library of Congress, but, more fundamentally, the modern poetry collection—by virtue of its connection to a general midcentury archival culture—formally paralleled the New Critical understanding of the poem.

The New Critical poem and the modern poetry collection can in fact both be understood as different manifestations of an underlying striving for cultural unity in an increasingly heterogeneous world, made more evident through the diversity of mass print. As Tate explains in his preface to *Sixty American Poets*:

> What use this check list will have I cannot foresee, beyond the pious and even ritualistic justification, frequently asserted by scholars, that bibliographies make it easier to "study" the works of a poet or the poetry of an age. The existence of the present check list witnesses my own participation in this belief or, if you will, illusion, which it doubtless is if "study" means more academic theses and more books on shelves which fail to arrest the roving eclecticism of the scholar at some point where he will read the poetry. It is my impression that poets in the past, before the era of Teutonic efficiency in letters, had to make their own way, and they did it without benefit of library science. There is no harm in this "science"; there may be in it some good; but I think that no one should suppose that it can "do something for literature" unless the society sustaining the literature has already done it, or is doing it, and the "science" is a mere instrument of that deeper will. The powerful predatory, at best acquisitive "procedures" of our libraries and museums may be only our sort of Alexandrianism; or it may be something better.[106]

While allowing for a kind of literary scholarship aided by library science, Tate ultimately remains skeptical that such "roving eclecticism" can get one to the heart of the poem or poetic tradition in the way that close attention to the text can. If libraries merely become other Alexandrias, they will be next to worthless because they have not valued, selected from, and organized what is best in modern poetry. They have the chance to do this, but only insofar as they tap into the cultural values of an organic society that sustains this poetry, the deep processes of which are revealed through intense close reading.[107] In their direct intervention into the book and manuscript collecting practices at the Library of Congress and elsewhere, however, Tate and the New Critics provide a material basis for the canon that enabled this close reading of both the poem and the society that conditioned it.[108]

In this light, it is important to recognize that while the institutionalized modern poetry archive offers real possibilities for poetic recovery and a reimagining of the poetic canon, it was a product of its New Critical moment in ways that we have not fully recognized. From their inception, the modern poetry library and archive were bound by the collector's notions of selectivity based in objective value and arrangement in service of an organic whole that has occluded many poets and poetic connections from critical examination. In an effort to correct for this history, literary and cultural critics must continue to investigate extrainstitutional archival sites—including periodicals and scrapbooks themselves—and new critical methods informed by the digital archive that promise to expand and even fundamentally alter our understandings of poetic modernism.

Coda

Remaking Poetic Modernism after a Culture of Mass Print

It is perhaps fitting that a book focused on the role of mass print in the making of poetic modernism concludes with a few words on the importance of both mass print and modern poetry in our current digital age. I do not mean to eulogize a print form that is not yet dead (although its demise has been predicted for some years now), but neither do I pretend that we are living in a culture dominated by that print. Magazines have crumpled and newspapers have folded in the flickering of websites and blogs, or they have found new life in digital distribution. My daily reading, like that of many people, is now typically carried out through some varying combination of laptop, tablet, smartphone, and printed paper, in addition to the bought or borrowed books that still make the old shelves creak and buckle. In the present volume, I have focused my attention on an earlier time period, however, because I think that a study of mass print culture—and of poetic modernism as a collection of responses to that culture—has something important and otherwise unobtainable to say about the here and now.

It hardly seems an accident that many of the scholars I have engaged with throughout this book have recently demonstrated interest in notions of modernist collecting and in previously marginalized textual constructions. Such attention to older media and fading historical moments strikes me as a refracted attempt at understanding our cultural zeitgeist in ways that can't quite be tackled head on. As I suggested in the introduction, scholars interested in media archaeology and comparative textual studies (mining the deep furrows cut by such scholars as Friedrich Kittler and Marshall McLuhan) would likely agree. As Jussi Parikka suggests, media archaeology is "a way to investigate the new media cultures through insights from past media, often with an emphasis on the forgotten, the quirky, the non-obvious apparatuses, practices, and inventions."[1] I can hardly think of a better way to describe the lasting and unpredictable impact of a mass print form like the scrapbook or the mass-circulation magazine on the media of today.

What insights, then, might these textual forms bring to our current media moment? As I argued in previous chapters, these forms are built out of heterogeneous, multimedia elements and must be understood as both collections of texts and as complex textual constructions in their own right. Making meaning out of these media objects requires the linking of texts or parts of texts on and across multiple pages, an activity that we have come to associate with the hop-skip of hypertext. (It should be noted that in both print and digital texts this is not simply a formal attribute but very often economically driven, with the demand that one flip or click through pages of advertising to get back to the main text of interest.) Interactivity, which has come to be seen as a staple of the digital, is present in older print-media forms through back-page crossword puzzles and other such games and through acts of cutting and pasting. And crowdsourcing, which has contributed to the making of so many online texts, also characterized a turn-of-the-century snippet culture that relied on many readers and editors contributing to a common cause.

We might likewise scratch beneath the digital's glossy surface to consider the extent to which print forms have anticipated the material-technological structures that make so much of our newest media possible. Foremost among these structures is the electronic database. Lev Manovich has argued for the database as an innovative literary genre, aligned with new media and the computer age, claiming that "the database represents the world as a list of items, and it refuses to order this list. In contrast, a narrative creates a cause-and-effect trajectory of seemingly unordered items (events). Therefore, database and narrative are natural enemies. Competing for the same territory of human culture, each claims an exclusive right to make meaning out of the world."[2] Some critics have challenged Manovich's division as too simplistic and inattentive to narrative's own fractured history, and we can recognize that these distinctions are not fundamentally different from those that governed the closed, narrativized collection and the haphazard accumulation that I have described throughout this book.[3] Still, the database intensifies this accumulation so that we might argue for a continuity of "archival effects" and archival affects that prompts us to look to the past for historical guidance.[4]

Similarly, as Wendy Chun has argued, electronic media foreground notions of regenerative memory as means to an enduring ephemeral and suggest that computer memory "is a storage medium *like* paper, but not quite. Both degenerate, revealing the limitations of the simile."[5] For me, though, this degeneration actually strengthens the simile. It may be that the pages of the collected book—protected as they are through private and public conservation—are ultimately a failed storage medium. But, like the computer's code, the ephemeral scraps that are reprinted in such snippet journals as *Tit-Bits* or that are pasted into the personal scrapbook, to perhaps again be reprinted or quoted in another text, do not only materially degenerate but also linguistically regenerate in other forms so that they might endure. It is with the help of the electronic database that we have started to recognize the extent to which such "viral texts" dominated mass print.[6]

Mass print objects may not function in exactly the same way as do their digital counterparts—and certainly not to the same degree (I can click a "like" button much faster than I can mail a letter of appreciation)—but there are definite connections that beg to be further explored. The very term "digital," after all, suggests a working with the hand's nimble digits, as do some of our more obvious lingering phrases like "cut and paste."[7] As Matt Kirschenbaum has convincingly argued, this is more than metaphor. There is a very real material and social substrate to the electronic text that demands we act to ensure its accessibility and preservation.[8] This foregrounding of the text's material dimension might also help explain why there has been a sustained—perhaps even increasing—interest in book history and bibliography in recent years, exemplified by numerous book series, degree programs, professional associations, and rare book schools. While such disciplinary formations might suggest that there are some Luddites out there desperately seeking refuge from life's incessant twitterings in a nobler, dustier past, the fact that book history is so often imbricated with studies of newer digital media—and that there are many other examples of the new and old in tandem, from artist's books' remediation of the digital to scholars' turns to textual encoding—suggests that the situation is more complex.

We might recall an already outdated example that nevertheless suggests some source of the interest. In 2007, shortly after releasing the second version (edition?) of the Kindle, Amazon.com founder Jeff Bezos remarked in a *Newsweek* interview that the "key feature of a book is that *it disappears*. . . . I've actually asked myself, 'Why do I love these physical objects?' . . . 'Why do I love the smell of glue and ink?' The answer is that I associate that smell with all those worlds I have been transported to. What we love is the words and ideas."[9] Such a statement, and the very idea of book burning implied in the title of the device and its proprietary format, is bound to prompt resistance. Maybe we just don't like losing our stuff—be it ink, glue, or a long textual tradition. Or worse yet, we don't like seeing it in front of our noses and being told it isn't really there. In this context, an interest in book history and bibliography echoes earlier attempts by many modern bibliophiles to keep in the foreground the mediating social, economic, and material structures that newer media have often threatened to conceal.

But even as we remain attentive to the material text, as book connoisseurs and collectors have done before us, we must remain skeptical of the overly restricted book collection. As I have argued throughout, we might understand book collecting and scrapbooking as examples of residual and emergent collecting practices and in doing so be particularly attentive to the ways in which haphazard accumulation undermines the possibility of a complete and closed collection. This transition, I have suggested, was taking place in modernism's long decades with respect to a culture of mass print, and it would seem that by now the dream of such a collection has distantly receded into the rear view. It is difficult to trace the Internet's sinewy webs for even a short amount of time, or to scan the books and other items available through HathiTrust (hathitrust.org) or the Digital Public Library of America (dp.la), without feeling that the beautifully arrayed gentleman's library is just a bit quaint.

We would do well to keep this in mind as we increasingly embrace strategies of distant reading. Such digital techniques as topic modeling and text mining offer incredible opportunities to step back from the individual text and to gain a bird's-eye perspective on thousands or millions of texts, which in turn prompts us to consider the dominant literary and cultural discourses binding writers and readers into shared historical moments and across time. But it isn't everything. Not even close. We must remain attentive to the ways in which previous economic, political, and aesthetic priorities of preservation exhibited in the mass print archive might continue to govern current practices of digital preservation and access. Which individuals and institutions are being privileged here, and which are being left out? We must also keep in mind that distance flattens perspective. The modern poem poses particular challenges for distant reading in that poems are not mere bags of words but complex formal and rhetorical structures marked by such features as meter and figurative language that complicate and qualify surface meaning. How can distant reading practices be effectively adapted to—or used in combination with—traditional close reading practices so that we register the accrual of not only content meaning but also formal meaning?

It would seem that, taken within an expansive media framework, mass print might still have much to say about textual culture today. But why be concerned with poetic modernism? This is, of course, a more specific form of the fundamental question that haunts all literary study: Why study the literary past at all? There are, as far as I can see, at least two reasons for investigating our literary history. One is that it gives particular insight into a historical moment that can't be achieved through other means; the other is that it might help us better understand our current literary and cultural expressions. To take the first point: if we are to thoroughly study mass print culture as a historical example for our own time, we must be attentive to more than individual forms, practices, and practitioners. We must strive to understand how people made sense of the overall culture of which they were a part. This is one of the reasons that I have been interested not only in the history of mass print media forms, or in how these were manipulated in a host of collecting practices, but ultimately in how people framed their relationship to mass print through new poetic texts, institutions, and modes of reception. Poetry has long been considered a privileged discourse for negotiating linguistic and aesthetic meaning, and, in its strivings to "make it new," poetic modernism itself mediates a culture of mass print in ways that resonate with us today. My attention to such issues as value, genre, form, reproduction, and institutionalization in previous chapters has offered some further insight into poetic modernism, and literature more generally, providing examples of how people have imagined their basic cultural priorities through poetry.

Second, a study of poetic modernism may help us better understand contemporary literary and cultural texts. If, as Jessica Pressman has argued, a particular strain of electronic texts currently being produced might be said to exhibit a "digital modernism" in its form and function, we would do well to revisit what we mean by "modernism," even as we contend with "the digital" as a rapidly changing qualifying term.[10] From my vantage point, Pressman's definition of modernism as a particular creative strategy (not temporally bound to the early twentieth century) is restricted in ways that are not at all atypical for studies of modernism but that I have been pushing against throughout this book. The decision to label recent texts modern can be attributed in part to their own self-conscious relationship to such modernist figures as Ezra Pound, but it is also dependent upon a particular investment in modernism itself, marked by the old standby criteria of difficulty, ambivalence, and textual complexity that demand certain sustained close reading strategies to uncover meaning. This restricted definition threatens to marginalize a great deal of literary and cultural production, however, including much of the popular poetry I have examined.

As I suggested in the last chapter, however, if we are to remain attentive to this poetry and effectively trace our literary history, we need to more clearly confront the constructedness of the archive through which it is preserved and accessed. I trust that the more the archive of modernism is expanded and read—especially as it is mined or sifted through in the digital surrogates of magazines, newspapers, and other ephemera—the more we will expand our notions of modernism in light of such markers as economics, readership, and general cultural impact. In an effort to contribute to such an expansion, this volume has been invested not only in the oft-neglected popular but also—through a juxtaposition of the popular to those figures, texts, media, and print institutions that have been most central to the modernist narrative—in accounting for how we have frequently come to privilege difficulty, ambiguity, and the isolated text at the expense of other creative and interpretive strategies. In doing so, this book has attempted to clear the brush for critical roads not yet taken and has pointed to the ways in which an expansive poetic modernism, largely conditioned by and mediated through the collecting of mass print, helps to frame our evolving understanding of the past—even as it prompts us to reimagine our current cultural moment and the possibilities for our future.

Notes

Introduction

1. Garvey, *Writing with Scissors*, 20.
2. Chasar, *Everyday Reading*, 32.
3. Eliot, "Address to the Members of the London Library."
4. Lynch, *Loving Literature*.
5. A. A. Hopkins, "Song of the Printing-Press," pasted into *The Literary Junk-Book*, ed. John M. Wing (1903-c.1912), John M. Wing Collection, Newberry Library, Chicago, 27 (hereafter *LJB*).
6. Richard Ohmann has made a compelling case with respect to magazines in particular in *Selling Culture*.
7. "Book Lore," *Book Lore* 1 (December 1884-May 1885): 1-2.
8. In one particularly amusing story, a collector finds that he has completed his collection except for that one impossible find, the first Shakespeare. As luck would have it, however, he finds a man who owns the book with a daughter of marrying age. The collector decides to pursue the daughter in hopes of attaining the book and begins to fall in love with the girl, realizing that perhaps "after-all, some flesh-and-blood women were desirable, and any girl whose future was bound up with that first edition must be interesting." In a final twist, the bride tells her husband she burned the book on the morning of their marriage. Aaron Mason, "The Book That He Married," *Book Lover: A Magazine of Book Lore* 1, no. 1 (Autumn 1899): 12-13 (hereafter *BL*).
9. Harper, *Book-Lovers Bibliomaniacs and Book Clubs*, 13.
10. These magazines include *Bibliographer* (London: Elliot Stock, 1882-1884); *Bookmart* (Pittsburgh: Bookmart, 1883-1890); *The Bibliographer* (New York: n.p., 1902-1903); *Literature* (London: Times, 1897-1902); *The Book Lover: A Monthly Journal for Those Interested in Rare and Standard Books, Portraits and Views for Extra-Illustration, Autograph Letters and Historical Documents* (New York: William Evarts Benjamin, 1888-1890); *The Book Lover: A Magazine of Book Lore, Being a Miscellany of Curiously Interesting and Generally Unknown Facts about the World's Literature and*

Literary People; Now Newly Arranged with Incidental Divertissement, and All Very Delightful to Read (San Francisco, New York: Book-Lover Press, 1899-1904); *Bookworm: An Illustrated Treasury of Old-Time Literature* (London: E. Stock, 1888-1894); *The Library: A Magazine of Bibliography and Literature, the Organ of the Library Association of the United Kingdom* (London: Elliot Stock, 1889-); *Book-Lover's Almanac* (New York: Duprat, 1893-1897); *Literary Collector: A Monthly Magazine of Booklore and Bibliography* (New York: G. D. Smith, 1900-1905); *The Bibliographer* (New York: Dodd, Mead, 1902-1903); and *The Bibliophile: A Magazine and Review for the Collector, Student and General Reader* (London: Bibliophile, 1908-1909).

11. Shaddy, *Books and Book Collecting in America*.

12. For more on the aesthetics of collecting, see Potvin and Myzelev, *Material Cultures*. See Belk, *Collecting in a Consumer Society*, for an anthropological analysis of the shift from a society of "limited goods" to one of "unlimited goods."

13. For more on the rise of the museum and the public collection, see Pearse, *Museums, Objects and Collections*, which analyzes how objects take on meaning in a museum context; and Conn, *Museums and American Intellectual Life*, which traces the history of the American museum in the late nineteenth and early twentieth centuries.

14. Braddock, *Collecting as Modernist Practice*.

15. Daniel M. Tredwell, "Privately Illustrated Books: A Plea for Bibliomania," *Book Lover* 1, no. 3 (Spring 1900): 267.

16. H. T. Peck, quoted in "Is Cheap Literature Cheapening Literature?," *BL* 1, no. 3 (Spring 1900): 288.

17. "Popular Books," *Book Lore* 6 (June-November 1887): 44.

18. Augustine Birrell, "Is It Possible to Tell a Good Book from a Bad One?," *BL* 1, no. 4 (Summer 1900): 447.

19. Henri Pene Du Bois, "Too Many Books," *Literary Collector* 1, no. 1 (1900): 18-19 (hereafter *LC*).

20. *L/B*, 76-78. Pasted from Virginia M. Arford, "Extra Illustrating of Books," *Sketch Book* (n.d.): 98-100.

21. J. H. Slater, "Principles of Book Collecting," *BL* 2, no. 9 (November-December 1901): 416.

22. As one collector notes, to "look upon the books of scholar or poet is to see the place in which he sharpened, if he did not forge, his thought. When he has scored the margin with comment or reflection, he has imparted something of himself to the printed page." There was a corresponding increase in the monetary value of the book as well. As H. J. Jackson has argued in *Marginalia*, these markings were not only traces of association but also often examples of learning and criticism of the primary text, suggesting ways in which the reader can manipulate the linguistic codes of a book as well.

23. *BL* 1, no. 4 (Summer 1900): 458.

24. Old Bookworm, "Books and Their Worms," *Bookworm* 2 (December 1889-November 1890): 192.

25. *BL* 1, no. 1 (Autumn 1899): 99.

26. Harper, *Book-Lovers Bibliomaniacs and Book Clubs*.

27. As Kevin J. H. Dettmar has observed, the gentleman's library gave "easier access to the symbolic capital represented by privately owned books [and] made it all the more likely that those not born into literary culture would mistake this symbolic for cultural capital, as the end in itself rather than a means to that end." Dettmar, "Bookcases, Slipcases, Uncut Leaves," 5-24.

28. T. J. Cobden-Sanderson, "The Ideal Book," *BL* 2, no. 10 (January-February 1901): 517.

29. Tredwell, "Privately Illustrated Books," 267. Coincidentally, the Brooklyn Bridge would be a provocative trope for many modern poets, including William Carlos Williams, Marianne Moore, and Hart Crane, who would synthesize the images and metaphors of the external world, and of poets preceding them, as they developed new poetic structures.

30. Benjamin, *Arcades*, 204-5.

31. As Susan Stewart explains, the collection in general "seeks a form of self-enclosure which is possible because of its ahistoricism. The collection replaces history with classification, with order beyond the realm of temporality. In the collection, time is not something to be restored to an origin; rather, all time is made simultaneous or synchronous within the collector's world." Stewart, *On Longing*, 151.

32. Benjamin, *Arcades*, 207.

33. *Oxford English Dictionary Online*, s.v. "scrap," accessed December 7, 2015, www.oed.com. It is a bit anachronistic to refer to nineteenth-century scrapbook making as "scrapbooking" and to those making such books as "scrapbookers," in that the terms don't frequently appear in the discourse of the time. I do so, however, as a convenient shorthand and to underscore the agency of scrapbook makers, as well as the continuity between nineteenth- and twentieth-century scrapbook processes.

34. Poole, *Manuscript Gleanings and Literary Scrap Book*, 3.

35. For more on Mark Twain's scrapbook innovations, see Garvey, *Writing with Scissors*.

36. For more on the history of commonplace books, see Havens, *Commonplace Books*; and Allan, *Commonplace Books and Reading in Georgian England*.

37. Meredith L. McGill has argued that the "temporal, national, and generic miscellaneousness of Emerson and Thoreau's commonplace book, and their untroubled circulation of poetry in partial, unidentified, and misquoted form, makes salient our own impulse to periodize, our need to make sense of literary texts within national, developmental frameworks, and our concern with originality and textual integrity." McGill, "Common Places," 358. As Cary Nelson notes in response, McGill's critique (more radically extending beyond the canonically privileged authors McGill cites)

can be applied as well to "commonplace books constructed as scrapbooks—with poems and portions of poems clipped from newspapers and glued on pages," whose cultural importance reaches into the twentieth century. Nelson, "Temporality of Commonplaces," 375.

38. For more on Victorian photo collage, see Siegel, *Playing with Pictures*.

39. W. L. Andrews, "Of the 'Extra-illustration' of Books," *Book Lover's Almanac* 3 (1895): 11; A.H.J., "Reflections of a Book Lover," *LC* 4, no. 5 (September 1902): 52.

40. "Extra Illustrating in New York," *Bookworm* 6 (December 1892-November 1893): 177.

41. Ibid., 181.

42. W. M. F. Round, "Enriching Books," *BL* 2, no. 9 (November-December 1901): 448. Reprinted from *New York Times*.

43. Garvey breaks this category into four general types: "young children's picture scrapbooks, often with cloth pages; compilations of favorite bits of poetry and newspaper clippings; more personal memorabilia books; and trade card scrapbooks," focusing her attention on this last type as a primer for learning to interact with magazine advertising. Garvey, *Adman in the Parlor*, 28.

44. Tucker, Ott, and Buckler, *Scrapbook in American Life*, 3.

45. Helfand, *Scrapbooks*, xix.

46. Charles F. Lummis, "Important Uses of the Scrapbook," *Writer* 12, no. 7 (July 1910): 97. Reprinted from *Journal of Education*.

47. William Henry Scott Family Papers, Manuscript Collection 1082, BV: 1, MARBL, Emory University. The scrapbook is pasted into the *Digest of Appropriations* from the Forty-Seventh US Congress, ironically underscoring the lack of appropriations for former slaves. I am grateful to Randall Burkett for directing me to this volume.

48. These publications included the *Missouri Republican, Cincinnati Communicator, Washington Gazette, Connecticut Gazette, Chicago Tribune, National Republican, Commercial Gazette, Boston Advocate, St. Louis Republican, Philadelphia Enquirer, New York Evening Post, Sun, Boston Evening Traveler, Boston Daily Advertiser, Atlanta Constitution, Macon Daily Telegraph, New Mississippian, Times Democrat, New York Times, Meridian Daily News, Washington Critic, New York Tribune, Tri-Weekly Dispatch, National Tribune, National Echo, Index,* and *Evening Star*.

49. For more on postbellum print culture, see Loughran, *Republic in Print*.

50. As Andreas Huyssen has argued, the "great divide" between mass and high culture was largely a gendered divide, where "the political, psychological, and aesthetic discourse around the turn of the century consistently and obsessively genders mass culture and the masses as feminine, while high culture, whether traditional or modern, clearly remains the privileged realm of male activities." Huyssen, *After the Great Divide*, 47. He goes on to claim that the real problem with this distinction is not

devaluing that which is gendered feminine but "rather the persistent gendering as feminine of that which it devalues" (53).

51. Although Garvey rightly notes that "women and men deserve equal blame or credit for nearly all types of clipped collections," she also concedes that "some nineteenth-century writers insisted on gendering scrapbooks." Garvey, *Writing with Scissors*, 10. Garvey makes this observation elsewhere in explaining that scrapbooking instructions that often appear in books aimed at girls or a gender-neutral audience are absent in books for boys, and that trade-card scrapbooks likewise encouraged gender-specific training in arranging and decorating. Garvey, *Adman in the Parlor*, 26, 43.

52. Chasar has observed that "the intentional, sustained reading of poetry and the making of poetry scrapbooks came to be viewed within popular culture as a distinctly domestic and feminine activity on par with housekeeping." Chasar, *Everyday Reading*, 58.

53. Quoted in Ohmann, *Selling Culture*, 225.

54. Garvey, *Writing with Scissors*, 172-206.

55. C.F.B., "Importance of Keeping a Scrapbook," *Writer* 27, no. 2 (February 1904): 29. Quoted in *New York Mail and Express*.

56. One article that has considered this issue to a limited extent is Marsh's "Thaddeus Coleman Pound's 'Newspaper Scrapbook' as a Source for *The Cantos*," 163-93.

57. "In Defense of Snippets," *BL* 1, no. 4 (Summer 1900): 454.

58. As Garvey has noted, nineteenth-century scrapbooking mirrored the more public clipping and recirculation of items that newspaper editors practiced. Garvey, *Writing with Scissors*, 4.

59. Raymond Blathwayt, "Lions in Their Dens: George Newnes at Putney," *Idler Magazine: An Illustrated Monthly*, ed. Jerome K. Jerome & Robert Barr, 3 (February-July 1893): 165.

60. Cook, *Literary Recreations*, 128. The lasting recognition of this fact is evident in the note appended to the copy of the first volume of the magazine that I consulted—a Google Books reproduction of a copy kept at the Bodleian Library—which attests, "I have just purchased a complete set of the first year (52 numbers) of 'Tit-Bits' 1881. This is both rare and important as being the precursor of so much of modern journalism (much though we may deplore this phase of modern life)."

61. McDonald, *British Literary Culture and Publishing Practice*, 146.

62. Kenner, *Sinking Island*, 35.

63. McGill, *American Literature and the Culture of Reprinting*.

64. George Newnes, "Tit-Bits," *Tit-Bits* 1, no. 1 (October 22, 1881): 1.

65. James Joyce, *Ulysses*, 56.

66. Ibid.

67. Jackson, "George Newnes and the 'Loyal Tit-Bitites,'" 12-13.

68. W.E.H., "Ex Libris: Tit-Bit Tyrranus," *Pall-Mall Magazine* 19 (September-December 1899): 581-86.

69. "The Literature of Snippets," *BL* 1, no. 4 (Summer 1900): 452-453.

70. Harold Rome, "On Not Reading Newspapers and Things," in *LJB*, 33.

71. H. Elsdale, "Why Are Our Brains Deteriorating?," *Nineteenth Century* 270 (August 1899): 267.

72. Cook, *Literary Recreations*, 130.

73. "Something New in Magazine Making," *Scrap Book* 1, no. 1 (March 1906): 1. I am thankful to Sean Latham for directing me to this magazine.

74. Ibid., 2.

75. "Marvelous Reception," *Scrap Book* 1, no. 2 (April 1906): 194. This success can be attributed in large part to the $75,000 advertising campaign that preceded the first issue.

76. Ibid., 196.

77. "Volume I of 'The Scrap Book' to Be Bound," *Scrap Book* 2, no. 4 (December 1906): 640.

78. Ibid.

79. "Even This Shall Pass Away," *Scrap Book* 2, no. 3 (November 1906): 438.

80. Susan Marr Spaulding, "Fate," *Scrap Book* 1, no. 1 (March 1906): 91. The last name would be corrected to "Spalding" in the October 1906 issue.

81. "A Rescued Poem: 'The Scrap Book' Resurrects from Distressing Obscurity a Gem That Might Otherwise Have Been Lost to Posterity," *Scrap Book* 1, no. 2 (April 1906): 257.

82. Walt Whitman, "O Captain! My Captain!," *Scrap Book* 2, no. 6 (February 1907): 801-802. Alfred, Lord Tennyson, "The Eagle," *Scrap Book* 2, no. 4 (December 1906): 590.

83. "Autumn and the Poets," *Scrap Book* 2, no. 3 (November 1906): 356-57.

84. "The Foreloper," *Scrap Book* 7, no. 6 (June 1909): 1041.

85. "An Irish Poem by Whittier," *Scrap Book* 7, no. 6 (June 1909): 1094.

86. Frank A. Munsey, "To the Readers of the *Scrap Book*," *Scrap Book* 4, no. 1 (July 1907): 88. The new two-part magazine would cost twenty-five cents, more than twice the cost of the ten-cent *Scrap Book* but less than the cost of two fifteen-cent magazines.

87. Ibid., 90.

88. "To the Readers of the *Scrap Book*," *Scrap Book* 6, no. 3. Insert between pages 486 and 487, printed on blue paper.

89. Quoted in Buck-Morss, *Dialectics of Seeing*, 165. As Buck-Morss explains, the concept of allegory allows Benjamin to "make visibly palpable the experience of a world in fragments, in which the passing of time means not progress but disintegration" (18). Benjamin's fascination with the allegorical can be traced to his early work on the German *Trauerspiel*, but as he suggests in "Paris, Capital of the Nineteenth

Century," this medieval concretization has its modern counterpart, where just as in the seventeenth century, "the canon of dialectical imagery came to be allegory, in the nineteenth it is novelty" typified by the magazine and newspaper press. Benjamin, "Paris, Capital of the Nineteenth Century," 158.

90. Benjamin, *Arcades*, 211.
91. Baudrillard, *System of Objects*, 88.
92. Benjamin, *Arcades*, 211.
93. "Collecting of Books," LJB, 39.
94. *Old Corner Library Scrap Book*; LJB.
95. Benjamin, "Theses on the Philosophy of History," 258.
96. Thosas Tapper, "What Clippings to Keep," *Writer* 3, no. 11 (November 1889): 248-249.
97. Raymond Williams, "Base and Superstructure in Marxist Cultural Theory," 3-16.
98. Jameson, *Marxism and Form*, 72.
99. Adorno and Horkheimer, "Culture Industry," 127.
100. Benjamin, "Work of Art," 21.
101. My understanding of the ways in which individuals can make meaning through mass culture is largely indebted to the work of British cultural studies theorists, including Dick Hebdige and Stuart Hall.
102. Huyssen, *After the Great Divide*. In arguing for a great divide, Huyssen draws, in part, on what Peter Bürger has seen as a separation of modernism from the historical *avant-garde*. Bürger, *Theory of the Avant-Garde*.
103. Darnton, "What Is the History of Books?," 65-83. As with any generative model, Darnton's circuit of book production has had its critics. Carl Kaestle and Janice Radway, for example, have argued that Darnton's social history doesn't go far enough in explaining nineteenth-century "cultures of print," a term they employ to resonate with the "print culture" of the last five hundred or so years but also to suggest a supersaturation of print throughout the public sphere, so that culture itself is *of* print. As they claim, the metaphor of the circuit "implies a view from above that homes in on the object being circulated rather than the social actors involved in the process, on the social milieu within which they operated, and their complex reasons for involving themselves in the culture of print in the first place." Kaestle and Radway, "Framework for the History of Publishing and Reading in the United States," 18.
104. Some attention has been given to collecting by Thomas R. Adams and Nicholas Barker, who have noted that Darnton's communications circuit is less a "book history" than a social history of people interacting with books and as such neglects to consider (among other things) what happens to the book when it is not in constant contact with historical actors, as when a book is buried for decades in an old shop, waiting to be rescued and given new life in a collection. Because they are less invested in how people interact with books, however, Adams and Barker have rela-

tively little to say about collecting practices themselves. Thomas R. Adams and Nicholas Barker, "New Model for the Study of the Book," 5–43.

105. Gitelman, *Paper Knowledge*.

106. Parikka, *What Is Media Archaeology?* Also see Huhtamo and Parikka, *Media Archaeology*.

107. Hayles and Pressman, *Comparative Textual Media*.

108. Guillory, "Genesis of the Media Concept," 359.

109. Ibid., 361.

110. Braddock, *Collecting as Modernist Practice*, 6–7.

111. Michael Davidson coins the portmanteau "palimptext" to describe "modern writing's intertextual and material character, its graphic rendering of multiple layers of signification. The term also suggests the need for a historicist perspective in which textual layers refer not only to previous texts but to the discursive frame of the present in which they are seen." Davidson, *Ghostlier Demarcations*, 9. McGann emphasizes poetry's foregrounding of the textual condition in the *Textual Condition*, 10. Rachel Blau DuPlessis argues for a "social philology" that "claims that the social materials (both specific and general politics, attitudes, subjectivities, ideologies, discourses, debates) are activated and situated within the deepest texture of, the sharpest specificities of, the poetic text: on the level of word choice, crypt word, impacted etymologies, segmentivity and line break, the stanza, the image, diction, sound, genre, the 'events' and speakers selected inside the work (enounced), and the rhetorical tactics of the thing on the page (enunciation)." DuPlessis, *Genders, Races and Religious Cultures in Modern American Poetry*, 12.

112. Bornstein, *Material Modernism*, 7.

113. The politics of the New Formalism have been most extensively examined in Theile and Tredennick, *New Formalisms and Literary Theory*. As Paul B. Armstrong asserts in an essay that productively reads the achievements of New Criticism against those of New Historicism, although the profession has frequently pitted form and history against one another, the "otherness of a literary work—its challenge as well as its appeal—is inextricably both formal and historical." Armstrong, "Form and History," 195. Susan J. Wolfson has similarly argued that even at the height of New Historicism, it was not "attention to form per se that was discredited; it was the impulse to regard it as the product of a historically disinterested, internally coherent aesthetics." Wolfson, "Reading for Form," 2. This special issue, edited by Wolfson and Marshall Brown, and the subsequent book collection, *Reading for Form*, based on the issue, remain two influential forays into New Formalism.

114. This is a kind of reading that Lawrence Rainey has associated with modernism, observing that "the effect of modernism was not so much to encourage reading as to render it superfluous. What modernism required was not the individual reader but a new and uneasy amalgam of the investor, the collector and the patron" speculating on the bear and bull markets of literary value. Rainey, *Institutions of Modernism*, 56.

115. Sherzer, "American Editions of Shakespeare," 633-96; Tupper, "Textual Criticism as a Pseudo-Science," 164-81; Root, "Publication before Printing," 417-31; Shipherd, "Play-Publishing in Elizabethan Times," 580-600.

116. Fruit, "Plea for the Study of Literature from the Aesthetic Standpoint," 33-34.

117. Wernaer, "New Constructive Criticism," 431.

118. Price, "New Function of Modern Language Teaching," 84-85.

119. Rainey, *Institutions of Modernism*.

120. Palgrave, *Golden Treasury* (1861), n.p.

121. Mao and Walkowitz, "Changing Profession," 737-48.

122. The key text on this front remains Cary Nelson's *Repression and Recovery*.

123. Wollaeger with Eatough, *Oxford Handbook of Global Modernisms*. Bulson, "Little Magazine, World Form," 267-87.

124. Ramazani, *Transnational Poetics*.

125. Hart, *Nations of Nothing but Poetry*.

126. Walsh, *Geopoetics of Modernism*.

127. McGill, *Traffic in Poems*.

128. Woolf, *Mr. Bennett and Mrs. Brown*, 4.

Chapter One. As Good as Gold

1. British Library Catalogue.

2. Alan Golding has traced the closely related historicizing and inspirational impulses that typified American poetry anthologies throughout the nineteenth century in *From Outlaw to Classic*, 6.

3. As Jeremy Braddock has argued, because of its increasing emphasis on social practice, "the occasional, coterie, or interventionist anthology endured, indeed flourished, as a salient provisional institution." Braddock, *Collecting as Modernist Practice*, 16.

4. Arthur Waugh, "Concerning Anthologies," *BL* 2, no. 2 (Spring 1901): 239.

5. Cheever, *American Common-Place Book of Poetry*.

6. The briefest of lists would include Beauchamp, *Poems of Revolt*; Clarke, *Treasury of War Poetry*; Cook, *An Anthology of Humorous Verse*; Hooper, *Rhymes of the Rockies*; Leonard, *Book of Light Verse*; Richards, *Melody of the Earth*; and Wells, *Vers de Société Anthology*.

7. Smith, *Contingencies of Value*.

8. Markham, *Book of Poetry*, x.

9. Waugh, "Concerning Anthologies," 239.

10. Palgrave, *Golden Treasury*, n.p. Unless otherwise noted, all citations are to the 1861 edition.

11. Ibid. These readers, whom Palgrave neglects to mention by name, were Thomas

Woolner and George Miller. For more on this and Palgrave's personal biases, see Latané, "Treasure Sub Rosa," 135-43.

12. As Linda H. Peterson explains, the exclusion of many women from *The Golden Treasury* can be attributed less to Palgrave's particular editorial stance than to a critical situation where a recent focus on women in poetry collections, anthologies, and biographies had the paradoxical effect of separating them from the poetic tradition at large. Peterson, "Anthologizing Women," 193-209.

13. Waugh, "Concerning Anthologies," 239.

14. Palgrave, *Golden Treasury*, n.p.

15. Ibid.

16. Waugh, "Concerning Anthologies," 240.

17. Ibid., 240-41.

18. Anne Ferry notes that the spatial dimension of the anthology has long been rooted in the arrangement of books and, by the mid-nineteenth century, "the localizing figure of a library had become a persuasive way to imagine an anthology in the changed cultural situation when home libraries on a much humbler scale than the private collections amassed after the Restoration had become familiar and comfortable spaces." Ferry, *Tradition and the Individual Poem*, 29.

19. Advertising circular, Stone and Kimball Collection (hereafter SK), Newberry Library, Chicago.

20. Stone to family, ca. 25 March 1893; Stone to Ned, ca. 6 April 1893, SK.

21. Prospectus, "The Book Lover," Autumn 1893. Quoting *Publisher's Weekly*, September 9, 1893, SK, 311.

22. Megan L. Benton focuses on these early decades of the twentieth century in *Beauty and the Book*.

23. Sawyer, *Leon's Catalogue of First Editions of American Authors*; Slater, *Early Editions*; Foley, *American Authors*; Arnold, *Record of First Editions*.

24. "Original Editions," *Bookworm* 2 (December 1888-November 1889): 293.

25. George F. Carter, "First Editions: A Phase of Book Collecting," *LC* 7, no. 2 (December 1903): 40.

26. "Boards, Uncut," *New York Times*, September 16, 1899. Historical *New York Times* Index, BR616. Reprinted in *BL* 1, no. 2 (Winter 1899-1900): 177.

27. According to N. N. Feltes, value for the turn-of-the-century collector "is constructed both of 'rarity,' which is simply an exceptionality ensured by chronological priority, and of 'completeness' in relation to some 'sentimental,' or personal, biographical criterion." Feltes, *Literary Capital*, 39.

28. Slater, *How to Collect Books*, 3.

29. Feltes, *Literary Capital*, 40.

30. This notion corresponds to what Outka has called the "originary authentic," where one feels that one is "not buying the general, but the genuine, the first model from which others might be made." The originary authentic is a corollary to the phe-

nomenon of the "commodified authentic" that lies at the heart of modernism—a paradox of "a constructed, marketed aesthetic of things that might be easily obtained and exchanged, infused with the contrary images of stability, permanence, and the noncommercial." Outka, *Consuming Traditions*, 9.

31. "Éditions De Luxe," *New York Times*, April 8, 1883. Historical *New York Times* Index, 8.

32. "Morris's Books and Rich Collectors," *New York Times*, January 26, 1901. Historical *New York Times* Index, BR8.

33. As Feltes notes, "even a contemporary book might also immediately attain 'value,' for value in books as physical objects was, since the nineties, a structure constituted by priority on as many scales as possible, along with some sentimental (i.e., arbitrary) 'literary' relationship, or 'association.'" Feltes, *Literary Capital*, 40.

34. C. F. Cazenove, "To a Young Collector," *BL* 2, no. 8 (Summer 1901): 359.

35. Palgrave, *Golden Treasury*, n.p.

36. Alfred, Lord Tennyson, *Lyrical Poems*, ed. Francis Turner Palgrave (London: Macmillan, 1885), viii.

37. Palgrave to Macmillan, n.d., Palgrave (Francis Turner) Correspondence with Macmillan and Co., 54977: 97, British Library Manuscript Collections (hereafter Palgrave/Macmillan).

38. Reprinted in Palgrave, *Golden Treasury* (1916).

39. Ibid.

40. Palgrave to Macmillan, 14 January 1890, Palgrave/Macmillan: 208-11. All underlining represents Palgrave's emphasis.

41. Robert Browning to Palgrave, 19 October 1864, Palgrave (Francis Turner) Correspondence and Papers, Add 45741: 28.

42. Palgrave to Craik, 26 October 1890, Palgrave/Macmillan: 216.

43. Palgrave to Craik, 10 December 1890, Palgrave/Macmillan: 220-21.

44. Palgrave to Macmillan, 14 May 1891, Palgrave/Macmillan: 227-28. As Megan Nelson notes, Palgrave referred to this as the second edition (when in fact it was the fourth), afraid to label the second and third editions as such because it would discourage the purchase of stock on hand. He also insisted that the first edition (meaning the first three editions) continue to be advertised, so that the 1891 edition was seen as more of a supplement than a replacement of the original. Nelson, "Frances Turner Palgrave," 160.

45. Palgrave to Macmillan, 15 November 1880, Palgrave/Macmillan: 125-26.

46. Palgrave to Craik, 20 October 1890, Palgrave/Macmillan: 214-15.

47. Palgrave to Craik, 10 December 1890, Palgrave/Macmillan: 220-21; Palgrave to Craik, 13 December 1891, Palgrave/Macmillan: 234.

48. Palgrave, *Golden Treasury*, Second Series, n.p.

49. Ibid.

50. Nelson, "Francis Turner Palgrave," 162.

51. The Copyright Act of 1842 allowed an author or editor to retain copyright of a written work for forty-two years or life plus seven years, whichever was greater, which meant that copyright on the original *Golden Treasury* expired seven years after Palgrave's death in 1897. This may partly account for the popularity of the original edition over the enlarged and expanded edition and the Second Series, which were still under copyright.

52. Palgrave and Rhys, *Palgrave's Golden Treasury*, vii, viii, xi.

53. Lewis, *Golden Treasury of the Best Songs and Lyrical Poems*, 15.

54. Oscar Williams, *Little Treasury of Modern Poetry*, 21.

55. Clarke, *New Treasury of War Poetry*; Knowles, *Treasury of Humorous Poetry*; Chadwick and Chadwick, *Treasury of Helpful Verse*.

56. Untermeyer, *Book of Living Verse*, v.

57. Squire, *Cambridge Book of Lesser Poets*; Collins, *Treasury of Minor British Poetry*.

58. *Silver Poets of the Seventeenth Century* suggests that "the word silver in the title of this volume, where minor might perhaps have been expected, marks its editor's resolve to distinguish without disparagement and to admire without extravagance. It acknowledges a distinction between this particular assembly of poets and their more eminent contemporaries and near-contemporaries, while implying that the least we can claim for them is a silver-tongued eloquence. Nor will the judicious reader complain if he finds, as he will, some golden verses here." Bullett, *Silver Poets of the Seventeenth Century*, v. *The Bronze Treasury* exclaims that "the great poet receives, and rightly deserves, the practical world's highest veneration and worship. The rest—of whom this book is made up—deserve the world's sympathy and pity—that it seldomer gives than is good for it." Kemp, *Bronze Treasury*, 5.

59. Rhys, *Golden Treasury of Longer Poems*; Jones, *Shorter Golden Book of Narrative Verse*; Lentricchia, *Modernist Quartet*, 55–56.

60. The poem, taken from the description of the Mona Lisa in *The Renaissance*, challenges the boundaries between poetry and prose. Pound, *Des Imagistes*; Yeats, *Oxford Book of Modern Verse*.

61. Knowles, *Golden Treasury of American Songs and Lyrics*, viii.

62. Stephen, *Golden Treasury of Canadian Verse*; MacDiarmid, *Golden Treasury of Scottish Poetry*.

63. Yeats, *Book of Irish Verse*, xv.

64. Rhys, *New Golden Treasury of Songs and Lyrics*; Rhys, *Additional Poems to Palgrave's Golden Treasury*, vii.

65. Oscar Williams, *F. T. Palgrave's The Golden Treasury*, xi, xii.

66. Brewster, *Golden Treasury*, vi.

67. Binyon, *Golden Treasury of Modern Lyrics*, v.

68. Collins, *Treasury of English Verse New and Old*, v.

69. Williams, *F. T. Palgrave's The Golden Treasury*, xi.

70. Wheeler, *Golden Treasury*, xi.

71. Van Dyke, *Little Masterpieces of Poetry*, v, vii.

72. Riding and Graves, *Survey of Modernist Poetry* and *A Pamphlet Against Anthologies*, 67.

73. Braddock, *Collecting as Modernist Practice*, 21.

74. Riding and Graves, *Survey of Modernist Poetry* and *A Pamphlet Against Anthologies*, 186, 201.

75. Ibid., xvii, xvi, xix.

76. Ibid., xi. Already feeling the backlash and criticism of what had been characterized and caricatured as New Criticism, Brooks and Warren wrote a postscript to the 1950 edition, explaining that, in the pedagogical climate of the previous decade:

> the chief need was for a sharp focus on the poem itself. At that time it seemed expedient to provide that focus, and to leave to implication the relationship of the poem to its historical background, to its place in the context of the poet's work, and to biographical and historical study generally. The years that have followed have indicated that these relationships could not safely be left to implication. Some teachers have felt that *Understanding Poetry* implied a disregard for historical and biographical study. . . . In this revised edition, therefore, though we continue to insist upon the need for a sharp focus upon the poem itself, we have tried to relate criticism to other literary studies. Specifically, we have attempted to view the poem in relation to its historical situation and in relation to the body of the poet's work (xxi).

By the third edition, issued in 1960, the "Letter to the Teacher" was cut altogether.

77. Ibid., xv.

78. Brooks, *Modern Poetry and the Tradition*, xxviii.

79. Ridler, *Little Book of Modern Verse*, 5, 8.

80. Eliot, "Tradition and the Individual Talent," 44.

81. Waugh, "Concerning Anthologies," 240-41. Anne Ferry notes that Eliot is able to "reconcile his language for describing tradition as a simultaneous order and a flowing current, because in an anthology poems exist together in a space where there is no before or after except as they locate places in the book." Ferry, *Tradition and the Individual Poem*, 254-55.

82. Eliot, "Tradition and the Individual Talent," 44.

83. Ibid., 50-51.

84. As John Guillory has argued, in an effort to sidestep the "canon wars" of the 1980s and 1990s, the literary canon should always be taken as an imaginary list that can never appear complete and uncontested, "even in the form of the omnibus anthology." What is concrete, he argues, is "the syllabus, the list of works one reads in a given class, or the curriculum, the list of works one reads in a program of study. . . . So far from being the case that the canon determines the syllabus in the simplest sense that the syllabus is constrained to select only from canonical works, it is much

more historically accurate to say that the syllabus posits the existence of the canon as its imaginary totality." Guillory, *Cultural Capital*, 30-31. Even more concrete than the syllabus or the curriculum, however, are those books that are actually being read and discussed. Chief among these books have been anthologies—especially *Understanding Poetry*. Insofar as it is a basis of the syllabus, *Understanding Poetry* posits the poetic canon as its imaginary totality that is then merely selected from in the classroom. In this respect, the poetry anthology's involvement in the canon wars goes back at least to the New Critics, if not to Palgrave himself.

Chapter Two. Making Modern *Poetry*

1. Circular, October 1917, *Poetry: A Magazine of Verse* Records 1895-1961, Special Collections Research Center, University of Chicago Library (hereafter PR).

2. For more on the "renaissance of printing," see McGann, *Black Riders*.

3. Hoffman, Allen, and Ulrich, *Little Magazine*, 5-6.

4. Latham and Scholes, "Rise of Periodical Studies," 517-31. This turn to modern periodical studies is exemplified by such books as Scholes and Wulfman, *Modernism in the Magazines*; as well as by such sites as the Modernist Journals Project (http://www.modjourn.org/). Focusing more clearly on the little magazines, Mark S. Morrisson has questioned the separation of the aesthetic and the commercial, arguing that modern literary magazines often inhabited a "counterpublic sphere," adopting the rhetorical and advertising strategies of mass-circulation magazines. Morrisson, *Public Face of Modernism*.

5. Suzanne W. Churchill has argued that modernist experimentation in literary form, most evident in the popularization of free verse, went hand in hand with social critique—a coupling that is often lost when poems are studied in isolation. Churchill, *Little Magazine "Others."* More recently John Timberman Newcomb has explored the political agenda of *Others* and *Seven Arts*, while recovering the experimental mission of the *Masses* in *How Did Poetry Survive?* On the role of women magazine editors, see Cahill, *Harriet Monroe*; Ellen Williams, *Harriet Monroe and the Poetry Renaissance*; Marek, *Women Editing Modernism*; and Newcomb, *How Did Poetry Survive?*

6. Ezra Pound, "To Whistler, American," *Poetry* 1, no. 1 (October 1912): 8.

7. Pound certainly was influenced by Whitman, though, as evidenced in the proclamation in "A Pact" that "I make truce with you, Walt Whitman—/I have detested you long enough." Ezra Pound, "A Pact," *Poetry* 2, no. 1 (April 1913): 11.

8. Pound, *Gaudier-Brzeska*, 151.

9. Newcomb, *How Did Poetry Survive?*, 37.

10. Harriet Monroe, "Motives of the Magazine," *Poetry* 1, no. 1 (October 1912): 26.

11. "*Poetry* recognizes poetry as a vital force, as changeable and fluid as life itself. Like the ideal art exhibition, it offers the best contemporary work of all schools, conservative and radical." Circular, late 1915 or 1916, PR.

12. "On the Reading of Poems," *Poetry* 1, no. 1 (October 1912): 25.

13. Benjamin, "Work of Art," 21, 24.

14. Harriet Monroe, "Comments and Reviews: Incarnations," *Poetry* 2, no. 3 (June 1913): 101-4.

15. In this manner *Poetry* resembles another magazine that sought to present a relatively auratic art object, Alfred Stieglitz's *Camera Work* (1903-1917).

16. Circular, October 1917, PR.

17. "Broad Margins," *Book Lore* 6 (June 1887-November 1887): 42.

18. The extreme case of such lavishness is the famous "blank issue" of the *Little Review*, where nothing was deemed fit to print.

19. Pound to Monroe, 11 October 1912, PR. Reprinted in Parisi and Young, *Dear Editor*, 47.

20. To take just the magazine's first two years (demonstrating how quickly *Poetry* would be identified with the fledgling movement), poems that could roughly be categorized as Imagist include Richard Aldington's "ΧΟΡΙΚΟΕ," "To a Greek Marble," and "Au Vieux Jardin" (*Poetry* 1, no. 2 [November 1912]: 39, 42, 43); H.D.'s "Verses, Translations, and Reflections from 'The Anthology'" that would include "Hermes of the Ways," "Priapus," and "Epigram" (*Poetry* 1, no. 4 [January 1913]: 118-22); F. S. Flint's "Four Poems in Unrhymed Cadence" (*Poetry* 2, no. 4 [July 1913]: 136-39); sections of Skipwith Cannéll's "Poems in Prose and Verse: A Sequence" (*Poetry* 2, no. 5 [August 1913]: 171-76); Ezra Pound's "Poems," which include "Ancora," "Surgit Fama: Fragment from an unwritable play," "The Choice," "April," "Gentildonna," "Lustra," and "Xenia" (*Poetry* 3, no. 2 [November 1913]: 53-60); Aldington's "Poems" (*Poetry* 3, no. 4 [January 1914]: 133-36); H.D.'s "Hermonax" and "Acon" (*Poetry* 3, no. 5 [February 1914]: 164-65, 165-66); Carl Sandburg's "Chicago" and "The Hammer" (*Poetry* 3, no. 6 [March 1914]: 191-92, 194); Amy Lowell's "Poems," especially "The Cyclists" and "A Lady" (*Poetry* 4, no. 1 [April 1914]: 1-11); Joyce Kilmer's rhyming but aphoristic and image-driven "Easter" (*Poetry* 4, no. 1 [April 1914]: 14); Sandburg's "Iron" (*Poetry* 4, no. 3 [June 1914]: 95); and Pound's "To ΚΑΛὸΝ," "The Bellaires," "Salvationists," "Amitiés" and "Abu Salammamm—A Song of Empire" (*Poetry* 4, no. 5 [August 1914]: 169-70, 170-72, 172-73, 174-75, 176-77).

21. Arrowsmith, "Transcultural Roots of Modernism," 27-42.

22. Pound, "A Few Don'ts by an Imagiste," *Poetry* 1, no. 6 (March 1913): 200-206; F. S. Flint, "Imagisme," *Poetry* 1, no. 6 (March 1913): 198-200.

23. Alice Corbin Henderson, Review of *Des Imagistes: An Anthology*, by Ezra Pound, *Poetry* 5, no. 1 (January 1916): 38-40.

24. Connoisseurship is central to what Louis Menand has pointed to as an extreme fetishization of the poem-object, where, "in its enthusiasm for ridding itself of the literary, Imagism ended by getting rid of everything *but* the literary; it moved the quality of literariness to the center of the poem, and then began to trim away what was left around the edges." Menand, *Discovering Modernism*, 61.

25. Ezra Pound, "In a Station of the Metro," *Poetry* 2, no. 1 (April 1913): 12.
26. Pound, *Gaudier-Brzeska*, 103.
27. Ellis, "Punctuation of 'In a Station of the Metro,'" 201-7.
28. At the time of the poem's initial publication, Pound was considering at least two other versions of "In a Station of the Metro" (both, significantly, with "Metro" offset by quotation marks, suggesting its novelty and foreignness). The reverse sides of two pages from a letter Pound sent to Monroe in April 1913, regarding the "Contemporania" series soon to be published, reveal two crossed-out versions:

The apparition of these faces in the crowd :
 Petals on a wet black bough .

And

The apparition of these faces in the crowd :
 Petals on a wet   ,black bough .

Like the printed version, both alternative versions display the importance of spacing and the poem's isolation on the page. Even the less radical first version has double spaces between words, slowing down the reading pace. It also maintains the space before the punctuation that ends each line. Pound to Monroe, April 1913, PR.

29. Pound to Monroe, March 10, 1913. Reprinted in Parisi and Young, *Dear Editor*, 57.
30. Pound to Monroe, March 1913, PR. Reprinted in Parisi and Young, *Dear Editor*, 58.
31. Chasar, *Everyday Reading*, 159.
32. Pound, *Gaudier-Brzeska*, 101.
33. Todorov, "Origin of Genres," 199-200.
34. Harriet Monroe, "The Open Door," *Poetry* 1, no. 2 (November 1912): 62-64.
35. Harriet Monroe, "Give Him Room," *Poetry* 6, no. 2 (February 1918): 81-84.
36. Narrative poems in the first two years would include Nicholas Vachel Lindsay's "General William Booth Enters into Heaven" (*Poetry* 1, no. 4 [January 1913]: 101-3); W. B. Yeats's, "The Two Kings" (*Poetry* 3, no. 1 [October, 1913]: 1-10); Robert Frost's "The Code—Heroics" (*Poetry* 3, no. 5 [February 1914]: 167-71); Ford Maddox Hueffer's three-part poem "On Heaven" (*Poetry* 4, no. 3 [June 1914]: 75-94); Lindsay's "Poems to Be Chanted" (*Poetry* 4, no. 4 [July 1914]: 123-40); and Constance Lindsay Skinner's "Songs of the Coast-Dwellers" (*Poetry* 5, no. 1 [October 1914]: 1-19).
37. Prose poems in the first two years would include the concluding section 14 from Rabindranath [Rabindra Nath] Tagore's "Poems" (*Poetry* 2, no. 3 [June 1913]: 81-91); sections of Skipwith Cannéll's "Poems in Prose and Verse: A Sequence" (*Poetry* 2, no. 5 [August 1913]: 171-76); Allen Upward's prose poem sequence, "Scented

Leaves—From a Chinese Jar" (*Poetry* 2, no. 6 [September 1913]: 191-99); John Cournos's "The Rose" (*Poetry* 3, no. 4 [January 1914]: 132); and Amy Lowell's "The Forsaken" (*Poetry* 4, no. 1 [April 1914]: 9-11).

38. Poem sequences in the first two years would include Skipwith Cannéll's "Poems in Prose and Verse: A Sequence" (*Poetry* 2, no. 5 [August 1913]: 171-76); Allen Upward's "Scented Leaves—From a Chinese Jar" (*Poetry* 2, no. 6 [September 1913]: 191-99); John Gould Fletcher's "Irradiations" (*Poetry* 3, no. 3 [December, 1913]: 85-91); Orrick Johns's "Songs of Deliverance" (*Poetry* 3, no. 5 [February 1914]: 172-78); Padraic Colum's "Three Irish Spinning Songs" (*Poetry* 3, no. 6 [March 1914]: 208-11); A. J. Russell's "The House of Takumi: Poem Sequence From the Japanese" (*Poetry* 4, no. 1 [April 1914]: 18-21); Cannéll's "Monoliths" (*Poetry* 4, no. 6 [September 1914]: 207-10); John Gould Fletcher's "The Blue Symphony" (*Poetry* 4, no. 6 [September 1914]: 211-15); and Constance Lindsay Skinner's "Songs of the Coast-Dwellers" (*Poetry* 5, no. 1 [October 1914]: 1-19). As Newcomb has suggested, such sequences represent some of the most significant, critically underappreciated forms of the "New Poetry."

39. Edgar Lee Masters, "What Is Poetry?" *Poetry* 6, no. 6 (September 1915): 307-8.

40. Harriet Monroe, "Reviews," *Poetry* 1, no. 4 (January 1913): 131-34.

41. The magazine would claim in a January 1915 circular, *Contemporary Poetry and the Universities*, that, of late, "the modern drama and the modern novel have been considered not wholly unworthy of academic consideration, but modern poetry and modern art remain the outcasts and pariahs of the institutions of formal education." PR.

42. Monroe, "Open Door," 63.

43. Circular, Summer 1912, PR.

44. Circular, late 1915 or 1916, PR.

45. As John Frow has argued, a textual frame helps define the ambivalent edges of a text as it works to cut it off from the outside world and define it against its other. For this reason, "the frame enclosing any piece of text is both a set of material determinants and a metaphor for the frame structure of genre." This frame, which can be of varying thickness, "radiates in two directions simultaneously: on the one hand, it 'quotes' the text within a context where it is assigned a particular function; on the other, it conducts the trace of the excluded non-aesthetic area inward, so that the delimited space of the text is structured by its limit and becomes significant because of the restrictions operated by the frame." Frow, *Genre*, 106-7.

46. For more on family resemblances, see Ludwig Wittgenstein's *Philosophical Investigations*.

47. This is not an absolutely rigid frame, however, as is evident in the magazine's subtitle, *A Magazine of Verse*. The reference to verse suggests anxiety over the extent

to which form and genre are dialectically related: genre is dependent on a rigidity of form evacuated of individual intention, and genre is always in danger of succumbing to set form.

48. Monroe, "Motives," 27.

49. Circular, September 1912, PR. In a Summer 1912 circular sent to prospective poets, *Poetry* would claim that "while the ordinary magazines must minister to a large public little interested in poetry, this magazine will appeal to, and it may be hoped, will develop, a public primarily interested in poetry as an art, as the highest, most complete expression of truth and beauty.... We hope to print poems of greater length and of more intimate and serious character than the other magazines can afford to use." PR.

50. Letter to Harriet Monroe in Spring or Summer 1913, by Ezra Pound, copyright 2015 by Mary de Rachewiltz and the Estate of Omar S. Pound. Reprinted by permission of New Directions Publishing Corp.

51. As Harriet Monroe would write in her eulogy to the magazine's founder, Herbert Stone, who died on board the *Lusitania*, "*The Chap-Book*—too short-lived, alas!—was not only witty and clever beyond all its contemporaries, but it led them all in literary discernment and distinction." Harriet Monroe, "Aere Perennius," *Poetry* 6, no. 4 (July 1915): 197.

52. Ruth Hall, "Liebig's Extract of Orthodoxy," *Chap-Book* 8, no. 11 (April 15, 1898): 445.

53. Brodhead, *Cultures of Letters*.

54. In an effort to underscore editorial decisions as to what counted as poetry, I have chosen to include only those poems that were indexed as poems under such headings as "poetry" or "verse." In doing so, I exclude a great deal of light verse from my analysis, which, as I explain later in this chapter, was often relegated to the back pages and not considered worthy of being called poetry or verse. Similarly, I don't account for the many poems used in advertisements, which were frequently excerpted from bound volumes. To include these other poems would significantly increase the number of poems I have graphed. As is standard, the journal volumes (or reproductions of bound volumes) that I have consulted to attain these numbers were bound two per year: May–October and November–April. As such, for the *Atlantic* and *Harper's* graphs, the year actually encompasses two months from the previous year in place of that year's last two months (e.g., the year 1909 goes from November 1908 to October 1909). While this discrepancy could potentially impact studies of individual years, it has little effect on my long view.

55. For a longer historical comparison, a cumulative index for *Harper's Monthly Magazine*, covering 1850–1885, lists 1,815 poems, an average of about 52 poems per year or 26 poems per volume.

56. How many poems is up for debate. The *Century* published much more light

verse than did the other two magazines, though, as I have indicated, this verse has only been counted if it was originally identified as poetry or verse.

57. Newcomb, *Would Poetry Disappear?*, 47.
58. "Have Great Poets Become Impossible?" *Harper's* 1 (1836): 340-43. "Lack of Poetry in America," *Harper's* 1 (1836): 403-4.
59. W. L. Shoemaker, "Untitled," *BL* 1, no. 4 (Summer 1900): 416.
60. Meredith Nicholson, "Wide Margins," *Atlantic* 90 (1902): 440.
61. Newcomb, *How Did Poetry Survive?*
62. S. E. Kiser, "The Special Column," *Writer* 14, no. 12 (December 1901): 180.
63. Carolyn Wells, "Fin de Siècle," *BL* 1, no. 3 (Spring 1900): 381.
64. *Life* 1, no. 1 (January 4, 1883): 1.
65. For more on heteroglossia and novelization, see Bakhtin, *Dialogic Imagination*.
66. *Life* 60, no. 1563 (October 10, 1912).
67. Ibid., 1945.
68. Ibid. 1949.
69. The poem is not an unproblematic endorsement of the movement, however, claiming with a Byronic flourish that you are a suffragist

> if you can hear the truth about the Suffrage
> Twisted about by Antis in defense,
> While you anew in acrimonious huff rage,
> And use the same old worn-out arguments. (Ibid. 1962-63)

70. Ibid. 1957.
71. The issue includes advertisements for Locomobile, Packard Trucks, Studebaker '20, the Oakland Platform, and the White Berlin Limousine. Ibid., 1939, 1944, 1965, 1967, 1981.
72. *Life* 60, no. 1562 (October 3, 1912): 1888.
73. *Life* 60, no. 1570 (November 28, 1912).
74. *Life* 61, no. 1576 (January 9, 1913).
75. *Life* 60, no. 1571 (December 5, 1912).
76. Ibid., 2362-63.
77. Ibid., 2373.
78. Ibid., 2375.
79. Rosalie Jonas, "Brother Baptis' on Woman's Suffrage," *Crisis* 4, no. 5 (September 1912): 247.
80. Rosalie Jonas, "The Foundling Hospital," *Poetry* 3, no. 3 (December 1913): 91-92.
81. Jean Toomer, "Banking Coal," *Crisis* 24, no. 2 (June 1922): 64-65.
82. W. E. B. Du Bois, "Opinions of W. E. B. Du Bois," *Crisis* 24, no. 2 (June 1922): 55-56.

83. Jesse Fauset, "As to Books," *Crisis* 24, no. 2 (June 1922): 66–67.
84. McKay, *Complete Poems*, xxxvi.
85. Claude McKay, "America," *Crisis* 24, no. 2 (June 1922): 80.
86. Ibid., 81.
87. *Times Literary Supplement*, June 21, 1919, PR.
88. Promotional materials, PR.
89. *Poetry* would cite a number of glowing reviews in its early years that suggest its early influence on the little magazines. A circular celebrating its first five years (and drumming up support to keep the enterprise going) quotes from the *New York Tribune* (Sunday, July 8, 1917): "The best magazine of poetry in the English language is not published in London (where dwells Mr. Masefield), not in Dublin (where every Sinn Feiner is a poet), nor yet in New York; but in Chicago, Illinois—loop, levee, stockyards and all. It is called *Poetry* (by honest right) and is edited by Miss Harriet Monroe." A later circular, "Are You a Connoisseur of Art? Keep Up with the Times—Read Poetry" (probably circulated in 1921), quotes from a number of newspapers. The *New York Times Sunday Tribune* (January 9, 1921) states, "Thanks to a rare coincidence of poise and generous imagination, of sense and sensitiveness, it ranks as easily the best vehicle of poetry in the English language." The *Chicago Evening Post*, commenting on *Poetry*'s eighth birthday, acknowledges that "*Poetry* is, so far as we know, unique in the length of its life, recognized position and rigorous artistic standard." Even the *Times* (London; November 25, 1920) admits that "it has published, as it honestly claims, much of the best experimental poetry written by Americans in the past eight years. . . . They have succeeded in their primary design—to create a poetry which should be American in thought, feeling, and form. That is after all, a distinct achievement." Such reviews are no doubt selective, but they begin to suggest *Poetry*'s impact on little magazines and on poetic modernism. All cited from PR.
90. Solomon Frank, *Writer* 33, no. 4 (April 1921): 53.

Chapter Three. Scrapping Modernism

1. Muriel Rukeyser, "A Crystal for the Metaphysical," *Saturday Review of Literature*, October 1, 1966, 81. Moore is featured on the issue's front cover.
2. Moore, *What Are Years?*, 46.
3. Several critics have pointed to the importance of allusion and quotation for modern poetry. Elizabeth Gregory provides a useful overview of poetic allusion in her analysis of the modern quoting poem in *Quotations and Modern American Poetry*. As Leonard Diepeveen argues, modern quoting poems characteristically "incorporate phrases in the new poetic text that precisely duplicate the verbal patterns of the original source, stealing for the new poem the conceptual content and the texture of a previously existing text." Diepeveen, *Changing Voices*, 2. Claudette Sartiliot, following Derrida, discusses the (re)iterability of modern citation in *Citation and Modernity*.

4. As Cristanne Miller has observed, quotation "functions as the ultimately equalizing or democratic structure in Moore's poems: here she both acknowledges that others' words contributed to her thought in verse as importantly as (or more than) her own, and she uses precisely the same mechanism to mark ephemeral and canonical or elite sources." Miller, *Marianne Moore*, 176-77. It is important to note, however, that, through her acknowledgment of both literary and popular texts, Moore is also able to manipulate their intertextual meaning and thus paradoxically call attention to her own literary authority.

5. Perloff, *Futurist Moment*, xviii.

6. Ibid., 72.

7. For a more recent incarnation of this argument, see Costello, *Planets on Tables*, 53-54. The argument has been especially problematic for studies of Marianne Moore. Elisabeth Joyce, for example, commenting on articles that Moore clipped from the New York Armory Show and pasted into one of her early scrapbooks, argues that

> these articles compose a semicollage of the response to the show by presenting quotations from various critics with little or no introduction. Moore expresses her affinity to collage not only by this simple collection of articles about the cubist artists but also by her reshaping of these articles, her cutting out, rearranging, and altering them. There was no work of collage in the Armory Show because Picasso was just making his first one, *Still Life with Chair Caning*, in 1912, when the show's curators were formulating the exhibition, but the impetus to develop collage techniques was apparent already in the cubist formulation. Moore reveals the influence of the visual arts not only through her scrapbook but through her use of collage in her poetry, especially in "Marriage" and "An Octopus."

Elisabeth W. Joyce, *Cultural Critique and Abstraction*, 65. To her credit, Joyce is one of the few critics to have considered Moore's scrapbooks in relation to her poetic production. In upholding a received history of collage, however, she fails to fully acknowledge that while the scrapbooks bear some functional relation to the art of the Armory Show, they are themselves potent sites of popular collage independent of the visual *avant-garde*.

In an effort to get a grip on Moore's disciplinary digressions, her manipulation of paratextual elements and her strategies of juxtaposition and quotation, other critics have likewise compared her poems to the work of various *avant-garde* visual artists. See Leavell, *Marianne Moore and the Visual Arts*; Falcetta, "Acts of Containment," 124-44; Reddy, *Changing Subjects*.

8. For more on the influence of the New York literary and artistic community on Moore's writing, see Miller, *Cultures of Modernism*.

9. In considering Moore's more popular forms of textual collage, Victoria Bazin has argued for Moore as a feminized Benjaminian collector (along lines I draw in chapter 1) so that in the "storehouse of textual fragments Moore collected throughout her

life, woman is a composite site of conflicting cultural views that rarely cohere. These contradictions are played out in Moore's complex poetic compositions" that challenge hierarchical traditions through textual excess. Bazin, *Marianne Moore and the Cultures of Modernity*, 13. Likewise, Suzanne W. Churchill has argued that "in her dealings with little magazines that sought to claim her as their own, Moore began to recognize ephemera as productive forms of evasion: a refusal to be fixed, labeled, or categorized, especially by gender." She goes on to suggest that Moore's notebooks would form "colorful verbal collages" that would influence her use of quotations and multiple points of view, allowing her to develop a "conversational poetics." Churchill, *Little Magazine "Others,"* 144, 155.

10. Helfand, *Scrapbooks*, 47.

11. Tucker, Ott, and Buckler, *Scrapbook in American Life*, 16.

12. Marianne Warner Moore to John Warner Moore, 21 February 1908, in Bazin, *Marianne Moore*, 13.

13. Moore to John Warner Moore, 3 March 1911, in Moore, *Letters*, 87.

14. Moore to John Warner Moore, 3 October 1915, in Moore, *Letters*, 100.

15. Moore, *Becoming Marianne Moore*, 370 (hereafter *BMM*). The poem was first published in *Bruno's Weekly* (October 7, 1916) and was found through Princeton University's *Blue Mountain Project* at http://bluemountain.princeton.edu.

16. *BMM*, 103.

17. Marianne Moore, "Apropos of Mice," *Bruno's Weekly* (October 7, 1916), http://bluemountain.princeton.edu/bluemtn/cgi-bin/bluemtn?a=d&d=bmtnaaq19161007-01.1.7&e=-------en-20--1--txt-IN-----.

18. *BMM*, 64.

19. Ibid., 347.

20. Marianne Moore, "Scrapbook One," constructed during 1909-1913, "Scrapbook Two," constructed during 1913-1914, and "The Daily Scale" (Summer 1911) (hereafter DS) are held at the Marianne Moore Collection, Rosenbach Museum and Library, Philadelphia.

21. Willis, *Marianne Moore*, 7. Leavell, *Holding On Upside Down*. Leavell touches on these scrapbooks and Moore's scrappy practices in chapter 9, "An Intramural Rat, 1911-1914," 111-27.

22. These sources include newspapers such as the *Philadelphia Record*, the *Evening Sun*, the *London Spectator*, the *Boston Evening Transcript*, and the *New York Times*, which correspond to Moore's places of residence. The magazines *Printer's Pie* and *Punch* point to Moore's sense of humor, *McBride, Nast & Company* underscores her interest in travel, *Current Opinion* highlights her interest in politics, and *Literary Digest* her interest in art and literature—though these categories overlap in all of these publications.

23. Willis, *Marianne Moore*, 5.

24. *Transcript*, n.d., "Scrapbook One," cellophane insert between pages 17 and 19. "The Octopus," in *Poems of Marianne Moore*, 167-72 (hereafter *PMM*).

25. Moore, "England," in *PMM*, 141-42.

26. Evelyn Underhill, "A London Flower Show," *Literary Digest*, May 30, 1914. "Scrapbook Two," 48. Quoted from *London New Weekly*.

27. *BMM*, 47.

28. Leonard Diepeveen has claimed that because Moore "primarily uses quotations contemporaneous with the poem she is creating (or, at least, the temporal differences from the quoting text are not important), because she doesn't heavily depend on contrasting the quotation's original rhetorical function with its function in its new setting, and because these quotations only marginally attempt to impinge on the social world of the reader, Moore's poems, much more than those of Cummings, Pound, and Eliot, only tangentially relate to the reader's political world." Diepeveen, *Changing Voices*, 67. I would suggest that it is precisely because she draws on the world at large, mediated through mass printed texts, rather than a restrictive canon of insular literary and cultural works, however, that her work has pressing political implications. Critics have become increasingly attentive to Moore's political bent, though. As Patrick Redding has argued, Moore was a deeply democratic poet but one for whom knowledge and the cultivation of aesthetic sensibility leads to a culture of equality—challenging some long-held assumptions about the conservative bent to Moore's poetry and the assumed link between aesthetics and elitism. Redding, "'One must make a distinction, however,'" 296-332.

29. Consider, for example, the dark joke of "Marriage," in which a visitor replies to the declaration that "I should like to be alone": "'I should also like to be alone; / why not be alone together?'" *BMM*, 116. As jokes like "Examples" from the "Scrapbook Two" cellophane inserted between 17 and 19 suggest, humor, like poetry, is for Moore an exploitation of the possibilities of language. In addition to pointing out what Moore can expect in her chosen profession, the joke relishes in redundancy:

> LITTLE WILLIE—Pa, what's a redundancy of expression?
>
> PA—Using more words than are necessary to express one's meaning, such as "wealthy plumber," "poor poet," "idle rich," etc.

Another joke, "The Slang of the Day," "Scrapbook One," 30, draws its power from puns:

> "A—Awful Hot, ain't it?" "Yes, awful!" (*pause*.)
>
> "A—Awful Jolly Floor, ain't it?" "Yes, awful!" (*pause*.)
>
> "A—A—Awful Jolly Sad about the poor Duchess, ain't it?" "Yes—Quite too awful—" (*And so forth.*)

For more on Moore and humor, see Trousdale, "Humor Saves," 122-38.

30. *Life* 63, no. 1641 (April 9, 1914), "Scrapbook Two," 20.

31. "The Parent's Book," April 19, 1914(?), "Scrapbook Two." "A Jelly-Fish," *PMM*, 14.

32. Cecire, "Marianne Moore's Precision," 101.

33. "Scrapbook One," 96.

34. "Scrapbook Two," 63.

35. Ibid.

36. *PMM*, 119.

37. *BMM*, 113.

38. Ibid.

39. Ibid., 108.

40. Ibid., 164-68.

41. Ibid., 174.

42. Ibid., 155, 379.

43. "Scrapbook One," 72.

44. Ibid., 88-89.

45. *PMM*, 175. Or, if we include the two-line title, the poem becomes a free verse sonnet with the quotation coming half-way through line 7, at the traditional Miltonic turn. To view the poem as a sonnet—which I am inclined to do—brings to mind another sonnet where a quotation within a quotation is at the heart of the poem: Shelley's "Ozymandias."

46. *PMM*, 183-84.

47. Ibid., 190-94.

48. Ibid., 101.

49. "Scrapbook One," 87.

50. Moore would make this pun in such poems as "Fear is Hope" when she declares

Holiday
and day of wrath shall be as one, wound in a device
of Moorish gorgeousness. (*BMM*, 57)

51. Pasted from Walter Conrad Arensberg, "Out of Doors," *Literary Digest*, May 10, 1914.

52. Pasted from *Literary Digest*, May 8, 1914.

53. "A London Flower Show" opens with the description: "Here is a daffodil, / Six-winged, as seraphs are." Among other poems, wing imagery appears in "A Talisman," *PMM*, 22; and "To Military Progress," *PMM*, 81.

54. For example, in a letter kept in "Scrapbook One," 23, suggesting a Lake Placid tryst, Moore voices her frustration with the technology when she made the following typos:

How is the worst I ever heard of
This machine is tge worst imitation of a typewre
This is the worst ever.

Pound and Cummings make use of the typewriter in their letters and poems as an instrument for foregrounding language's visible dimensions. In *The Waste Land*, Eliot exhibits anxiety over modern automatic technologies such as the typewriter and phonograph. For more on the impact of the typewriter on modernism, see Kittler, *Gramophone, Film, Typewriter*.

55. Moore, "The Steeple-Jack," *Complete Poems*, 5 (hereafter *CP*). Moore, "The Pangolin," *CP*, 118.

56. DS, 8.

57. Ibid.

58. "Sojourn in the Whale" is the title for a poem about the Irish troubles already referred to, but Moore also titles a series of letters about New York City sent to her brother in December 1915 "Sojourn in the Whale," suggesting a metaphorical connection between Ireland and New York and her own Jonah-like adventure in the metropolis.

59. DS, 17.

60. Rollo Britten, "Was It Not Day Just Now?" *Harvard Monthly* 53, no. 3 (December 1911), accessed April 27, 2012, through Google Books.

61. The article, reprinted from the *Boston Journal*, appeared in the September 1, 1895, edition of the *New York Times*.

62. Ibid.

63. As Lisa M. Steinman characteristically puts it, Moore's "collections of images quite purposefully are designed in their heterogeneity, their diverse origins, and the rapidity with which they are replaced to resist an Eliotic totalization." Steinman, "Marianne Moore and Literary Tradition," 109. Similarly, Bazin has argued that Moore's poems "offer an alternative to Eliot's vision of modernity as a wasteland insisting upon the value of the fragment as fragment rather than as part of a unified tradition." Bazin, *Marianne Moore*, 11.

64. According to Lawrence Rainey, *The Waste Land* "has as much to do with Grail Legends and vegetation rituals as *Ulysses* has with the rickety schema that Joyce concocted as he neared the end of his masterpiece. Both writers, as publication approached, worried that their works might seem too disordered, too structureless for contemporary readers and critics, and each responded by hinting that his work was governed by an arcane logic that could be reconstructed." Rainey, *Revisiting "The Waste Land,"* 49.

65. Eliot, "Address to the Members of the London Library."

66. As Rainey has shown by comparing poetic lines with contemporary letters

through an exhaustive analysis of such bibliographical features as the color, weight, watermarks, and chain-lines of Eliot's different papers, the poems and fragments that would ultimately feed into the poem date from as far back as October 1913, with much of the composition taking place during 1921-1922. Rainey, *Revisiting "The Waste Land."*

67. Conrad Aiken, "An Anatomy of Melancholy," *New Republic* 33 (February 7, 1923): 294-95. Quoted in Rainey, *Revisiting "The Waste Land,"* 114.

68. Edmund Wilson, "The Poetry of Drouth," *Dial* 73, no. 6 (December 1922): 611-16. Quoted in Rainey, *Revisiting "The Waste Land,"* 112 (emphasis mine).

69. Ibid.

70. Jennifer Sorensen Emery-Peck notes this connection in "Tom and Vivien Eliot Do Narrative in Different Voices," 331-58.

71. T. S. Eliot, review of *Poems*, by Marianne Moore, *Dial* (December 1923): 594. Found in David E. Chinitz, *T. S. Eliot and the Cultural Divide* (Chicago: University of Chicago Press, 2003).

72. Eliot to Moore, 14 April 1921, in Eliot, *Letters*, 442.

73. Eliot, Review of *Poems*, by Marianne Moore, 595.

74. Ibid., 597.

75. Ibid.

76. O'Driscoll, "Ezra Pound's *Cantos*," 173-89.

77. O'Driscoll, "Dead Catalogues," 17-18.

78. Pound, "Canto CXVI," in *Cantos*, 816.

79. Ibid., 817.

80. Williams to Marianne Moore, June 19, 1951, in Williams, *Selected Letters*, 304.

Chapter Four. Selecting Modernism

1. There was only ever one person named Faber, but such things seem to demand an "and."

2. Akroyd, *T. S. Eliot*, 222. As Suman Gupta has argued, "Eliot's search for 'genius' as a publisher (particularly of poetry), and his role in the construction of Faber and Faber as the principal institutional legitimizer of such 'genius,' may be regarded as a final consolidation of a certain spirit of literary modernism," although Gupta also recognizes in the rejection of potential Faber poets a set of consistent editorial principles rooted in the command over meter and language, "intensity" and "aural" quality, precision or tautness of expression, and a subject worthy of such expression, which serves to ground such genius. Gupta, "In Search of Genius," 35-36.

3. Schuchard, "T. S. Eliot at Fabers," 84.

4. The list includes volumes by W. H. Auden, Christopher Isherwood, Louis MacNeice, Roy Campbell, Idris Davies, Walter De La Mare, Ronald Duncan, William Empson, Edwin Muir, Norman Nicholson, Herbert Read, Keidrych Rhys, Anne Ridler,

Lynette Roberts, Michael Roberts, A. L. Rowse, Stephen Spender, Henry Treece, Vernon Watkins, Robert Lowell, Sylvia Plath, Ted Hughes, and Thom Gunn.

5. Reader's report on Roy Campbell's Miscellaneous Poems, March 3, 1956. Quoted in Schuchard, "T. S. Eliot at Fabers," 79.

6. Ibid., vii.

7. Ibid.

8. Pound, *Selected Poems*, xxvi. Listed under "Poetry" is *A Lume Spento, Personae, Exultations, Canzoni, Ripostes, Lustra, Quia Pauper Amavi, Hugh Selwyn Mauberley*, and *XVI Cantos*. Under "Prose" is *Gaudier-Brzeska: A Memoir, Noh: A Study of the Classical Stage of Japan, Passages from the Letters of John Butler Yeats, Pavannes and Divisions, Instigations*, and *Antheil: And the Treatise on Harmony*.

9. Texts are italicized as they appear in Eliot's table of contents.

10. Ibid., vii.

11. Quoted in Gallup, *Ezra Pound*, 11. Pound, *Provença*. The title of the English volume would become *Canzoni*.

12. For a complete account of the four versions of *Lustra*, see Wilson "*Lustra*," 57–79.

13. Pound, *Quia Pauper Amavi*; Pound, *Hugh Selwyn Mauberley*.

14. The cut Pound poems were "Echoes I, II," "An Immortality," "Salve Pontifex," and "Effects of Music upon a Company of People: I. Deux Movements; II. From a Thing by Schumann." The cut Hulme poems were "Autumn," "Mana Aboda," "Above the Dock," "The Embankment," and "Conversion."

15. As Gallup notes, "The Alchemist" first appears in *Umbra: The Early Poems of Ezra Pound*, though in manuscript form in 1912. *Ezra Pound*, A20.

16. Pound to Elkin Matthews, 30 May 1916. Pound is referring specifically to the censored British edition of *Lustra*. Quoted in Wilson, "*Lustra*," 63.

17. Stephen Wilson, for example, claims that Eliot was "so solicitous of the order of *Personae* that he placed in an appendix the early poems that he wished to include but which Pound had omitted." Wilson, "*Lustra*," 69.

18. The added poems were "In Tempore Senectutius," "Camaraderie," "An Idyll for Glaucus," "Canzon: The Yearly Slain," "Korè," and "Canzon: of Incense." The cut poems were "Ballad of the Goodly Fere," "Mr. Housman's Message," "Translations and Adaptations from Heine," "Au Solon," "Au Jardin," "Silet," "In Exitum Cuiusdam," "Les Millwin," "The Bellaires," "The New Cake of Soap," "Tempora," "To Formianus' Young Lady Friend," "Our Contemporaries," "Salutation the Third," "Monumentum Aere, Etc.," "Come My Cantilations," "Before Sleep," "Post Mortum Conspectu," "Fratres Minores," "Cantico Del Sole," "Hugh Selwyn Mauberley," *Homage to Sextus Propertius* (1917), and "Cantus Planus."

19. Pound, *Selected Poems*, xxiii.

20. Ibid., xxiv.

21. Ibid., xx.

22. Ibid.

23. Ibid., xxii.

24. Ibid.

25. Eliot to Moore, 5 January 1934. Quoted in Goodridge, *Hints and Disguises*, 107.

26. Goodridge, *Hints and Disguises*, 107.

27. Kappel, "Presenting Miss Moore, Modernist," 130-32.

28. Sheile Kineke has argued that Eliot "furnished armor against Moore's female gender and sexuality for her colleagues and critics," so that Moore would not be seen as a feminine, sentimental poet and would be understood as masculine by default. Kineke further argues that Eliot acted as a kind of father figure for Moore. Given Moore's influence on Eliot, I am skeptical that either Moore or Eliot would have agreed, but I take Kineke's larger point that Moore was not only defeminized through a severed connection with the feminized mass print culture that informed her work but also was actively masculinized as a modernist poet in the process. Kineke, "T. S. Eliot, Marianne Moore, and the Gendered Operations of Literary Sponsorship," 134-35.

29. These attitudes characterize Moore's correspondence with Eliot and others who hoped to publish her work, paralleling what Cristanne Miller has observed in Moore's poems as the construction of an "alternative kind of authority that depends precisely on lack of self-assertion, the foregrounding of a questioning attitude, and an equalizing, constantly shifting access to the positions of expert and judge. While appearing to belittle herself, she instead shifts the terms of value by which one judges what is worth hearing." Miller, *Marianne Moore*, 5. It also suggests what Evan Kindley has pointed to as Moore's antagonism against the critical agonism that characterized modern critical discourse. Kindley, "Picking and Choosing," 685-713.

30. Moore to Eliot, 18 January 1934, in Moore, *Letters*, 317.

31. Eliot to Moore, 31 January 1934, Moore Collection, Series V, Box 17, folder 25, Rosenbach Museum and Library.

32. Moore to Eliot 15 February 1934, Moore Collection, Series V, Box 17, folder 25, Rosenbach Museum and Library.

33. Eliot to Moore, 27 February 1934, Moore Collection, Series V, Box 17, folder 25, Rosenbach Museum and Library.

34. Moore to Eliot, 16 May 1934, in Moore, *Selected Letters*, 322-23.

35. Eliot to Moore, 28 June 1934. Quoted in Goodridge, *Hints and Disguises*, 110.

36. Moore to Eliot, 28 June 1934. Quoted in Goodridge, *Hints and Disguises*, 110.

37. Moore, *Selected Poems*, viii (hereafter *SP*).

38. Ibid., vii-viii.

39. Moore, *Complete Poems*, 36.

40. Bornstein, *Material Modernism*, 36.

41. Ibid.

42. *SP*, x.

43. Ibid.

44. Ibid., xi.

45. Eliot to Moore, 31 January 1934. Quoted in Stapleton, *Marianne Moore*, 98.

46. *SP*, xiv.

47. Moore to Eliot, 4 May 1934, and Eliot to Moore, 20 June 1934, Moore Collection, Series V, Box 17, folder 25, Rosenbach Museum and Library.

48. Eliot to Moore, 20 June 1934, Moore Collection, Series V, Box 17, folder 25, Rosenbach Museum and Library.

49. Kappel, "Presenting Miss Moore," 141.

50. Ibid., 144.

51. For more on this depoliticization, see Bornstein, *Material Modernism*, 105.

52. Bornstein, *Material Modernism*, 99.

53. Quoted in ibid.

54. As Kappel has rightly noted, given his aesthetic and political implications, Eliot's charge to "settle the order of the contents" was really "a radical unsettling, a thorough rearrangement that had enormous consequences about the way in which the first three decades, or nearly so, of Moore's poetry forever after appeared before the public." Kappel, "Presenting Miss Moore," 134.

55. Eliot, "Unfading Genius of Rudyard Kipling," 9-12; repr. Gilbert, *Kipling and the Critics*, 119.

56. Ibid.

57. David Chinitz is one critic who has highlighted Eliot's fascination with popular textual forms, such as nursery rhymes and ragtime jazz.

58. Eliot, "Defects of Kipling," 3.

59. Ibid., 2, 3.

60. Eliot to J. Donald Adams, 1960. Quoted in ibid., 5.

61. Eliot, "Kipling Redivivus," 298.

62. Ibid., 297.

63. Ibid., 298.

64. Ibid.

65. Ibid.

66. September 1936 reader's report on David Jones's *In Parenthesis*. Quoted in Schuchard, "T. S. Eliot at Fabers," 75.

67. Kipling, *A Choice* (1941), 9. References are to the first edition unless otherwise noted.

68. Ibid., 13.

69. Ibid.

70. Ibid., 15, 13.

71. For more on this, see Schuchard, "T. S. Eliot at Fabers."

72. Kipling, *A Choice*, 13.

73. Kipling, *A Choice* (1963).
74. Cookson, "T. S. Eliot on Rudyard Kipling," 5.
75. Orwell, "Rudyard Kipling," 110.
76. Ibid., 111.
77. Ibid., 112.
78. Ibid., 100.
79. Ibid., 104.
80. Kipling, *A Choice*, 7.
81. Esty, *A Shrinking Island*, 113.
82. Ibid., 115.
83. Kipling, *A Choice*, 27
84. Esty, *Shrinking Island*, 133.
85. Eliot, "Social Function of Poetry," 7.
86. Muir, *Selected Poems*.
87. Eliot to Faber, 22 March 1925. Quoted in Schuchard, "T. S. Eliot at Fabers," 70.
88. For more on these reviews see Harding, *Criterion*.
89. Rainey, *Revisiting "The Waste Land,"* 98.
90. Barnhisel, *James Laughlin, New Directions, and the Remaking of Ezra Pound*.
91. Eliot to Moore, 5 January 1934, Moore Collection, Series V, Box 17, folder 25, Rosenbach Museum and Library.
92. Ibid.
93. Eliot to Weaver, 9 November 1928, Harriet Shaw Weaver Papers, Volume IX, General Correspondence 1922-1960, 57353: 110, British Library.
94. Eliot to Messrs. Macmillan, 13 September 1938, Macmillan Archive, 54895: 135, British Library.
95. As the Faber archives mostly remain closed to scholars at the moment, such isolated examples can only give a glimpse into how influential Eliot's editorial practices may have been on other firms, but this influence will be further fleshed out as materials are increasingly made available.
96. Moore to Eliot, 18 June 1950, Moore Collection, Series V, Box 18, folder 1, Rosenbach Museum and Library.
97. Eliot to Moore, 15 August 1950, Moore Collection, Series V, Box 18, folder 2, Rosenbach Museum and Library.
98. Moore to H. S. Latham, 30 September 1950, Manuscripts Collection, New York Public Library (hereafter NYPL). As Moore explained to Eliot about Macmillan, "I should be glad to have the Company issue the material if it very much wishes to—that if in view of the fact that my SELECTED POEMS languished, it does not wish to venture, it would be a help to me to offer the material elsewhere i.e. let you offer it as you kindly have offered to do." 30 September 1950, Moore Collection, Series V, Box 18, folder 2, Rosenbach Museum and Library.
99. Moore to H. S. Latham, vice president of Macmillan, 13 October 1950, NYPL.

100. Latham to Peter du Sautoy, 19 October 1950, Moore Collection, Series V, Box 19, folder 25, Rosenbach Museum and Library.

101. Moore to Latham, 13 October 1950, NYPL; Moore to du Sautoy, 11 November 1950, Moore Collection, Series V, Box 19, folder 25, Rosenbach Museum and Library.

102. Canadian copyright is a whole other vexing issue that I don't have space to discuss here, except to say that it has yet to be sufficiently explored in relation to either US or UK copyright agreements.

103. Latham to Moore, 3 December 1951, Moore Collection, Series V, Box 38, folder 27, Rosenbach Museum and Library.

104. Moore to Eliot, 20 July 1950, Moore Collection, Series V, Box 18, folder 1, Rosenbach Museum and Library.

105. Latham to Moore, 7 December 1951, Moore Collection, Series V, Box 38, folder 27, Rosenbach Museum and Library.

106. Ibid.

107. Section 31 of An Act to Amend and Consolidate the Acts Respecting Copyright, 1909.

108. Moore to Latham, 11 December 1951, NYPL; Latham to Moore, 11 December 1951; Moore to Latham, 12 December 1951.

Chapter Five. Instituting Modernism

1. Joseph Auslander was appointed as the first Consultant in Poetry at the Library of Congress in 1937.

2. David C. Mearns worked for the library from 1918 to 1967 and at the time was director of the Reference Department.

3. Tate to MacLeish, 29 September 1943, Archibald MacLeish Papers, Box 21: Tate, Allen, 1941-1952, 1961, Library of Congress.

4. Manoff, "Theories of the Archive from Across the Disciplines," 10.

5. Foucault, *Archaeology of Knowledge*, 145.

6. Ibid., 146 (emphases in original).

7. Derrida, *Archive Fever*, 16-17.

8. Steedman, *Dust*.

9. LaCapra, *History in Transit*, 25.

10. Greetham, "Who's In, Who's Out," 8.

11. "Wie aus der Natur der politischen Papiere das Staatsarchivs seinen Charakter und den besonderen in ihm wirkenden Geist erhielt, so wird in diesen Räumen gleichsam ein genius loci sich ausbilden; aus der Natur des Nachlasses bedeutender Schriftsteller wird der Charakter und das *Gesetz der Archive* sich entwickeln." Wilhelm Dilthey, "Archive für Literatur," *Deutsche Rundschau* 58 (1889): 367. Quoted in Thaler, "Some Remarks on the Aesthetics of the Archive."

12. "Wir verstehen ein Werk aus dem Zusammenhang, in welchem es in der Seele seines Verfassers enstand, und wir verstehen diesen lebendigen seelischen Zusammenhang aus den einzelnen Werken. Diesem Zirkel in der hermeneutischen Operation entrinnen wir völlig nur da, wo Entwürfe und Briefe zwischen den vereinzelt und kühl dastehenden Druckwerken einen inneren lebensvollen Zusammenhang herstellen." Dilthey, "Archive für Literatur." Quoted in Hutchinson and Weller, "Guest Editor's Introduction," 136.

13. Wright, "Archival Classification," 173.
14. Jimerson, *Archives Power*, 19.
15. Doehaerd, "Remarks on Contemporary Archives," 323-24.
16. Genicot, "Problem of Modern Archives," 333.
17. Brooks, "Selection of Records for Preservation," 223.
18. Martin, "Use of Cataloging Techniques," 318.
19. Buck, "Let's Look at the Record," 112-13.
20. Kahn, "Librarians and Archivists," 247.
21. Recent horror stories of Google Books and others doing just this to scan books and make them indexed documents suggest one way in which the metaphor has been powerfully literalized.
22. Garrison, "Relation of Historical Manuscripts to Archival Materials," 97-105.
23. Leland, "First Conference of Archivists," 111, 116.
24. Brooks, "First Decade of the Society of American Archivists," 119.
25. Ibid., 121.
26. Cappon, "Archival Profession and the Society of American Archivists," 197.
27. Cappon, "Historical Manuscripts as Archives," 103, 104.
28. Cochran et al., "Report of Ad Hoc Committee," 230-32.
29. Tate to the Librarian [of Congress], 29 November 1943, "Manuscript Acquisitions 1943-64," Central Archives, Poetry Office 22, Admin and General Records (1934-1965), Library of Congress (hereafter LOC Poetry Office).
30. This letter and the responses are in the LOC Poetry Office, Box 130, "Sixty American Poets" folder. Among the thirty-four libraries that replied to Tate's letter were Brown University; Dartmouth College Library; Fisk University Library; Harvard College Library; the Jones Library, Amherst; New York University; the Newberry Library; Northwestern University, Charles Deering Library; the Public Library of the City of Boston; the University of Iowa; Stanford University; Syracuse University, School of Library Science; the University of Buffalo, Lockwood Memorial Library; University of California, William Andrews Clark Memorial Library; the University of Chicago; the University of North Carolina, Chapel Hill; the University of Texas; University of Virginia, Charlottesville, Alderman Library; the General Library, the University of Wisconsin; Wellesley College Library; Wesleyan University, Olin Library; Williams College; and Yale University Library.
31. These poets were Léonie Adams, James Agee, Conrad Aiken, Hilda Doolittle

Aldington, Howard Baker, Stephen Vincent Benét, John Peale Bishop, Richard P. Blackmur, Louise Bogan, Malcolm Cowley, Hart Crane, Edward Estlin Cummings, Donald Davidson, Richard Eberhart, Thomas Stearns Eliot, Paul Engle, Kenneth Fearing, Kimball Flaccus, John Gould Fletcher, Robert Frost, Horace Gregory, Langston Hughes, Robinson Jeffers, James Weldon Johnson, Alfred Kreymborg, William Ellery Leonard, Nicholas Vachel Lindsay, Amy Lowell, Archibald MacLeish, Norman Macleod, Edgar Lee Masters, Marianne Moore, Merrill Moore, Howard Nutt, Ezra Pound, Frederic Prokosch, Howard Phelps Putnam, John Crowe Ransom, Laura Riding, Edwin Arlington Robinson, Muriel Rukeyser, Carl Sandburg, Delmore Schwartz, Karl Shapiro, Gertrude Stein, Wallace Stevens, Jesse Stuart, Genevieve Taggard, Allen Tate, Sara Teasdale, Mark Van Doren, Robert Penn Warren, James Whaler, John Wheelwright, William Carlos Williams, Yvor Winters, Elinor Wylie, and Marya Zaturenska.

32. Tate, *Sixty American Poets*, iii.

33. Ibid., iii-iv.

34. Ibid., 177, 61.

35. Mearns, "Note," in Tate, *Sixty American Poets*, ii.

36. Tate notes that "catalogues and published sources only have been consulted, this check list has obvious and unavoidable limitations. To the titles listed in the Union Catalogue of the Library of Congress have been added others found in the United States Catalogue and Cumulative Book Index, in Millett's Contemporary American Authors, in Merle Johnson's American First Editions (revised by Joseph Blanck, 1942), and in individual bibliographies which are listed here under the various poets." Tate, *Sixty American Poets*, v. While this accounting may not be exhaustive, it would likely yield a fairly accurate portrait. Reprints, however, were regrettably not included.

37. Ibid., vi.

38. Bernhard Knollenberg to Tate, 22 October 1943, LOC Poetry Office 130, "Tate, Allen, Sixty American Poets."

39. Donald Coney to Tate, 14 October 1943, LOC Poetry Office 130, "Tate, Allen, Sixty American Poets."

40. Alida M. Stephens to Tate, 4 October 1943, LOC Poetry Office 130, "Tate, Allen, Sixty American Poets."

41. Nathaniel L. Goodrich at Dartmouth College Library to Tate, 4 October 1943; Charles R. Green at the Jones Library, Amherst, to Tate, 5 October 1943, LOC Poetry Office 130, "Tate, Allen, Sixty American Poets."

42. Metcalf to Tate, 6 October 1943, LOC Poetry Office 130, "Tate, Allen, Sixty American Poets." These collections were those of Conrad Aiken, E. E. Cummings, James Weldon Johnson, Alfred Kreymborg, Vachel Lindsay, Amy Lowell, Archibald MacLeish, Edgar Lee Masters, Edwin Arlington Robinson, Carl Sandburg, Genevieve Taggard, and Sara Teasdale, as well as the T. S. Eliot collection in the Eliot house.

43. McCombs to Tate, 9 October 1943, LOC Poetry Office 130, "Tate, Allen, Sixty American Poets."

44. Stanley Pargellis to Tate, 4 October 1943, LOC Poetry Office 130, "Tate, Allen, Sixty American Poets."

45. Ralph A. Beals to Tate, October 19, 1943, LOC Poetry Office 130, "Tate, Allen, Sixty American Poets."

46. "The Harriet Monroe Library of Modern Poetry," *Courier*, no. 10 (May 1938), Friends of the Library, Box 1, University of Chicago Library.

47. Ibid.

48. Lew Sarett to the director of the library, 28 April 1938. Reprinted in "The Harriet Monroe Library of Modern Poetry." Reprinted in Judith Bond, "A Place for Poetry," *University of Chicago Magazine* (November 1958): 5. PR, Box 144, Folder 9.

49. Ibid.

50. As stipulated in a codicil to her will (January 14, 1933), Harriet Monroe Collection, Box 6, Folder 7, University of Chicago Library.

51. Monroe, "Birthday Reflections," 31-36.

52. Harriet Monroe Collection, Box 6, Folder 2, University of Chicago Library.

53. Abbott to Tate, 13 October 1943. LOC Poetry Office 130, "Tate, Allen, Sixty American Poets."

54. Ibid. Of the poets on Tate's list, Abbott pointed to (often extensive) holdings of manuscripts and letters for Hilda Doolittle Aldington, John Peale Bishop, Louise Bogan, Malcolm Cowley, Richard Eberhart, Paul Engle, Kenneth Fearing, Kimball Flaccus, John Gould Fletcher, Robert Frost, Langston Hughes, Robinson Jeffers, Nicholas Vachel Lindsay, Amy Lowell, Edgar Lee Masters, Marianne Moore, Ezra Pound, Frederic Prokosch, Muriel Rukeyser, Karl Shapiro, Wallace Stevens, Genevieve Taggard, Sara Teasdale, Mark Van Doren, John Wheelwright, William Carlos Williams, Yvor Winters, and Elinor Wylie.

55. Braddock, *Collecting as Modernist Practice*, 216.

56. Abbott, "Poet's Workshop," 11.

57. Abbott, "Poetry in the Making," 258.

58. Abbott, introduction to *Poets at Work*, 32 (hereafter *PAW*).

59. Abbott, "Poet's Workshop," 11.

60. Abbott, *PAW*, 5-7.

61. Abbott found it most productive to have face-to-face conversations with poets and with the assistance of the Carnegie Corporation traveled to England for three months collecting manuscripts.

62. Abbott, *PAW*, 13. Braddock quotes from the response at length and contends that Pound—who did in fact keep his drafts, correspondences, and other ephemera—was responding to Buffalo (and I would say Chicago as well) as an *institution*, rather than as a fellow collector. Braddock, *Collecting as Modernist Practice*, 226-27.

63. Moore to Anna Russell, 22 June 1958, Poetry Collection, University of Buffalo.

64. Box 290: "Moore, Marianne-Moore, Merrill," 13 November 1994, University Libraries, University History, University of Buffalo.

65. Williams to Abbott, 8 March 1942, MPC, 868.

66. Williams to Abbott, 15 May 1942, MPC, 869. Reprinted in Williams, *Selected Letters*, 195.

67. Williams to Abbott, 26 May 1943, MPC, 873.

68. Williams to Abbott, 25 July 1943, MPC, 874.

69. Williams to Abbott, 13 August 1943, MPC, 875.

70. Williams to Abbott, 9 May 1946, MPC, 888.

71. Williams to Abbott, 24 June 1947, MPC, 914.

72. Arnheim, "Psychological Notes on the Poetical Process," 125.

73. Auden, "Squares and Oblongs," in *PAW*, 165.

74. Stauffer, "Genesis, or The Poet as Maker," in *PAW*, 47, 53, 81.

75. Abbott, "Poetry in the Making," 262.

76. Abbott, *PAW*, 9, 25-26.

77. *Literary Papers and Manuscripts: A Plea for their Preservation in the National Archives*, LOC Poetry Office 22, "MSS. Acq. 43-64."

78. Ibid.

79. Ibid.

80. Ibid.

81. Anderson, *Imagined Communities*. As Trish Loughran has argued, a coherent American print culture was largely an antebellum phenomenon—though it was in full force by the rise of the national modern poetry archive in the 1940s. Loughran, *Republic in Print*. This archive might be said to extend the project of the nineteenth-century public library and archive as a political technology central to the formation of a liberal mode of governmentality, such as Patrick Joyce has argued for in "Politics of the Liberal Archive," 35-49. Moreover, as Richard Harvey Brown and Beth Davis-Brown have argued, even ostensibly apolitical processes, such as collection development, classification, and access, can become deeply ideological flexings of state power. Brown and Davis-Brown, "Making of Memory," 17-32.

82. Conrad Aiken, 24 January 1952, LOC Poetry Office 22, "MSS. Acq. 43-64."

83. Conrad Aiken, 8 April 1952, LOC Poetry Office 22, "MSS Acq. 43-64."

84. Randall Jarrell, Consultant in Poetry, to Henry J. DuBester, chief, General Reference and Bibliography Division, 8 November 1956, LOC Poetry Office 22, "MSS. Acq. 43-64."

85. Jarrell, "Essays on Robert Frost."

86. Wystan Hugh Auden, E. E. Cummings, Allen Tate, Robert Penn Warren, Conrad Aiken, Robinson Jeffers, Carl Sandburg, Archibald MacLeish, Léonie Adams, Louise Bogan, and Ogden Nash.

87. Elizabeth Bishop, Robert Lowell, Karl Shapiro, Theodore Roethke, Richard

Wilbur, Katherine Hoskins, Delmore Schwartz, Louis Simpson, John Berryman, and Adrienne Cecile Rich.

88. Office memorandum from chief, Manuscripts Division, to associate director, Reference Department, 3 January 1957, Subject: Papers of Contemporary Literary Figures with Particular Reference to Mr. Jarrell's Memorandum of November 8, 1956, LOC Poetry Office 22, "MSS. Acq. 43-64."

89. "Program for acquisition of literary papers—Summary of Discussion on February 7, 1957," Roy P. Besler, associate director, Reference Department, to Henry J. Dubester, chief, General Reference and Bibliography Division, February 11, 1957, LOC Poetry Office 22, "MSS. Acq. 43-64."

90. Ibid.

91. Office memorandum from Phyllis E. Armstrong, assistant to the Consultant in Poetry, to Burton W. Adkinson, director, Reference Department, 13 February 1951, LOC Poetry Office 24, "Poetry Magazine."

92. Robert G. Gooch to Conrad Aiken, 12 March 1951. Aiken to Shapiro, 26 September 1951. LOC Poetry Office 24, "Poetry Magazine."

93. Shapiro to Aiken, October 4, 1951, LOC Poetry Office 24, "Poetry Magazine."

94. Aiken to Shapiro, 10 October 1951, LOC Poetry Office 24, "Poetry Magazine."

95. "Program for acquisition of literary papers."

96. Randall Jarrell to Léonie Adams, 10 February 1958, LOC Poetry Office 22, "MSS. Acq. 43-64."

97. Shapiro, "Letter to American Poets and Libraries," 573-74.

98. Ibid.

99. "Librarian Replies," 574-75.

100. Peckham, "Manuscript Repositories and the National Register," 320.

101. Ibid., 321.

102. Land, "National Union Catalog of Manuscript Collections," 201. The University of North Carolina did not respond, and the University of Texas replied that it had an insufficient staff to supply the information necessary or to enable it to give tentative support to the project.

103. The Digital Public Library of America (dp.la) is one such archive.

104. Tate, "Tension in Poetry," 72.

105. Brooks and Warren, *Understanding Poetry*, xv.

106. Tate, *Sixty American Poets*, iv-v.

107. For more on the relationship between New Critical close reading and conceptions of organic society, see Jancovich, *Cultural Politics of the New Criticism*.

108. This library intervention supports Walter Kalaidjian's claim that "the New Critical agenda had wider cultural ambitions that—tied to the cultural elitism of the high modernists—sought to intervene in the shaping of everyday life in twentieth-century America." Kalaidjian, *Edge of Modernism*, 153.

Coda

1. Parikka, *What Is Media Archaeology?*, Kindle edition, 2.

2. Manovich, *Language of New Media*, 225. Manovich proceeds to argue that the database "becomes the center of the creative process in the computer age. Historically, the artist made a unique work within a particular medium. Therefore the interface and the work were the same; in other words, the level of the interface did not exist. With new media, the content of the work and the interface are separated. It is therefore possible to create different interfaces on the same material" (227). As I have repeatedly demonstrated, however, the same linguistic text can be and frequently is expressed in any number of bibliographical interfaces. These interfaces—a paperback and a leather-bound folio, for example—help determine a text's meaning, value, and form. It takes longer to reprint a book than to change the font, color, and layout of a computer screen, but the two processes are not fundamentally different.

3. Jerome McGann recognizes the dialectical history of these forms when he challenges Manovich's easy binary, pointing out that there were many ways in which narrative was fractured throughout the twentieth century, as does N. Katherine Hayles in her suggestion that, rather than natural enemies, "narrative and database are more properly seen as natural symbionts" in a complex ecology of forms. McGann, "Database, Interface and Archival Fever," 1589; Hayles, "Narrative and Database," 1603.

4. Manoff, "Archive and Database as Metaphor," 385-98.

5. Chun, "Enduring Ephemeral," 165 (emphasis in original).

6. For more on such viral texts, see the digital project, *Viral Texts: Mapping Networks of Reprinting in 19th-Century Newspapers and Magazines*, http://viraltexts.org/.

7. David Kirby has offered the term "digimodernism" to describe our current media moment. The dominant features that he suggests distinguish digital modernism from postmodernism—onwardness; haphazardness; evanescence; reformulation and intermediation of textual roles; anonymous, multiple, and social authorship; the fluid-bounded text—would seem to characterize mass print to a great extent as well. Kirby, *Digimodernism*, 51-53.

8. Kirschenbaum, *Mechanisms*.

9. Levy, "Future of Reading."

10. Pressman, *Digital Modernism*.

Bibliography

Archival Collections

Central Archives. Poetry Office, Admin and General Records (1934-1965). Library of Congress.
Friends of the Library Records, 1933-1945. University of Chicago.
Hutchins (Patricia) Correspondence, 57726. British Library Manuscript Collections.
London Library Papers. London Library.
MacLeish, Archibald, Papers. Library of Congress.
Macmillan Archive, 54786-56035. British Library Manuscript Collections.
Manuscripts Collection. New York Public Library.
Monroe, Harriet, Collection. Special Collections Research Center, University of Chicago Library.
Moore, Marianne, Collection. Rosenbach Museum and Library, Philadelphia.
Palgrave (Francis Turner) Correspondence and Papers, 45741. British Library Manuscript Collections.
Palgrave (Francis Turner) Correspondence with Macmillan and Co., 54977. British Library Manuscript Collections.
Poetry: A Magazine of Verse Records 1895-1961. Special Collections Research Center. University of Chicago Library.
Poetry Bookshop Papers, 57752. British Library Manuscript Collections.
The Poetry Collection of the University Libraries. University at Buffalo. The State University of New York.
Raymond Danowski Poetry Library. Manuscript Collection. Manuscript, Archives, and Rare Book Library (MARBL). Emory University.
Scott, William Henry, Family Papers. Manuscript Collection. Manuscript, Archives, and Rare Book Library (MARBL). Emory University.
Stone and Kimball Collection. Newberry Library, Chicago.
University Libraries. University at Buffalo, the State University of New York.
Weaver, Harriet Shaw Papers, 57345-57352. British Library Manuscript Collections.

Wing, John M., Collection, Newberry Library, Chicago.
Yeats (William Butler) Correspondence with Macmillan and Co. 1913-1939, 55003. British Library Manuscript Collections.

Printed Materials

Abbott, Charles David. Introduction to *Poets at Work: Essays Based on the Modern Poetry Collection at the Lockwood Memorial Library, University of Buffalo*, 1-36. New York: Harcourt, Brace: 1948.

———. "Poetry in the Making." *Poetry* 55, no. 5 (February 1940): 258-66.

———. "Poet's Workshop." *Saturday Review of Literature*, April 25, 1942, 10-11, 14.

An Act to Amend and Consolidate the Acts Respecting Copyright. 1909. http://copyright.gov/history/1909act.pdf.

Adams, Thomas R., and Nicholas Barker. "A New Model for the Study of the Book." In *A Potencie of Life: Books in Society: The Clark Lectures, 1986-1987*, edited by Nicholas Barker, 5-43. London: British Library, 2001.

Adorno, Theodor W., and Max Horkheimer. "The Culture Industry: Enlightenment as Mass Deception." In *Dialectic of Enlightenment*, translated by John Cumming, 120-167. New York: Continuum, 2001.

Akroyd, Peter. *T. S. Eliot: A Life*. Riverside, NJ: Simon & Schuster, 1984.

Alcott, A. Bronson. "Influence of a Library." *Book Lover: A Magazine of Book Lore* 1, no. 2 (Winter 1899-1900): 153.

Ali, Shahid Agha. *T. S. Eliot as Editor*. Ann Arbor, MI: UMI Research, 1986.

Allan, David. *Commonplace Books and Reading in Georgian England*. Cambridge: Cambridge University Press, 2010.

Anderson, Benedict. *Imagined Communities: Reflections on the Origin and Spread of Nationalism*. London: Verso, 1983.

Armstrong, Paul B. "Form and History: Reading as an Aesthetic Experience and Historical Act." *Modern Language Quarterly* 69, no. 2 (June 2008): 195-219.

Arnheim, Rudolf. "Psychological Notes on the Poetical Process." In *Poets at Work: Essays Based on the Modern Poetry Collection at the Lockwood Memorial Library, University of Buffalo*, edited by Charles David Abbott, 125. New York: Harcourt, Brace: 1948.

Arnold, William Harris, ed. *A Record of First Editions of Bryant, Emerson, Hawthorne, Holmes, Longfellow, Lowell, Thoreau, Whittier*. Jamaica, NY: Marion, 1901.

Arrowsmith, Rupert Richard. "The Transcultural Roots of Modernism: Imagist Poetry, Japanese Visual Culture, and the Western Museum System." *Modernism/modernity* 18, no. 1 (January 2011): 27-42.

Auden, W. H. "Squares and Oblongs." In *Poets at Work: Essays Based on the Modern Poetry Collection at the Lockwood Memorial Library, University of Buffalo*, edited by Charles David Abbott, 165. New York: Harcourt, Brace: 1948.

Bibliography

Baker, Nicholson. *Double Fold: Libraries and the Assault on Paper*. New York: Vintage, 2002.

Bakhtin, M. M. *The Dialogic Imagination: Four Essays*. Austin: University of Texas Press, 1992.

Banash, David. "From Advertising to the Avant-Garde: Rethinking the Invention of Collage." *Postmodern Culture* 14, no. 2 (2004).

Barnhisel, Gregory. *James Laughlin, New Directions, and the Remaking of Ezra Pound*. Amherst: University of Massachusetts Press, 2005.

Baudrillard, Jean. *The System of Objects*. New York: Verso, 1996.

Bazin, Victoria. *Marianne Moore and the Cultures of Modernity*. Surrey: Ashgate, 2010.

Beauchamp, Joan, ed. *Poems of Revolt: A Twentieth Century Anthology*. London: Labour, 1924.

Belk, Russell W. *Collecting in a Consumer Society*. New York: Routledge, 1995.

Benjamin, Walter. *The Arcades Project*. Edited by Rolf Tiedemann. Translated by Howard Eiland and Kevin McLaughlin. Cambridge, MA: Belknap Press of Harvard University Press, 1999.

———. "Paris, Capital of the Nineteenth Century." In *Reflections: Essays, Aphorisms, Autobiographical Writings*, edited by Peter Demetz, 146-62. New York: Schocken, 1978.

———. "Theses on the Philosophy of History." In *Illuminations: Essays and Reflections*, edited by Hannah Arendt, 253-64. New York: Schocken, 1969.

———. "The Work of Art in the Age of Its Technological Reproducibility, Second Version." In *The Work of Art in the Age of Its Technological Reproducibility and Other Writings on Media*, 19-55. Cambridge, MA: Belknap Press of Harvard University Press, 2008.

Benton, Megan L. *Beauty and the Book: Fine Editions and Cultural Distinction in America*. New Haven, CT: Yale University Press, 2000.

Binyon, Laurence, ed. *The Golden Treasury of Modern Lyrics*. New York: Macmillan, 1924.

Bond, Judith. "A Place for Poetry." *University of Chicago Magazine* (November 1958): 4-7.

Bornstein, George. *Material Modernism: The Politics of the Page*. Cambridge: Cambridge University Press, 2001.

Braddock, Jeremy. *Collecting as Modernist Practice*. Baltimore: Johns Hopkins University Press, 2012.

Brewster, William T., ed. *The Golden Treasury Selected from the Best Songs and Lyrical Poems in the English Language*. Rev. and enlarged. Two vols. in one. New York: Macmillan, 1937.

Brodhead, Richard H. *Cultures of Letters: Scenes of Reading and Writing in Nineteenth-Century America*. Chicago: University of Chicago Press, 1993.

Brooks, Cleanth. *Modern Poetry and the Tradition*. Chapel Hill: University of North Carolina Press, 1939.

Brooks, Cleanth, and Robert Penn Warren, eds. *Understanding Poetry: An Anthology for College Students*. New York: Henry Holt, 1950.
Brooks, Philip Coolidge. "The First Decade of the Society of American Archivists." *American Archivist* 10, no. 2 (April 1947): 115-28.
———. "The Selection of Records for Preservation." *American Archivist* 3, no. 4 (October 1940): 221-34.
Brown, Richard Harvey, and Beth Davis-Brown. "The Making of Memory: The Politics of Archives, Libraries, and Museums in the Construction of National Consciousness." *History of the Human Sciences* 11, no. 4 (1998): 17-32.
Buck, Solon J. "Let's Look at the Record." *American Archivist* 8, no. 2 (April 1945): 109-14.
Buck-Morss, Susan. *The Dialectics of Seeing: Walter Benjamin and the Arcades Project*. Cambridge, MA: MIT Press, 1999.
Bullett, Gerald, ed. *Silver Poets of the Seventeenth Century*. London: J. M. Dent, 1947.
Bulson, Eric. "Little Magazine, World Form." In *The Oxford Handbook of Global Modernisms*, edited by Mark Wollaeger with Matt Eatough, 267-87. Oxford: Oxford University Press, 2012.
Bürger, Peter. *Theory of the Avant-Garde*. Minneapolis: University of Minnesota Press, 1984.
Burnley, James. *Summits of Success: How They Have Been Reached with Sketches of the Careers of Some Notable Climbers*. Philadelphia: J. B. Lippincott; London: Grant Richards, 1902.
Burton, Antoinette, ed. *Archive Stories: Facts, Fictions, and the Writing of History*. Durham, NC: Duke University Press, 2005.
Cahill, Daniel J. *Harriet Monroe*. New York: Twayne, 1973.
Cappon, Lester J. "The Archival Profession and the Society of American Archivists." *American Archivist* 15, no. 3 (July 1952): 195-204.
———. "Historical Manuscripts as Archives: Some Definitions and Their Application." *American Archivist* 19, no. 2 (April 1956): 101-10.
Cecire, Natalia. "Marianne Moore's Precision." *Arizona Quarterly: A Journal of American Literature, Culture, and Theory* 67, no. 4 (Winter 2011): 83-110.
Chadwick, John White, and Annie Hathaway Chadwick, eds. *A Treasury of Helpful Verse*. Boston: L. C. Page, 1896.
Chasar, Mike. *Everyday Reading: Poetry and Popular Culture in Modern America*. New York: Columbia, 2012.
Cheever, George B. *The American Common-Place Book of Poetry: With Occasional Notes*. Boston: American Stationers', 1831.
Chinitz, David E. *T. S. Eliot and the Cultural Divide*. Chicago: University of Chicago Press, 2003.
Chun, Wendy Hui Kyong. "The Enduring Ephemeral, or the Future Is a Memory." *Critical Inquiry* 35, no. 1 (Autumn 2008): 148-71.

Churchill, Suzanne W. *The Little Magazine "Others" and the Renovation of Modern American Poetry*. Aldershot: Ashgate, 2006.

Clarke, George Herbert, ed. *The New Treasury of War Poetry*. New York: Literary Classics, 1943.

———, ed. *A Treasury of War Poetry: British and American Poems of the World War*. Boston: Houghton Mifflin, 1917.

Clough, Arthur Hugh. *Poems: With a Memoir*. London: Macmillan, 1874.

Cochran, Thomas C., Howard K. Beale, Katharine E. Brand, George E. Mowry, and Alice E. Smith. "Report of Ad Hoc Committee on Manuscripts Set Up by the American Historical Association in December 1948." *American Archivist* 14, no. 3 (July 1951): 229-40.

Collins, A. S., ed. *Treasury of English Verse New and Old*. London: University Tutorial Press, 1931.

Collins, J. Churton, ed. *A Treasury of Minor British Poetry*. London: Edward Arnold, 1896.

Conn, Stephen. *Museums and American Intellectual Life, 1876-1926*. Chicago: University of Chicago Press, 1998.

Cook, Edward Tyas. *Literary Recreations*. London: Macmillan, 1918.

Cook, Theodore A., ed. *An Anthology of Humorous Verse*. London: Hutchinson, 1906.

Cookson, George. "T. S. Eliot on Rudyard Kipling." *English: The Journal of the English Association* 4, no. 19 (1942): 4-7.

Costello, Bonnie. *Planets on Tables: Poetry, Still Life and the Turning World*. Ithaca, NY: Cornell University Press, 2008.

Cresswell, L. G. "A Literary Double Acrostic." *Book Lore* 5 (December 1886-May 1887): 97.

Darnton, Robert. "What Is the History of Books?" *Daedalus* 111, no. 3 (Fall 1982): 65-83.

Davidson, Michael. *Ghostlier Demarcations: Modern Poetry and the Material Word*. Berkeley: University of California Press, 1997.

Derrida, Jacques. *Archive Fever: A Freudian Impression*. Translated by Eric Prenowitz. Chicago: University of Chicago Press, 1995.

Dettmar, Kevin J. H. "Bookcases, Slipcases, Uncut Leaves: The Anxiety of the Gentleman's Library." *Novel* 39, no. 1 (Fall 2005): 5-24.

Dickie, Margaret. *On the Modernist Long Poem*. Iowa City: University of Iowa Press, 1986.

Diepeveen, Leonard. *Changing Voices: The Modern Quoting Poem*. Ann Arbor: University of Michigan Press, 1993.

Dilthey, Wilhelm. "Archive für Literatur." *Deutsche Rundschau* 58 (1889): 360-75.

Doehaerd, Renée. "Remarks on Contemporary Archives." Translated by Mrs. Magurn. *American Archivist* 13, no. 4 (October 1950): 323-28.

DuPlessis, Rachel Blau. *Genders, Races and Religious Cultures in Modern American Poetry*. Cambridge: Cambridge University Press, 2001.

Eagleton, Terry. *How to Read a Poem*. Oxford: Blackwell, 2007.
Ellis, Steve. "The Punctuation of 'In a Station of the Metro.'" *Paideuma* 17, nos. 2-3 (Fall-Winter 1988): 201-7.
Eliot, T. S. "An Address to the Members of the London Library by T. S. Eliot, O.M., on the Occasion of His Assuming the Office of President of the Library." Delivered at the Annual General Meeting of Members in the Reading Room, July 22, 1952. London: Queen Ann, 1952.
———. "The Defects of Kipling." Reprinted in *Essays in Criticism: A Quarterly Journal Founded by F. W. Bateson* 51, no. 1 (January 2001): 1-7.
———. "Kipling Redivivus." *Aethenaeum*, May 19, 1919, 297-98.
———. *Letters of T. S. Eliot, 1898-1922*. Vol. 1. Rev. ed. Edited by Valerie Eliot and Hugh Haughton. New Haven, CT: Yale University Press, 2011.
———. "Opening of the New University Library, 12th May, 1959." *The University of Sheffield Reprint from the Fifty-Fourth Annual Report to the Court of Governors, Session 1958-1959*.
———. "The Social Function of Poetry." In *On Poets and Poetry*, 3-16. New York: Noonday Press, 1961.
———. "Tradition and the Individual Talent." In *The Sacred Wood: Essays on Poetry and Criticism*, 42-53. London: Methuen, 1920.
———. "The Unfading Genius of Rudyard Kipling." *Kipling Journal* 26, no. 129 (March 1959): 9-12. Reprinted in *Kipling and the Critics*, edited by Elliot L. Gilbert, 118-23. New York: New York University Press, 1965.
———. *The Waste Land*. A facsimile and transcript of the original drafts including the annotations of Ezra Pound. Edited by Valerie Eliot. New York: Harcourt, 1971.
Emery-Peck, Jennifer Sorensen. "Tom and Vivien Eliot Do Narrative in Different Voices: Mixing Genres in *The Waste Land*'s Pub." *Narrative* 16, no. 3 (October 2008): 331-58.
Esty, Jed. *A Shrinking Island: Modernism and National Culture in England*. Princeton, NJ: Princeton University Press, 2004.
Eysteinsson, Astradur. *The Concept of Modernism*. Ithaca, NY: Cornell University Press, 1990.
Falcetta, Jennie-Rebecca. "Acts of Containment: Marianne Moore, Joseph Cornell, and the Poetics of Enclosure." *Journal of Modern Literature* 29 (Summer 2006): 124-44.
Feltes, N. N. *Literary Capital and the Late Victorian Novel*. Madison: University of Wisconsin Press, 1993.
Ferry, Anne. *Tradition and the Individual Poem: An Inquiry into Anthologies*. Palo Alto, CA: Stanford University Press, 2001.
Foley, P. K. *American Authors, 1795-1895: A Bibliography of First and Notable Editions Chronologically Arranged*. Boston: Printed for subscribers, 1895.
Foucault, Michel. *Archaeology of Knowledge*. London: Taylor and Francis, 2013.

Bibliography

Fowler, Alastair. *Kinds of Literature: An Introduction to the Theory of Genres and Modes*. Cambridge, MA: Harvard University Press, 1982.

Frow, John. *Genre*. London: Routledge, 2006.

Fruit, John P. "A Plea for the Study of Literature from the Aesthetic Standpoint." *PMLA* 6, no. 1 (1891): 29-40.

Gallup, Donald. *Ezra Pound: A Bibliography*. Charlottesville: University of Virginia Press, 1983.

Garrison, Curtis W. "The Relation of Historical Manuscripts to Archival Materials." *American Archivist* 2, no. 2 (April 1939): 97-105.

Garvey, Ellen Gruber. *The Adman in the Parlor: Magazines and the Gendering of Consumer Culture, 1880s to 1910s*. New York: Oxford University Press, 1996.

———. "Anonymity, Authorship, and Recirculation: A Civil War Episode." *Book History* 9 (2006): 159-78.

———. "Imitation is the Sincerest Form of Appropriation: Scrapbooks and Extra-Illustration." *Common-Place* 7, no. 3, April 2007. Accessed March 3, 2010. http://www.common-place.org.

———. "Scrapbook, Wish Book, Prayer Book: Trade-Card Scrapbooks and the Missionary Work of Advertising." In *The Scrapbook in American Life*, edited by Susan Tucker, Katherine Ott, and Patricia P. Buckler, 97-115. Philadelphia: Temple University Press, 2006.

———. *Writing with Scissors: American Scrapbooks from the Civil War to the Harlem Renaissance*. Oxford: Oxford University Press, 2013.

Genicot, Léopold. "The Problem of Modern Archives." Translated by Mrs. Magurn. *American Archivist* 13, no. 4 (October 1950): 329-39.

Gilburt, Joseph. "Fiction: Some Hard Facts about It." In *Library: A Magazine of Bibliography and Library Literature*, edited by J. Y. W. Macalister, F.S.A., 172-73. London: Library Bureau, 1898.

Gioia, Dana. *Disappearing Ink: Poetry at the End of Print Culture*. St. Paul, MN: Graywolf, 2004.

Gitelman, Lisa. *Paper Knowledge: Toward a Media History of Documents*. Durham, NC: Duke University Press, 2014.

Golding, Alan C. "The *Dial*, the *Little Review*, and the Dialogics of Modernism." *American Periodicals* 15, no. 1 (Winter 2005): 42-55.

———. *From Outlaw to Classic: Canons in American Poetry*. Madison: University of Wisconsin Press, 1995.

Goodridge, Celeste. *Hints and Disguises: Marianne Moore and Her Contemporaries*. Iowa City: University of Iowa Press, 1989.

Graff, Gerald. *Professing Literature: An Institutional History*. Chicago: University of Chicago Press, 1987.

Greetham, David. "'Who's In, Who's Out': The Cultural Poetics of Archival Exclusion." *Studies in the Literary Imagination* 32, no. 1 (Spring 1999): 1-28.

Gregory, Elizabeth. *Quotations and Modern American Poetry: Imaginary Gardens with Real Toads*. Houston: Rice University Press, 1996.

Guillory, John. *Cultural Capital: The Problem of Literary Canon Formation*. Chicago: University of Chicago Press, 1993.

———. "Genesis of the Media Concept." *Critical Inquiry* 36, no. 2 (Winter 2010): 321-62.

Gupta, Suman. "In Search of Genius: T. S. Eliot as Publisher." *Journal of Modern Literature* 27, no. 5 (Fall 2003): 26-35.

Hagar, J. Henry. "A Word about Quotations." *Writer* 5 (February 1891): 28.

Hall, Stuart. "Encoding/Decoding." In *Culture, Media, Language: Working Papers in Cultural Studies, 1972-1979*, edited by Stuart Hall, Dorothy Hobson, Andrew Lowe, and Paul Willis, 107-16. London: Hutchinson, 1980.

Hansen, Jim. "Formalism and Its Malcontents: Benjamin and de Man on the Function of Allegory." *New Literary History* 35, no. 4 (Autumn 2004): 663-83.

Harding, Jason. *The Criterion: Cultural Politics and Periodical Networks in Inter-War Britain*. Oxford: Oxford University Press, 2002.

Harper, Henry H. *Book-Lovers Bibliomaniacs and Book Clubs*. Cambridge: Riverside, 1904.

Harrison, Henry, ed. *The Sacco-Vanzetti Anthology of Verse*. New York: Henry Harrison, 1927.

Hart, Matthew. *Nations of Nothing but Poetry: Modernism, Transnationalism, and Synthetic Vernacular Writing*. Oxford: Oxford University Press, 2010.

Havens, Earle. *Commonplace Books: A History of Manuscripts and Printed Books from Antiquity to the Twentieth Century*. New Haven, CT: Beinecke, 2001.

Hayles, N. Katherine. "Narrative and Database: Natural Symbionts." *PMLA* 122, no. 5 (October 2007): 1603-8.

Hayles, N. Katherine, and Jessica Pressman, eds. *Comparative Textual Media: Transforming the Humanities in the Postprint Era*. Minneapolis: University of Minnesota Press, 2013.

Helfand, Jessica. *Scrapbooks: An American History*. New Haven, CT: Yale University Press, 2008.

Hoffman, Frederick J., Charles Allen, and Carolyn F. Ulrich. *The Little Magazine: A History and a Bibliography*. Princeton, NJ: Princeton University Press, 1946.

Hooper, Shadrick K., ed. *Rhymes of the Rockies; or, What Poets Have Found to Say of the Beautiful Scenery on the Denver and Rio Grande Railroad, the Scenic Line of the World*. Chicago: Poole Bros., 1896.

Hopkins, A. A. "Song of the Printing-Press." Pasted into *The Literary Junk-Book*, edited by John M. Wing (1903-c.1912), 27. John M. Wing Collection. Newberry Library, Chicago.

Howsam, Leslie. *Old Books and New Histories: An Orientation to Studies in Book and Print Culture*. Toronto: University of Toronto Press, 2006.

Hubbard, Elbert. *Elbert Hubbard's Scrap Book: Containing the Inspired and Inspiring Selections, Gathered during a Lifetime of Discriminating Reading for His Own Use*. East Aurora, NY: Roycroft, 1923.

Huhtamo, Erkki, and Jussi Parikkam. *Media Archaeology: Approaches, Applications, and Implications*. Berkeley: University of California Press, 2011.

Hutchinson, Ben, and Shane Weller. "Guest Editor's Introduction: Archive Time." *Comparative Critical Studies* 8, nos. 2-3 (2011): 133-53.

Hutchinson, Thomas. "Sonnets in the Library." *Book Lover: A Magazine of Book Lore* (July-August 1903): 203.

Huyssen, Andreas. *After the Great Divide: Modernism, Mass Culture, Postmodernism*. Bloomington: Indiana University Press, 1986.

Jackson, H. J. *Marginalia: Readers Writing in Books*. New Haven, CT: Yale University Press, 2001.

Jackson, Kate. "George Newnes and the 'Loyal Tit-Bitites': Editorial Identity and Textual Interaction in *Tit-Bits*." In *Nineteenth-Century Media and the Construction of Identities*, edited by Laurel Brake, Bill Bell, and David Finkelstein, 11-26. London: Palgrave, 2000.

Jameson, Fredric. *Marxism and Form: Twentieth-Century Dialectical Theories of Literature*. Princeton, NJ: Princeton University Press, 1972.

——. *The Political Unconscious: Narrative as a Socially Symbolic Act*. Ithaca, NY: Cornell University Press, 1981.

——. *Postmodernism; or, the Cultural Logic of Late Capitalism*. Durham, NC: Duke University Press, 1991.

Jancovich, Mark. *The Cultural Politics of the New Criticism*. Cambridge: Cambridge University Press, 1993.

Jarrell, Randall. "Essays on Robert Frost." In *Poetry and the Age*. New York: Vintage, 1953.

Jimerson, Randall C. *Archives Power: Memory, Accountability, and Social Justice*. Chicago: Society of American Archivists, 2009.

Jones, Frank, ed. *The Shorter Golden Book of Narrative Verse*. London: Blackie & Son, 1943.

Joyce, Elisabeth W. *Cultural Critique and Abstraction: Marianne Moore and the Avant-Garde*. Lewisburg, PA: Bucknell University Press, 1998.

Joyce, James. *Ulysses*. New York: Random House, 1986.

Joyce, Patrick. "The Politics of the Liberal Archive." *History of the Human Sciences* 12, no. 2 (1999): 35-49.

Kaestle, Carl F., and Janice A. Radway. "A Framework for the History of Publishing and Reading in the United States, 1880-1940." In *A History of the Book in America, Print in Motion: The Expansion of Publishing and Reading in the United States, 1880-1940*, edited by Carl F. Kaestle and Janice A. Radway, 7-21. Chapel Hill: University of North Carolina Press, 2009.

Kahn, Herman. "Librarians and Archivists—Some Aspects of Their Partnership." *American Archivist* 7, no. 4 (October 1944): 243-51.

Kalaidjian, Walter. *The Edge of Modernism: American Poetry and the Traumatic Past.* Baltimore: Johns Hopkins University Press, 2006.

Kappel, Andrew J. "Presenting Miss Moore, Modernist: T. S. Eliot's Edition of Marianne Moore's *Selected Poems.*" *Journal of Modern Literature* 19, no. 1 (Summer 1994): 129-50.

Kaufman, Robert. "Everybody Hates Kant: Blakean Formalism and the Symmetries of Laura Moriarty." *Modern Language Quarterly* 61, no. 6 (March 2000): 131-55.

Kelly, A. W. "Soliloquy of the Old Scissors." Pasted into *The Literary Junk-Book*, ed. John M. Wing (1903-c.1912), 29, John M. Wing Collection, Newberry Library, Chicago.

Kemp, Harry, ed. *The Bronze Treasury: An Anthology of 81 Obscure English Poets Together with Their Biographical Portraits.* New York: Macaulay, 1927.

Kenner, Hugh. *A Sinking Island: The Modern English Writers.* Baltimore: Johns Hopkins University Press, 1987.

Kindley, Evan. "Picking and Choosing: Marianne Moore among the Agonists." *ELH* 79, no. 3 (Fall 2012): 685-713.

Kineke, Sheila. "T. S. Eliot, Marianne Moore, and the Gendered Operations of Literary Sponsorship." *Journal of Modern Literature* 21, no. 1 (Summer 1997): 134-35.

Kipling, Rudyard. *A Choice of Kipling's Verse.* Edited and with an introduction by T. S. Eliot. London: Faber and Faber, 1941. Reprinted in 1963, 1983.

Kirby, David. *Digimodernism: How New Technologies Dismantle the Postmodern and Reconfigure Our Culture.* New York: Continuum, 2009.

Kirschenbaum, Matt. *Mechanisms: New Media and the Forensic Imagination.* Cambridge, MA: MIT Press, 2008.

Kittler, Friedrich A. *Gramophone, Film, Typewriter.* Translated by Geoffrey Winthrop-Young and Michael Wutz. Palo Alto, CA: Stanford University Press, 1999.

Knowles, Frederic Lawrence, ed. *The Golden Treasury of American Songs and Lyrics.* Boston: L. C. Page, 1911.

———. *A Treasury of Humorous Poetry, Being a Compilation of Witty, Facetious, and Satirical Verse Selected from the Writings of British and American Poets.* Boston: Dana Estes, 1902.

LaCapra, Dominick. *History in Transit: Experience, Identity, Critical Theory.* Ithaca, NY: Cornell University Press, 2004.

Land, Robert H. "The National Union Catalog of Manuscript Collections." *American Archivist* 17, no. 3 (July 1954): 195-207.

Latané, David E., Jr. "Treasure Sub Rosa: An Introduction." *Victorian Poetry* 37, no. 2 (Summer 1999): 135-43.

Latham, Sean, and Robert Scholes. "The Rise of Periodical Studies." *PMLA* 121, no. 2 (2006): 517-31.

Leavell, Linda. *Holding On Upside Down: The Life and Work of Marianne Moore*. New York: Farrar, Strauss and Giroux, 2013.

———. *Marianne Moore and the Visual Arts: Prismatic Color*. Baton Rouge: Louisiana State University Press, 1995.

Leland, Waldo Gifford. "The First Conference of Archivists, December 1909: The Beginnings of a Profession." *American Archivist* 13, no. 2 (April 1950): 109-20.

Lentricchia, Frank. *Modernist Quartet*. Cambridge: Cambridge University Press, 1994.

Leonard, R. M., ed. *A Book of Light Verse*. London: Henry Frowde, Oxford University Press, 1910.

Levy, Steven. "The Future of Reading." *Newsweek*, November 26, 2007, 57-64.

Lewis, C. Day, ed. *The Golden Treasury of the Best Songs and Lyrical Poems in the English Language*. London: Collins, 1954.

Loughran, Trish. *The Republic in Print: Print Culture in the Age of U.S. Nation Building, 1770-1870*. New York: Columbia University Press, 2009.

Lummis, Charles F. "Important Uses of the Scrapbook." *Writer* 12, no. 7 (July 1910): 97. Reprinted from *Journal of Education*.

Lynch, Deidre Shauna. *Loving Literature: A Cultural History*. Chicago: University of Chicago Press, 2015.

MacDiarmid, Hugh, ed. *The Golden Treasury of Scottish Poetry*. London: Macmillan, 1941.

Manning, Susan, ed. *Transatlantic Literary Studies: A Reader*. Baltimore: Johns Hopkins University Press, 2007.

Manoff, Marlene. "Archive and Database as Metaphor: Theorizing the Historical Record." *portal: Libraries and the Academy* 10, no. 4 (2010): 385-98.

———. "Theories of the Archive from across the Disciplines." *portal: Libraries and the Academy* 4, no. 1 (2004): 9-25.

Manovich, Lev. *The Language of New Media*. Cambridge, MA: MIT Press, 2001.

Mao, Douglas, and Rebecca L. Walkowitz. "The Changing Profession: The New Modernist Studies." *PMLA* 123, no. 3 (2008): 737-48.

Marek, Jayne. *Women Editing Modernism: "Little" Magazines and Literary History*. Lexington: University Press of Kentucky, 1995.

Markham, Edwin, ed. *The Book of Poetry: Collected from the Whole Field of British and American Poetry; Also Translations of Important Poems from Foreign Languages*. New York: Wm. H. Wise, 1928.

Marsh, Alec. "Thaddeus Coleman Pound's 'Newspaper Scrapbook' as a Source for *The Cantos*." *Paideuma: A Journal Devoted to Ezra Pound Scholarship* 24 (Fall-Winter 1995): 163-93.

Martin, Dorothy V. "Use of Cataloging Techniques in Work with Records and Manuscripts." *American Archivist* 18, no. 4 (October 1955): 317-36.

McDonald, Peter D. *British Literary Culture and Publishing Practice, 1880-1914*. Cambridge: Cambridge University Press, 1997.

McGann, Jerome. *Black Riders: The Visible Language of Modernism*. Princeton, NJ: Princeton University Press, 1993.
———. "Database, Interface and Archival Fever." *PMLA* 122, no. 5 (October 2007): 1588-92.
———. *The Textual Condition*. Princeton, NJ: Princeton University Press, 1991.
McGill, Meredith L. *American Literature and the Culture of Reprinting, 1834-1853*. Philadelphia: University of Pennsylvania Press, 2002.
———. "Common Places: Poetry, Illocality, and Temporal Dislocation in Thoreau's *A Week on the Concord and Merrimack Rivers*." *American Literary History* 19, no. 2 (Summer 2007): 357-74.
———, ed. *The Traffic in Poems: Nineteenth-Century Poetry and Transatlantic Exchange*. New Brunswick, NJ: Rutgers University Press, 2008.
McKay, Claude. *The Complete Poems of Claude McKay*. Edited by William J. Maxwell. Urbana: University of Illinois Press, 2004.
McKenzie, D. F. *Bibliography and the Sociology of Texts*. Cambridge: Cambridge University Press, 1999.
Mearns, David C. "A Librarian Replies." *American Library Association Bulletin* 52 (September 1958): 574-75.
———. "Note." In *Sixty American Poets: 1896-1944*, edited by Allen Tate, ii. Washington, DC: Library of Congress General Reference and Bibliography Division, 1945.
Menand, Louis. *Discovering Modernism: T. S. Eliot and His Context*. New York: Oxford University Press, 1987.
Meynell, Francis. *The Week-End Book*. London: Nonesuch Press, 1928.
Miller, Cristanne. *Cultures of Modernism: Marianne Moore, Mina Loy, & Elsa Lasker-Schüler; Gender and Literary Community in New York and Berlin*. Ann Arbor: University of Michigan Press: 2005.
———. *Marianne Moore: Questions of Authority*. Cambridge, MA: Harvard University Press, 1995.
Monroe, Harriet. "Birthday Reflections." *Poetry* 39, no. 1 (October 1931): 31-36.
Moore, Marianne. *Becoming Marianne Moore: The Early Poems, 1907-1924*. Edited by Robin G. Schulze. Berkeley: University of California Press, 2002.
———. *The Complete Poems of Marianne Moore*. New York: Penguin, 1994.
———. "The Daily Scale" (Summer 1911). Marianne Moore Collection. Rosenbach Museum and Library. Moore X:07.
———. *The Poems of Marianne Moore*. Edited by Grace Schulman. New York: Viking, 2003.
———. "Scrapbook One" (1909-1913). Marianne Moore Collection. Rosenbach Museum and Library. Moore X:02.
———. "Scrapbook Two" (1913-1914). Marianne Moore Collection. Rosenbach Museum and Library. Moore X:05.

———. *The Selected Letters of Marianne Moore*. Edited by Bonnie Costello, Celeste Goodridge, and Cristanne Miller. New York: Knopf, 1997.

———. *Selected Poems*. Edited by T. S. Eliot. New York: Macmillan, 1935.

———. *What Are Years?* New York: Macmillan, 1941.

Morrisson, Mark S. *The Public Face of Modernism: Little Magazines, Audiences, and Reception, 1905-1920*. Madison: University of Wisconsin Press, 2001.

Muir, Edwin. *Selected Poems*. Edited by T. S. Eliot. London: Faber and Faber, 1965.

Munsey, Frank A. "To the Readers of the *Scrap Book*." *Scrap Book* 4, no. 1 (July 1907): 88-91.

———. "To the Readers of the *Scrap Book*." *Scrap Book* 6, no. 3 (September 1908). Insert between pages 486 and 487.

Nelson, Cary. *Repression and Recovery: Modern American Poetry and the Politics of Cultural Memory, 1910-1945*. Madison: University of Wisconsin Press, 1989.

———. *Revolutionary Memory: Recovering the Poetry of the American Left*. New York: Routledge, 2001.

———. "The Temporality of Commonplaces: A Response to Meredith McGill." *American Literary History* 19, no. 2 (Summer 2007): 375-80.

Nelson, Megan Jane. "Francis Turner Palgrave and *The Golden Treasury*." PhD diss., University of British Columbia, 1985.

Newcomb, John Timberman. "Eliot as Publisher." In *A Companion to T. S. Eliot*, edited by David E. Chinitz, 399-410. Hoboken, NJ: Wiley Blackwell, 2009.

———. *How Did Poetry Survive? The Making of Modern American Verse* (Urbana: University of Illinois Press, 2012.

———. "Poetry's Opening Door." *American Periodicals* 15, no. 1 (Winter 2005): 6-22.

———. *Would Poetry Disappear? American Verse and the Crisis of Modernity*. Columbus: Ohio State University Press, 2004.

New York Times. "Nuggets." January 29, 1894. Historical *New York Times* Index, 4.

O'Driscoll, Michael. "'Dead Catalogues': Ezra Pound's *Guide to Kulchur* & the Archival Consciousness of Modernism." *Global Review* 1, no. 1 (2013): 1-29.

———. "Ezra Pound's *Cantos*: 'A Memorial to Archivists and Librarians.'" *Studies in the Literary Imagination* 32, no. 1 (Spring 1999): 173-89.

Ohmann, Richard. *Selling Culture: Magazines, Markets, and Class at the Turn of the Century*. London: Verso, 1996.

Old Corner Library Scrap Book: About Books, Bibliography, Book-Plates, Libraries, and Other Things, Picked up Here and There, by a Philosopher. Chicago: Pasted at the Old Corner, 1899.

O'N., H. D. "To Moribund Members." In *Cautionary Verses for the London Library* (printed card). London: London Library, April 1934.

Orwell, George. "Rudyard Kipling." In *Critical Essays*, 100-113. London: Secker and Warburg, 1946.

Outka, Elizabeth. *Consuming Traditions: Modernity, Modernism and the Commodified Authentic*. Oxford: Oxford University Press, 2009.

Palgrave, Francis Turner, ed. *The Golden Treasury of the Best Songs and Lyrical Poems in the English Language*. London: Macmillan, 1861.

——. *The Golden Treasury of the Best Songs and Lyrical Poems in the English Language*. Second Series. London: Macmillan, 1897.

——. *The Golden Treasury of Songs and Lyrics*. With illustrations by Maxfield Parrish. New York: Duffield, 1911.

——. *The Golden Treasury of the Best Songs and Lyrical Poems in the English Language*. New York: Macmillan, 1916.

Palgrave, Francis Turner, and Ernest Rhys, eds. *Palgrave's Golden Treasury*. Everyman's Library. London: J. M. Dent, 1906.

Palgrave, Gwenllian. *Francis Turner Palgrave*. London, 1899.

"Palgrave Macmillan: Our History." Accessed March 25, 2016. https://www.palgrave.com/gp/about-us/our-history.

Parikka, Jussi. *What Is Media Archaeology?* Cambridge: Polity, 2012; 2013, Kindle edition.

Parisi, Joseph, and Stephen Young, eds. *Dear Editor: A History of Poetry in Letters; The First Fifty Years, 1912-1962*. New York: W. W. Norton, 2002.

Pearse, Susan. *Museums, Objects and Collections: A Cultural Study*. Washington, DC: Smithsonian, 1992.

Peckham, Howard H. "Manuscript Repositories and the National Register." *American Archivist* 17, no. 4 (October 1954): 319-24.

Perloff, Marjorie. *The Futurist Moment: Avant-Garde, Avant Guerre, and the Language of Rupture*. Chicago: University of Chicago Press, 1986.

Peterson, Linda H. "Anthologizing Women: Women Poets in Early Victorian Collections of Lyric." *Victorian Poetry* 37, no. 2 (Summer 1999): 193-209.

Poole, John. *Manuscript Gleanings and Literary Scrap Book, Original and Select*. London: Newgate, 1830.

Potvin, John, and Alla Myzelev, eds. *Material Cultures, 1740-1920: The Meanings and Pleasures of Collecting*. Farnham, UK: Ashgate, 2009.

Pound, Ezra. *The Cantos of Ezra Pound*. New York: New Directions, 1993.

——, ed. *Des Imagistes, An Anthology*. London: Poetry Bookshop, 1914.

——. *Gaudier-Brzeska*. London: Bodley Head, 1916.

——. *Hugh Selwyn Mauberley*. London: Ovid Press, 1920.

——. *Personae: The Collected Poems of Ezra Pound, including Ripostes, Lustra, Homage to Sextus Propertius, H. S. Mauberley*. New York: Boni & Liveright, 1926.

——. *Poems, 1918-21 including Three Portraits and Four Cantos by Ezra Pound*. New York: Boni & Liveright, 1921.

——. *Provença: Poems Selected from Personae, Exultations, and Canzoniere of Ezra Pound*. Boston: Small, Maynard, 1910.

———. *Quia Pauper Amavi*. London: Egoist, 1919.
———. "The Renaissance III." *Poetry* 6, no. 2 (May 1915): 84-91.
———. *Selected Poems*. Edited by T. S. Eliot. London: Faber, 1928.
———. *Selected Poems*. Edited by T. S. Eliot. London: Faber & Faber, 1948.
———. *Umbra: The Early Poems of Ezra Pound: All that he now wishes to keep in circulation from "Personae," "Exultations," "Ripostes," etc*. With translations from Guido Cavalcanti and Arnault Daniel and poems by the late T. E. Hulme. London: Elkin Matthews, 1920.
Pressman, Jessica. *Digital Modernism: Making It New in Mew Media*. Oxford: Oxford University Press, 2014.
Price, Thomas R. "The New Function of Modern Language Teaching." *PMLA* 16, no. 1 (1901): 77-91.
Rainey, Lawrence. *Institutions of Modernism: Literary Elites & Public Culture*. New Haven, CT: Yale University Press, 1998.
———. *Revisiting "The Waste Land."* New Haven, CT: Yale University Press, 2005.
Ramazani, Jahan. *A Transnational Poetics*. Chicago: University of Chicago Press, 2009.
Redding, Patrick. "'One must make a distinction, however': Marianne Moore and Democratic Taste." *Twentieth-Century Literature* 58, no. 2 (Summer 2012): 296-332.
Reddy, Srikanth. *Changing Subjects: Digressions in Modern American Poetry*. Oxford: Oxford University Press, 2012.
Reed, David. *The Popular Magazine in Britain and the United States, 1880-1960*. Toronto: University of Toronto Press, 1997.
Rhys, Ernest, ed. *Additional Poems to Palgrave's Golden Treasury*. New York: Macmillan, 1928.
———. *The Golden Treasury of Longer Poems*. Everyman's Library. London: J. M. Dent, 1921.
———. *The New Golden Treasury of Songs and Lyrics*. Everyman's Library. London: J. M. Dent, 1914.
Richards, Mrs. Waldo [Gertrude Moore], ed. *The Melody of the Earth: An Anthology of Garden and Nature Poems from Present-Day Poets*. Boston: Houghton Mifflin, 1918.
Riding, Laura, and Robert Graves. *A Survey of Modernist Poetry* and *A Pamphlet Against Anthologies*. Edited by Charles Mundye and Patrick McGuinness. Manchester: Carcanet, 2002.
Ridler, Anne, ed. *A Little Book of Modern Verse*. London: Faber and Faber, 1941.
Root, Robert K. "Publication before Printing." *PMLA* 28, no. 3 (1913): 417-31.
Sartiliot, Claudette. *Citation and Modernity: Derrida, Joyce and Brecht*. Norman: University of Oklahoma Press, 1993.
Sawyer, Walter Leon. *Leon's Catalogue of First Editions of American Authors*. New York, 1885.

Sayre, Henry M. *The Visual Text of William Carlos Williams*. Urbana: University of Illinois Press, 1983.

Scholes, Robert. *The Rise and Fall of English: Reconstructing English as a Discipline*. New Haven, CT: Yale University Press, 1998.

Scholes, Robert, and Clifford Wulfman. *Modernism in the Magazines: An Introduction*. New Haven, CT: Yale University Press, 2010.

Schuchard, Ronald. "T. S. Eliot at Fabers: Book Reports, Blurbs, Young Poets." *Areté: The Arts Tri-Quarterly* (Spring/Autumn 2007): 63-87.

Shaddy, Robert A. *Books and Book Collecting in America, 1890-1930*. Lewiston, NY: Edwin Mellen, 2000.

Shapiro, Karl. "A Letter to American Poets and Libraries." *American Library Association Bulletin* 52 (September 1958): 573-74.

Shaw, Thomas. "First Editions as an Investment." *First Edition* and *Book Collector* 1, no. 2 (September-October 1924): 95.

Sherzer, Jane. "American Editions of Shakespeare: 1753-1866." *PMLA* 22, no. 4 (1907): 633-96.

Shipherd, H. Robinson, "Play-Publishing in Elizabethan Times." *PMLA* 34, no. 4 (1919): 580-600.

Siegel, Elizabeth. *Playing with Pictures: The Art of Victorian Photocollage*. Chicago: Art Institute of Chicago, distributed by Yale University Press, 2009.

Slater, J. H. *Early Editions: A Bibliographical Survey of the Works of Some Popular Modern Authors*. London: Kegan Paul, Trench, Trubner, 1894.

———. *How to Collect Books*. London: G. Bell, 1905; Chiswick, n.d.

———. "Principles of Book Collecting." *Book Lover: A Magazine of Book Lore* 2, no. 9 (November-December 1901): 416-18.

———. *Round and About the Bookstalls: A Guide for the Book-Hunter*. London: L. Upcott Gill, 1891.

Smith, Barbara Herrnstein. *Contingencies of Value: Alternative Perspectives for Critical Theory*. Cambridge, MA: Harvard University Press, 1988.

Spieker, Sven. *The Big Archive: Art from Bureaucracy*. Cambridge, MA: MIT Press, 2008.

Squire, J. C., ed. *The Cambridge Book of Lesser Poets*. Cambridge: Cambridge University Press, 1927.

Stapleton, Laurence. *Marianne Moore: The Poet's Advance*. Princeton, NJ: Princeton University Press, 1978.

Stauffer, Donald A. "Genesis, or The Poet as Maker." In *Poets at Work: Essays Based on the Modern Poetry Collection at the Lockwood Memorial Library, University of Buffalo*, edited by Charles David Abbott, 37-82. New York: Harcourt, Brace: 1948.

Steedman, Carolyn. *Dust: The Archive and Cultural History*. New Brunswick, NJ: Rutgers University Press, 2002.

Steinman, Lisa M. "Marianne Moore and Literary Tradition." In *Gendered Modernisms:*

American Women Poets and Their Readers, edited by Margaret Dickie and Thomas J. Travisano, 97-116. Philadelphia: University of Pennsylvania Press, 1996.

Stephen, Alexander Maitland, ed. *The Golden Treasury of Canadian Verse*. Toronto: J. M. Dent, 1931.

Stewart, Susan. *On Longing: The Narratives of the Miniature, the Gigantic, the Souvenir, the Collection*. Durham, NC: Duke University Press, 1993.

Stokes, Claudia. "Copyrighting American History: International Copyright and the Periodization of the Nineteenth Century." *American Literature* 77, no. 2 (June 2005): 291-317.

Stone, Herbert. *First Editions of American Authors: A Manual for Book Lovers*. Compiled by Herbert Stuart Stone. Cambridge, MA: Stone & Kimball, 1893.

Tate, Allen, ed. *Sixty American Poets: 1896-1944*. Washington, DC: Library of Congress General Reference and Bibliography Division, 1945.

———. "Tension in Poetry." In *Reason in Madness: Critical Essays*, 62-81. New York: G. P. Putnam's Sons, 1941.

Tennyson, Alfred Lord. *Lyrical Poems*. Edited by Francis Turner Palgrave. London: Macmillan, 1885.

Thaler, Jürgen. "Some Remarks on the Aesthetics of the Archive." Delivered at the Twelfth International Conference of the British Comparative Literature Association. "Archive," University of Kent, Canterbury, UK, July 5-8, 2010. Translated by Christoph Nöthlings. http://vlb.vorarlberg.at/fileadmin/vlb/downloads/pdf/thaler_archives.pdf.

Theile, Verena, and Linda Tredennick, eds. *New Formalisms and Literary Theory*. Basingstoke, UK: Palgrave Macmillan, 2013.

Todorov, Tzvetan. "The Origin of Genres." In *Modern Genre Theory*, edited by David Duff, 193-209. Essex: Longman, 2001.

Trousdale, Rachel. "'Humor Saves Steps': Laughter and Humanity in Marianne Moore." *Journal of Modern Literature* 35, no. 3 (Spring 2012): 122-38.

Tucker, Susan, Katherine Ott, and Patricia P. Buckler, eds. *The Scrapbook in American Life*. Philadelphia: Temple University Press, 2006.

Tupper, Frederick, Jr. "Textual Criticism as a Pseudo-Science." *PMLA* 25, no. 1 (1910): 164-81.

Untermeyer, Louis, ed. *The Book of Living Verse: English and American Poetry from the Thirteenth Century to the Present Day*. New York: Harcourt, Brace, 1932.

———. *A Treasury of Great Poems, English and American, from the Foundations of the English Spirit to the Outstanding Poetry of Our Own Time with Lives of the Poets and Historical Settings Selected and Integrated*. New York: Simon and Schuster, 1942.

Van Dyke, Henry. *Little Masterpieces of Poetry: A Book of British and American Verse*. Garden City, NY: Doubleday, Page, 1923.

Verne, G. H. "First Editions of Living Authors." *FEBC* 1, no. 2 (September-October 1924): 73-74.

Walsh, Rebecca. *The Geopoetics of Modernism*. Gainesville: University Press of Florida, 2015.

———, ed. *A Vers de Société Anthology*. New York: Scribner, 1907.

Wernaer, Robert M. "The New Constructive Criticism." *PMLA* 22, no. 3 (1907): 421–45.

Wheeler, C. B., ed. *The Golden Treasury of the Best Songs and Lyrical Poems in the English Language*. Selected and arranged by Francis Turner Palgrave with additional poems and some contemporary poems. New York: Oxford University Press, 1928.

Williams, Ellen. *Harriet Monroe and the Poetry Renaissance*. Urbana: University of Illinois Press, 1977.

Williams, Oscar, ed. *F. T. Palgrave's The Golden Treasury of the Best Songs and Lyrical Poems*. A modern edition revised, enlarged, and brought up to date by Oscar Williams. New York: New American Library, 1953.

———. *A Little Treasury of Modern Poetry, English & American*. New York: Scribner, 1946.

Williams, Raymond. "Base and Superstructure in Marxist Cultural Theory." *New Left Review* 82 (November–December 1973): 3–16.

Williams, William Carlos. *The Selected Letters of William Carlos Williams*. Edited by John C. Thirwall. New York: New Directions, 1957.

Willis, Patricia C. *Marianne Moore: Vision into Verse*. Philadelphia: Rosenbach Museum and Library, 1987.

Wilson, Stephen. "*Lustra*: Work and Text." In *Rebound: The American Poetry Book*, edited by Michael Hinds and Stephen Matterson, 57–79. New York: Rodopi, 2004.

Wing, John M. *The Literary Junk-Book* (1903–c.1912). John M. Wing Collection. Newberry Library, Chicago.

Wittgenstein, Ludwig. *Philosophical Investigations*. The German text, with an English Translation by G. E. M. Anscombe, P. M. S. Hacker, and Joachim Schulte. Rev. 4th ed. Edited by P. M. S. Hacker and Joachim Schulte. Chichester: Wiley-Blackwell, 2009.

Wolfson, Susan J. "Reading for Form." *Modern Language Quarterly* 61, no. 1 (March 2000): 1–16.

———, ed. *Reading for Form*. Seattle: University of Washington Press, 2006.

Wollaeger, Mark, ed., with Matt Eatough. *The Oxford Handbook of Global Modernisms*. Oxford: Oxford University Press, 2012.

Woolf, Virginia. *Mr. Bennett and Mrs. Brown*. London: Hogarth, 1928.

Wright, Almon R. "Archival Classification." *American Archivist* 3, no. 3 (July 1940): 173–86.

Yeats, W. B., ed. *A Book of Irish Verse*. Selected from modern writers with an introduction and notes. London: Methuen, 1900.

———. *The Oxford Book of Modern Verse, 1892–1935*. Oxford: Oxford University Press, 1936.

Index

Page numbers in *italics* refer to figures.

Abbott, Charles D., 184-88, 189
accumulation. *See* book collecting; scrapbooking
Adorno, Theodor, 31
advertising: in "The Daily Scale," 130; in *Scrap Book,* 28
aestheticization of poems, 25, 73, 90, 102, 104
"age of bulk," 173-74
Aiken, Conrad, 137-38, 172, 191-92, 193, 194
Alcott, A. Bronson, 6
Aldington, Richard, 77
allegory, 27, 28, 30
Anderson, Benedict, 191
anthologies: book collecting compared to, 49, 54; canon wars and, 219-20n84; contemporary poems in, 53-59, 63, 64; critique of, 64-65; as ideal collections, 46-49; little magazines compared to, 73; as manufacturing value, 49-53; material manipulation and, 45; modernist interventionist, 46, 64, 65, 69; Moore on, 136; objective literary value and, 46, 47-48, 56, 61, 64-65, 69-70; overview of, 30; Palgrave influence on, 59-65; *Understanding Poetry,* 66-67, 198. See also *Golden Treasury of Song and Lyrics, The*
archival consciousness of Pound, 139
archival logic in book collecting, 175-76
archival profession, institutionalization of, 176

archival unit, 174-75
archives: definitions of, 169-70; dominating force of, 170; keeping collections together principle of, 193-94; literary, 171; as memorializing repository, 191; winnowing of materials in, 170-71; work of destruction and, 174. *See also* modern archives; modern poetry archives
Arensberg, Walter Conrad, "Out of Doors," 126
Arnheim, Rudolf, 188
Arnold, Matthew, 54
Atlantic Monthly: poems in, 87, *88*; "The Starling," 90-91, *91*; "Wide Margins," 89-90
Auden, W. H., 141, 161, 188
"Auguries of Innocence" (Blake), 133, *134*
aura: Benjamin on, 76; of poems, 36
auratic quality, 51
authorial intention and first editions, 50-51
author portfolios, 16
avant-garde collage: masculinized visual, 106, *107*; Moore and, 126; novelization and, 93; scrapbook and, 108

Bacon, Francis, 15
Balkan Wars, 115, 117
Baudrillard, Jean, 27-28
"Beneficiary, The" (Kauffman), 94-97, *95*
Benjamin, Walter: on allegory, 27, 28; on book collecting, 13-14; concept of aura of, 36; "Work of Art," 31, 76

Bergson, Henri, 77
Besler, Roy, 193, 194
Bezos, Jeff, 202-3
bibliographical elements, fetishization of, 11, 27-28, 32
bibliographic codes and linguistic codes, 32, 36
bibliography, interest in, 202-3
bibliomania, 9
Binyon, Laurence, 63
Bishop, Elizabeth, 113
Blake, William, "Auguries of Innocence," 133, 134
Bodley Head, 52
book collecting: in age of mass print, 6-14; anthologies compared to, 49, 54; archival logic in, 175-76; as collecting practice, 4, 26-31; Eliot on, 2-4; first editions, 50-51, 52-53, 57; institutionalization of, 181; little magazines compared to, 73; overly restricted, 203
book history, interest in, 202-3
Book Lore (magazine), 9
books: archival units compared to, 175; as arrangement of parts, 12-13; Bezos on, 202-3; commonplace, 14-15, 47; communications circuit of, 32-33; extra-illustrated, 15-16, 135; handcrafted, 8-9, 11; materiality of, compared to text of, 11-12; rare, market for, 51-52; value, and production of, 162-63. *See also* book collecting; first editions
bookworms, 11-12
Bornstein, George, 36, 149
Braddock, Jeremy, 10, 35, 64, 172, 184
Brewster, William T., 63
Britten, Rollo, "Was It Not Day Just Now?," 131-32, 133
Britton, Lucy A. (Mixer), scrapbook of, 1-2, *3*
Brodhead, Richard, 87
Brooks, Cleanth: *Modern Poetry and the Tradition*, 67; *Understanding Poetry*, 66, 67, 198
Browning, Robert, 55-56
Buck, Solon J., 174-75

canon: Guillory on, 219-20n84; of poetic modernism, 42, 172, 173

Cantos, The (Pound), 74, 107, 139, 143, 144
Carney, Julia Fletcher, "Little Drops of Water," 132-33
Century Illustrated Monthly, 87, *88*
Chap-Book, 86
Chasar, Mike, 2, 207n2, 211n52, 222n31
"Chicago" (Sandburg), 102-3
Children's Treasury of English Song, The, 54-55, 57
Choice of Kipling's Verse, A (Kipling), 152-61, 153
Chun, Wendy, 201-2
clippings, scrapbooks of, 18
closed collections, 27-29
close reading, 65
closure, axis of, 26-29
collage: artistic, and scrapbooking, 108, 126; "Coon That Won't Come Down, The" (Moore), 124-26, *125*; paper, 15; photo, 15, 107. *See also avant-garde* collage
collage poems, 40, 136-40. *See also* Moore, Marianne; poetic collage
Collected Poems (Moore), 152, 164-67
collecting, culture of, 10
collecting practices: continuum of, 26-31; gender and, 7; mediation and, 35; overview of, 4-6. *See also* book collecting; scrapbooking
Collins, A. S., 63
Colum, Padraic, 118-19
commodified authentic, 52
commonplace books, 14-15, 47
communications circuit of books, 32-33
comparative study of textual media, 34-35, 200
completeness, indexed ahistorical, of collections, 14
"Concerning Anthologies" (Waugh), 46-47, 48-49, 65
conservation. *See* book collecting
contemporary poems in anthologies, 53-59, 63, 64
copyright, international, 166-67
Copyright Act of 1842, 218n51
Cornell, Joseph, 107
Crane, Hart, 109, 179
Cresswell, L. G., 53
Crisis magazine, 98-102
Criterion, 161-62, 163

Index

crowdsourcing, 21-22, 34, 201
Crystal Palace exhibitions, 10
Cuala Press, 52
cultural capital of book collecting, 12
cultural unity and Eliot, 142-43
culture: of collecting, 10; high and mass, divide between, 31-32, 210-11n50; of reprinting, 115. *See also* mass culture; mass print culture; snippet culture
"culture industry," 31
Cummings, E. E., 109, 128-29, 179
cutting and pasting: artistic, 15; in *The Golden Treasury*, 45; by Moore, 122-24, *123*

"Daily Scale, The" (Moore), 127-35, *128*, *134*
Darnton, Robert, 32
databases, electronic, 201
"Defects of Kipling, The" (Eliot), 154
Delaney, Mary, 15
Derrida, Jacques, *Archive Fever*, 170
Diepeveen, Leonard, 106
digital age and mass print culture, 200-205
Digital Public Library of America, 203
Dillon, George, 183
Dilthey, Wilhelm, 171
distant reading, 203-4
Doehaerd, Renée, 174
Du Bois, W. E. B., on coal, 99-100
du Sautoy, Peter, 164, 165

Eastman, Max, "At the Aquarium," 115-16
economic transformations and mass print culture, 8
Egoist Press, 162, 163
electronic media, 201-2
Eliot, T. S.: on anthologies, 67-68; on book collecting, 2-4; *Criterion* and, 161; cultural unity and, 142-43; "The Defects of Kipling," 154; as editor, 69, 142; Faber and, 141, 163, 164, 165; high modernism and, 136; *The Idea of a Christian Society*, 158; Jarrell on, 192; "Kipling Redivivus," 154; MacDiarmid and, 163-64; Moore and, 138-39, 142, 147, 165; *Notes towards the Definition of Culture*, 159; poetic modernism and, 141-42, 167; review of works of Moore by, 138-39; selected poems of Kipling and, 152-60, *153*;

Selected Poems of Moore and, 147-52, *153*; *Selected Poems* of Muir and, 159; *Selected Poems* of Pound and, 143, 145-47; "The Social Function of Poetry," 159; Tate and, 179; "Tradition and the Individual Talent," 138, 146; typewriter and, 128-29; *The Waste Land*, 4, 69, 107, 136-38, 158
emergent cultural practices, 30-31
enjambment by Moore, 122-24, *123*
Esty, Jed, 158
Everyman's Library, 54, 59-60, *60*
extra-illustrated books, 15-16, 135

Faber Library Series, 160
Faber publishing house, 141, 148, 160-67
Fauset, Jesse, 100, 102
Feltes, N. N., 51
fetishization: of bibliographical elements, 11, 27-28, 32; of old and rare books, 9
first editions: collecting of, 50-51, 52-53, 57; Eliot and, 137
First Editions of American Authors (Stone), 49-50
Firuski, Maurice, 137
Flint, F. S., 77
Foucault, Michel, *Archaeology of Knowledge*, 169-70
framing of texts: genre and, 223n45; in *Life* magazine, 94, *95*; modernism and, 73; in *Poetry*, 73-81, *79*, 84; of *Poetry* within field of periodical production, 85-92; in "quality journals," 89-91, *91*
Frost, Robert, 55, 179, 182, 192
Fruit, John P., 37

Garvey, Ellen Gruber, 1
Garvey, Marcus, 101
gender: collage poetry and, 108; collecting practices and, 7; discourse of scrapbooking and, 17-18; divide between mass and high culture and, 210-11n50
general media framework, 34
genre: archives and, 172, 189; feminizing of, 18; modern poetic, 73; poetic, 81-85, 103. *See also* verse, distinction between poetry and
genuineness, Eliot on, 149
Gitelman, Lisa, 33
globalism and poetry, 42-43

Golden Treasury of Song and Lyrics, The (Palgrave): Everyman's edition of, 59-60, *60*; influence and legacy of, 59-65; overview of, 39, 45; preface to, 47, 55; Second Series, 53-59, 63; selection problem for, 55-56
Golden Treasury Series of books, 54
good bad poetry, 157-58
Goodridge, Celeste, 147
grangerized books, 15-16
Graves, Robert, 64-65
Greetham, David, 170-71
Gris, Juan, 15
Guillory, John, 34, 35, 219-20n84

Hagar, J. Henry, 109
Hall, Donald, 161
Harding, Jason, 161
Harlem Renaissance, 99
Harmsworth, Alfred and Cecil B., 20
Harper's Monthly Magazine, 87, *88*, 88-89
Hart, Matthew, 42
Harvard College Library, 182
HathiTrust, 203
Hayles, N. Katherine, 34
H.D. (Hilda Doolittle), 5, 77, 108, 109
Helfand, Jessica, 108
Henderson, Alice Corbin, 78
high culture, divide between mass culture and, 31-32, 210-11n50
high modernism, 136, 137, 142
Historical Manuscripts Commission, 176
historical phenomena, book collecting and scrapbooking as, 30
historical sense, 67-68
Hogarth Press, 137, 162
Horkheimer, Max, 31
Housman, A. E., 191
Hubbard, Elbert, 9
Hughes, Langston, 180
Hughes, Ted, 141, 161
Hulme, T. E., 77
Hutchinson, Thomas, 6
Huyssen, Andreas, 32
hypertext, 201

Idea of a Christian Society, The (Eliot), 158
Imagism, 77-81, *79*, 82
imperialism and Kipling, 158

"In a Station of the Metro" (Pound), 78-81, *79*
information media, 6
institutionalization: of archival profession, 176; of book collecting, 181; of literary archive, 171; of modern poetry, 47; of poetic modernism, 103, 140, 162. *See also* Library of Congress; modern poetry archives; Poetry Collection, University of Buffalo; University of Chicago, *Poetry* archives of
interactivity, 34, 201
Ireland, material embodiment and criticism of, by Moore, 117-20, *118*

Jameson, Fredric, 30
James Weldon Johnson Memorial Collection of Negro Arts and Letters, Yale, 172
Jarrell, Randall, 172, 192-93, 194
Jonas, Rosalie: "Brother Baptis' on Woman's Suffrage," 98-99; "The Foundling Hospital," 99
Joyce, James, *Ulysses*, 21

Kappel, Andrew J., 150-51
Kauffman, Ruth, "The Beneficiary," 94-97, *95*
Kelly, A. W., 19
Kelmscott Press, 9, 52, 60
Kenner, Hugh, 20
Kimball, Hannibal, 50
Kipling, Rudyard: *A Choice of Kipling's Verse*, 152-61, *153*; Eliot and, 142, 155; Orwell and, 157
"Kipling Redivivus" (Eliot), 154
Kirschenbaum, Matt, 202
Kittler, Friedrich, 34, 200
Knowles, Frederic Lawrence, 62

LaCapra, Dominick, 170
Latham, H. S., 164, 165, 166
Laughlin, James, 162, 188
Leavell, Linda, *Holding On Upside Down*, 112
Lentricchia, Frank, 62
Lewis, C. Day, 60-61
libraries, 4, 10, 12, 13. *See also* modern poetry archives
Library of Congress: consultants for, 172; Division of Manuscripts, 168-69, 190;

modern poetry collection of, 190-96; national register of manuscripts of, 196-97; New Criticism and, 198-99; Tate proposal for, 178-81
Life magazine: "The Beneficiary," 94-97, *95*; poems in, 92-98
linguistic codes and bibliographic codes, 32, 36
literacy, functional and cultural, 23
literary archive, 171
literary history: New Criticism and, 173; reasons to study, 204-5; *Scrap Book* and, 24
Literary Junk-Book, The, 28
literary modernism and *Tit-Bits,* 20, 21
literature, as cheapened by mass print culture, 10-11
lithography, 7
little magazines. *See* magazines, little
Longfellow, Henry, 54
long modernism, 43-44
Loughran, Trish, 210n49, 241n81
Lowell, Amy, 5, 78, 90-91, *91,* 109
Lowell, Robert, 141
Loy, Mina, 108
Lynch, Deidre Shauna, 7

MacDiarmid, Hugh, *Mature Art,* 163-64
MacLeish, Archibald, 168, 173
Macmillan, 162, 163, 164-65, 166
MacNeice, Louis, 161
Madge, Charles, 161
magazines: bibliographic, 9-10; binding services for, 23-24; dialogic, scrapbooking compared to, 73; marginalization of poems in, 87-89, 91-92; *Scrap Book,* 28; scrapbooking, 19-20. *See also* periodicals; *specific magazines*
magazines, little: *Chap-Book,* 86; format of, 104; importance of, 71-73; overview of, 39-40. See also *Poetry: A Magazine of Verse*
Manoff, Marlene, 169
Manovich, Lev, 201
manuscript curators, 176-77
Manuscript Gleanings and Literary Scrap Book, Original and Select (Poole), 14
manuscript repositories, 197
manuscripts, literary: definition of, 178; national register of, 196-97; Tate proposal for collection of, 178-81; ties between modern archives and, 176-77; value of, 194-96
Mao, Douglas, 42
marginalization: of mass print culture, 43-44; of poems, 69-70, 87-89, 91-92
Markham, Edwin, 47
"Marriage" (Moore), 121-22, 135, 138, 148, 229n29
Marsden, Dora, 163
mass culture: forging identity within and through, 31-32; high culture and, 17-18, 75
mass print culture: book collecting in age of, 6-14; collecting practices and, 4-6; digital age and, 200-205; emergence of, 1, 7-8; marginalization of, 43-44; mediating, 31-35; scrapbooking in age of, 14-18; snippet culture and, 19-26
Masters, Edgar Lee, 83
Maxwell, William J., 100-101
McGill, Meredith, 21, 43
McKay, Claude: "America," 100-102; "Without Honor," 101
McLuhan, Marshall, 200
Mearns, David C., 180, 193, 194, 195-96
media: electronic, 201-2; general media framework, 34; information, 6; textual, comparative study of, 34-35, 200
media archaeology, 34, 200
mediating mass print culture, 31-35
memory, regenerative, 201-2
Millay, Edna St. Vincent, 5, 109
Milton, John, 15
modern archives: "age of bulk" and, 173; book collections compared to, 175-76; as organic wholes, 197; Tate and, 178; ties between manuscripts and, 176-77. *See also* modern poetry archives
modernism: as creative strategy, 204-5; framing of texts and, 73; high, 127, 136, 142; literary, 20, 21; little magazines and, 71-73; long, 43-44; period of, 2; Rainey on, 214n114. *See also* poetic modernism
modernist interventionist anthology, 46, 64, 65, 69
modern poems: in digital age, 200; distant reading and, 203-4; primary objectives of, 36; quotation in, 105-6, 120-21, 123-24,

modern poems (*continued*)
126-27. See also *Poetry: A Magazine of Verse*

modern poetry archives: in age of bulk, 173-78; literary critics and, 192-93; at midpoint of twentieth century, 181-82; New Criticism and, 197-99; organic unity and, 172-73, 197-99; overview of, 41; rise of, 169; scope of, 171-72; Stauffer on, 189; at University of Buffalo, 172, 181, 184-88, 189; at University of Chicago, 181, 182-84, 193-94

Monro, Harold, 77

Monroe, Harriet: on *Chap-Book*, 224n52; collection of, at University of Chicago, 181, 182-84, 193-94; editorial "Reviews" of, 83; Imagism and, 78; "The Motive of the Magazine," 75, 85-86; on Open Door policy, 82. See also *Poetry: A Magazine of Verse*

Moore, Marianne: anchoring and, 115, 122, 125; on anthology, 136; "Apropos of Mice," 110, 146; artistic collage and, 126; "'The Bricks are Fallen Down . . . ,'" 123; captions and phrases inserted by, 124-25; *Collected Poems*, 152, 164-67; conflation of poems by, 131-34; "The Coon That Won't Come Down" collage, 124-26, *125*; "The Daily Scale," 127-35, *128, 134*; "Diligence is to Magic as Progress is to Flight," 110; Eliot and, 138-39, 142, 147, 165; extra-illustrated books of, 135; "The Fish," 151; formal strategies in poems of, 120; "'He Wrote The History Book,'" 124; "Holes Bored in a Workbag by the Scissors," 109-10; importing and, 120-21; "In This Age of Hard Trying, Nonchalance Is Good And," 121; "The Jerboa," 124; juxtaposition principle of, 115-17, 119, 121-22; "Leaves of a Magazine," 110-11; "Marriage," 121-22, 135, 138, 148, 229n29; "A Note on the Notes," 105-6; "Novices," 120; "An Octopus," 121, 135; organization of scrapbooks of, 114; "The Pangolin," 129; pasting-over and enjambment by, 122-24, *123*, 126-27; *Poems*, 129, 138; "Poetry," 149; politics of, 113, *116*, 117, 151; quotations in poems of, 120-21, 123-24; response to Abbott by, 186; "Scrapbook One," 115-17, *116*; scrapbooks of, 18, 29, 107-8, 111-14; "Scrapbook Two," 117-20, *118*; scrappy poetics of, 107, 114-27, 136, 138, 139; "Sea Unicorns and Land Unicorns," 121; *Selected Poems*, 147-52, *153*, 160; selection principles in scrapbooks of, 115; "Sojourn in the Whale," 120, 151, 231n58; "The Steeple-Jack," 124, 129, 150-51; Tate and, 179; textual accumulation process of, 113; "Those Various Scalpels," 110; "To a Bandoliera," 130-31; "To a Cantankerous Poet Ignoring His Compeers . . . ," 113; "To a Snail," 121; triangulation of multiple sources by, 117; on writing, 105

Morris, William, 9

"Motive of the Magazine, The" (Monroe), 75, 85-86

Muir, Edwin, *Selected Poems*, 159

Munsey, Frank A., 19, 23, 26

National Archives, 176, 190-97
national register of manuscripts, 196-97
Nelson, Megan, 58-59
Newberry Library, Chicago, 182, 193-94
Newcomb, John Timberman, 23n38, 87, 220n5
New Criticism: close reading practices of, 65; conception of poem of, 197-98; individual poems and, 142; methodology of, 48; modern poetry canon and, 172, 173; organic form and, 37, 173; poetic assumptions and, 103; scrapbooking and, 5; *Understanding Poetry* and, 66, 67
New Directions, 162
New Formalism, 214n113
New Historicism, 214n113
Newnes, George, 20, 21
New York University libraries, 182
Notes towards the Definition of Culture (Eliot), 159
novelization of page in *Life* magazine, 93

objective literary value: anthologies and, 46, 47-48, 56, 61, 64-65, 69-70; Moore and, 129; volumes of collected poems and, 142
O'Driscoll, Michael, 139
Old Corner Library Scrap Book, 28

Index

O'N., H. D., 181
open collections, 27-29
order, axis of, 27
organic literary form, 37-38
organic unity of modern poetry archives, 172-73, 197-99
organization: of anthology of Palgrave, 48-49; of literary archives, 171; of modern archives, 174-75, 177-78; of poems of Kipling, 159-60; of poems of Moore, 150-52; of poems of Pound, 143-44, 145-47, 151-52; of scrapbooks, 114; of scrapbooks of Moore, 114
Orwell, George, 157, 158
Outka, Elizabeth, 52
Oxford Handbook of Global Modernisms, The, 42

Palgrave, Francis Turner: on arrangement of anthology, 48-49; on Golden Treasury Series, 54; material manipulation and, 45; objective literary value and, 47-48; selection principles for anthology of, 45-46, 48, 55-56, 69. See also *Golden Treasury of Song and Lyrics, The*
paper: cutting and pasting of, 15, 45, 122-24, *123*; development of machine-made wood, 7
paper collage, 15
Parikka, Jussi, 200
Paterson (W. C. Williams), 107, 140, 186
Pearson, Cyril Arthur, 20
"performing archivalness," 1
Periodical of the Modern Language Association (PMLA), 37
periodicals: Faber and, 161-62; "quality journals," 85-92. See also magazines
Perloff, Marjorie, 106
permanence: axis of, 29-30; books and potential for, 11; Eliot on, 149
personal scrapbooks, 16-18
photo collage, 15, 107
PMLA (*Periodical of the Modern Language Association*), 37
Poe, Edgar Allan, 74
poems: aestheticization of, 25, 73, 90, 102, 104; aura of, 36; bibliographically based, 8; collage, 40, 136-40; contemporary, in anthologies, 53-59, 63, 64; in *Crisis* magazine, 98-102; dynamic wholeness of, 198; form of, 36-37; in *Life* magazine, 93-98, *95*; "literary immortality" and, 24-25; marginalization of, 69-70, 87-89, 91-92; in "quality journals," 85-92; revisions of, 162; in scrapbooks, 1-2. See also modern poems; poetry; volumes of selected poems; *specific poems*
Poems (Moore), 129, 138
poetic collage: gender and, 108; Perloff on, 106; Rukeyser on, 105; views of, 106-7. See also collage poems; Moore, Marianne
poetic modernism: canon of, 172; culture of mass print and, 4-5; dimensions of, 5; Eliot and, 141-42; expansion of beyond canon, 42; Faber publishing firm and, 141; influence of *Poetry* on, 102-4; overview of, 36-44; reasons to study, 204-5; scrapbooking and, 127; Tate and material possibilities of, 181; as transnational and transatlantic, 42-43; use of term, 38. See also anthologies; collage poems; magazines, little; modern poetry archives; poetic collage; volumes of selected poems; *specific poets*
"poetics of scrapbooking," 2
poetry: distinction between verse and, 81-85, 103, 146; good bad, 157-58; transnationalism and, 42-43, 166-67. See also poems
Poetry: A Magazine of Verse: appearance of, 71; archives of, at University of Chicago, 181, 182-84, 193-94; cover page of, *72*; distinction between poetry and verse and, 82-85; editorials in, 75, 83, 85-86; first issue of, 73-74; Imagism and, 77-78, 82; "In a Station of the Metro," 78-81, *79*; influence and legacy of, 102-4; isolating format of, 75-77; modern poetry and, 179; overview of, 39-40; Pound and, 71, 75, 77; reading strategy for, 84
Poetry Collection, University of Buffalo, 172, 181, 184-88, 189
poetry scrapbooks, 18
Poets at Work (Abbott), 188
politics: of Kipling, 158; of Moore, 113, *116*, 117, 151
polyphonic prose, 84
Poole, John, 14

Pound, Ezra: *The Cantos,* 74, 107, 139, 143, 144; *Des Imagistes,* 62; Eliot and, 142; Imagism and, 77-78; "In a Station of the Metro," 78-81, *79;* Jarrell on, 192; *Lustra of Ezra Pound with Earlier Poems,* 144; on Monroe Collection at University of Chicago, 183-84; *Personae,* 143, 144-45; *Poems, 1918-21,* 144; on poetry in magazines, 86; *Poetry* magazine and, 71, 77; *Provença,* 143-44; response to Abbott by, 186; *Selected Poems* of, 143-47, 151-52, 160; Tate and, 179; "To Whistler, American," 73-75; typewriter and, 128-29; *Umbra,* 144; W. C. Williams and, 187-88
Pressman, Jessica, 34, 204
print: as early example of mass culture, 31-32; media forms and, 33-34; reprinting, culture of, 115; terminology and, 33. *See also* mass print culture
print media forms: history of, 204; interactivity and, 201. *See also* anthologies; books; first editions; magazines; volumes of selected poems
print-media objects, 4, 6
productive potential of scrapbooking, 108
professional scrapbooks, 16
prose, 83-84
Public Archives Commission, 176
publishing: connection between scrapbooking and, 18, 19-20; Faber, Eliot, and, 160-67; international copyright and, 166-67; transnational network of, 164

quotation in modern poetry, 105-6, 120-21, 123-24, 126-27

radial reading, 134-35
Rainey, Lawrence, 38, 136, 138, 162
Ramazani, Jahan, 42
Ransom, John Crowe, 179, 180, 192
rare books: fetishization of, 9; market for, 51-52
reading publics, 20
reading strategies: close reading, 65; for collage poems, 140; distant reading, 203-4; for *Life,* 96-98; organic form and, 37-38; for *Poetry,* 84; radial reading, 134-35; for sentence-level formal innovations of Moore, 123-24

regenerative memory, 201-2
reprinting, culture of, 115
reproduction: canon of modernist poems and, 41; copyright and, 166-67; mass textual, 10; mechanical, 51, 71; New Criticism and, 103; of poetic modernism, 140; *Scrap Book* and, 24
residual cultural practices, 30-31
Rhys, Ernest, 59-60
Riding, Laura, 64-65
Ridler, Anne, *A Little Book of Modern Verse,* 67
Roberts, Michael, 161
Robinson, Edwin Arlington, 179, 182, 191
Rosenbach Library, 111, 186
Roycroft Press, 9
Rukeyser, Muriel, 105

Sandburg, Carl, 78, 102-3
Sarett, Lew, 183
Sassoon, Siegfried, 160
Sawyer, Mary, "Mary Had a Little Lamb," 2, *3*
scarcity: format of *Poetry* and, 77; logic of, 51-52, 57; manufactured, 68
scholars and collectors, 11-13
Scott, William H., 17
Scrap Book (magazine), 23-26, 28
scrapbooking: in age of mass print, 4, 14-18; Britton example of, 1-2, *3;* as collecting practice, 4, 26-31; dialogic magazines compared to, 73; as feminized negotiation of mass textual culture, 135; mode of reading of, 38; Moore and, 18, 29, 107-8, 111-14, 115-20, *116, 118;* snippet culture and, 19-26
scrap publications, 127-35
scrappy poetics: of Eliot, 136-38; of Moore, 107, 114-27, 136, 138, 139; of Pound, 139; of W. C. Williams, 140
Selected Poems (Moore), 147-52, *153,* 160
Selected Poems (Pound), 142-43, 145-47, 151-52, 160
selection principles: for anthology of Palgrave, 45-46, 48, 55-56, 69; of modern archives, 174, 177-78; for Poetry Collection at University of Buffalo, 189; in scrapbooks of Moore, 115
Shakespeare, William, *Measure for Measure,* 119

Index

Shapiro, Karl, 193-94, 195
Shaw, George Bernard, 122
Sixty American Poets, 1896-1944 (Tate), 179-81, 198
Slater, J. H., 11, 51
snippet culture, 19-26, 111
"Social Function of Poetry, The" (Eliot), 159
social transformations and mass print culture, 7-8
Society of American Archivists, 176
"Song of the Printing-Press," 8
Spaulding, Susan Marr, "Fate," 24-25
Spender, Stephen, 161
"Squares and Oblongs" (Auden), 188
Stauffer, Donald, 189
Steedman, Carolyn, 170
stereotyping, 7
Stevens, Wallace, 30, 78, 179
Stieglitz, Alfred, 107
Stone, Herbert, *First Editions of American Authors*, 49-50
Street, A. G., 160
symbolic capital of contents of books, 12

Tate, Allen, 168-69, 172, 173, 178-80, 198
telegraph, 33
Tennyson, Alfred and *Golden Treasury*, 48
text of books, compared to materiality of, 11-12
texts. *See* framing of texts
textual accumulation, Moore process of, 113
textual media, comparative study of, 34-35, 200
Thomas, Dylan, 195
Tietjens, Eunice, 183
Tit-Bits from All the Most Interesting Books, Periodicals and Newspapers in the World, 20-23
Todorov, Tzvetan, 82
Toomer, Jean, "Banking Coal," 99, 100
"To Whistler, American" (Pound), 73-75
"Tradition and the Individual Talent" (Eliot), 138, 146
transmission process, 149
transnationalism and poetry, 42-43, 166-67
Tredwell, Daniel, 10, 13
Twain, Mark, 14, 50-51
typecasting, improvements in, 7
typewriter, 128-29, 132, 173

Understanding Poetry (Brooks and Warren), 66-67, 198
unit, archival, 174-75
unity: cultural, 142-43; organic, 172-73, 197-99; textual, 149-51, 155, 156
University of Buffalo, Poetry Collection of, 172, 181, 184-88, 189
University of Chicago, *Poetry* archives of, 181, 182-84, 193-94
University of Texas at Austin, 182
Untermeyer, Louis, 61

value: book production and, 162-63; manufactured, 49-53; of manuscripts, correspondence, and ephemera of poets, 194-96; marginalia and, 208n22. *See also* objective literary value
Van Dyke, Henry: *Little Masterpieces of Poetry*, 64; "What America Means to Me," 1-2
verse, distinction between poetry and, 81-85, 103, 146
vers libre, 62, 73, 81, 84, 151
Victorian lyric, challenge to, 62
visual *avant-garde*, 106, 107, 135
volumes of selected poems: book production and, 162-63; Faber and, 160-61; of Kipling, 152-61, *153*; legal view of, 166; as model for nation-state, 142-43; of Moore, 147-52, *153*, 160; objective literary value and, 142; overview of, 40-41; periodical production and, 161-62; of Pound, 143-47, 151-52, 160; transmission through, 149

Walker, John Brisben, 18
Walkowitz, Rebecca, 42
Walsh, Rebecca, 42
Warren, Robert Penn, 66, 67, 198
"Was It Not Day Just Now?" (Britten), 131-32, *133*
Waste Land, The (Eliot), 4, 69, 107, 136-38, 158
Waugh, Arthur: "Concerning Anthologies," 46-47, 48-49, 65; on *The Golden Treasury*, 68
Weaver, Harriet Shaw, 163
Wells, Carolyn: "Fin de Siècle," 92; "Ifs for Women," 96

Wheelock, John Hall, 183
Whitman, Walt, 50-51, 74, 117, 191
Williams, Oscar, 61, 62-63
Williams, Raymond, 30
Williams, William Carlos: *Paterson,* 107, 140, 186; on poems, 90; *Poetry* magazine and, 78; response to Abbott by, 186-87; Tate on, 180
Willis, Patricia, 111-12

Wilson, Edmund, 138
Woolf, Virginia, 43, 137
Worcester, Dean Conant, 122-23, *123*
"Work of Art" (Benjamin), 31, 76
worksheets, Abbott interest in, 184-86

Yale University library, 182
Yeats, John "Jack" Butler, 117-18, *118*
Yeats, William Butler, 62, 65, 71, 118-19